Memoirs
of
Huseyn Shaheed
Suhrawardy

Memoirs
of
Huseyn Shaheed
Suhrawardy

with

a brief account of his life and work

Edited by

Mohammad H.R. Talukdar

Foreword by

Kamal Hossain

OXFORD
UNIVERSITY PRESS

OXFORD
UNIVERSITY PRESS

Great Clarendon Street, Oxford OX2 6DP

Oxford University Press is a department of the University of Oxford.
It furthers the University's objective of excellence in research, scholarship,
and education by publishing worldwide in

Oxford New York

Auckland Cape Town Dar es Salaam Hong Kong Karachi
Kuala Lumpur Madrid Melbourne Mexico City Nairobi
New Delhi Shanghai Taipei Toronto

with offices in

Argentina Austria Brazil Chile Czech Republic France Greece
Guatemala Hungary Italy Japan Poland Portugal Singapore
South Korea Switzerland Turkey Ukraine Vietnam

Oxford is a registered trade mark of Oxford University Press
in the UK and in certain other countries including Pakistan.

ISBN 978-0-19-547722-1

This edition by Oxford University Press 2009

Typeset in Times
Printed in Pakistan by
Kagzi Printers, Karachi.
Published by
Ameena Saiyid, Oxford University Press
No. 38, Sector 15, Korangi Industrial Area, PO Box 8214
Karachi-74900, Pakistan.

Dedicated to the
fond memories of
my beloved parents

Contents

Editor's Note   xi
Foreword   xiii
Recollections   xvii
Preface   xxi

PART I: LIFE AND WORK   1

FAMILY BACKGROUND   1
Suhrawardy order of saints   1
Renaissance movement in Bengal   2
EDUCATION AND FAMILY LIFE   6
HINDU-MUSLIM UNITY   8
The Khilafat Movement   8
The Bengal Pact   9
1926 Riots   10
A SEPARATIST MUSLIM LEADER   12
A leader of Muslim India   14
Independent Muslim Party   15
BPML General Secretary   15
1936 GENERAL ELECTIONS   16
Labour and Commerce Minister   16
Civil Supplies Minister   18
    1943 Famine   18
1946 GENERAL ELECTIONS   20
Prime Minister of Bengal   21
    Delhi convention   22
    Direct Action Day   23
    Appointment of Punjabi police   25
    Peace emissary   26
PARTITION OF INDIA   26
The only alternative to prolonged civil war   27

GREATER BENGAL SCHEME   27
The loss of Calcutta   31
MISSION WITH GANDHI   32
Ban on Suhrawardy's entry into East Bengal   35
A FIGHTER FOR DEMOCRACY   36
Slaughter of democracy   36
Birth of bureaucracy   38
Emergence of fascism   39
Formation of the Awami League   40
Language movement   42
Jukto Front   44
    The Front ministry   45
Constitutional crisis   46
Law Minister   47
    Principle of parity   48
The first constitution framed   50
PRIME MINISTER   51
Speedy domestic measures   52
    Joint electorate   52
    A fair trial for democracy   53
    Economic policies   53
Spirited foreign policy   54
    Neighbours   55
    Muslim World   56
    Pakistan's security   58
    American arms aid use   60
    Kashmir dispute   60
Resignation   62
MILITARY DICTATORSHIP   66
EBDOed and jailed   66
A FALLEN WARRIOR OF DEMOCRACY   69
Democracy untried   74

PART II: MEMOIRS   77

MILITARY OLIGARCHY   77
An unholy policy   77

FRUSTRATION AND FAILURE 78
The First Constituent Assembly 78
Matchless generosity of East Bengal 79
Reluctance to frame constitution 80
INTRIGUE AND CHICANERY 82
Frequent changes in government 82
Elections to West Pakistan legislatures rigged 83
National Assembly dissolved 85
Law Minister to avoid dictatorship 86
Offer of Prime Ministership subtly upset 89
One Unit as a solid front against East Pakistan 91
Reluctant creation of the Republican Party 93
The minority Sarkar ministry 94
Prime Minister of Pakistan 95
The hard core of the NAP 96
MAJOR CONTRIBUTION 99
Muslim League victory in 1946 104
COMMUNAL HARMONY 106
Peace Mission in India 107
Peace Mission in East Bengal 110
Unseated in the Assembly 111
MOVEMENT FOR DEMOCRACY 112
Creation of opposition 112
Military alliances to defend democracy 114
The NAP blackmails 118
Resignation 119
Over emphasizing religion in politics 122
Awami League support to Republicans 125
Mirza's tangled maze of politics favouring revolution 126
OCTOBER REVOLUTION 127
Second October Revolution 128
Reforms with little bearing on democracy 129
Demoralization of the Civil Service 137
Astronomical waste of public funds 140
Ayub's Islamization programme questioned 141
American aid ignores East Pakistan 143

East Pakistan press strangulated   145
A facade of democracy   146
Disparity in capital development   154
East Pakistan progressively impoverished   156
Grievances of East Pakistan   157
Courageous opposition in West Pakistan   164
Pakistan's future at stake   165
Suhrawardy arrested   166
One-man constitution imposed   169
The President resiled from his pet theories   172
Suhrawardy's release demanded   173
The nine signatories   176
DEMOCRATIZATION OF THE CONSTITUTION   177
Ayub's measures examined   179
Obstructions to holding public meeting   189
League convention with a bad start   190
The main revolutionary principle abandoned   193
Repeated obstructions to holding public meeting   195
Bhashani's double-dealing   197
President's enmity and vengeance   199
ALTERNATIVES SUGGESTED TO SAVE PAKISTAN   201
Party interests predominate   204
SEPARATION INEVITABLE   205
Appeals to President Ayub   205
Last efforts to stand united   206
Further disability on politicians   210
Political life at a standstill   212
Mass upheaval in East Pakistan feared   214

    Appendix I   215
    Appendix II   223
    Appendix III   224
    Notes   226
    Index   243

Editor's Note

Immediately after the *Memoirs* were first published in 1987, the book received wide appreciation from BBC, VOA, and Bangladesh Television and all national dailies and periodicals critically reviewed the book calling it a unique publication and assessing it as the best book of that year. The English daily, *The New Nation*, and the Bengali Monthly *Desh* serialized the *Memoirs*. Suhrawardy Smriti Sangsad rewarded the Editor for publishing the *Memoirs* that had remained hitherto unknown until the book was published.

In this edition while I had nothing to do with the *Memoirs* of Huseyn Shaheed Suhrawardy re-produced in Part II, an effort has been made to bring the material up to date and to introduce necessary emendations in Part I. Due consideration was given to critical comments published as reviews — among which that of Professor Sirajul Islam of the Department of English, Dhaka University, was the most comprehensive, published in the editorial column of the popular Bengali daily *Sangbad* — that elicited great attention and interest of the literary circle. He commented upon the last paragraph in Part I of the book, where I inadvertently called the liberation war a civil war. I realized my mistake immediately and corrected it in the subsequent Bangla editions for the vast majority of its Bengali readers.

The services of all these reviewers are herewith gratefully acknowledged.

Mohammad H.R. Talukdar

Foreword

These unfinished memoirs were written in the last year of Huseyn Shaheed Suhrawardy's life—1963. They are a first draft of what would have been a much larger work. His active involvement in major events in the subcontinent, spanning a period of over 40 years, would have ensured that. Indeed I recall my meeting with him in London in September 1963, when he gave me the first hundred or so pages of these memoirs to read. He indicated that they were only a tentative first draft, which were to be elaborated into a full-fledged work.

Two features of this work need underlining. They are unfinished and are not conventional memoirs. Conventional memoirs are written by one who has completed his life's work and sets about to recollect it in tranquillity.

In 1963 the work of Huseyn Shaheed Suhrawardy's life was far from finished. Nor was the luxury of tranquillity available to him. He was detained in prison for the first time in his life in 1962. After his release he launched and led a vigorous movement for restoration of democracy, in the course of which he suffered a severe heart attack. He went abroad for treatment and, while in convalescence, death overtook him in the solitude of exile. The funeral procession which received his coffin in Dhaka was perhaps the largest that had ever assembled till that time. Millions poured into the capital from the remote corners of the countryside—on foot, on boats, on trains and buses—in a silent and moving demonstration of their reverence and affection. No more convincing testimony could be presented of the enduring confidence which the people placed in him and of the sway he continued to hold over their hearts and minds till the end of his life.

Suhrawardy's achievements were not inconsiderable. He had been Chief Minister of a united Bengal and Prime Minister of Pakistan. He led his party (the Muslim League) to a historic election victory in 1946 which entitles him to be recognized as one of the founders of Pakistan. The first years of Pakistan, however, found him not in high public office but working with Mahatma Gandhi in India to restore communal harmony in areas convulsed by Hindu-Muslim riots. When he came to Pakistan it was to play a critical role in establishing a democratic opposition to the Muslim League which had begun to manifest anti-people tendencies and to assume an authoritarian character. Working for popular unity, he was one of the architects of the United Front which decisively routed the Muslim League in the elections held in East Bengal in 1954, and marked the emergence of the Awami League as a major political force. He became Prime Minister in 1956 for barely thirteen months. The remainder of his life was spent in a relentless struggle to establish democracy in the face of the military rule which was imposed in Pakistan in 1958.

Like his memoirs, his life's work remained unfinished. At the core of his politics was an unshakeable commitment to democracy and a profound faith in the capacity of people, through their efforts, to control their destiny. The irreconcilable conflict between this commitment and military rule against which he had to contend during the last years of his life is one of the principal themes of his memoirs. When he died Pakistan was still ruled by a Field Marshal, albeit behind a civilian facade, and democracy still remained an unrealized goal.

In the opening pages, he describes the situation then prevailing, in terms which have remarkable contemporary relevance:

> ...even where democracies have theoretically been restored in their ding-dong battle against such military dictatorships, they have in fact never been free but have always been directed and controlled by the military, who, once having tasted blood, find it advantageous and necessary in their vested, as well as newly acquired, interests to keep civilian power in subordination. Military officers, high and low, were put in charge of important administrative civilian posts for which they were untrained and unfit.... Not only retired but also active military personnel, high and low, and members of their families were rewarded with posts, lands, licences, permits and pecuniary advantages commensurate with their ranks, their influence, or their family connections. The military, therefore, are as a class interested in the continuance of a system so beneficial to them, and a body of disciplined personnel is thus ready and prepared to exert itself to the full to maintain its gains and privileges.... Hence experience shows, and illustrations are not wanting, that military dictatorships tend to perpetuate themselves, overtly and covertly.

His faith in people's power is documented by the importance he attached to building up popular organizations at the grass-root. His initiation in politics was through building up organizations of urban workers—jute and textile mill workers, rickshaw-pullers and hotel employees—in and around Calcutta. This approach was applied by him to the building up of the mass rural base of the Muslim League in Bengal.

These memoirs, despite being fragmentary, provide some valuable insights into Suhrawardy's politics and his personality. His tribute to Deshbandhu Chittaranjan Das provides an insight into his political values, thus:

> In the initial stages I was loosely associated with the Congress and was the Deputy Mayor of Calcutta with Deshbandhu C.R. Das as Mayor. He was the greatest Bengali, may I say Indian, scarcely less in stature than Mahatma Gandhi, I have

ever had the good fortune to know. He was endowed with wide vision, he was wholly non-communal, generous to a fault, courageous and capable of unparalleled self-sacrifice. His intellectual attainments and keen insight were of the highest order. As an advocate he commanded fabulous fees—which he laid at the feet of his country. Towards the end of his days he renounced his profession, devoted himself to politics and the service of his country, and died a pauper overwhelmed with debts. I believe with many that had he lived he would have been able to guide the destiny of India along channels that would have eliminated the causes of conflict and bitterness, which had bedevilled the relationship between Hindus and Muslims, and which for want of a just solution, led to the partition of India and the creation of Pakistan.

The depth of his understanding of emerging political forces is reflected in a record of his discussions with his closest political lieutenant:

Mujibur Rahman, in particular, is fretting very strongly. He is prepared to accept the objective of democracy for Pakistan as the sole issue. He also feels that since, for the time being at least, I am the only person who can mobilize the masses in East Pakistan and capture their imagination, it is advisable to work under my umbrella. *But he has doubts that national unity and national integration will solve the problems of East Pakistan.*

In this last sentence is anticipated the future course of politics, which would see the launching of the six-point demand for autonomy, the growth of Bengali nationalism, and ultimately the emergence of sovereign, independent Bangladesh.

In another passage, while describing his own efforts for realization of popular aspirations within the framework of united Pakistan, he recognized the growing alienation of Bengalis and the inevitability of a violent upheaval, once the possibility of peaceful change was denied, thus:

By all accounts there is general political stagnation and the question remains how it can be ended. The general theory is that when constitutional avenues are blocked, people find a way to adopt unconstitutional measures—in short, a revolution. Whether such a revolution is possible in view of the tremendous disparity between the armed forces and the people is doubtful. One contingency which we were probably approaching was the mass upheaval in East Pakistan against West Pakistan which would have included the Army, the West Pakistan industrialists and even the non-Bengali refugee element. This would have led to bloody riots and murders and would have been based on sheer hatred. I have succeeded in stemming this, but we have yet to see if it is entirely extinguished. If not, desperation may once more light the smouldering fires and destroy me in the process as well.

He did not live to see the conflagration which was to burst forth from those smouldering fires and the convulsions and violence of 1971, which were foreshadowed prophetically in the concluding lines of these memoirs.

The Bengali people are still engaged in the quest for freedom and justice—for democracy and people's supremacy—goals towards which Suhrawardy—and after him Bangabandhu Sheikh Mujibur Rahman—had led them. These goals are still unrealized. In the struggle which continues for their realization, these memoirs should serve as a powerful source of inspiration.

Kamal Hossain
19 July 1987

Recollections

On 5 December 1963, at 5 a.m., the phone at my home in London rang with a tone of ominous foreboding. I was still awake, studying hard for my BA finals from London University, trying to cram three years work into the few remaining months left before I sat my examinations. I realized the call heralded something of pressing urgency as, even by the standards of a casual, student life no one rang up for a chat at 5 o'clock in the morning. The news was shattering, though I suppose, in all honesty, not totally unexpected. The call was from Francois Jabres, a long-standing friend of my family, phoning from Beirut to tell me the news that my father was dead.

My father had stayed with me during the previous six months, convalescing, after suffering two severe heart attacks, at the house that I shared with some fellow Pakistani students, who were also studying at English universities. This six months was perhaps the most productive period of our relationship and certainly the longest that we have spent together, uninterrupted, since I was a small child in Calcutta before Partition. During this time I saw the multi-dimensional facets of his personality given full expression. I saw the courage he displayed, combating the painful angina attacks with which he was intermittently afflicted, each one of which, one feared, may have been his last. Even more poignantly, I recall the humour he displayed on such occasions. After experiencing one such attack during a game of bridge and, whilst my friends and I were literally carrying him in a cradle of arms to his bed, he said in barely audible tones, through teeth clenched with pain, 'Damn, and I had a strong one-no-trump opening bid'. On other occasions, while he was convalescing in bed or working on these memoirs, he would answer the phone at his bed-side and, if the calls were for me or my flatmates, would introduce himself as our secretary and take the message, writing it down in his immaculate hand-writing, making sure that the name of the caller was spelt correctly and the message crystal clear. If the voice at the other end was female, he would stay on the line for twenty minutes to half an hour, charming the caller, without giving away who he was, and most of us were lucky not to lose our girlfriends, before they had even met him. Though considerably older than my friends, who were the same age as myself, he was able to communicate with them so easily that they used to enjoy sitting and arguing with him, being gently corrected in their arguments, picked up on factual errors, whilst he quietly admonished them for their prejudices, which were the product of youthful arrogance and inexperience. Nor was this tutoring biased in my favour.

I recall on one occasion getting into one of those perennial arguments with my friends, who all hailed from West Pakistan, about the economic discrepancy that prevailed between the two wings and the exploitation of the East wing by the centre, authoritatively supporting my argument with some pretty impressive figures, depicting the disparity between the foreign exchange earnings of the East wing and the commensurate paucity of reinvestment and the dreadful reduction in the development of the fishery and jute industries. My father had come into the room during my harangue and quietly watched my performance. Fuelled by both his presence and the fervour of my argument, I assailed my friends with even more towering rhetoric and ended with a peroration that, had it been delivered at the Paltan Maidan, would have brought the crowd to its feet. Everyone sat in stunned silence and then one of my friends asked my father whether what I had said was true, to which he quietly responded, 'not quite'. Whereupon, equally quietly but, oh so succinctly, he proceeded to rip my argument to shreds, logically and factually and replaced it with an historic and evolutionary dissertation, which endorsed the genius of my exposition but put it into a perspective of reality, elevating it from the level of demagoguery, prejudice and even ignorance, which, I have to say, for many years often distorted the real issues and justification of suspicion and betrayal that the Bengali people felt towards the vested interests of West Pakistan and, even more insidiously, which dictated how decent, well-meaning and fair-minded West Pakistanis felt about the people of East Pakistan.

I was there with him as countless Bengalis and Pakistanis came to my house from all over England to see him, which the somewhat conservative residents of Hampstead Garden suburbs, whose only intercourse with subcontinentals in those days was being waited on in an Indian or Pakistani restaurant, found totally bewildering.

I was there when Ayub Khan sent a special envoy to meet him, offering him the vice-presidency, with assurances of a move towards the restoration of full democracy if would accept the position. He replied that had Ayub made this offer three years before he may well have accepted but by 1963 too much blood had flowed under the bridge and President's reputation had become so tainted that it was now impossible.

I was there when Sheikh Mujibur Rahman came to visit him, to beg him to revive the Awami League, since there was talk of some of the other parties reviving and Mujib was frightened that the Awami League might lose its potency if it remained dormant. He rejected this plea, saying that he had given his word to the other leaders of the NDF that he would not revive the party without consulting them—a point I had to stress quite vehemently a few months later in Dhaka when, at a high-level meeting of the Awami League at Manik Mia's house, shortly after my father's funeral, this subject was being passionately argued.

Most of the time, however, was spent helping him to collate the memoirs on which he had started working. Towards the end of his stay with me he had completed the first draft, with numerous handwritten amendments. In short, that is what is published in its entirety in this book. Whilst they are concise, they are nevertheless, a recondite commentary of his assessment and involvement in the politics of Pakistan from its birth to the time of his death. They recount much of what had not been said before and, more surprisingly, what has not been said since. The tragedy is considering what the end-product might have been had he had the time to pursue the normal evolutionary stages of any literary creation. How much more was there to be said had he had access to objective criticism and been able to work on the second, third and fourth drafts? Yet the relevance of that analysis in the context of the political events of today is so frighteningly apposite that there is a disconcerting feeling of *deja vu*.

I think many people will feel disappointed and even a little cheated that he did not deal more extensively with those dramatic, colourful and, alas, frequently historically-distorted years leading up to partition. His work during that period and that of the Bengal Muslim League, which have been so shamelessly vilified in supposedly profound and erudite histories, through the media of films and television series, which, heavily financed by the Indian government, have depicted him and the Muslims of India, particularly of Bengal, as the villains of Partition, compared with the incorruptibility and fairplay of Mountbatten and Nehru. The fact that he has concentrated, for the most part, on the political events relating to Pakistan, was quite obviously determined by the knowledge that they were current and vibrant and, had his comments been reproduced more promptly, may well have tarnished the sanctimonious image which Ayub and his brilliant propaganda machine had so adroitly created.

For a variety of reasons there was a lengthy delay before the papers came into my possession again. By the time this had happened and I was able to have them re-typed the political equations in the country had altered. The war with India had disturbed the status quo and Ayub's seeming invincibility was showing signs of strain. British publishers whom I approached felt that the memoirs should be used as the basis for a greater work on Pakistan or a biography of my father and not published in their isolated form. Obviously, no Pakistani publisher or press was willing to touch them at that time.

When Mohammad H.R. Talukdar approached me for permission to use them I became interested when he indicated that he wished to write a short history of my father's life, family background and political career. This seemed to me the perfect correlative to the memoirs. Mr Talukdar's work is not meant to be an in-depth and comprehensive analysis and account but it provides information about the salient features of my father's life and career, much of which is new and illuminating and I hope very much, as I am sure Mr Talukdar does, that this book may encourage other historians to delve into the archives and repositories, mainly centred in India, and produce more detailed biographies which may describe the life and times of one of the great political figures of this century, putting into perspective his true role in the history of the Indian subcontinent.

Rashid Suhrawardy
30 April 1987

Preface

Writing a comprehensive account of the life and achievements of Huseyn Shaheed Suhrawardy (1892–1963) is an almost impossible task and I have not attempted this. What I have endeavoured to do is to present a brief narration of the political events of his time and his association with, and role in, moulding these events, also attempting to provide some of the missing links in the study of his political memoirs. These memoirs, which have been faithfully reproduced in the second part of this book, were still being worked on at the time of his death. This should be considered when one is reading them.

A copy of Suhrawardy's memoirs came into my possession while I was in Karachi and was writing pamphlets on the heroes of the struggle for independence for the Pakistan government. I visited Lakham House—the Karachi residence of his only daughter, Begum Akhter Jahan and her husband, Shah Ahmad Sulaiman several times. Begum Sulaiman showed me many rare documents, including her illustrious father's memoirs, which tell us the story of Suhrawardy's role in the final phase of our struggle for freedom from the British Raj. We also find in his memoirs the relentless struggle he waged for the establishment of democracy and the rule of law in Pakistan. However, the memoirs were incomplete; missing pages provoked me to collect a fuller version, which Begum Sulaiman had already mentioned but could not provide me with at the time. I had, also, no time to wait because of my planned repatriation from Pakistan following the creation of Bangladesh in 1971, and I proceeded to publish the incomplete memoirs.

As if by providence, when I requested Dr Kamal Hossain to write a foreword to this book, he instantly offered me a copy of the fuller, much more detailed version than I had collected from Suhrawardy's daughter, at the same time asking me to obtain Suhrawardy's surviving son, Rashid Suhrawardy's, approval which I did. I most gratefully acknowledge this magnanimous offer of his copy with permission to publish here and for writing the foreword to this book.

Rashid Suhrawardy, while offering me his best wishes, stated the circumstances surrounding his father's memoirs that deserve our special attention and I quote:

At the time of his death in Beirut the Pakistan government gave instructions for his papers to be seized, obviously because they had gleaned information that he had commenced working on his memoirs, which were going to be highly embarrassing and injurious to the reputations of Ayub. A friend of ours, a Mr Francois Jabres, who resided in Beirut, phoned me in London to give me the sad news of my father's death and also to advise me to cable the Lebanese authorities, instructing them to hold all my father's belongings and papers until I arrived, which stymied the Pakistan authorities' attempts to gain access to my father's papers. I left the papers with Monsieur Jabres before accompanying my father's body to Pakistan and picked them up on my return to England. I gave a copy of the memoirs to Kamal in 1975, requesting him to see if he could use his influence in having them published, or if they could be of any service or aid to any potential researcher.

Publication of this book has been possible only with the encouragement and moral support of Professor Salahuddin Ahmed of the University of Dhaka and Mohiuddin Ahmed, Managing Director of the University Press Limited, Dhaka. Professor Ahmed happens to be one of my beloved teachers. Once he came down from Dhaka to my Joydebpur residence, painstakingly went through my collection and planned their publication. He also reviewed the manuscript and offered valuable suggestions which I incorporated with gratitude; I am ever grateful to him for his help and encouragement.

Rashid Suhrawardy also read the final draft, gave his 'Recollections' and a copy of the letter his illustrious father wrote from jail to President Ayub (Appendix I). A.M.A. Muhit made available to me the original copy of Rashid Suhrawardy's letter addressed to the Provisional Government of Bangladesh, supporting the liberation struggle (Appendix II). Shahida, Sulaiman's only child, then a law student, had also her own collections on her maternal grandfather, especially foreign newspaper comments on the Kashmir debate at the United Nations and American arms commitment to Pakistan. These are valuable documents and I owe them my grateful thanks.

For the introduction I heavily depended upon the Ittefaq edition on Suhrawardy. It contains a rare collection of Suhrawardy's parliamentary and public speeches and writings on him. I also owe gratitude to Shamsul Alam, PhD, and M.A. Wadud, for offering me to consult their collections on Suhrawardy. Innumerable friends and colleagues and all those who wished me well, I offer them my sincerest thanks.

M.A. Mannan, PhD, Director General of the Bangladesh Rice Research Institute and my office chief, kindly granted me about 3 months leave to complete this work and I also owe him my gratitude.

To Charles T. Brackney, my colleague, who most willingly gave his editorial inputs, I owe him my heart-felt gratitude. I also thank Manoj Mandol and Nurun Nahar, who proofread and Ashraf Uddin and M.A. Baten, who typed the entire manuscript with great care.

Last but not least, I am grateful to my wife Laily Rahman and my children, Khokan, Shapon, Ratna, and Babu, without whose constant encouragement and patient bearing of my long absence from their midst I could not have completed this work.

Mohammad H.R. Talukdar

PART I

Life and Work

FAMILY BACKGROUND

Huseyn Shaheed Suhrawardy was born on 8 September 1892 into an illustrious Muslim family from Midnapore in West Bengal, India. The ancestral home of the family was Suhraward, a city in Iraq, from which it assumed its surname Suhrawardy.[1] The founder of the family in Iraq was Sheikh Shahabuddin Omar bin Mohammad Us-Suhrawardy (1145–1235).[2] He was the chief disciple of Ghous al-Azam Hazrat Abd al-Qadir al-Jilani.[3] He himself was a vastly learned man and philosopher. His *Aa'oraful Ma'rif* is a masterpiece of Islamic learning.

According to family tradition, Sheikh Shahabuddin Suhrawardy was descended from his father's side from Hazrat Abu Bakr Siddiq, the first Caliph of Islam. From his mother's side he was descended from Hazrat Ali bin Abu Talib and Bibi Fatima. Hazrat Ali was a son-in-law of the holy prophet and the fourth Caliph of Islam. He was, therefore, both a Siddiqui and a Syed.[4]

SUHRAWARDIA ORDER OF SAINTS

Sheikh Shahabuddin Suhrawardy also founded the Suhrawardia Order of Saints and sent out his sons and disciples to Iran, Turan, Turkestan, Sindh, Hindustan and Bangladesh to preach Islam.[5] Suhrawardia preachers had come to the subcontinent long before the Chistia Sheikhs arrived.[6] Sheikh Bahauddin Zakaria Multani, one of the Sheikhs of this Order, spread Islam in the subcontinent.[7] It is said that Sultan Alauddin Mohammad Shah Khilji (1296–1316), along with his ministers and courtiers, received Maulana Rukunuddin Suhrawardy, a grandson of Sheikh Bahauddin Zakaria Multani, at the Delhi Gate, and descending from the royal horse, kissed his feet.[8] Two of Sheikh Shahabuddin Suhrawardy's daughters, Bihi Nur and Bibi Nur, are buried at the Delhi Chistia graveyard. Their *mazar* is still known as Bihi-Nur-Ki Dargah. Shamsul Arifin, popularly known as Turkman Shah, was another of Sheikh Shahabuddin's sons. He settled in Delhi. The Turkman Gate in the old part of Delhi still bears his name. Another illustrious scion of this family married a daughter of Sultan Bahlol Lodi (1451–1489), the founder of the Afghan Lodi dynasty of Delhi.[9] The founder of the Nizam Shahi dynasty of

Hyderabad, Deccan, Nizam ul-Mulk Asaf Jang (1724), is also said to descend from the Suhrawardy family.[10]

In addition, the Sufi saints of Maner Sharif, Bihar Sharif, Gour and Pandua in West Bengal belonged to the Suhrawardy Order.[11] Sheikh Sharfuddin Bihari, who received his education at Sonargaon, the one-time Muslim capital of Bengal near Dhaka, also belonged to this family. According to H. E. Staplestone, Hazrat Shah Jalal also belonged to this illustrious family.[12] He came to Sylhet with 360 disciples to preach Islam in Gour, Pandua, Rangpur, Dinajpur, Sylhet and in many other parts of Bangladesh. Sheikh Shahabuddin Suhrawardy had so dedicated himself to preaching Islam that reminiscences of his devotion are still extant in many parts of Turkestan.[13] The Khanqa of Sheikh Zainuddin Suhrawardy can still be seen just outside Tashkent, the capital of Uzbekistan.

RENAISSANCE MOVEMENT IN BENGAL

The Suhrawardy family of Midnapore, West Bengal, pioneered the Islamic renaissance movement in Bengal.[14] The name of Maulana Obaidullah al-Obaidi Suhrawardy (1834–1886) is immediately remembered in this connection. He was a versatile genius and linguist. Probably he had no parallel during his time; he was called the *Bahrul Ulum* or the sea of knowledge for his profound eruditon.[15] Maulana al-Obaidi received his early education in Arabic and Persian. Later in his life he acquired proficiency in English and advocated the cause of English education and modern sciences among Muslim youths of his time.[16] In 1864, he received an award for an essay entitled 'Reciprocal influence of Mohammadan and European Civilizations.'[17] The prize was awarded by Charles Trevelyan. The essay was first published in 1865 and reissued in 1877.

Maulana al-Obaidi's first appointment as a public servant was as Head Munshi in the Translation Department of the Viceregal Legislative Council in Delhi. He was next appointed Anglo-Arabic Professor of Hoogli college. Syed Ameer Ali, one of his most favourite students, a one-time member of the British Privy Council and a renowned historian, later wrote in his memoirs: 'Every Sunday morning Moulvi Obaidullah, the Persian Professor, and I breakfasted with the Syed (Syed Ahmad Khan of Aligarh) and scarcely ever left before one o'clock. We ranged over the whole region of oriental history and philosophy. He (Obaidullah) was a scholarly man conversant in English.'[18] In 1867, Obaidullah al-Obaidi Suhrawardy and Syed Ameer Ali jointly published a translation of Syed Keramat Ali's *Makhazul Ulum*.[19] While at Hoogli, Maulana al-Obaidi also published his Anglo-Arabic Grammar in 1873 for students of the affiliated colleges of the University of Calcutta. Maulana Al-Obaidi also wrote *Dasturi Farsi Amoz*, a Persian grammar, written on the model of grammars in European languages. His collection of poems, *Dewan-i-Obaidi*, were first published in 1886. A poet from Shiraz wrote of the Maulana that, even though he was not born in Persia, his command of the Persian language was almost equal to that of a native of Shiraz.[20] Some of his *Qassidas* (poems) in praise of Dhaka can be compared with the best in Persian poetry.

Maulana Obaidullah al-Obaidi Suhrawardy was appointed the first superintendent of Dhaka Aliya Madrasah when it was established on 16 March 1874.[21] He held this post until his death twelve years later. This was one of the three madrasahs established out of the Mohsin fund on the pleadings of Nawab Abdul Latif to open the doors of modern education to Muslim boys.[22] It was then the only institute in eastern Bengal which taught English to Muslim students.

The Maulana was a man of progressive ideas and heartily supported Syed Ahmad Khan and his liberal movement.[23] The Syed was very pleased to find an enthusiastic supporter of his views in the far eastern corner of India. Maulana Obaidullah al-Obaidi regularly contributed to *Tahzibul Akhlaq*, the journal started by the Syed for the propagation of his progressive views.[24] He was also one of the first directors of the Mohammadan Anglo-Arabic College, Aligarh.[25]

Maulana al-Obaidi participated in the renaissance movement in East Bengal.[26] In 1863, Nawab Abdul Latif had founded the Mohammadan Literary Society in Calcutta in order to spread modern education among Muslims.[27] Syed Ameer Ali's Central National Mohammadan Association, founded in 1877, was also located in Calcutta.[28] To meet the need for such a society in Dhaka, Maulana al-Obaidi founded the Friends' Association for the betterment of Bengali Muslims on 13 December 1879.[29] He became its secretary. Not much is known of this association except for a passing reference to it in the *Navapanjika* published by the East Bengal Press on 10 March 1880.[30]

In addition to founding this association, Maulana al-Obaidi cooperated with a group of enthusiasts of Dhaka College in founding the Dhaka Mohammadan Friend's Association on 24 February 1883.[31] He became its chief patron. Indeed, it was his inspiration that made its establishment possible, and until his death in early 1886, it used to sit in session in the Dhaka Aliya Madrasah where he was its superintendent. Its aim was the betterment of the Muslim society in Bengal and the spread of English education among Muslim men and women. Owing to financial difficulties the association devoted its first few years to spreading education among Muslim women only. Each member of this association used to pay a monthly fee of two annas. Within a period of three years membership rose to 162 from 23 at the time of its foundation.

For the spread of education among Muslim women, the association prepared a syllabus and conducted examinations for students up to class V. Candidates could answer either in Bengali or Urdu and appear at examination in their own homes under the supervision of their guardians who could also recommend oral examiners. The association seemed to have been active until 1887. That it had dedicated itself during this short period to the overall improvement of Bengali Muslims is proved by the secretary's report for 1887.[32]

These were the contributions of Maulana Obaidullah al-Obaidi towards awakening the national consciousness of Bengali Muslims. More than a hundred years ago, in 1865, he wrote:

> Supposing that there exists any contradiction between the modern scientific truths and our scripture, we should consult our sacred writings for our moral instructions and guidance towards salvation, not for scientific investigation.[33]

Advocating reforms in government madrasah education, he observed further that

> The course of studies in government madrasahs should be remodelled. Studies should be confined to easy texts of all branches of Arabic learning leaving out the cumbersome methods of teaching commentaries, which abound in quibbles, thus saving the student's time from being wasted in sifting out metaphysical questions which are of no practical use and giving him facility for learning modern science through the English language.[34]

Maulana al-Obaidi died in 1886 while prostrated saying his prayers and is buried near the Shahi Mosque inside the Lalbagh Fort.

Maulana al-Obaidi was the maternal grandfather of Huseyn Shaheed Suhrawardy. Shaheed Suhrawardy's paternal grandfather, Maulana Mobarak Ali Suhrawardy, a famous lawyer and Sadar-i-ala of Bhagalpur in Bihar, was al-Obaidi's only real brother. Their father was Aminuddin Suhrawardy. Shaheed Suhrawardy's father, Barrister Zahidur Rahman Zahid, popularly known as Zahid Suhrawardy, was a judge of the High Court of Calcutta. He had, however, started his career as an advocate of the district court of the 24 Parganas in West Bengal. After practising law for four years, he was enlisted as an advocate at the appellate division of the Calcutta High Court. In those days conditions for admission to the London Inns of Court could be relaxed for those who had practised law in a High Court in India. Zahid Suhrawardy seized upon this opportunity and went to London to study law which he completed with distinction.[35] He joined the Calcutta High Court Bar but was appointed to the position of judge for the Small Causes Court.

He later resigned from the post to become a member of the Bengal Legislative Assembly. He was knighted after his retirement from the Bar.[36]

Suhrawardy's mother, Begum Khozesta Akhter Banu, the eldest daughter of Maulana al-Obaidi, had learned Persian, Arabic, Urdu, and English from her father and was the first Muslim woman to pass the Senior Cambridge Examination.[37] She also graduated with honours in Persian literature from the Indian Board of Examinations. The University of Calcutta later appointed her as an examiner for Urdu literature.[38] She was the only Indian lady to receive this honour.[39] Although a veiled lady, Khozesta Akhter Banu was a great advocate of women's education and a social worker. She wrote *Aina-e-Ibrat*, a valuable book on women's education. The University of Calcutta had approved the book for its affiliated colleges. In 1909, she founded the Suhrawardia Girls School in Calcutta. Lady Minto, wife of the Viceroy of India, inaugurated this school. In sympathy for the poor she frequently visited the *bustees* (slums) to provide them with education and teach them health and sanitation. While she was thus engaged in social work she caught influenza and died on 12 January 1919.

Begum Khozesta Akhter Banu had four brothers: Mamun Suhrawardy, Abdullah al-Mamun Suhrawardy, Hassan Suhrawardy, and Mahmud Suhrawardy. Mamun Suhrawardy died immediately after his graduation. The other three brothers earned high reputations for their learning and public work. Abdullah al-Mamun Suhrawardy studied law in England and obtained the degrees of PhD, LLD and Dlit from Oxford University. He joined the English Bar. While in England he was greatly influenced by Jamaluddin Afghani's Pan Islamic thought and founded in 1905 the Pan Islamic Society in London.[40] Attracted by his dedication to Islam, Sultan Abdul Hamid of Turkey honoured him by awarding the title of *Majidia*.[41] The Shah of Iran also endowed him with the title of *Iftekharul Millat* or the Pride of the Muslims.[42] On his return to India, Abdullah al-Mamun Suhrawardy joined the Lahore Islamia College as its principal and later joined the Calcutta High Court Bar, but soon resigned to accept an appointment as Tagore Professor of Law at the University of Calcutta.[43] At that time the professorship was considered a very prestigious post and carried a handsome salary. In 1911 the Balkan War began and he established the Red Crescent Society in Calcutta to provide assistance for Turkish war victims.[44] At the request of the governments of the United Kingdom and the United States of America, respectively, he prepared constitutions for the Muslims of Gambia and the Philippines.[45] He married into the family of Tipu Sultan of Mysore; he had no issue.

Suhrawardy's third uncle, Lt.-Col. Sir Hassan Suhrawardy, DSC, LLD, FRCS, was the first Muslim Vice-Chancellor of the University of Calcutta. He was also a member of the Viceroy's advisory board. Hassan Suhrawardy was actively associated with the foundation of the Muslim Cultural Centre and the Regent Park Mosque in London.[46] He married a daughter of the Nawab of Dhaka, Syed Mohammad Azad. Another daughter of the Nawab was married to A.K. Fazlul Huq. Hassan Suhrawardy's only daughter, Shaista Begum, was married to Mohammad Ikramullah, ICS, High Commissioner and Ambassador of Pakistan to the United Kingdom, Canada, and France and Foreign Secretary of Pakistan between 1958 and 1962. Shaista Begum was elected as a member of the First Constituent Assembly and a delegate to the United Nations and, after her husband's death in 1963, was appointed Ambassador to Morocco. The fourth uncle, Mahmud Suhrawardy, was a member of the Indian Council of States.

Suhrawardy's elder and only brother, Professor Hassan Shahid Suhrawardy, after graduating with honours from Oxford University, proceeded to Russia for further studies. He was much liked and admired by the intellectual and artistic circles and became professor of English at Moscow University. After the Russian Revolution he escaped with the Russian refugees. He worked with Konstantin Stanislavsky in the Moscow Arts Theatre. Professor Shahid was a great linguist of the subcontinent and was fluent in more than a dozen languages. Before the partition of India in 1947 he was Professor of Fine Arts at Calcutta University. Later he became a member of the Bengal and then of the Pakistan Public Service Commissions. Because of his association with Russian refugees the British at one stage looked upon him with suspicion. This, however, was allayed by Robert Bridges' vouching for him.

EDUCATION AND FAMILY LIFE

Huseyn Shaheed Suhrawardy received his early education from his mother and from his maternal uncle, Sir Abdullah al-Mamun Suhrawardy. Later he entered the Calcutta Aliya Madrasah and graduated with honours in science from St Xavier's College. In fulfilment of his mother's wishes, he obtained the degree of Master of Arts in Arabic from Calcutta University in 1913. That same year he left for England for higher studies and graduated in science with honours from the University of Oxford. He also received his BCL degree from this university and was called to the Bar from Grey's Inn in 1918.

Suhrawardy married Sir Abdur Rahim's daughter, Begum Naiz Fatima, in 1920. Sir Abdur Rahim was a judge of the Calcutta High Court, a member of the Governor's Executive Council and President of the Indian Legislative Assembly. Their married life lasted only three years. Begum Naiz died in 1922. By her, Suhrawardy had a son and a daughter. The son, Shahab

Suhrawardy, died in London in 1940 while pursuing his studies at Oxford. The daughter, Akhter Jahan Suhrawardia, was married to Sir Mohammad Sulaiman's son, Shah Ahmad Sulaiman. Sir Mohammad Sulaiman was Chief Justice of the Allahabad High Court, Vice-Chancellor of Allahabad University and a judge of the Federal Court of India. He was also reputed to be a talented mathematician. Begum Akhter Sulaiman died in Karachi in 1982 and is survived by her only daughter, Shahida Munni, who is also a barrister.

In 1940, nearly eighteen years after Naiz Fatima's death, Suhrawardy married Vera Tiscenko, a former actress of the Moscow Arts Theatre, who had met Professor Shahid Suhrawardy when he was directing at the Moscow Arts Theatre and who had invited her to come to India, after she and her family had had to flee Russia after the Revolution. Previously married to a brilliant Russian surgeon, she had led a life almost as colourful and unusual as the man she was soon to marry. Originally caught up in the Russian Revolution, she was in Germany when Hitler seized power, in Italy when Mussolini came to power and in Spain during the civil war. In all these countries she was an alien and had to flee, often in the most dramatic and perilous circumstances. She was now to be in India during that country's hectic struggle for independence.

A mixture of Suhrawardy's all-consuming commitment to this struggle and the obvious social, linguistic, and cultural difficulties encountered by a lady of her background, put an understandable strain on their marriage and in 1946 they separated, with the decree nisi becoming final in 1951. Neither was to marry again. Their only issue, Rashid, as a result of this divorce, was brought up in England and after being educated at Charterhouse, Oxford and London universities chose, with his father's blessing, to follow in his mother's footsteps and, after graduating, with top honours, from the Royal Academy of Dramatic Art, is now pursuing a career of a professional actor in England and has spent a number of years with the Royal Shakespeare Company. There can be no doubt that this decision would have disappointed Suhrawardy, who would, obviously, have wanted his only son to follow him into the law or politics but it is typical of the man that he commented, in support of Rashid's decision, that had circumstances been different he would have loved to have been an actor, himself. If fact, anyone who had the privilege of witnessing his brilliant performances in a court of law or on the platform of a mass political meeting, with his rich baritone voice resonating, would not have found this an unreasonable proposition at all.

HINDU-MUSLIM UNITY

Suhrawardy returned home sometime in 1920 and was immediately involved in the political movements of the day. Three most important factors probably dictated Suhrawardy's rather quick entry into politics.

First, the relationship between the caste Hindus and the Muslims was rapidly deteriorating. Although the Bengali Muslims had a clear edge in numbers over their Hindu compatriots, they could not compete politically and economically with them. The caste Hindus had become educationally more advanced and occupied all important government and business positions and thus had acquired economic and political control over the Muslims who became mainly agriculturists along with the low-caste Hindus.

Sitting at the nerve-centre of politics in Calcutta, Suhrawardy saw this helplessness how his community who constituted the majority in the countryside but were a minority in the cities and towns stood neglected at every stage of their life.

Therefore, alongside his law practice Suhrawardy chose the dirty road to politics—the only way to rehabilitate them socially and politically. Thus, forced circumstantially young Suhrawardy broke away[47] from the erudite family tradition, otherwise no one before or after him participated in politics.

Second, although the All-India Muslim League (AIML) was founded in Dhaka in 1906 to protect, among others, Muslim interests in Bengal and defend the 1905 partition of Bengal, it had lost all credibility in the land of its birth being limited to a few armchair politicians of western provinces.

Third, the First World War (1914–1919) had just ended, leaving the vast Turkish Empire spread over Eastern Europe, North Africa and Western Asia, dismembered and the Caliphate threatened with abolishment. The Muslims of India had supported Turkey during its war in the Balkans (1911–1912) and had continued the support through the Great War when it broke out in 1914. They were naturally worried over the fate of the only existing Muslim power upon which they could look with pride as a source of inspiration and had started the Khilafat movement to support it as well as to strengthen their own freedom struggle.

THE KHILAFAT MOVEMENT

The Khilafat movement, the most spectacular movement of the day, was then raging all over India under the dynamic leadership of the Ali Brothers—the vibrant Maulana Mohammad Ali and the phlegmatic Showkat Ali. Gandhi took advantage of the situation and supported the Muslims in their demand for restoration of the Khilafat in Turkey. The Khilafat committee soon changed its composition from a middleclass organization into one representing the masses. Many persons who were members of the Khilafat committee were also members of the Congress with considerable cooperation between the two organizations. The Ali Brothers cooperated with Gandhi throughout and attempted to effect a conciliation between the conflicting claims and demands of the Hindus and Muslims. Several conferences were held through the initiative, particularly of the great Bengali leader, Deshbandhu C.R. Das, who was the foremost criminal lawyer in Calcutta. Suhrawardy accepted the Ali Brothers as his political mentors and, as secretary to the Calcutta Khilafat committee, humbly worked for it as their right-hand man in Bengal to unify and organize the Muslims of Bengal.

THE BENGAL PACT

Only a year later, in 1921, Suhrawardy was elected to the Bengal Legislative Assembly from the Khidirpur industrial area.[48] He had, with his Oxford background, a strong leaning towards independence and critical politics. He consequently adopted an independent attitude in the debates opposing the government in a reasoned but trenchant manner. During this time the British government placed the Whipping Bill before the Assembly and Suhrawardy, as an opposition leader, attacked it creating a big sensation among the younger generation.[49] He cautioned the British government that

> Indians are not animals; they are as good human beings as their white masters. They have the same amount of feelings as the British. Like all other civilized peoples of the world, they also have the same sense of self-respect. Maddened with power the British might have managed to get the bill passed with assistance from nominated members of the Assembly, but that would have been against humanity. We were not slaves. We surrendered to the animal power of the British, but history would testify that in the past we were superior in accordance with the standards of civilization.[50]

Congress leaders recognized Suhrawardy's bold stand and considered him a valuable asset in their opposition to the government. This also helped Suhrawardy to come closer to C.R. Das and convince him of the need for Hindu-Muslim unity before embarking on the movement to fight for freedom. Das also honestly believed that achievement of freedom would be impossible unless the Muslims were given their due share in administration. A statesman of the highest order, he was absolutely neutral and commanded respect equally from the Hindus and the Muslims of Bengal. He also conceived the idea of Bengali nationalism and in 1923 entered into an agreement with the Bengali Muslims.[51] Known as the Bengal pact, the agreement accepted the Muslim majority in Bengal, the principle of separate electorates and expansion of facilities for the education of Muslim students. The pact further stipulated equal Muslim representation in all elective bodies in Bengal, including the legislative assembly and the appointment of Muslims in public bodies until they reached parity with the Hindus. It also ensured the post of Mayor of Calcutta to a Muslim every third year. The vested Hindu groups opposed the pact, but C.R. Das managed to get it approved by both the provincial and the Indian National Congress.[52]

Das also believed in liberal democracy and left the Congress Party when he found his views clashing with the majority of its members. He, therefore, formed the Swaraj Party in 1923 to enter the Bengal Legislative Assembly where he could use it as a forum for the struggle for freedom.[53] He had so much faith in Suhrawardy that he appointed him Deputy leader of his Swaraj Party. Probably in 1924 the Calcutta municipality was elevated to a corporation and the Swaraj Party captured a majority of seats in the 1924 Calcutta corporation election.[54] Although he was never in Congress, in accordance with a stipulation of the Bengal pact, Shaheed Suhrawardy was elected the first Deputy Mayor of the Congress-ridden corporation while C.R. Das became the Mayor.[55] Prior to him no Muslim had ever been appointed to that post. In those days the corporation exerted great influence on local political affairs and Shaheed Suhrawardy, in his capacity as the Deputy Mayor, did his best to eradicate Hindu monopoly in the corporation. Even this qualified success was no slight achievement for Suhrawardy as he had just begun his political career.

1926 RIOTS

As long as C.R. Das was alive, the Bengal pact was never violated. After his death in 1925 Subash Chandra Bose and Suhrawardy renewed the pact.[56] But Das's death changed not only the entire complexion of political life in Bengal, but in the whole of India. Suhrawardy believed that had Das lived longer he would have 'eliminated the causes of Hindu-Muslim conflict and bitterness' that 'led to the partition of India and creation of Pakistan.'[57] In 1926, a Muslim killed Rajpal, the author of *Rangila Rasool*, resulting in anti-Muslim riots that broke out that year.[58] During the riots Suhrawardy moved from one corner of the city to another at great risk to his own life to save the unprotected people and restore order in the riot-torn city. He did all that he could to stem the riots and to bring about peace between the Hindus and the Muslims.

The Hindus had all the advantages during the riots. Not only did they constitute 78 per cent of the population of Calcutta but also both the higher and the lower ranks of the Calcutta police. The armed police were manned almost entirely by them, and this resulted in the Muslims being slaughtered in many places. However, in spite of their weaker position and greater losses, the Muslims were mostly indicted in criminal cases: as many as 64 Muslims were indicted in murder cases whereas only one Hindu was so involved. Arrangements had to be made to feed the affected Muslims in their localities, as, not only were they surrounded by Hindus, but also Hindu tradesmen in Muslim localities had left their businesses behind, locked and unattended, and no food was available. Arrangements had also to be made to defend those Muslims who were indicted in criminal cases. Suhrawardy, then a young lawyer, fought a desperate legal battle on their behalf and through his forensic skill and application got all of them acquitted, including one condemned to death by hanging.[59] He persuaded the Muslim dock workers, mostly from East Bengal, to contribute generous donations to help the riot-afflicted penurious Muslims. His close contact with the dock workers and *bustee* dwellers also helped him to understand their problems at close hand. These people also considered him to be one of them. From this moment on Suhrawardy became directly associated with the labour movement in Bengal. During the communal riots, although Suhrawardy was constantly risking his life to rescue the Hindus from Muslim localities and the Muslims from Hindu localities in the face of murderous mobs, a section of the Hindus had started a false and malicious propaganda against Suhrawardy which led ultimately to his resignation from the Deputy Mayoralty in 1927.

In 1927, as a result of this riot, attempts were made at a high level to bring about a rapprochement between the Hindus and the Muslims. A peace conference of Hindu and Muslim representatives from all over India met at Simla with the Maharajah of Alwar presiding. Both Mohammad Ali Jinnah and Suhrawardy attended that meeting as Muslim representatives.[60] The points of contention centred mainly on the question of cow slaughter and the playing of music before mosques, points which were regarded as the main symptoms of the discord that led to most of the riots in 1926.

Firstly, the Hindus insisted that Muslims should not slaughter cows, which they considered to be sacred and worshipped, elevating cows to the position of mother. The Muslims, however, insisted on slaughtering cows because that was their main protein source; beef was cheaper than mutton, fish or fowl. It was also convenient for them to sacrifice cows during the Eid ul Azha festival when animals were sacrificed in the name of Allah to commemorate the manner in which Abraham was prevented from slaughtering his own son, Ismail. Seven persons could receive religious benediction for each cow sacrificed, whereas the sacrifice of a goat or a sheep conferred religious benediction on only one person. The Muslims were prepared to conduct the slaughter and the sacrifice removed from the public gaze and to convey the beef under cover, but this did not allay the objection of the Hindus who took serious exception to cow slaughter in any form, particularly during this festival. Cows were slaughtered in abattoirs in the towns, but in the villages, they were slaughtered at any convenient place, usually by the roadside where the meat could be readily sold.

Secondly, the Hindus insisted on playing music when passing along a thoroughfare, even if there was a mosque on that thoroughfare and even if prayers were being conducted at that time. The Muslims insisted that music should be stopped when passing a mosque. This had become a custom when the Muslims were in power, particularly in those areas where they were in a vast majority, as in parts of East Bengal. Some were prepared to come to an understanding with a section of the Hindus on the basis that music would not be played when the congregational prayer in mosques was actually in progress. But the extreme section of the Muslims insisted that music should be stopped before mosques at all times as prayers could be held and were actually held throughout the day. Conversely, the extreme section of the Hindus insisted that they had the right of a citizen to pass along the thoroughfare and play music at all times. The government found a via media by ordering that music could be played before a mosque, except during congregational prayer time and in those places where the custom was to stop music at all times. The Hindus retaliated by playing music before mosques louder than ever, often provocatively, for longer periods.

A SEPARATIST MUSLIM LEADER

The 1927 meeting at Simla yielded no results and Jinnah told Suhrawardy privately that he considered the Hindus to be extremely unreasonable.[61] At that time Jinnah was in the Congress and it appeared that he might be able to play the role of a mediator between the Hindus and the Muslims. He, therefore, tried to take a middle road on Hindu-Muslim issues, advocating the principle of joint electorate. But failure of the Simla Peace Conference convinced Suhrawardy that 'the talk of Hindu-Muslim unity was a myth', that 'the Hindus wanted nothing but complete surrender from the Muslims as the price of unity.'[62] From now on Suhrawardy adopted the clear stand of a separatist Muslim leader, fighting for the survival and progress of the Muslims as a community.

The Lucknow Pact signed in 1916 had already accepted the principle of separate electorates introduced by the 1909 Reforms Act and accordingly had provided that seats in the legislature be apportioned between the Hindus and the Muslims, that the Muslims would be elected by a Muslim electorate and non-Muslims by a general electorate of all non-Muslims. Muslims felt that in a joint electorate the Hindus, with their greater numbers, as well as their political predominance, would always be able to elect those Muslims who were under their influence. Hence the significance of Muslim representation would be both lost and betrayed.

After the failure of the Simla Peace Conference, Jinnah worked out his Delhi formula, demanding the acceptance of a Muslim majority in the Bengal legislature and in other Muslim majority provinces, one-third Muslim representation at the centre and introduction of reforms in the North-West Frontier Province (NWFP) in lieu of foregoing the Muslim demand for separate electorates. Shaheed Suhrawardy and his uncle, Abdullah al-Mamun Suhrawardy, opposed this formula too and another attempt to impose a joint electorate on the Muslims failed.[63] The celebrated poet Allama Iqbal also agreed with Suhrawardy that Muslims could never forego their demand for a separate electorate.[64] Suhrawardy was also the first person to oppose the Motilal Nehru Report published in 1928.[65] The Report advocated a joint electorate with reservation of seats for the Muslims of Bengal and the Punjab. Most Muslim leaders considered the Report acceptable and joined the Congress.[66] But Suhrawardy did not agree. He did not consider that conditions were conducive for a joint electorate system which could only be practicable when some degree of understanding had been achieved between Muslims and Hindus and their mutual claims and rights were accommodated.[67] He held a conference in Calcutta where the Report was repudiated and denounced. Sheikh Mujibur Rahman, his closest political disciple, later wrote that acceptance of this formula (The Nehru Report), in the absence of Suhrawardy's opposition, would have cut at the very root of the future of the Muslims, as far as the movement for Pakistan at the subsequent stage was concerned.[68]

Between 1923 and 1926, Suhrawardy was also associated with youth organizations, and after 1927, with the labour movement. Quite a number of revolutionaries were infiltrating labour organizations and attempting to exploit them for political purposes. Suhrawardy established constitutional trade unions along the British lines. His National Labour Federation, founded in 1927, in no time enjoyed a large membership throughout the country. Trade unionism was an uphill task as employers were very chary of acceding to legitimate labour demands and did so only after strikes and disorders. Suhrawardy was successful in setting up as many as thirty-six trade union organizations in almost every concern, such as jute and cotton mills and sea-going labour at all its branches, ensuring that disputes between employers and labourers were brought to the negotiation table before more drastic measures were taken.

The resulting breach between Hindus and Muslims after the 1926 riots had its effects on the labour movements too. While the majority of the Muslim labourers joined his constitutional trade union organizations, the majority of the Hindu labourers joined what they deemed to be the more

progressive communist-inspired labour organizations, which did not believe
in organized trade unionism but in agitation.

A LEADER OF MUSLIM INDIA

As General Secretary of the Khilafat committee, Suhrawardy had already
acquired considerable influence over the Muslims of Calcutta. He now,
gradually but surely, acquired a reputation as a leader of Muslim India. In
1928, Motilal Nehru presided over the Congress session in Calcutta.[69] M.A.
Ansari chaired the Indian National Conference, also in Calcutta, at this time.
Obviously, as a challenge, the same week Shaheed Suhrawardy organized
the All-India Khilafat Conference with Maulana Mohammad Ali presiding.[70]
He also organized the first All-Bengal Muslim Conference in Calcutta in
1928.[71] At this time the Muslim League was divided into what was then
known as the Shafi League and the Jinnah League. To patch up the
differences, Muslim leaders belonging to these opposing groups met at Delhi
in December 1928. The conference, presided over by Sir Sultan Ahmad and
His Highness The Aga Khan passed a resolution incorporating the Muslim
demand for a separate electorate. The Ali brothers and Suhrawardy also
attended the conference.

In 1931, North Bengal suffered the calamity of a disastrous flood.
Suhrawardy went all out to alleviate the sufferings of the flood-stricken
people.[72] It was here he came in contact with Maulana Abdul Hamid Khan
Bhashani who had convened a peasant conference at Sirajganj. Suhrawardy
inaugurated it. That same year the All-India Muslim Volunteers' Conference
was held in Bombay. The next year, the All-India Muslim Conference was
held in Calcutta.[73] Suhrawardy presided over the first and acted as the
chairman of the reception committee in the second. When another batch of
constitutional reforms became due and the Linlithgow Commission was
appointed, Shaheed Suhrawardy appeared before the Commission in London
in 1933 as a representative of the Muslim conference.[74]

A new Government of India Act was passed in 1935, embodying further
constitutional reforms. It created wholly elected legislatures and abolished
diarchy but maintained separate electorates. Jinnah then finally returned to
India and joined the Muslim League, assumed the leadership of the Muslims
and adopted an anti-Congress attitude. He began to contact Muslim leaders
of differing shades, especially of the Muslim majority provinces. It enabled
him to unite the Muslims of India under the banner of the Muslim League
and transform it from its middle class-restricted membership into a mass
organization, similar to—but set against—the Congress which the Muslims
considered to be a Hindu organization dominated by Gandhi. Many important
Muslims, however, continued to be associated with it. Jinnah finally gained

a firm footing in the confidence of the Muslims when Maulana Showkat Ali gave his blessings and called upon all Muslims to accept his leadership.

INDEPENDENT MUSLIM PARTY

During 1935 and 1936, Shaheed Suhrawardy organized the *tabliq* and *seerat*, and a number of other conferences designed to build up public opinion in favour of independence. At the same time, he launched a movement to boycott the Calcutta corporation.[75] In fact, he made Calcutta, the nerve-centre of Indian politics, his political fort.[76] He also started a mass organization in Bengal, which he called the Independent Muslim Party (IMP) with the same membership fee as that on which Jinnah subsequently organized the Muslim League.[77] Founded in early 1936, Suhrawardy himself became its general secretary and Khwaja Nazimuddin its president. He set up its branches all over Bengal and selected candidates to contest the 1936 election on his party tickets.

BPML GENERAL SECRETARY

It was a very bad time for the Muslim League in Bengal where it was already reduced to a party of armchair politicians. Fazlul Huq had broken away from the Muslim League and organized the Krishak Proja Party (KPP) to contest the 1936 election.[78] Most Muslim leaders had also joined the IMP. To meet this situation the Muslim business community of Calcutta, led by the Ispahanis, invited Jinnah and advised him that unless Shaheed Suhrawardy was persuaded to join the League, it had no future in Bengal.[79] Jinnah understood the gravity of the situation and sent Khwaja Nazimuddin, Khwaja Khairuddin, Abul Hassan, Hassan Ispahani, and Abdur Rahman Siddique to persuade Suhrawardy to join the Muslim League.[80] They requested him on behalf of Jinnah to convert his organization to the Bengal branch of the Muslim League. Suhrawardy hesitated to do so for a number of reasons, but subsequently agreed in view of the fact that the Muslim League was an all-India organization. He affiliated his organization to the AIML of which Jinnah was the President and thus became the General Secretary of the Bengal Provincial Muslim League (BPML) in 1936.[81] The Ispahanis had their own party, the New Muslim Majlish, and they too merged their party along with the IMP.[82]

In a belated attempt to get Suhrawardy to merge with their party certain friends of His Highness The Aga Khan approached him to become organizer of the Muslim Conference which was His Highness's party.[83] He convinced them that it was better to shut down their organization and cooperate with Jinnah. They followed his perceptive advice.

1936 GENERAL ELECTIONS

After the introduction of provincial autonomy in the 1935 Act, the first general election was to be held in 1936. It was practically the first attempt to hold elections on such a large-scale and with so many voters. Most of the Muslim candidates stood as independents. The election was, however, a straight fight between the BPML and the KPP for 119 Muslim seats in a House of 250. Fazlul Huq approached the electorate with an assurance of *dal-bhat* (ordinary meals) and a 14-point manifesto promising, among others, abolition of *zamindari* without compensation, universal free primary education without taxation and full provincial autonomy, supported by the larger group of the peasantry and a progressive section of the educated middle class.[84] To fight Fazlul Huq's KPP, a BMPL Parliamentary Board was set up with Suhrawardy as its General Secretary. But compared to KPP leaders, who had mass contact with the rural people, no one in the BPML, with the exception of Maulana Akram Khan, 'felt at home in a predominantly Bengali speaking Muslim gathering.'[85] The Maulana brought out the first Muslim Bengali daily, *The Daily Azad*, and it played a great role in popularizing the Muslim League in Bengal.

Shaheed Suhrawardy, who had already proved his mettle as an able organizer, organized the election campaigns urging the electorate for Muslim solidarity.[86] His untiring effort and hard work rewarded him when he secured 39 of the 119 Muslim seats.[87] He himself was elected from two constituencies; he surrendered one in favour of Khwaja Nazimuddin who, after being defeated in his own constituency by A.K. Fazlul Huq, was elected through a by-election. Fortunately for the BPML, 21 independent members, of the 44 elected, joined it. The Congress also captured 60 general seats. Fazlul Huq's KPP captured 36 seats and 18 independent members joined his party. However, even though he had the smallest group in the House, Fazlul Huq manoeuvred and was invited to form the ministry when the Muslim League offered him the Prime Ministership to ward off the danger of a Congress-KPP coalition. Fazlul Huq soon joined the Muslim League and was elected President of the BPML.

LABOUR AND COMMERCE MINISTER

Suhrawardy joined the Proja-League Coalition government that Fazlul Huq formed in April 1937 as Minister for Labour and Commerce. Subsequently, he held several other portfolios, one after another, including that of Finance when the Finance Minister, a Hindu, resigned. During this ministry, as a trade union leader himself, he got the Bengal Provincial Assembly to adopt the Labour Welfare Act and the Maternity Benefit Act.[88] Later, these Acts were constitutionally adopted all over India. Suhrawardy also did everything possible for his organization and, by working with Fazlul Huq, began to learn more about people in the rural areas, their problems and their language and they began to get to know him. The two leaders worked closely on behalf of the downtrodden members of the province. The Muslim middle class and the peasantry felt greatly relieved when the Muslim League government established the Debt Settlement Board and passed the Money Lenders Act and various tenancy laws, including the Bengal Tenancy Amendment Bill of 1938. Suhrawardy sent a memorandum to the Governor on 9 May, stressing upon the urgent need of the Tenancy Amendment Bill being passed into law. He wrote:

> The entire Muslim party in the legislature which also includes landlords and intermediate landlords, not only supports the measure but considers that it has not gone far enough. The scheduled caste party equally supports the measure. The vast majority of persons whose rights are affected support the measure; only an infinitesimal portion does not. If these are not conceded much worse and much more drastic measures are bound to follow. If, by mischance, the bill is not passed into law, there is no doubt that an era of revolution and of seething discontent, which will take the form of a no-rent campaign, coupled with violence and incendiarism, which nothing whatsoever can check. In the name of justice and peace and to prevent a far greater calamity, the bill should be passed into law.[89]

For the first time, since Akbar the Great annexed Bengal to the Mughal Empire in 1576, Bengalis had a government of their own choice and it acquitted itself effectively.[90]

Meanwhile, as the struggle for freedom was gaining momentum, Muslim League leaders gathered at Lahore and passed the historic Lahore Resolution on 23 March 1940. Moved by A.K. Fazlul Huq, it provided for two sovereign Muslim states in the East (Bengal and Assam) and in the West (Punjab, Sindh, Balochistan and the NWFP) of India where Muslims predominated. Suhrawardy attended the Lahore Session as the spokesman for the Bengal delegation and fought against the federation idea, embodied in the Government of India Act 1935 and advocated by the Congress. The federal government, he argued, had a natural tendency to move towards centralization and as the federal government of India, with control over defence, foreign policy and finance, was bound to be dominated by the Hindus, it would centralize all power, reducing autonomy to a paper scheme.[91] He insisted that each of the provinces in the Muslim majority areas be accepted as a sovereign state.

Shaheed Suhrawardy's role in the freedom struggle reached its zenith during the crucial period of 1940–47. In 1941, only a year after the Lahore Resolution was passed, Fazlul Huq fell out with Jinnah and resigned from the Muslim League.[92] This led the Muslim League to withdraw its support from the ministry the day Pearl Harbour was bombed by the Japanese on 7 December, creating political upheavals in the province.

Fazlul Huq constituted his second coalition ministry, with Hindu Mahasabha and Forward Bloc support. He took Shyama Prasad Mukherjee, a prominent Hindu Mahasabha leader, as his deputy. The inclusion of this man in the ministry antagonized the Muslims. Suhrawardy seized upon this godsent opportunity, addressed hundreds of rural meetings and appealed to the Muslim masses for support. The Muslim student community stood behind him to fight Fazlul Huq's coalition ministry. The Muslim middle class, now more conscious of their political rights, resolved to fight the caste Hindus. People hurled rotten eggs and tomatoes at the once uncrowned monarch of Bengal and welcomed him with black flags wherever he went. For the first time in his long political career Fazlul Huq found himself isolated from the Muslim masses. Within a year many KPP members crossed the floor and joined the Muslim League Parliamentary Party. During the tenure of this ministry there were two vacancies in the Muslim seats and two by-elections were held. Suhrawardy organized the campaign on behalf of the Muslim League; Fazlul Huq did so on behalf of his party. But in both by-elections the latter suffered signal defeats and the deposits of his candidates were confiscated, showing that the Muslims were in no mood to compromise with the Hindus and that they supported the struggle which the Muslim League was waging for their rights. They also showed that the people of Bengal were politically conscious and that coercion, blandishment, or government patronage did not affect their morale to any degree.

By the beginning of 1943 the Muslim League had gathered sufficient strength at the expense of the Shyama-Huq ministry, the latter having now lost all its influence both inside and outside the House. Finally, an acrimonious exchange of letters with the British Governor led to Huq's downfall on 29 March 1943.[93]

The abnormal situation elsewhere, beyond his control, proved injurious to Fazlul Huq. The Second World War was on. The Japanese were knocking at the door and a Japanese invasion of Bengal seemed imminent. The Congress had started the Quit India movement. A severe famine hit Bengal because of the war. Strikes, riots and lawlessness afflicted the country and the administration seemed incapable of coping with the situation.

CIVIL SUPPLIES MINISTER

1943 famine. Suhrawardy joined the Khwaja Nazimuddin ministry as Civil Supplies Minister when it was formed on 24 April after the fall of the

Shyama-Huq ministry. The main task of the ministry in general, and Suhrawardy in particular, was to combat the famine.

The famine was caused by human ineptitude and the deliberate manipulation and incompetence of the British Raj. Fazlul Huq, as the Prime Minister of Bengal, had bought all foodgrain at high prices which never dropped. He had, in December 1942, at a Delhi Food Conference, declared that there was no danger of shortage of foodgrain in Bengal, and the Indian government, accordingly, made no preparations to send foodgrain to Bengal.[94] From the opposition benches, Suhrawardy had protested vehemently that, owing to the failure of crops for two seasons, a serious famine was impending.[95]

Suhrawardy had an uphill task. Sheikh Mujibur Rahman, while praising the role of Suhrawardy in combating the famine, gives a pathetic picture of the situation.[96] He says that the foodgrain was not available, even for money. The Japanese occupation of Burma exacerbated the situation as Burma was the principal supplier of foodgrain to Bengal. The movement of foodgrain from surplus to deficit areas within the province itself was impeded because the rolling stock had for the most part been taken over by the army, who were preparing a counter-attack in Burma. Large river craft which conveyed the foodgrain along the broad rivers of Bengal had been sunk by the government in pursuance of what was known as the Denial Policy against an anticipated Japanese invasion. Soldiers stationed in various parts of Bengal had priority call on the foodgrain and on supplementary foods like eggs, chickens, bananas, coconuts, vegetables and pulses. Inter-district and inter-provincial cordoning and the hostility of the central government Food Minister, Sree Nivas, who had just succeeded Sir Azizul Huq, further impeded Suhrawardy's efforts to procure food for the civil population.[97]

But Suhrawardy was not the type of man to surrender without a fight. Immediately after taking his oath of office, in a radio broadcast, he told his listeners that he believed that around 20 million people would be affected and half of them might die of starvation, since there had been no arrangement for the procurement of rice.[98] He, however, assured the country that he would do everything possible to save as many human lives as possible. With two experts, loaned by the central government, he sat for days and nights and drew up a scheme to combat the famine. Accordingly, he fought the central government and forced it to allocate foodgrain from the surplus provinces, many of them a considerable distance from Bengal. These supplies did not reach Bengal in adequate quantities, largely on account of the war movement and the difficulties of procurement. He sent officers to surplus areas, such as the Punjab, to procure foodgrain with partial success.

Subsequently, it was agreed that the movement of foodgrain should be more or less on a regional basis, and foodgrain was allocated from Assam,

Bihar, Orissa and the eastern states of CP. For a variety of reasons Suhrawardy had great difficulty in procuring foodgrain from these regions, but he set up a new organization for procurement and despatch and Assam reluctantly sent the major portion of its contribution. Orissa also sent its allotment. The procurement in the eastern regions was difficult but to some extent successful. Bihar, which had been allocated the largest quota, refused to send any foodgrain.[99] It first complained that the assessment by the central government was incorrect. It forcibly unloaded on the platform foodgrain purchased by Bengal government agents. Its refusal was greatly dictated by the fact that it had a Congress government, which did not wish to assist the Muslim League government of Bengal in spite of the deteriorating conditions and deaths due to starvation in that province. Therefore, the amount of foodgrain collected was insufficient to meet even the minimum requirements. Moreover, no one had any real knowledge of rationing, distribution or procurement, or of the concomitant problems and Suhrawardy had to improvise, directing and controlling proceedings through a combination of common sense, inventiveness and astuteness. He opened ration shops for city dwellers, who could buy food and, for poor villagers, free gruel kitchens for mass feeding. For the medical treatment of those famished people, who fell easy prey to diarrhoeal diseases, he opened auxiliary hospitals throughout the country.

Even the sternest of his critics will admit that without Suhrawardy's capable handling of the problem many millions of people would have lost their lives from starvation. Nevertheless, nearly 5 million people died in the famine, which provoked Zainul Abedin to sketch in charcoal the pathetic famine scenes that immortalized the famine as well as his name.[100]

1946 GENERAL ELECTIONS

During 1945 and 1946 central and provincial elections were held on the Pakistan issue. It was another big challenge to the Muslim League in Bengal. Jinnah was not invited to visit Bengal to prevent him from interfering with the Parliamentary Board as he had done in Sindh.[101] He did, however, once pass through Bengal by train on his way to Sylhet but did not address any wayside gatherings. Liaquat Ali Khan, also, only once visited the Gafargaon constituency in greater Mymensingh district, but its Muslim League candidate was miserably defeated.

Therefore, the onerous responsibility to organize the general election in Bengal had fallen on Suhrawardy. He, as General Secretary of the BPML, was in charge of elections and virtually organized operations single-handedly, helped by a number of staunchly loyal workers. He again boldly accepted the challenge, toured the remotest parts of the country and mobilized the

Muslim masses so that when the fateful election came, the BPML captured 114 of the 119 Muslim seats of the Provincial Assembly.[102] Fazlul Huq again contested the BPML with his KPP but could capture only five seats. The general election fought on the issue of Pakistan resulted in a complete victory for the Muslim League in Bengal.

PRIME MINISTER OF BENGAL

The victory of the Muslim League in Bengal was Suhrawardy's personal triumph for which he received a congratulatory message from Jinnah.[103] On 3 April 1946, he was elected leader of the Parliamentary group. Subsequently, he formed a ministry on 24 April which turned out to be the only Muslim League government in the whole of the subcontinent. A notable and early decision of his government was to release all political prisoners, who had been held without trial. During the one and half years of his government no one was taken into custody on political grounds. He did the same thing in Pakistan when he formed a coalition government at the centre in 1956 with his small party of Awami Leaguers, setting a unique example in the history of Asia and of Africa. But the most daring act was perhaps the release in 1946 of the Chittagong Armoury Raid convicts, sentenced to long-term imprisonment, earning him the people's gratitude.

The Muslim League victory in Bengal proved to be decisive in the movement for freedom. It saved the Muslim League from an impending disaster and the demand for Pakistan from becoming ineffectual. The three other overwhelmingly Muslim majority provinces—the Punjab, Sindh and the NWFP—had voted against Pakistan which put Jinnah in a very awkward position. Jinnah had a difficult task in trying to convince the British and the Hindus that the Muslims wanted Pakistan when he had failed signally in three out of the four Muslim majority provinces to secure their support, although the Muslims in the Muslim minority provinces solidly voted for the Muslim League.

It was Jinnah who brought Pakistan into being, but it was Suhrawardy, without question, who supplied him with the weapon to fight for Pakistan. 'Had Suhrawardy not won the general election in 1946, in the light of total failure of the Muslim League in all the other Muslim majority provinces, there would have been no Pakistan.'[104] Regarding the importance of the Muslim League victory in Bengal and Suhrawardy's role in it, Islam says that 'His contributions to the creation of the new country was second to none. He belonged to Bengal but he was the leader of Muslim India. It is history that the Muslim League victory in Bengal in 1946 made all the difference for the creation of Pakistan. It was Suhrawardy who was the architect of the Muslim League victory in Bengal which paved the way for the partition of

India. It was Suhrawardy who, by his sustained hard work, created among the Muslims of Bengal a religious zeal for Pakistan—a kind of zeal which made Pakistan inevitable.'[105] But for the victory of the Muslim League in Bengal, the British would have left the destiny of India in the hands of the Congress.

Delhi convention. The election now over, on 7 April 1946, Jinnah invited all central and provincial body members to a convention at Delhi's Mohammadan Anglo-Arabic College ground. The convention was called at the suggestion of Suhrawardy, who wrote to Jinnah in order to decide the issue of the Muslim League's right to nominate the full Muslim quota in the interim central cabinet, which the Congress had challenged.[106] Of the 480 councillors, 450 attended the convention. Held on 9–10 April under Jinnah's chairmanship, the convention of Muslim councillors, although ostensibly sitting to decide on the Muslim quota in the interim central government, changed the content of the Lahore Resolution, which had demanded the creation of two sovereign Muslim states. The General Secretary of the Muslim League, Nawabzada Liaquat Ali Khan, at Jinnah's instance, corrected the word 'states' for state as a typographical error, ignoring loud protestations from Bengali councillors, the most vocal of whom were Maulana Abdul Hamid Khan Bhashani, President of the Assam Provincial Muslim League, and Abul Hashim, General Secretary of the Bengal Provincial Muslim League.[107]

Bengal questioned the right of the Convention of Councillors to change the decision of a resolution that had been adopted by a full body of Muslim representatives, but Jinnah was adamant for one Pakistan, when he saw his dream within sight. Evidently, he ignored the geographical incongruity and the basic differences between the two peoples and their ways of life: Urdu was the *lingua franca* of the Muslims of the provinces west of Bengal, while Bengali Muslims, who alone maintained their separate identity, spoke and read in Bengali. They also differed in their respective traditions, social systems, food and dress. The only common bond was religion and even though this may have been a good enough reason to fight for freedom from a common enemy it certainly was not a good enough reason to live together as one nation. Furthermore, the struggle for Muslim emancipation that originated in Bengal was not fought on religious grounds alone; economic emancipation from the more advanced and affluent Hindus, the Hindu *zamindars* (landlords) and *mahajans* (money-lenders), was much more important to them.[108] But, for the Muslims of western India, religious considerations were as, if not more, important as the economic factor.

Why Suhrawardy, who had never wanted a partitioned Bengal, agreed to this change, has puzzled many people to this day. We should not, however, forget that the 1946 Resolution was the end-product of the existing political circumstances, created by the passing of the Lahore-termed 'Pakistan' Resolution in 1940 and the holding of the 1946 general election on the issue of Pakistan. The demand for the two sovereign Muslim states was as quickly forgotten as the people of Bengal forgot Fazlul Huq, when they discovered that their greater demand for freedom from Hindu domination became threatened by the Congress demand for Akhanda Bharat (undivided India). The failure of the three other Muslim majority provinces to return a Muslim League government had already weakened Jinnah's arguments for Pakistan. Suhrawardy was astute enough to realize that Pakistan would never be created in the foreseeable future if Bengal stood firm on its stand of a separate sovereign state and would play straight into the hands of the Congress. As Prime Minister of the only Muslim League government in the subcontinent much depended on him and he acted as an all-India nationalist Muslim leader to firstly create the state of Pakistan but did not, at the same time, withdraw the principle of a separate sovereign state in eastern India. Thus, on the day the resolution was moved, he suggested in his confidential note to the Cabinet delegation that 'the British would find it to their advantage to deal with two or three, or more central authorities than one.'[109]

In moving the Resolution, Suhrawardy declared that in this subcontinent there was no path for Muslims other than the Muslim League and no ambition before them other than Pakistan (Appendix III).[110] He observed: 'Britain wants to hand over power to the Indians and the Cabinet Mission is here to find out suitable machinery for the transfer of power. Congress tells the British:

Give us power, we shall sweep away all opposition. We shall suppress the Muslims. We shall bring the scheduled caste to heel and we shall annihilate the *adivasis*. Give us the police, your army and arms and we shall reproduce an Armageddon in the name of a united India.' This I call insanity induced by the lust for power.... We do not intend to start a civil war but we want a land where we can live in peace. We are a nation and, we believe, we have something to contribute to the civilization of the world. But, are the British and the Congress prepared to give us Pakistan peacefully and with grace? If not, then, are the Muslims prepared to fight? I have long pondered over these questions. Let me now honestly declare that every Muslim of Bengal is ready and prepared to lay down his life for Pakistan. Now I call upon you, Mr Jinnah, to test us.[111]

Direct Action Day. At this time, betraying the Muslim cause, the Viceroy called upon Pandit Nehru to form an interim government which he did, but the Muslim League refused to participate in it. Jinnah even cancelled his talks with Lord Wavell, the Viceroy, and proclaimed 16 August as Direct Action Day.[112] The one-member majority Muslim League government in

Sindh, formed after the assassination of the Congress Chief Minister Allahbux, was also asked, but, because it was a shaky government, its Muslim League members could not be trusted. So, all the risks of the Direct Action Day fell on the Bengal government. On that day Muslims were expected to gather in large numbers to proclaim their adherence to the concept of Pakistan. Shaheed Suhrawardy declared a holiday for that day in Calcutta.

On a previous occasion, when no holiday had been proclaimed, there had been disturbances between Hindus and Muslims; people were dragged out of their cars and insulted. Now Hindus objected to the proclamation of a holiday and made extensive, secret preparations to attack Muslims. Neither the Intelligence Branch concerned with the activities of terrorists and revolutionaries, nor the Criminal Investigation Department, both of which were manned almost wholly by Hindus, gave the Prime Minister any information regarding these preparations and he was caught unawares.[113] On 16 August at the Ochterlony Monument Maidan, whilst he was addressing a crowd, gathered from all parts of Calcutta and the suburbs, he received news that processions were being obstructed and attacked by the Hindus and anti-Muslim riots were taking place in many areas. It was the Muslim holy month of Ramadan (fasting). Suhrawardy ordered the Muslims to disperse and go back to their homes. The crowd was very large, many with children in their laps, having come from all over the city, from the neighbouring areas of Howrah and the 24 Parganas, and from the Jute and Cotton Mill areas. As the crowd was returning home they were set upon by the Hindus, provoking an anti-Muslim riot on a scale far greater than the one in 1926.

The Commissioner of Police, a Britisher, did not know Calcutta and its problems and was unable to deal with the situation with only a small police force. The Riot Commission, which was set up by the British government as a result of the riot, reports that immediately after the riot began the Prime Minister rushed to Lalbazar Police Headquarters to attain first hand information and, being apprised of the grave situation, demanded deployment of the army on the very first day of the riot.[114] But Governor Burrows rejected the demand, primarily to divert the strong anti-British sentiments generated during the Rashid Ali Day, observed in Calcutta in June 1945 and which he hoped would worsen Hindu-Muslim relations.[115] Captain Ali was a member of the Indian National Army, which had been created by Subash Chandra Bose to fight the British during the Second World War. He was caught, tried and sentenced to a seven-year jail term. Captain Ali had sought Muslim League support during his trial and Suhrawardy, defying a government ban, headed a large protest procession, along with other top League and Congress leaders.[116]

The Governor also turned down Suhrawardy's suggestion to put pickets between Hindu and Muslim localities, creating a bulwark which would help to separate the two communities (a suggestion adopted much later, when the damage had already been done and a number of Muslim localities had been destroyed and thousands of Muslims massacred). Instead, Burrows heeded the advice of the Commissioner of Police that the civil power was capable of dealing with the situation and that there was no need to deploy the army. It was only when Suhrawardy threatened to resign that the Governor reluctantly pretended to agree and three or four days later merely ordered the army to stand by. Suhrawardy, accompanying the Governor and the army commander on a tour of inspection on 18 August, showed them an area of Calcutta, Suvabazaar, which was strewn with the bodies of dead Muslims. This was predominantly a Hindu area, with some Muslim houses and shops. The army had had no knowledge that this was a riot area and the Commissioner of Police, himself, had had no information that there had been riots there. It was a 'big discovery' of 'wholesale slaughter' of Muslims and the Governor and the General were deeply shocked.[117]

Appointment of Punjabi police. At that time Calcutta was a city of six million people but it had only a 1200-man police force of whom only 63 were Muslims.[118] Of the officers, with the exception of one Deputy Commissioner and one Officer-in-Charge, the remainder were Hindus.[119] The riot had spread so far that even government officials were not beyond direct involvement. The 1200-man police force was, therefore, not only too small to cope with the situation but suspect in its loyalty as well. In this situation Suhrawardy decided to appoint 1,200 trained Muslim Punjabi Sepahis to achieve equity in the balance of the city's police force.[120] Hindu leaders protested against this to the Governor, who asked Suhrawardy to desist from recruiting Muslim Punjabi Sepahis. Instead, he suggested recruitment of the same number of trained Muslim Bengali Sepahis. Suhrawardy argued that trained Muslim Bengali Sepahis could not easily be found and that he needed trained forces immediately to contain the riots. He also argued that the police force of Calcutta was composed of Gurkhas, Sikhs, Rajputs and Jats, and there was no Hindu Bengali. He agreed to appoint an equal number of Muslim and Hindu Bengalis only after dismissing the existing force. However, the Governor did not agree to this proposal and urged him not to appoint trained Muslim Punjabi Sepahis. Burrows finally consented to his proposal only when the Prime Minister again threatened to resign on this issue.[121] Suhrawardy immediately recruited 1,200 trained Muslim Punjabi Sepahis to keep a balance in the police force and ordered Muslim Officers-in-Charge to be posted in 21 of the 22 *thanas*. He personally took charge of the Police Control Room from one British Officer and mobilized the police force himself to quell the riots.

There were hundreds of occasions when Suhrawardy himself, often clandestinely clad in the uniform of a European military officer, drove through the affected localities to save the lives of the defenceless victims, Muslims and Hindus alike. Suhrawardy's critic, Hassan Ispahani, while giving a pen-picture of this carnage, praises his role in bringing the riot under control. He says: 'I have not seen a man work so hard and act so swiftly to try and control a conflagration as Suhrawardy did.'[122] During the riots he arranged free lodging and food for many Hindu families, including ninety-five Hindustani milkmen, his own Hindu haircutter Nogen Sheel and Hindu washerman Kunja Dhopa.[123] Among Suhrawardy's trusted personal attendants was Shibu, also a Hindu from Orissa, who served him most faithfully even during those troubled years. Peace soon returned to the riot-torn city.

Peace emissary. The riots perturbed the British government. Viceroy Lord Wavell visited Calcutta on 25 August and saw the carnage himself.[124] The Muslim community of Calcutta covered the city with thousands of posters, symbolically written in red ink, charging him with the responsibility for the riot and calling upon him to leave.[125] Dhaka received him with the same slogans. The Viceroy wanted to know from Prime Minister Suhrawardy how he could be held responsible for the riot.[126] Suhrawardy explained that the riot was a consequence of the formation of the interim government without Muslim League representation and the deeply-held Muslim belief of a deliberate British creation of Hindu-Muslim misunderstanding as a rationale to hand over power only to the Congress Party.[127] He further warned that what had happened in Calcutta would repeat itself all over India unless the British government changed its policy. Suhrawardy also convinced him that a united India was impossible and cooperation of the Muslim League was essential if India was to be saved from civil war. Before he left Bengal, Lord Wavell asked Suhrawardy to work as an emissary between himself and Jinnah.[128]

Suhrawardy saw Jinnah in Bombay on 6 September and Lord Wavell in Delhi two days later, and succeeded in bringing about a rapprochement between them. They first met on 16 September in Delhi. Lord Wavell assured Jinnah that he was ready to accept the Muslim League demand, and the Muslim League announced on 15 October its decision to join the interim government headed by Pandit Nehru.[129] On this occasion Jinnah admitted that Suhrawardy had saved the country from a perilous situation.[130]

PARTITION OF INDIA

Jinnah's Direct Action strategy, bathed in the blood of the Muslims of Calcutta, won him a great political victory and made Pakistan inevitable. The momentum increased in pace by the threat of continued civil war elsewhere on the subcontinent as a direct repercussion of the Great Calcutta Killing.

The British, who, in the beginning, had encouraged disunity between the Hindus and the Muslims to perpetuate their rule, soon found the situation getting out of control. Therefore, on 24 February 1947, the Attlee government announced that the British would withdraw not later than June 1948, even if that meant partitioning India and replaced Wavell by Lord Mountbatten as its agent for the final phase.

The Only Alternative to Prolonged Civil War

The Mountbattens arrived in March. They infused a new spirit into Indo-British relations from the moment of their arrival and 'captured the imagination and affection of Nehru from the start' to the detriment of the Muslims.[131] The new Viceroy believed in a united India, but soon convinced himself that Pakistan was inevitable. The spectres of civil war and anarchy finally convinced all but Gandhi that partition must be accepted as the only alternative to a prolonged civil war. On 3 June, Mountbatten announced a plan to partition India and to secure British withdrawal in a headlong rush within the incredible time of ten weeks, settling on 14 August 1947 as the day of reckoning.[132] Cyril Radcliffe, a judge of the High Court of England, whom Jinnah knew personally and on whose integrity he had great reliance, was sent from England to partition Bengal and the Punjab, settle boundaries, and to suggest a scheme for the partition of India. He drew up a plan for the partition of Bengal and the Punjab. However, Muslims held that he altered his proposals at the direct instigation of Lord Mountbatten by incorporating the Muslim majority district of Gurdaspur and Batala tehsil with East Punjab (India) to provide an Indian territory which would be contiguous to Kashmir. Muslims had considerable reservations about the manner in which Radcliffe partitioned the Punjab and Bengal, but since Jinnah had agreed to accept the verdict in advance, nothing could be done about it.

Radcliffe also suggested a referendum in Sylhet (a Muslim majority district of the province of Assam) and in the NWFP (a Muslim majority province under Congress rule) as to which state these two areas wished to join. When the referenda were held, these two areas voted for Pakistan.

GREATER BENGAL SCHEME

When the partition plan was accepted, Shaheed Suhrawardy fought against the partition of Bengal on the grounds that it was a Muslim majority province. Suhrawardy declared that the partition of India was inevitable, but

Bengal should remain indivisible.[133] Jinnah also asserted that on no account would he accept 'a truncated, moth-eaten Pakistan.'[134] Partition of Bengal meant the loss of Calcutta, built mainly on the resources of East Bengal. The alternative to partition was an independent Bengal. Suhrawardy is both accused of and credited with the sponsoring of the sovereign, or, what is also known as, the Greater Bengal Scheme. There is a full document on this scheme published by Maulana Raghib Ahsan, a member of the AIML Working Committee.[135]

The British decision to partition Bengal was finalized in mid-May with Mountbatten, in close consultation with V.P. Menon, the only Indian on the Viceroy's staff and Congress leaders, especially Pandit Nehru and Sirdar Patel.[136] However, the Mountbatten plan, partitioning Bengal with Calcutta in West Bengal, was already known to the AIML High Command by April.[137] When the Muslim League government of Bengal refused to accept the plan, Jinnah asked Suhrawardy to work for a sovereign, independent Bengal.[138] Suhrawardy immediately started negotiations with the Congress leaders of Bengal for a mutually agreed scheme to ward off the dangers of the partition of Bengal.

The Muslim League leaders of Bengal had, for some time now, been discussing the issue. It was during the Jinnah-Gandhi Bombay talks in 1944 that Jinnah himself had first asked the BPML to express its views on the future form, shape and boundaries of East Pakistan.[139] The members of the BPML Working Committee held several secret meetings in mid-August at Suhrawardy's private residence in Calcutta and emerged with three alternate proposals:

- Raghib Ahsan's confederation or federation of Bengal, Assam and Jharkhand of the Chotonagpur *adivasis;*
- Fazlur Rahman's proposal for the formation of East Pakistan composed of Bengal and the Surma valley of Assam on the Curzon partition line, to ensure Muslim majority; and
- Hamidul Huq Choudhury's plan for a United Bengal and Assam as a unit of Pakistan.

The BPML Working Committee forwarded the three proposals to Jinnah at Bombay through a special messenger. What Jinnah's reaction was is not known, but members of the AIML Working Committee, including Abdul Matin Choudhury of Assam, definitely demanded the inclusion of the whole of Bengal and Assam into East Pakistan.[140]

In 1942, with the threat of the Japanese invasion of Bengal, the Cripps Plan had offered Indian union, giving provinces the right to secede.[141] Two years later Rajagopalachari offered self-determination for Muslims of the

Muslim majority provinces.[142] Then, in 1946, the Cabinet Mission refused to hand over power to two entirely sovereign states, where the two halves of Pakistan would be dependent on the goodwill of India and recommended a Union of India, divided into three sections, with the provinces having the right to secede.[143] During the last days of Lord Wavell's viceroyship news reached the Muslim League leaders that His Majesty's government might transfer power to the existing provincial governments.[144] On the basis of this prognostication, in the last week of February 1947, Abul Hashim and Sarat Chandra Bose discussed the plan for a sovereign, independent Bengal comprised of the Bengali-speaking people of eastern India from Purnea in Bihar to Assam in the furthest-east.[145] When the scheme was divulged, the Hindu Mahasabha demanded the partition of Bengal.[146] In March, the then Congress President Acharya Kripalani too demanded the partition of Bengal.[147] Gandhi, in reply to this, remarked that if Bengal was partitioned the communal problem would be a lasting feature of eastern India.[148] This stand encouraged the Bengali leaders to work out an agreed scheme for a Sovereign United Bengal.

Prime Minister Suhrawardy first openly proposed the scheme of a Sovereign United Bengal at a press conference on 27 April 1947 in Delhi.[149] Following discussions between Lord Mountbatten and Jinnah on 28 April, he returned to Calcutta and the same day met Sarat Chandra Bose of the Forward Bloc. Besides Suhrawardy, Khwaja Nazimuddin, Abul Hashim and Fazlur Rahman were also present.[150] The Muslim League formed a subcommittee consisting of Suhrawardy, Habibullah Bahar, Hamidul Huq Choudhury and Fazlur Rahman, with Nurul Amin as the convener, to negotiate with the Hindu leaders, especially Congress chief Surendra Mohan Ghosh, Congress Parliamentary leader Kiron Shankar Roy and Forward Bloc leader Sarat Chandra Bose.[151] A two-man delegation composed of Abul Hashim and Sarat Chandra Bose also met Gandhi on 12 May to discuss the Sovereign United Bengal scheme and received his blessing.[152] The East Bengal Hindus, commanding an overwhelming majority amongst the leaders of both Bengals in the Bengal Congress, the Bengal Legislative Assembly and the Bengal intelligentsia, were also against the partition of Bengal.[153] They questioned the wisdom of Hindu Mahasabha chief Mukherjee's arguments for partition. Seeing this reaction Suhrawardy at first offered the Hindus joint electorate, without reservation of seats for any community.[154] Later he modified the offer to include reservation of seats on a population basis for the Muslims, the high and the scheduled caste Hindus and other religious minorities. This offer was based on the Mohammad Ali formula, that is, a combination of joint and separate electorates. The offer also included the electoral principle that no candidate would be declared elected unless he polled at least 33 per cent of the votes of his own community.

Finally, the members of the Congress-League joint committee formally signed a tentative agreement on 20 May for a Sovereign United Bengal.[155] Suhrawardy forwarded the outline to Jinnah and Sarat Chandra Bose to Gandhi. Bose assured Mahatma Gandhi that both the Congress and the Muslim League parties in Bengal would ratify the tentative agreement, probably with some modifications.[156]

Surprisingly however, in reply to Bose's letter of 23 May forwarding the agreed outline, Gandhi advised him to give up the struggle for the unity of Bengal and to refrain from disrupting the atmosphere already created for the partition of Bengal.[157] Gandhi shifted from his stand after discussions with Nehru and Sirdar Patel who were both against the proposal, alleging it to be a trick designed to divide the caste and the scheduled caste Hindu leaders.[158]

Bose was shocked. He declared that if the partition of India was a sin, the vivisection of Mother Bengal would be a greater sin.[159] He reminded the Hindus of the great sacrifices they had once made in undoing the 1905 partition of Bengal and the ill-treatment C.R. Das and Netajee Subash Chandra Bose, his brother, had received from North Indian leaders. They had been forced to leave Congress and respectively form the Swaraj Party and the Forward Bloc. But Bose received no support from the powerful Hindu press and thus the demand for partition became stronger.

Sarat Chandra Bose and Kiron Shankar Roy also met Sirdar Patel at Dehradun. When the scheme was placed before Patel he rejected it outright as a trick by Suhrawardy for Bengal to join Pakistan.[160] He believed after this happened there would be no alternative for Assam but to join Pakistan. Patel, as the Home and States Minister of India, had by this time become all powerful in the Congress High Command and his opposition to the scheme meant a Congress veto. Later Patel, disclosing his secret deal with Viceroy Mountbatten, said that he had agreed to accept the partition of India and the creation of Pakistan on condition that Bengal was partitioned with Calcutta remaining in a West Bengal that belonged to India.[161] The wily Mountbatten circumscribed the Sovereign United Bengal scheme, laying as a primary condition, the total agreement to it by both the Congress and the Muslim League.[162] When the Congress ultimately rejected it, Jinnah agreed to the partition of Bengal.

The British had partitioned Bengal once before in 1905 but annulled it in 1911, convinced that Bengal was one political entity.[163] Based on this conviction, they offered the Cripps and the Mission plans. When they had assumed control of the province from the Muslims after the battle of Plassey in 1757, it was a vast domain, which comprised Bengal, Bihar and Orissa, but Mountbatten changed the course of history and partitioned the province in deference to Hindu wishes.

The caste Hindus rejected the scheme of a Sovereign United Bengal when the Muslims, who had successfully passed their first test of government by ably ruling the province for ten years (1937–1947), had demanded it. This rejection was difficult to comprehend since they, themselves, had vehemently opposed the partition of Bengal in 1905 and, through violence, had secured the annulment of the 1905 Act. One explanation may be that the formation of the Proja-League government in 1937 had disillusioned the caste Hindus, who then began to preach Indian nationalism.[164] Gradually, the two communities fell further apart with recrudescences of communal riots breaking out each year. An independent Bengal with a Muslim majority would mean the abolition of landlordism and nationalization of landholdings.[165] Since most caste Hindus belonged to the landed aristocracy, they disliked the Lahore Resolution, which had envisaged a separate Muslim state in eastern India and they opposed the Sovereign United Bengal scheme. Another factor was the lot that they had already cast with Hindu India, thereby sealing the fate of Bengali nationalism.

The religious solidarity seems to have also affected the Bengali Muslims. Fazlul Huq's proud declaration, at the Lahore session of the Muslim League in 1940, that 'he was a Muslim first and Bengali afterwards' had imbued the Bengali Muslims with the feeling of oneness with the Muslims, in the rest of India.[166] It thus, became impossible for both religious communities to untie their new-found bonds of nationhood with peoples beyond the frontiers of Bengal. In this manner they not only bartered away their birthright to decide their own fate by themselves but stood physically divided.

THE LOSS OF CALCUTTA

The partition council of Bengal was constituted in 1946 with an equal number of Muslim and Hindu members. Governor Sir Frederick Burrows was the chairman. Suhrawardy represented the Muslim League government on the council. He argued before the council that the Muslims of Calcutta were in the forefront of the struggle for freedom and had made great sacrifices for Pakistan.[167] The city was also built mainly with the resources of jute grown in East Bengal. He convinced the Labour Governor that East Bengal, as the major and principal section of the province and containing two-thirds of the population and of the area, had superior claims on Calcutta in the partition division. West Bengal was the minor, seceding party, wanting to break away from the main body. In no country did the seceding unit claim control over the headquarters of the main body. Moreover, the fate of Calcutta was still to be decided by the Boundary Commission. Therefore, the principal party, East Bengal, could not be deprived of the control of the capital, until such time as the Boundary Commission had decided its fate, working out all the intricacies of assets and liabilities and certainly not until full compensation to build a new capital had been paid. Governor Burrows found substance and force in the Premier's cogent arguments and promised to vote for his motion in case of a tie.[168] Most surprisingly, a Muslim cast his vote in favour of the Hindus, giving Calcutta to West Bengal.[169]

A section of the Dhaka group of the BPML was anxious to eliminate Calcutta from East Bengal in order to isolate Suhrawardy from its politics, especially since Calcutta was the stronghold of the Suhrawardy group.[170] They ironically saw no future for Calcutta. They rather envisaged it turning into a desolate town with the development of the port of Chittagong usurping its status and affluence.[171] These Muslim leaders moved to Dhaka, leaving Calcutta to its fate.

At this time, in June, immediately after the referendum in Sylhet, seventeen members from that district joined the Muslim League Parliamentary group and offered Prime Minister Suhrawardy their support in the election for the new parliamentary leadership provided he gave them the posts for three ministers and three parliamentary secretaries.[172] Suhrawardy totally rejected this conditional offer prior to an election. Disappointed, they approached Khwaja Nazimuddin, the other candidate for the post, who readily accepted their conditions and, with support from Liaquat Ali Khan, the General Secretary of the AIML, planned an election to elect him leader of the Parliamentary Party of the East Bengal Muslim League. Actually Jinnah had assured Suhrawardy that there would be no election for the parliamentary leadership of East Bengal and Suhrawardy had remained busy preparing briefs for advocates who would appear before the Boundary Commission on behalf of the Muslim League.[173] But Liaquat Ali Khan, who disliked Suhrawardy and was jealous of him, suddenly announced an election, not in the Punjab but in Bengal only, throwing in his support behind Khwaja Nazimuddin. Suhrawardy's defeat was a foregone conclusion. Khwaja Nazimuddin was elected leader and the Chief Minister-designate of East Bengal, with Dhaka as its capital. The claim for any compensation for the loss of Calcutta was thus quietly abandoned.[174]

Suhrawardy remained Prime Minister of Bengal until 13 August when he handed over the charge to the two newly elected parliamentary leaders of the two Bengals. P.C. Ghosh was elected leader of West Bengal.

MISSION WITH GANDHI

After the partition of India on 14 August 1947, the British army, manned by British soldiers who had been inducted into Calcutta and had been utilized to keep the peace, were withdrawn and replaced by Sikh soldiers. The

Punjabi Muslim armed police, whom Suhrawardy had appointed to make up for the deficiency in the armed police of Calcutta, also opted for East Bengal and left Calcutta. The Hindus of Calcutta took advantage of this and began planned attacks on different Muslim localities beginning in August 1947. There was a heavy exodus of terrified people from both India and Pakistan. Calcutta Muslims were in the middle of another nightmare and they asked Suhrawardy to stay with them. Suhrawardy could not refuse them in their most perilous time as they had stood solidly by him in all his movements for over a quarter of a century.[175]

Some time in early August, Mahatma Gandhi came to Calcutta on his way to Noakhali to be with its people on Independence Day and to assess the extent of the much-exaggerated loss of Hindu lives in communal riots there. M.A. Osmani, Calcutta Mayor and General Secretary of the City Muslim League, called on him and requested him to first establish peace in Calcutta before going to Noakhali.[176] He also took Gandhi to some of the ravaged areas. Gandhi was horrified at the appalling loss of life and property of the helpless Muslims and agreed with Osmani's suggestion to take Suhrawardy with him in a mission for peace on the subcontinent.[177] Shaheed Suhrawardy had just returned to Calcutta, after attending the AIML Working Committee meeting in Karachi. Osmani apprised him of what had transpired between him and Mahatma Gandhi. Suhrawardy, thereupon, met Gandhi in his Sodhpore *ashram* (hermitage) and convinced him of the prime need for peace on the subcontinent, to avert possible war between India and Pakistan, and to put a stop to communal riots. He also assured him of his full dedication to the cause of peace. From then on they dedicated themselves to fight unto death for peace. The Suhrawardy-Gandhi Peace Mission, also known as the Gandhi Peace Mission, aimed at making the majority community in each country responsible so that it could, by establishing a bond of friendship and cooperation with the minority community, remove all obstacles and mobilize the entire nation to the service of the state.[178]

In the Gandhi Peace Mission, Shaheed Suhrawardy worked and lived like a mendicant, at great risk to his life. He turned down five tempting offers from Jinnah in order to undertake the safety and salvation of Indian Muslims.[179] No other Muslim League leader came forward to save the helpless Indian Muslims. Thus, instead of going to Pakistan for a life of position and peace he attended, with Gandhi, colossal peace meetings in Calcutta and in other parts of West Bengal, East Punjab, Alwar, Bharatpur, Delhi and the United Provinces. Everywhere he asked Muslims to accept partition as a settled fact and live as loyal citizens of India.[180] Through the untiring and courageous efforts of the two of them, they were able to create a strong public opinion in India in favour of peace and communal harmony. The mission saved Pakistan from possible economic disaster by checking the potential unabated migration of Indian Muslims, sustained the integrity of East Bengal and saved the lives of millions of Indian Muslims.[181] But members of Hindu communal organizations, like the Rashtriya Swayamsevak Sangha (RSS), disliked the activities of the Gandhi Peace Mission. At one stage the extremist Hindus in Calcutta broke the peace and started killing Muslims. Mahatma Gandhi and Suhrawardy were both living in a dilapidated house at Beliaghatta at the time. A crowd of about 20,000 people approached the house with the intention of killing Suhrawardy. He faced them alone and told them: 'If you want to kill me, kill me now, but, before you kill me, you've got to give me your word that after me you'll kill no other Muslim.'[182] Hearing disturbances, Mahatma Gandhi came out of the residence and asked them to kill him first, before killing Suhrawardy.[183] It worked like magic and the crowd soon dispersed. Mahatma Gandhi condemned the attack and threatened to fast unto death unless the Hindus stopped killing Muslims.

When the nefarious plan to uproot the Indian Muslims and wreck Pakistan at its birth was thus foiled by the self-sacrifice of these two great leaders, extremist Hindus planned to kill them both.[184] Even then, defying all the threats to their lives, Suhrawardy and the Mahatma continued undeterred to work for peace. It would be true to say that with the exception of Gandhi, himself, there is no comparable instance, amongst contemporary politicians, of the magnitude of self-sacrifice and courage, demonstrated by Shaheed Suhrawardy during these and the coming months. For many this was his finest hour.

After establishing peace in Bengal, where the two-man boundary force was more valuable than the whole boundary force in the Punjab, Gandhi moved to Delhi in October to spend the last few weeks of his life in persuading, exhorting and commanding in the cause of communal harmony.[185] The holocaust in the west of India had been of even far greater dimensions, with whole villages exterminated and train-loads of Muslim migrants butchered as they huddled in the coaches.[186] Millions of frightened people were travelling in either direction. The great tide of the inward refugee movement in India had surged as far as Delhi, carrying with it bitterness and anti-Muslim feeling. They occupied many mosques in the old city and created consternation and panic among the remaining Muslim minority. In early January 1948, extremist Hindus, under the leadership of Sirdar Patel, raised serious objections to the cash payment of Rs500 million, payable to Pakistan as her share of the Partition, on the grounds of the Kashmir War that had broken out at this time. Suhrawardy had followed Gandhi to Delhi. He approached Gandhi and begged his intervention and the Mahatma, by persuasion and by a fast, secured the payment of the pledged sum to Pakistan as well as the evacuation by Hindu and Sikh refugees of the Muslim holy places and the safety of Muslim lives.[187]

These events further angered the RSS and its agents became more active in trying to kill the two of them. During these days Suhrawardy was staying with Gandhi at the Birla Bhavan in New Delhi. The RSS agents attempted to kill him here, but believing that Suhrawardy, with one eye open and one closed, a pose he affected when he was lost in deep meditation, was a different person, they left the place without harming him. On 20 January, they threw a bomb at a Gandhi prayer meeting in Birla Park. Finally, they succeeded in assassinating Mahatma Gandhi on 30 January 1948 when he was going to his usual prayer meeting. Following the assassination of Mahatma Gandhi, the RSS was banned, but with his death they created an unfillable void in the peace mission. For Suhrawardy, now alone, it was a dauting task indeed. He still continued Gandhi's peace mission and set up several Gandhi *samities* in Calcutta.

BAN ON SUHRAWARDY'S ENTRY INTO EAST BENGAL

But in East Bengal, its League Premier, Khwaja Nazimuddin, imposed, on 3 June 1948, a ban on his entry into the province as injurious to public peace, had him arrested and ousted him from Dhaka.[188] Khwaja Nazimuddin also charged him with attempting to reunite both Bengals.[189] In a press conference held in Calcutta on 5 June, Suhrawardy forcefully denied these charges as baseless and false and declared his avowed determination to continue his peace mission.[190] He challenged the Chief Minister's contention that there was no need for the peace mission in East Bengal. The need was very much there, he asserted, and would continue until the Hindu exodus stopped and the migrants returned home. Past conflict between the two warring communities had caused them to fight for freedom from two separate platforms. This bitterness continued, even after the creation of the two states based on religion. In fact, the need for the peace mission was far greater in East Bengal, where a large Hindu population lived, since their total migration to India would force upon the Indian government a policy of directing a total migration of the Muslim population to Pakistan. He recognized that the Pakistan government would be unable to absorb and rehabilitate such a large population.

Suhrawardy reminded Khwaja Nazimuddin that Pakistan was created for the safety of the 100 million Muslims of the subcontinent, not just for the safety of the 60 million Muslims of Pakistan. During British rule, Muslims had claimed that the solution to the minority problem could only be achieved through the establishment of Pakistan but were opposed by Hindu leaders. Therefore, Pakistan should now come forward to settle its minority problem. He believed that since the protection of the minority groups and maintenance of peace largely depended upon the goodwill of the majority community, the

Muslims of Pakistan and the Hindus of India should work for communal harmony in their respective countries. Many notable Hindu leaders were already working for peace in India. Had the leaders in Pakistan worked for communal harmony in Pakistan, he added, he would not have to organize special peace meetings in East Bengal and assure safety to minority Hindus.

Suhrawardy asked the Pakistan government to rescind its fascist attitude towards him and allow his peace mission to continue unhindered, for, whatever happened in Muslim East Bengal would surely have its repercussion in Hindu West Bengal and Hindu India and endanger the lives of the Muslim minority there. The ban on his entry could only logically be interpreted as the Pakistan government not wanting communal harmony.

In November 1947, Suhrawardy convened an All-India Muslim League convention in Calcutta.[191] Muslim League leaders remaining in India attended the convention. Suhrawardy accused them that when he had been engaged in relief work in the affected areas of East Punjab no League leader had stood by his side. That same year Suhrawardy also attended the last session of the AIML council session in Karachi with Jinnah presiding. At this session Suhrawardy proposed the formation of a national party in place of building another Muslim League, but no one gave much importance to his proposal.[192]

A FIGHTER FOR DEMOCRACY

Suhrawardy's ailing father, Sir Zahid Suhrawardy, died in early 1949 in Calcutta. This encouraged the Indian government to impose an enormous income tax on him and, on the flimsy grounds of non-payment, appropriated his entire property. Suhrawardy was penniless and since his entry into East Bengal was banned, he returned to Karachi on 5 March to witness his National Assembly seat retrospectively cancelled on the grounds of non-citizenship.[193] Babu Rajkumar Chakravarty, a Hindu member of the Assembly, permanently lived in Calcutta but his membership was not cancelled.[194] In fact, membership of no other person was cancelled. This saddened Suhrawardy a great deal, especially since he had been one of the architects of this Assembly.

SLAUGHTER OF DEMOCRACY

By the time Suhrawardy returned to Pakistan Jinnah was dead. He had been the Quaid-i-Azam, the father of the new nation and his death left Pakistan in the hands of mediocre and greedy politicians. This led to the emergence of fascism in Pakistan under the leadership of Prime Minister Liaquat Ali Khan.

But can we make him alone responsible for the slaughter of democracy in Pakistan? Although Jinnah professed democracy, did he himself practise it? On the achievement of Pakistan he, as AIML President fighting for Pakistan, became the first Governor General of Pakistan and appointed Nawabzada Liaquat Ali Khan, his General Secretary, as the first Prime Minister. Despite the fact that 56 per cent of the population of Pakistan lived in East Bengal, neither of the posts was given to a Bengali. As the architect of the Muslim League victory in Bengal that had made the creation of Pakistan possible, Suhrawardy was the rightful claimant to the post of Prime Minister. However, the AIML Central Working Committee, heavily dominated by the Urdu-speaking west, engineered dissension in the rank and file of the BPML and got it abolished (although the Punjab Muslim League was still allowed to exist) and contrived to establish a weak administration in Dhaka and keep Suhrawardy out of the power bloc in Pakistan.[195] This attitude was already evident when, for several years prior to independence, Jinnah and Liaquat Ali Khan were, respectively, routinely elected as the President and the General Secretary of the AIML. The national capital, which is the economic base of a country, was also set up in Karachi. And, although Bengali was the language of the majority of the people, Urdu was imposed as the only state language of Pakistan.

Jinnah lived for just over a year after Pakistan's creation; but as long as he was alive, Liaquat Ali Khan was Prime Minister in name only.[196] Under the federal parliamentary system of government, which Pakistan had accepted as its prototype, the Governor General was only the constitutional head of state and the real power was vested in the cabinet and a sovereign parliament. But when Jinnah, who was recognized as father of the new nation, assumed the position of the Governor General, both the cabinet and the parliament became impotent before his imperious personality. Thus, the constitutional head of state became the fountain-head of absolute power.[197] Whether or not Jinnah had deliberately sought this change, it happened with devastating results for the future when ruthless men inherited the mantle but did not possess the personality. The Transfer of Power Bill also empowered him to dismiss ministers. This Liaquat Ali Khan particularly disliked but he never dared to challenge it.[198] He also privately moaned when Jinnah appointed ministers without consulting him or parliament and made them responsible to the Governor General.

During this period Liaquat Ali Khan had a raging furnace burning within him. This was first manifested when, in the final months of his life, Jinnah became seriously ill and was sent to Ziarat for treatment. During his long stay there, the Prime Minister paid him a courtesy call on only one occasion and that only for a few minutes.[199] Subsequently, when the dying leader was brought back to Karachi, neither the Prime Minister nor any of his colleagues, went to see him at his residence.[200] Thus, through the assumption of arbitrary power for the Governor General by the father of the new nation, the first coup against democracy and the parliamentary system occurred in the political life of the country and opened the door to a series of civilian and military coups thereafter.[201]

Birth of Bureaucracy. Jinnah also fathered the growth of bureaucracy in Pakistan. He was aware that his lieutenants lacked administrative experience and he depended heavily upon bureaucrats for the administration of the new nation. Almost all of the 100 British-trained senior bureaucrats who had opted for Pakistan were non-Bengalis. They seized upon the absence of a powerful political party and the administrative inexperience and weaknesses of the politicians and began to rule Pakistan. Chowdhury Mohammad Ali, the first Secretary General of Pakistan and Aziz Ahmed, the first Chief Secretary of East Bengal, became the real masters of the country.[202] Ghulam Mohammad, head of the Punjabi group, Sir Zafrullah Khan and Nawab M.H. Gurmani were given positions in the cabinet.[203] Subsequently, Chowdhury Mohammad Ali, Ghulam Mohammad, and Defence Secretary Iskander Mirza, who later became enmeshed in the sordid struggle for political power, held the highest executive posts. However, Jinnah did not appoint a single bureaucrat-turned politician to a cabinet post from East Bengal.

The bureaucrats became so dominant that they both formulated state policy and executed it; their hold on the central government machinery was total. They also occupied all the positions of departmental secretaries of the East Bengal Secretariat and frustrated the demands and aspirations of the Bengalis. To consolidate their hold, they even joined hands with both the Muslim League politicians and the army; the latter was mostly drawn from the Punjab Plain. Although Karachi was the capital, the Punjabis, with the two sources of power—the army and the bureaucracy—solidly in their control, became the most powerful force in determining the fate of Pakistan. They knew that the Muslim League leaders in power did not represent the people and would never give the country a constitution, since this would result in their own elimination from the Pakistan political scene, they would, therefore, be obliged to support the bureaucrats for their very existence. Among them were non-Bengali, refugee politicians nominated to the Constituent Assembly from East Bengal. They chose to live permanently near the capital in West Pakistan and depended upon those spineless sons of the soil from East Bengal who themselves had no followers. With no army, no bureaucracy and few politicians to speak for them, the Bengalis remained unrepresented in central power politics and were powerless to prevent the insidious exploitation and economic pillaging of their province. For obvious reasons, it became strategically and economically of the utmost importance for the vested interests to keep the two widely separated provinces politically united.[204] Jinnah and Liaquat Ali Khan, both of whom were refugees, had no knowledge of the complex social, economic and cultural problems of the new state. Thus, they became easy prey to the will and machinations of the bureaucrats.

Of the total population of Pakistan, the minor provinces of West Pakistan—Sindh, Balochistan and the NWFP—together constituted only 7 per cent while East Bengal and Punjab, respectively, constituted 56 and 37 per cent. The minor provinces had their own problems but had no platform to voice their protestations. East Bengal, however, with a more highly educated, politically mature population, strongly protested against this conspiracy and demanded a general election and an immediate framing of a constitution recognizing the proposition of full provincial autonomy, based on the 1940 Lahore Resolution. Quite unjustly, however, the Bengalis were vilified and accused of being secessionists for making this demand and were charged with being influenced by the minority Hindu population, most of whom lived in East Bengal. The Punjabi-dominated bureaucrats were afraid that once a national constitution was framed, the Bengalis would attain political power and the systematic exploitation of East Bengal, as a colony, would cease. Bureaucracy continued its contemptible policy towards East Bengal, until Pakistan disintegrated, with the conspicuous exception of a 13-month respite during Suhrawardy's Prime Ministership, who, in attempting to curtail its influence, lost his own power.

Emergence of Fascism. Jinnah died on 11 September 1948 and Khwaja Nazimuddin, until then the Chief Minister of East Bengal, became the next Governor General. To achieve this exalted position he had sacrificed more than half a dozen parliamentary seats to West Pakistanis, thus making the majority province of East Bengal a minority in the Constituent Assembly.[205] He did this without consulting his own people and acquired a benign popularity in West Pakistan. Nawabzada Liaquat Ali Khan, as if to avenge himself upon Jinnah, made even the pliable new Governor General a mere show-boy and, pursuing the policy of divide and rule, established weak administrations in the provinces in order to assure subservience to himself. Furthermore, the Constituent Assembly, that had been brought into existence in 1947 to frame the country's constitution but had transparently failed to fulfill its obligation, was comprised of a coterie of eighty people, who appointed from amongst themselves governors general; ministers and ambassadors, and distributed state patronage.

Liaquat Ali Khan, who hailed from the United Province in India, had no political base in Pakistan and was always fearful of his ability to maintain power. Therefore, to consolidate his influence he became a megalomaniac and intolerant towards political opponents. He dismissed the Punjab Mamdot ministry and the Ayub Khuhro ministry in Sindh, and harassed them with the Public and Representative Offices (Disqualification Act) of 1949 (PRODA).[206] Hamidul Huq Choudhury belonged to his group but, after a slight disagreement with him, was dismissed from the government and compelled to face PRODA. Hamidul Huq Choudhury's *Pakistan Observer*, the leading Dhaka English daily, was banned. He became so paranoiac towards any form of opposition that on the occasion of the third anniversary of Pakistan (14 August 1950) he called Suhrawardy 'the dog let loose by India', dubbing him an Indian agent, and sent Maulana Abdul Hamid Khan Bhashani and Sheikh Mujibur Rahman to jail.[207] He appointed Chowdhury Khaliquzzaman, an elderly politician, president of the Pakistan Muslim League (PML), but, when differences between them arose, he sent League volunteers to stone his house. Chowdhury Khaliquzzaman resigned for his and his family's safety, whereupon the Prime Minister assumed the presidency of the ruling party as well, soon to convert the PML, the successor of the AIML, into a closed corporation.[208] In fact, Liaquat Ali Khan was moving steadily towards the establishment of a one-party state.[209]

FORMATION OF THE AWAMI LEAGUE

The exigency of the circumstances that prevailed demanded the creation of an opposition political party to create a constitutional movement to stem the increasing fascism in Pakistan. Suhrawardy believed in democracy and wished to establish a democratic system within the country.[210] A one-party state, suppressing all opposition, does not lend itself to a free expression of divergent opinions or to freedom of thought. He was also aware of the political maturity of the people of East Bengal and wanted their close association and involvement in state affairs.

In West Pakistan, already the Jinnah Muslim League of Iftikhar Ali Khan, the Nawab of Mamdot, and the Awami (People's) Muslim League of the Peer of Manoki Sharif, were putting up some opposition to the ruling PML Party. Suhrawardy was initially inclined to join them. Instead, however, he called his old Muslim League workers in East Bengal to a meeting on 23–24 June 1949 at Dhaka and formed the East Pakistan Awami Muslim League with Maulana Abdul Hamid Khan Bhashani as its president.[211] Maulana Raghib Ahsan presided over the meeting. In 1950, Suhrawardy also founded the Pakistan Awami Muslim League on an all-Pakistan basis with himself as its president and M.H. Usmani as its general secretary. Its doors were open to all Pakistanis so as to curb the fascist proclivity of the PML. Later he amalgamated his party with that of the Nawab of Mamdot to be known as the Jinnah Awami Muslim League. But Mamdot's personal ambitions caused this relationship to be dissolved in 1953. Suhrawardy renamed his party the Awami Muslim League. The word 'Muslim' was subsequently dropped in a council meeting held in January 1953 when he considered that the people of Pakistan were getting used to the idea of a common citizenship with other religious factions and that it was necessary for the strength and development of Pakistan that all its citizens cooperate, irrespective of religious leanings.[212]

While campaigning to enlist support for the newly-formed party, Suhrawardy forcefully repudiated the PML claim to be the creators of Pakistan. He asked how was it possible that a son could be born before the birth of his father, asserting that the PML was formed after the creation of Pakistan and referring to the dissolution of the AIML and the National Home Guards.[213] Suhrawardy took his lieutenants with him, toured every nook and corner of East Bengal, made the Awami League the most popular and powerful party in the province, and geared it fully to contest the provincial elections that were to be held in 1954. Nurul Amin, the Muslim League Chief Minister in East Bengal, under instructions from the centre, fabricated charges against Suhrawardy's supporters and detained them for months and even years, turning the newly-formed Awami League into a party of protest, which led the fight against the reactionary forces, centred in West Pakistan.[214] Thus, the power struggle between the Awami League and the Muslim League became, to all intents and purposes, a struggle between the two wings of Pakistan.[215] During this time student unrest was growing, with the University of Dhaka becoming the hotbed of agitation. In their opposition to the East Pakistan Muslim League (EPML) government, the students and the Awami League worked hand in glove.

The life of the East Pakistan provincial legislature should have expired much earlier. Provincial elections in West Pakistan were completed by 1951, but in East Bengal the life of the Provincial Assembly was perpetuated and annually extended by the central legislature. In spite of vacancies occurring from time to time, after the holding of only one by-election, which resulted in defeat for the Muslim League candidate, no further by-elections were held.[216] When the EPML was finally forced to announce an election date for the provincial assembly for 1954, as many as thirty-five seats were lying vacant in the East Bengal legislature.[217]

The EPML Party then came to be considered as a party of the West and its popularity and its claim to represent the people of East Bengal was lost. In fact, when Pakistan was achieved the inherent differences between the two peoples became quite evident. The people of East Bengal, who were more literate and had a greater degree of political sophistication, were frustrated by the centre's step-motherly behaviour towards them and its attempt to impose upon them an unfair constitution. Economic disparity, rooted in the unnatural creation of Pakistan, with the majority of the people living in the East but all economic bases and the capital of the country in the West, confirmed for many thinking Bengalis the essential unfairness and impracticability of the 1946 Resolution. The centre, separated by a hostile India, with her 1,500 mile landmass between the two wings of Pakistan, could never appreciate and understand the desires and feelings of the Bengalis and watched them with suspicion. West Pakistan, especially the Punjabis, considered the Bengali Muslims to be out-caste Hindus and half-Hindus, converted to Islam, and always looked down upon them.

LANGUAGE MOVEMENT

Added to this was the language issue. Although Bengali was the language of the majority of Pakistanis and logically could claim precedence as the only state language of Pakistan, in a totally undemocratic way Jinnah, Liaquat Ali Khan and other official bureaucrats of Pakistan imposed Urdu, the language of the refugees from India and spoken by only 6 per cent of the total population of Pakistan, as the only state language of Pakistan, for the sake of so-called national integrity.[218]

The language movement first began within the government when in the inaugural session of the Pakistan National Assembly held in February 1948, Dhirendranath Datta of Congress proposed that Bengali should be one of the official languages of Pakistan.[219] Later, Maulana Abdur Rashid Tarkabagish, another member from East Bengal, spoke in Bengali, in defiance of the Assembly rule.[220] However, Prime Minister Liaquat Ali Khan refused to accord Bengali a status equal to Urdu, saying that the language issue was motivated in order to divide the people of Pakistan.[221] This attitude created a deep unrest among the students and the intelligentsia in East Bengal who reacted openly and began to agitate to make Bengali the official language of East Bengal and one of the state languages of Pakistan. The agitation soon gained momentum and a Committee of Action was set up on 2 March 1948, demanding that Bengali be accepted as one of the state languages of Pakistan.[222] On 11 March, a province-wide strike was called and big processions were held. Khwaja Nazimuddin panicked and, on 15 March, signed an agreement accepting an eight-point demand of the students; this included the recognition of Bengali as the official language of East Bengal and one of the state languages of Pakistan.[223] The East Bengal Assembly was in session and it unanimously adopted a resolution, making Bengali the official language and medium of instruction in East Bengal.

However, on his arrival in Dhaka on 19 March, Jinnah refused to accept the terms agreed with the students, saying that they had been made under duress. In a meeting with the Action Committee members, he insisted upon

Family photograph. West Bengal. c. 1945. Standing from left to right: S.M. Doja. Shahid Suhrawardy. Khwaja Nasrullah. Huseyn Shaheed Suhrawardy. S.N. Baker ICS. Alim-ur-Rahman Khan.

Sitting from left to right: Nuru (K. Nasrullah's 2nd daughter). Nanni (K. Nasrullah's 3rd daughter). Mrs Akhter Sulaiman. Mrs Nasrullah. Mrs Amena Doja (on lap Mrs Sulaiman's daughter). Iffat (K. Nasrullah's eldest daughter). Moina (Sir A. F. Rahman's granddaughter). Rashid Suhrawardy.

Rashid Suhrawardy, 2001

Huseyn Shaheed Suhrawardy, c.1955

Sitting: Begum Shaista Ikramullah
Standing left to right: Huseyn Shaheed Suhrawardy, Shahid Suhrawardy, and M. Ikramullah
Paris, c.1953

Begum Akhter Sulaiman, c.1953

Shahid Suhrawardy, c.1953

one language for the whole of Pakistan, to enhance unity between the two wings.[224] He was told that Urdu was not the language of any province of Pakistan and that if unity had to be sought, then either Bengali, the language of the majority of the people of Pakistan, or English be accepted as the state language of Pakistan. Jinnah rejected these arguments and told the student delegation categorically that Pakistan should accept Urdu because India had accepted Hindi.[225] On 21 March, in a public meeting in Dhaka, Jinnah unrealistically declared that Urdu was to be the only state language of Pakistan.[226] He repeated his declaration at the annual convocation of Dhaka University only to be shouted down by the students present.[227] Never before, in his entire life, had he been treated with such hostility and contempt from fellow Muslims as he suffered on this occasion.

On 26 January 1952, Khwaja Nazimuddin, on his first official visit to Dhaka as the Prime Minister of Pakistan, at the All-Pakistan Muslim League Convention, again declared that 'Urdu and only Urdu shall be the state language of Pakistan.'[228] This escalated the student unrest and the statement provoked a province-wide strike called on 21 February, in support of their demand. Chief Minister Nurul Amin responded to the strike with police repression. The police opened fire on the unarmed striking students, in front of Dhaka Medical College, killing eight and injuring many.[229] The antipathy caused by the language dispute completely alienated the people of East Bengal from the centre and led to the growth of a regionalist movement, which eventually created Bangladesh.

The Muslim League leaders, who represented East Bengal, had no *locus standi*; furthermore, the centre would only recruit those who spoke for the West. Khwaja Nazimuddin, who had once been Prime Minister of Bengal before partition, could neither read nor write Bengali and at public meetings, which he rarely addressed, he always spoke in Bengali, reading from a text, which was written in Urdu. He was a Bengali *zamindar* of Kashmiri descent and was always considered to be a representative of the West. Maulana Abdul Hamid Khan Bhashani and Sher-e-Bangla A.K. Fazlul Huq were born Bengali and recognized as leaders of the masses. They spoke in their language and instinctively understood the feelings and grievances of the Bengali people.

Shaheed Suhrawardy's position was more difficult. Although his ancestors lived in Midnapore for more than two centuries, no one in his family could speak, read or write Bengali. Suhrawardy had learned the political facts of life from Khwaja Nazimuddin's defeat, in Nazimuddin's own *zamindari*, by A.K. Fazlul Huq in the 1937 Provincial Assembly election, that unless he learned Bengali, spoke in Bengali, thought of himself as a Bengali and demonstrated love for Bengal, he had no possibility for establishing himself in the hearts of the Bengalis and becoming their recognized leader. He also held the view: 'That I am a Bengali is a bigger truth than the truth that I am a Muslim.'[230] Therefore, he quickly learned Bengali and could freely speak it although his somewhat exotic accent was easily detectable. He had a deep and sincere feeling for the people and his early association with Bengal politics helped him endear himself to the masses wherever he went.

JUKTO FRONT

As the date for the 1954 general elections neared, the three public leaders—A.K. Fazlul Huq, Shaheed Suhrawardy and Maulana Bhashani—came to the forefront. Already, as early as September 1952, the Democratic Youth League and the East Pakistan Communist Party had proposed the formation of a United Front to fight the ruling EPML in the next provincial elections.[231] The progressive student organizations also campaigned for an anti-Muslim League alliance.[232] Finally, the May 1953 Awami League Council meeting resolved, in a move to fight the ruling EPML, to form a 'Jukto' (United) Front with other like-minded political groups.[233] Suhrawardy initiated the approach in order to check the advance towards fascism and to attempt to bring the true representatives of the people of East Bengal effectively into the Pakistan political arena. The party was formally established on 13 November 1953 in a public meeting held in Dhaka.[234] The Awami League, the largest party in the alliance, remained in the vanguard of the opposition. To commemorate the Martyr's day, 21 February, the Front fought the March 1954 election on a 21-point programme which, *inter alia,* stipulated to adopt Bengali as one of the state languages of Pakistan and promised autonomy for East Bengal, nationalization of the jute trade, introduction of free primary education, abolition of all rent-receiving interests in land and distribution of surplus lands among landless farmers.[235]

The party programme and the personalities of the Front leaders produced an unprecedented election hysteria with universal support. However, it was the organizing genius of Suhrawardy that achieved its landslide victory for the Front. It captured 215 of the 237 Muslim seats and conceded only nine to the ruling EPML, the rest going to independents.[236] Earlier, during the election campaign, in Jessore district, Suhrawardy had declared that the ruling party would get only nine seats and it won neither more nor less than Suhrawardy had predicted, which, to some degree, is an indicator of how well he had organized the campaign and to what extent he had got his finger on the pulse of the needs and wishes of the people.[237] Later, eight independent members joined the Front bringing the total number to 223. The Awami League, alone, had contested 140 Muslim seats and it won all of them. The EPML Chief Minister Nurul Amin and four of his cabinet colleagues met with ignominious defeats in their constituencies, while more than fifty other

Muslim Leaguers lost their deposits, amounting to what was a virtual 'bloodless revolution'.[238]

The victory of the Jukto Front was inevitable, because:[239]

- the Front was led by political giants like A.K. Fazlul Huq, Huseyn Shaheed Suhrawardy and Maulana Bhashani, whereas the EPML leadership was directed by the mediocre talents of Nurul Amin and his followers, who had already earned the people's wrath and odium in the province for their roles in the language movement;
- the Front had placed before the electorate a clear-cut 21-point programme and had stressed the economic problems of the province, whereas the League had no programme other than saying that both Pakistan and Islam were in danger; and
- the EPML had jailed hundreds of students and opposition political leaders and had a dreadful record of seven years of misrule and failure.

The Front Ministry. The Front's resounding victory brought upon it the centre's positive hostility. The emergence of a non-Muslim League power elite in East Bengal created fear in the PML ministry at the centre and provoked it into adopting a campaign of clandestine and insidious actions to nullify the election victory.[240] On 23 March, only a fortnight after the elections, it instigated Bengali-Bihari riots at the US-aided Chandroghona Paper Mills in Chittagong.[241] The riots proved ominous. After procrastinating for about a month Fazlul Huq was finally commissioned to form a ministry. He constituted a 3-member ministry on 3 April and immediately left for Calcutta where he, carried away by the enthusiastic welcome of its citizens, seemed to assert that he had been against the partition of India and the creation of Pakistan and was amenable to once again conjoining the two Bengals.[242] This statement sparked off a major drama and full-scale controversy and created a political crisis, which exacerbated the existing rivalry between the central power elite and the newly-elected power elite of East Bengal.[243] Fazlul Huq immediately withdrew his speech, excusing it as an aberration caused by age, made in a state of unmitigated elation, and expanded his ministry on 15 May to include the Awami League and other Front colleagues. But when the Front ministers were in the midst of taking their oath, news came in that pre-planned ethnic riots had again broken out, this time at the Adamjee Jute Mills, a non-Bengali concern, in Narayanganj industrial town, only a few miles from Dhaka.[244] The mill belonged to Maulana Bhashani's trade union organization and it had voted *en bloc* in support of the Front.

The central Prime Minister, Mohammad Ali Bogra, alleged that, because of heavy communist infiltration, Huq was unable to maintain law and order in the province.[245] Huq strongly denied this charge but, unfortunately, *The New York Times* correspondent, John P. Callahan, with deliberate malice, reported, on 23 May, that the Front Premier was working for the independence of his province.[246] Huq, at the time, was attending the Chief Ministers' conference in Karachi. He quickly contradicted the report as a 'perversion of truth.'[247] But the centre, feeling humiliated at the signal defeat its provincial counterpart had suffered, pretended to believe Callahan's 'gathered' news and, determined to dislodge the popular ministry, moved quickly to take advantage of the situation.[248] It branded Huq as a 'traitor', dismissed him, suppressed the Front ministry and promulgated Section 92-A of the constitution, substituting Governor's rule for ministerial rule on 29 May.[249] It also replaced Governor Khaliquzzaman by its hard-liner administrator, Defence Secretary Colonel (later Major General) Iskander Mirza. He quickly followed the imposition of Section 92-A with the arrest of a number of Front leaders and protesting students; as many as 3,000 people, including 35 Provincial Assembly members and a minister, Sheikh Mujibur Rahman, were arrested. The Chief Minister, himself, was put under house arrest.

The dramatic events moved smoothly and surely in the centre's favour and Callahan's report provided the final piece of ammunition to strike at the Front ministry. Furthermore, the Pak-US military pact signed on 19 May was inextricably linked with Huq's dismissal.[250] Suhrawardy, who was abroad for medical treatment, deplored the central government's action and urged the people of East Bengal to remain united.[251]

CONSTITUTIONAL CRISIS

At the centre, in an unprecedented move on 25 October 1954, Governor General Ghulam Mohammad abolished the sovereign parliament and asked Mohammad Ali Bogra to form a new ministry. He had become the third Prime Minister of Pakistan in April 1953, after the dismissal of Khwaja Nazimuddin, who had, in the greater interest of the country, stepped down from the post of Governor General to become Prime Minister on 17 October 1951, following the assassination of Nawabzada Liaquat Ali Khan on 16 October.

Ghulam Mohammad was a bureaucrat but had become the central Finance Minister in the Liaquat ministry and subsequently Governor General when Khwaja Nazimuddin relinquished his post to succeed Liaquat Ali Khan as Prime Minister. He had no experience in parliamentary democracy and he considered the office of the Prime Minister simply as the head of an executive body. Therefore, in complete disregard for parliamentary mores, he appointed and dismissed ministers. He appointed Mohammad Ali Bogra as Prime Minister although the latter was not even a member of parliament and was, at the time, Pakistan's ambassador to Washington. Again, when he suspected the strong possibility of his own removal, following the passing of a bill curtailing his special power to dismiss parliament and the cabinet, he quickly contacted a prominent Awami League leader, Ataur Rahman Khan, to obtain his views on the Jukto Front supporting him, in case he abolished the existing parliament and, with support from the army, the bureaucracy and the industrial magnates, sharply counter attacked, creating the greatest constitutional crisis Pakistan ever faced.[252]

Bogra was abroad at the time. Ghulam Mohammad ordered him to return to Karachi. When he arrived there without delay he found himself a virtual prisoner, was forced to agree to the dissolution of the National Assembly and his own ministry and, on his solemn assurance that he knew nothing of the secret conspiracy against the Governor General, broadcast a prepared speech as Prime Minister.[253] Ghulam Mohammad wanted a Bengali to justify his despotic act and Bogra agreed to do it. A 'Ministry of Talents' was formed with, among others, the Army Chief, General Ayub Khan, who joined the cabinet as Defence Minister. Iskander Mirza was recalled from East Bengal and made the Interior Minister.

LAW MINISTER

Suhrawardy was at the time undergoing medical treatment at the Kantonspital in Zurich. He had worked strenuously during the provincial elections and his health had seriously broken down. Ghulam Mohammad sent an emissary to Zurich, requesting him to return to Pakistan to eliminate the constitutional impasse that had occurred and to give some measure of verisimilitude to his government.[254] The emissary assured Suhrawardy of Ghulam Mohammad's intention to ultimately commission him as the Prime Minister and, although to begin with, he should join as a minister, he would, in fact, be the de facto Prime Minister of Pakistan, empowered to 'wash the dirty linen of the regime.'[255] Suhrawardy was confused because of the inclusion of General Mohammad Ayub Khan in the cabinet and replied that he would decide his course of action on returning home.[256]

Meanwhile, General Ayub and General Iskander Mirza communicated their dislike of Suhrawardy to Ghulam Mohammad.[257] They feared the release of the army generals who had been convicted for their attempted coup against Liaquat Ali Khan and who had been so brilliantly defended by Suhrawardy that they had escaped with their lives. Finding himself in an awkward situation, Ghulam Mohammad asked Bogra to rescue him.[258] Bogra had worked in Suhrawardy's cabinet in undivided Bengal and he too feared Suhrawardy's inclusion in the cabinet. So, he met Fazlul Huq and promised him and his Krishak Sramik Party (KSP) power in East Bengal in exchange for Huq's promise to challenge Suhrawardy's credentials to represent the people of East Bengal.[259] Thus, the two leaders of Bengal were 'kept apart to serve the ambitions of the ruling coterie.'[260]

Suhrawardy had no knowledge of this conspiracy against him, and he was not allowed to meet his colleagues in East Bengal when he returned to Karachi on 5 December. He was genuinely moved by Ghulam Mohammad's promises and the tears in his eyes and, surprising both friend and foe alike, he joined the Bogra ministry on 21 December, in order to try and restore parliamentary government and even more importantly to stave off the looming threat of military dictatorship in Pakistan.[261] The portfolio of law minister was of prodigious importance, as it fell upon him to untangle the web of questionable judicial decisions decreed by the Supreme Court.[262] However, Suhrawardy soon realized Ghulam Mohammad's dissimulation and was further handicapped when Abu Hossain Sarkar, Fazlul Huq's nominee, joined the cabinet as the Health Minister. He was not even consulted about the appointment. A series of broken promises prevented him from implementing the necessary changes in the country's administration and constitution, for which he had joined the cabinet in the first place.

Principle of parity. However, at a high-level conference, held at Murree, in 1955, Suhrawardy was responsible for the signing of the Murree pact, which stipulated five state principles.[263] Following the signing of the pact he successfully constituted a new central assembly, based on the principle of parity. Drawing inspiration from the Bengal pact signed in 1923 (p. 9) he ably convinced the people of East Bengal to forgo their majority and accept, with magnanimity, the principle of parity at the centre. On paper, the principle seemed unfair. East Bengal, with 56 per cent of Pakistan's population, enjoyed a clear majority and it was not easy for the Bengalis to agree to accept parity. In 1950, Prime Minister Liaquat Ali Khan had submitted the first Basic Principles Committee (BPC) Report, but East Bengal had rejected it as unacceptable because it was 'terribly anti-Bengali' and retained separate representation for elections to the federal and provincial legislatures.[264] The Report had also recommended Urdu as the only state language of Pakistan, but totally disregarded the principle of provincial autonomy. The next year Khwaja Nazimuddin submitted the second BPC Report and this time Punjab rejected it since it asked them to surrender portions of their territory to the minor provinces of West Pakistan. The situation worsened and martial law had to be imposed in the province, followed by the dismissal of the Punjab Daultana ministry. Finally, the

Nazimuddin ministry at the centre was also dismissed. Obviously, the problem of representation accentuated these events.

Suhrawardy is sometimes blamed for surrendering the majority rights of East Pakistan. Fazlul Huq and his KSP opposed him vigorously as in this he found an opportunity to make Suhrawardy unpopular. But despite Huq's fulmination that he was selling East Pakistan to West Pakistan, Suhrawardy was able to persuade the people of East Pakistan to accept parity. Without parity, he realized, the framing of a constitution was becoming increasingly impossible.

The principle of parity was established to remove the fear of majority domination and to ensure the rights of equal representation in all walks of national life, based on the philosophy of give and take.[265] Suhrawardy expected that parity would force members to vote through the manifesto of political parties and not parochially and would lead to the creation of national political parties. More importantly, parity recognized East and West Pakistan as two separate 'nations' (in a loose sense), groups or entities.[266] This recognition of regional individuality, coupled with geographical incongruity, made the granting of autonomy and the introduction of joint electorate an imperative need for East Pakistan. Suhrawardy pointed out that separate electorates would entitle the Hindu minority to a large number of parliamentary seats and entrust it with the balance of power between the two rival Muslim groups to the detriment of East Pakistan.[267] As a minority group, the Hindus would always remain united and organized while the Muslims, because of the growing antipathy between the two wings, would always be divided and therefore dependent on the minority Hindus. But under joint electorate the Hindus would be integrated into the Bengali nationhood, to participate in the solid front against attacks from the integrated West Pakistan. Therefore, parity was a price East Pakistan paid for autonomy and a joint electorate. Fortunately for East Pakistan, the Hindus refused to be considered a minority group and wholeheartedly supported Suhrawardy's move but had to wait until he became Prime Minister.

At this time the majority Muslim League Party, with the consent of Governor General Iskander Mirza, who had meanwhile replaced Ghulam Mohammad, offered Suhrawardy the Prime Ministership and they began to negotiate the selection of ministers and the distribution of portfolios.[268] However, when everything seemed settled and the BBC had even broadcast his name as the next Prime Minister, Iskander Mirza, with machiavellian chicanery, reneged on his offer. Chowdhury Mohammad Ali, who had agreed to Suhrawardy becoming Prime Minister, was now approached by Iskander Mirza and, sufficiently tempted, formed the next ministry on 11 August 1955 with A.K. Fazlul Huq lending his support. Huq became the Interior Minister and Suhrawardy the official leader of the opposition. Bogra went back to his former position in Washington.

THE FIRST CONSTITUTION FRAMED   •

The new ministry moved quickly to frame the country's first constitution and to hold general elections. From the opposition Front bench Suhrawardy offered his full support to the constitution makers. He wanted, he said, a constitution that would be acceptable equally to both wings, which would mark an end to the era of indirect elections, which would serve to rid the Assembly of unpopular and dishonest people who were holding responsible positions in the government, and which would achieve early general elections to establish democracy and ensure political stability.[269]

Referring to a suggestion of some West Pakistanis that if East Pakistan wished it could go its own way, he parried by arguing that although they were, broadly speaking, two different peoples, the memories of a common struggle and the belief that neither wing could survive without the other bound them together.[270] Religion was, in itself, a very loose unifying thread since, in reality, it was not strong enough to politically unite the culturally and linguistically desperate Muslim neighbours. He also brought to the attention of the Assembly the peculiar geographical composition of Pakistan, which, instead of being considered a problem, had blessed the country with a unique position.[271] On the one hand, Pakistan was linked with the Western World and the Muslim countries of the Middle East, as far west as West Africa, and, on the other, it could connect with Burma, Indonesia and other countries in the East. These wide communication links gave Pakistan prodigious scope to exert influence of great political significance and to emerge, in course of time, as one of the more powerful countries in the world. But once divided, he suggested, Pakistan would be able to exert little or no influence at either end. Therefore, Suhrawardy urged the government to develop equally both wings, grant provincial autonomy to East Pakistan and to appoint a committee of economic experts to examine and report on the deplorable state of her economy, which would then recommend measures for improving the situation; otherwise, he warned, an impending storm, growing out of neglect and frustration, would fiercely blow and engulf the province.[272] He, finally, maintained that if the Bengalis could show more understanding and the Punjabis see reason the future of Pakistan would be secure.

The constitution was finalized on 29 February 1956 and Suhrawardy signed it as the opposition leader. It was, in fact, the outcome of a compromise which had been reached between autonomist East Pakistan and centrist West Pakistan. The constitution recognized Bengali and Urdu as the two state languages of Pakistan and granted a large measure of provincial autonomy, but it deferred any decision on the introduction of joint electorate. Governor General Iskander Mirza signed the constitution only after receiving a written assurance that he would be appointed the first president of the new republic.[273] Accordingly, he was sworn in as the interim President on 5 March and the new constitution was enforced on 23 March, the date chosen to commemorate the 1940 Lahore Resolution, which had adopted the first draft constitution for the future homelands of India's Muslims.

Iskander Mirza had no peer in the art of political intrigue and knavery and when he became head of state it was generally accepted that the main source of his strength was General Ayub Khan, the Commander-in-Chief of the armed forces.[274] The President made full use of this assumption to enhance his own power and to sabotage his own constitution. Although trained at Sandhurst, Iskander Mirza had worked as a British political agent in the NWFP, where he wielded enormous power, and he had become a past master in setting one tribe against the other and bribing tribal leaders. Even after becoming the chief executive of the nation he could not jettison this habit and played the 'old frontier game' to remain in power. Thus, when he found his Prime Minister becoming a political leader, after the framing of the constitution, Iskander Mirza became alarmed. He started talking openly of controlled democracy.[275] The framers of the constitution themselves became alarmed by his reaction and, realizing that everything they had achieved was in perilous straits, moved quickly to hold early general elections. The President, sensing his possible isolation, manoeuvred to build his own political party within the Assembly and to try and avoid general elections. He encouraged Dr Khan Sahib, the elder brother of Khan Abdul Ghaffar Khan of the NWFP, to form the Republican Party. Overnight, the Muslim League members of West Pakistan *en masse* joined the 'Palace Party'. A Republican ministry was soon formed in West Pakistan.

At the centre, Chowdhury Mohammad Ali, whose options were either to join the Republican Party or to resign, chose the latter to prove his political integrity and he stepped down on 8 September 1956. The President asked Shaheed Suhrawardy, whom he had escorted from Dhaka, to form the next ministry. Suhrawardy was sworn in as the country's fifth Prime Minister on 12 September 1956, with Republican support, and his own 14-member minority Awami League Party and seven scheduled caste members from East Pakistan.

PRIME MINISTER

It looked like the dawn of a new era when Suhrawardy became Prime Minister of Pakistan. He gave immediate emphasis to three objectives:

- a general election in the country;
- elevating Pakistan's prestige in the sphere of international opinion and;
- equal treatment to the neglected regions of Pakistan.

SPEEDY DOMESTIC MEASURES

Within one month of his assumption of power, parliament was convened in Dhaka to resolve many problematic and delicate questions, including the electorate issue.[276]

Joint Electorate. Opening the debate on the electorate issue, Suhrawardy said that he had fought for separate electorate for the Muslims of British India as a weapon to fight for an independent homeland for the minority Indian Muslims, but a joint electorate should be the weapon now to consolidate the Pakistani nation, since both India and Pakistan had accepted the existence of their respective minorities. Suhrawardy explained that the 'two-nation theory was advanced by Muslims as a justification for the partition of India and the creation of a state made up of geographically contiguous units, where Muslims were numerically in a majority. Once that state was created the two-nation theory had lost its force even for the Muslims.'[277] If Pakistan should still keep the separate electorate system for its own minorities, he maintained, they could legally claim a separate homeland for themselves, comprised of those areas where they predominated. Since that was out of the question, joint electorate was the only logical answer to this problem. All the Muslim countries, he argued, believed Islam did not prescribe any electorate system and therefore calling joint electorate un-Islamic was baseless. No Muslim country, he added, had separate electorates for their own minorities.

Joint electorate means Hindus and Muslims would vote together to elect their representative. Did we not cast our votes jointly in electing the President of the Islamic Republic of Pakistan and the Speaker of the National Assembly, or do we not jointly vote on issues coming up for discussion in the House? he asked. In local body elections in East Pakistan the system had been practised for a long time, such as in the case of election of municipal committees, district and union boards and school and college governing bodies. Those who supported separate electorate feared Hindu domination in joint electorate. This fear, he said, was unfounded and unjustified as was manifested in the Khulna district where the Hindu-Muslim ratio was almost equal and, under separate electorate, eight Muslims and seven Hindus were returned in the provincial Assembly elections, whereas, in the 30-member district board, only two Hindus were returned under joint electorate. Therefore, if anyone stood to lose under this system, it was the Hindus who, nevertheless, were prepared to support joint electorate so that they might be regarded as Pakistanis and not just Hindus. Surprisingly, however, the fear of Hindu domination was voiced in that part of the country where the Hindus constituted barely 2 per cent of the local population.

Suhrawardy urged the people to consider the issue dispassionately and observe how the demand for separate electorate was rooted in a deep mistrust and hatred for the Hindus, emanating from partition days. This rift would take time to heal but we should begin the healing process immediately, he stressed. Since an exchange of the respective religious communities of India and Pakistan would transform Pakistan into a sea of human bodies, we should not lose sight of the truth and, therefore, offer the Hindus the considerations of equal honour and respect, creating in them the self-confidence, which is the rightful due of a citizen of Pakistan. This could happen only through equal participation in all state affairs. When the Hindus could enjoy equal rights and privileges, they would engage themselves equally in the task of building a nation.

Suhrawardy warned the supporters of separate electorates that their policy would only divide the nation but, in order to achieve a happy, prosperous, and strong Pakistan we needed the cooperation of the Hindus. Suhrawardy appealed to the people to support his policy in the greater interest of Pakistan. He vehemently declared that the electorate that had voted the government into power should not now be separated on religious grounds. Even the diehards of separate electorates could not decry him or his cogent reasoning. He introduced the Joint Electorate Bill in parliament which the House passed.

A Fair Trial for Democracy. Suhrawardy guaranteed equal citizenship to all, irrespective of religion, race, creed and culture.[278] Democracy that so long existed in name only was given a fair trial in East Pakistan. The Awami League government in East Pakistan, which came to power only six days before his own assumption of power at the centre, began in right earnest, in fulfilment of its obligation, the execution of the 21-point programme adopted as the election manifesto of the Jukto Front. It earned the people's respect by releasing all political prisoners and abolishing the Public Safety Act that had been frequently used by previous governments to intimidate opposition political leaders.[279] Unlike the previous governments, it faced the people, regularly called Assembly sessions, placed and passed bills and budgets, and held by-elections. Seven by-elections were held in which the Awami League won six and lost one; but it could not convince its central counterpart for more autonomy. When it pressed for more decentralization of power, Suhrawardy agreed, but only within the framework of the constitution.

Economic Policies. Suhrawardy adopted speedy economic measures to remove disparity in the East wing and in the smaller regions of West

Pakistan. This was the first time any government had attempted this. He reviewed the existing categories of imports and made provisions for the introduction of newcomers into the import trade, abolished the Chief Controller's Office in Karachi and set up three independent offices of the Controller of Exports and Imports, one each at Chittagong for East Pakistan, Lahore for West Pakistan and Karachi for the federal zone.[280] He also took steps to make sure that all foreign exchange earnings were divided equally between East and West Pakistan, and the federal zone.[281] He empowered the Chittagong and Lahore controllers to consult their respective provincial governments and issue licences.[282] The Controller of Karachi was advised to consult the federal commerce ministry for the issue of licences. He upgraded the Chittagong branch of the Central Supply and Development Department to meet East Pakistan demands and ensure supply, and placed it under the full control of an Additional Director General.[283] He also introduced a new financial year beginning July each year that gave East Pakistan executives enough time to complete construction and building works before the monsoon season.[284]

When the Awami League assumed power, famine was already looming large in different regions of East Pakistan. Within three days of the formation of his ministry, Suhrawardy visited the province to assess its needs and helped avert a repetition of the 1943 famine by quickly importing rice from Australia, Burma, Thailand and other countries.[285] The Awami League ministry in East Pakistan enjoyed full freedom and received his unreserved backing, and succeeded in meeting the threat of famine without any loss of lives. The government spent millions of rupees on test relief works to enable the landless peasants to earn a decent wage. The Awami League government also established the Films Development Corporation to assist the private sector improve the film industry, the Jute Marketing Corporation to boost the jute trade that earned about 70 per cent of Pakistan's foreign exchange, the Dhaka Improvement Trust and the Chittagong Development Authority for urbanization of these two fast growing cities, and the Inland Water Transport Authority for the development of waterways in this riverine province.[286] In consultation with the United Nations Secretary General, Suhrawardy appointed a mission under Krugg to find ways and means to prevent floods that regularly visited East Bengal.[287] Following the Krugg recommendations, an autonomous Water Development Board was set up mainly to deal with flooding.

SPIRITED FOREIGN POLICY

Suhrawardy is, however, chiefly remembered for his spirited foreign policy. Although he was in power only for a little over a year he was able to raise the status of Pakistan high in the zone of international opinion. In his first broadcast to the nation he declared that he would pursue an independent foreign policy, based on honesty and truth.[288] Four important factors influenced his policy:

First, Pakistan, at creation, had not received its share of either civil or military equipment from India and had come into being, economically underdeveloped with barely any industries. Therefore, it needed to develop and strengthen its military capacity, acquire ammunition and military equipment, and build up its industrial insufficiency.

Second, the communist powers were hostile to Pakistan, owing to India's flirtations with China and Russia, and because of Pakistan's subservient acceptance of American aid.

Third, when Suhrawardy became Prime Minister, Pakistan's foreign policy was weak and in disarray. Pakistan 'had no friends in Asia except Iraq, Turkey, Thailand and the Philippines, who were friendly because they were members of defence pacts. All neighbours—India, the USSR, China and Afghanistan—were hostile. Burma was unfriendly and Ceylon (Sri Lanka) indifferent to Pakistan.'[289]

Fourth, the Kashmir issue, which no Pakistani government could neglect, still remained unsolved.

The situation called for a foreign policy, based on the realities of the time and on Pakistan's essential needs. Hence, Suhrawardy extended the hand of friendship to all, attempted to counteract India's policy abroad, expose Nehru and help the cause of the Kashmiris. Thus, he summarized the basis of his foreign policy as 'Goodwill towards all and malice towards none.'[290]

Neighbours. Suhrawardy recognized that he could talk of Kashmir only from a position of strength. He, therefore, aimed at getting Asian and Russian support to try and find a solution to the Kashmir problem. This policy was initiated by visiting Pakistan's neighbours to improve relations and to gain friends. First he accepted an invitation from the Chinese government to visit their country in October 1956.[291] Suhrawardy was the first Pakistani head of government with enough courage and foresight to take such a step. Before him no leader had dared to open a dialogue with Chinese leaders, fearing adverse public reactions. While addressing a public meeting at the historic Paltan Maidan, he declared: 'I was the first to start this thing (Sino-Pakistan friendship). Until then no one had dared to do it. My predecessors would say: 'Gentlemen, we're afraid of doing this.' What is there to fear? If my mind is clear, if I have love in my heart, if I'm not jealous, of what should I be afraid? I fear none but Allah alone.'[292] Chinese Premier Chou En-Lai made a return visit to Pakistan. His historic reception in Dhaka was a memorable watermark in Sino-Pakistan relations. Suhrawardy convinced the Chinese leaders that even with different political systems they could live as friends and establish cultural and bilateral relations. Pakistan sent a high-level delegation to China and also received a Chinese trade delegation. The Dalai Lama's visit to India in 1956 had created misunderstanding between India and China and Suhrawardy seized full advantage of the situation.[293]

Suhrawardy visited Burma on his way to and from China, establishing direct contact with Burmese leaders. A high-level delegation visited Burma to negotiate and sign an agreement, defining mutual interests. A trade delegation also visited Burma, followed by the visit of a private mission, sent by the Friends' of Burma Society in Karachi. Pakistan was also represented at the 2500th anniversary celebration for Lord Buddha. Suhrawardy visited Japan in April 1957. A trade pact was negotiated and signed with Russia. A parliamentary delegation visited Russia and invited the Russians to participate in future Pakistan cultural and educational conferences.

Muslim World. Suhrawardy strongly questioned the efficacy of bringing together all emerging Muslim countries on to a common platform, since they were deeply divided amongst themselves and were weak economic and military powers.[294] While addressing the S.M. Hall students of the University of Dhaka he mused about the results of creating a Muslim bloc and said: However many zeroes we may add to each other, the answer will still be zero. Therefore, nothing positive will ever be produced by blindly adding a series of zeroes together. However, if we added a zero to one the total would be determined by how many zeroes we added to that one. Whether zeroes were added to the right or to the left of the one the result would always be bigger than a zero.[295]

By this equation Suhrawardy was referring to the military strength of the emerging Muslim nations, not their international reputations.[296] Compared with America, the United Kingdom or the USSR, the Muslim countries had no modern military potency with its concomitant supporting industrial technology and were considered to be incapable of repelling aggression or of becoming involved in international conflicts without outside help. He included Pakistan in this zero group, but his severe public assessment angered the Arab World, especially Egypt. During the Suez crisis Egypt rebuffed Pakistan's offer of an army contingent as a contribution to the United Nations peace-keeping force, organized to maintain peace following the withdrawal of the Franco-British and Israeli troops. Egypt also refused to receive Suhrawardy when he offered to visit their country to explain Pakistan's policies in relation to Arabs. But the biggest shock was Egypt's vote against Pakistan, when the Kashmir issue was debated at the United Nations.

The conflict was unfortunate, but not totally unexpected. Since independence, India had pursued an aggressive foreign policy in the Middle East and had been more successful than Pakistan in placating the Arabs. India appointed Muslim ambassadors to Arab nations, established strong trade links and engaged in vigorous anti-Baghdad pact propaganda, earning the gratitude of the Arabs. India succeeded in creating among the Arabs a negative attitude towards Pakistan for being too pro-Western in spite of the fact that India recognized and maintained trade links with Israel, whereas Pakistan had consistently refused to recognize the state of Israel. Suhrawardy was on a state visit to China when England, France, and Israel attacked Egypt. Immediately upon his return from China, he accused Israel of being an aggressor and condemned Britain and France for invading Egypt. Pakistan joined with Iran, Iraq and Turkey, the other three Muslim members of the Baghdad pact, to condemn the attack and prevailed upon Britain and France to immediately withdraw from Egyptian soil, in accordance with a United Nations Resolution.[297]

However, although Egypt failed to support Pakistan, Suhrawardy succeeded in obtaining the promise of support from all the other Arab states.[298] They now fully recognized Pakistan's problems and, although they themselves could not join the Baghdad pact, appreciated the steps Pakistan was taking for its self-defence. They objected to Iraq's membership, the only Arab country to join the pact, because they were still busy in managing the 'Arab horse' and believed in Arab unity, in preference to entering into any pact with non-Arab Muslim countries.[299] In his efforts to strengthen fraternal ties with all Muslim states, Suhrawardy received the Prime Ministers of the Federation of Malay States and Indonesia, two South-East Asian Muslim neighbours. The Malay Federation was scheduled to attain independence in August 1957. Pakistan sent a constitutional expert, as a member of the Malay Constitution Commission, to help draft the future constitution. In November 1956, Suhrawardy visited Iran and Lebanon, and Turkey the following January. At the invitation of the Saudi King, President Iskander Mirza visited the Kingdom of Saudi Arabia. A trade pact was negotiated and signed with Saudi Arabia and, as a gesture of goodwill, the Saudi Commerce Minister visited Pakistan.

Pakistan had never had good relations with its northern neighbour Afghanistan, the only country to vote against Pakistan's entry into the United Nations. This relationship reached its nadir in Kabul in 1955 when the Pakistan embassy was ransacked and the national flag pulled down and insulted. The Afghan government, closely allied to India, claimed sovereignty over a substantial portion of the Pushto-speaking NWFP of Pakistan. Relations vastly improved when Suhrawardy assumed power. President Iskander Mirza visited Kabul at the invitation of King Zahir Shah and Sardar Daud's subsequent visit to Pakistan further improved relations between the two countries. Suhrawardy paid a return visit to Afghanistan.

Suhrawardy was anxious to 'sit together, whenever possible, and exchange views and establish, if not political ties, such economic, cultural and religious ties as may advance our common outlook.'[300] He hoped that closer bonds among Muslim countries would lead naturally to the emergence of a power, mightier than a military force, that would be capable of guiding it to a more constructive role in the world.[301]

Pakistan's Security. Probably no government before his had thought of Pakistan's security as strongly as did Suhrawardy's. The lion's share (85%) of Pakistan's budget went on defence expenditure, yet there was no feeling of real security against foreign aggression. In fact, Pakistan, immediately after independence, suffered from the same degree of insecurity as severe as France suffered after the end of the First World War (1914–1919).[302] Therefore, Pakistan had joined the Baghdad pact in 1954 with Britain, the United States, and three neighbouring Muslim countries—Iran, Iraq and Turkey. In September 1955, Pakistan had joined the South-East Asia Treaty Organization (SEATO) with Australia, Britain, France, New Zealand, the Philippines, Thailand and the United States.

Indian Prime Minister Pandit Nehru attacked the pacts vigorously, claiming that the arms aid received under these two pacts would be directed against India and America would not supervise its deployment. India received American assurances of support should military-aid equipment, which the United States had provided to its allies, be used in an attack against its borders.[303] Suhrawardy, too, openly declared, time and again, that Pakistan would use American arms aid only for purposes of self-defence and would never use it against India or any other country, unless Pakistan was attacked. He wondered how Nehru, who always preached world peace and opposed imperialism and colonianism, could remain silent when Russia invaded Hungary on 23 October 1956 but was able to criticize the pacts Pakistan had joined for her self-defence. Furthermore, Nehru never criticized the Warsaw pact signed between Russia and its satellite East European Bloc nations, the Russo-Chinese arms aid pact or Russian arms aid to Syria. Nehru could condemn a small country like Pakistan because India was militarily secure and could stand on her own resources.

However, Suhrawardy wanted Pakistan and India to live in peace with each other for mutual progress. India was a vast and rich country with a large Muslim population. Therefore, he was totally against inciting India and thought it unwise even to consider his neighbour an enemy. But, at the same time, he wanted reciprocity and a quick solution to the Kashmir dispute and the new problems, caused by diverting the Ganges water flow from East Pakistan, the Brahmaputra flooding problem from Assam, and the canal water dispute in West Pakistan. He repeated the offer of a 'no-War pact' with India and even proposed dismissing the national army once these outstanding problems were solved.[304]

Pakistan's membership in the two defence pacts was not beyond criticism, even from within the country itself. There was strong public support for Pakistan to remaining neutral. The President of the East Pakistan Awami League, Maulana Abdul Hamid Khan Bhashani, broke away from his party on the question of remaining in these defence pacts of which he could not approve and formed his own National Awami Party (NAP). Differences between Suhrawardy and the Maulana over foreign policy came to the surface at the Kagmari conference held on 7–8 February 1957, which the latter had convened to decide the issue of Pakistan's foreign policy.[305] The Maulana had timed the conference to occur with the Security Council debate on the Kashmir issue. He also invited heads of several governments, including Pandit Jawaharlal Nehru of India, Chief Minister P.C. Ghosh of West Bengal and Indian intellectuals antipathetic to Suhrawardy. Suhrawardy strongly defended the pacts, arguing that Pakistan could hardly hope to become the Switzerland or the Sweden of Asia simply because of the peculiar geographical composition, with two wings separated by more than 1,500 miles of hostile Indian territory.[306] He posed the question as to how a country could talk of neutrality and remain isolated, when she was nakedly exposed to foreign aggression and was unable to repel it? On two occasions, in March 1950 and July 1951, when Pakistan stood helpless, India had deployed its armed forces all along the international border.[307] Pakistan could not sit back complacently in the face of this ever-present threat on her borders and needed security against such potential aggression.

Unfortunately, the decision to join these defence pacts had been made by only three persons—Ghulam Mohammad, Zafrullah Khan and General Ayub.[308] The cabinet learned about these pacts only after they were finalized. The people were not taken into the confidence of the trio because of the latter's lack of courage and foresight. Suhrawardy offered the first public statement on the subject, elaborately explaining that the two pacts were purely defensive and in no way directed against Russia and China, or even India, who were known to be militarily far more powerful than Pakistan.[309] Moreover, the Bandung conference, comprised of heads of the newly emergent states of Asia and of Africa, did not prohibit governments from entering into pacts for purposes of self-defence.[310] The two pacts brought in military, economic and food assistance, which Pakistan desperately needed, and helped to create links with other friendly and Commonwealth countries, and to enlist support on the Kashmir issue. Suhrawardy especially recognized American support as total, timely and worthy of a true friend, appreciating the fact that such action potentially jeopardized its role as a permanent member of the Security Council.[311]

American arms aid use. Apart from these earnest attempts, Suhrawardy sent trade and goodwill missions to several countries, including those of Eastern Europe. At the Commonwealth Prime Ministers' Conference, held in London in January 1957, he effectively explained Pakistan's problems to the other government heads. From London he went to the United States and impressed the same message upon the Eisenhower administration and the people of America. His extempore address to Congress was a masterly analysis of the world situation and was considered an oratorical *tour-de-force* bringing him a standing ovation. Suhrawardy was able to persuade the government of the United States to give its approval for the development of American military aid equipment against all aggression.[312]

Following his visit to the United States, Suhrawardy toured East Pakistan where he made speeches in favour of a pro-United States policy and sought and obtained support for his foreign policy from the vociferous Dhaka student community and his own party. On arrival at Lahore airport from his tour to East Pakistan, he reported to pressmen that American arms aid could be used against any aggression. From Peshawar, the United States ambassador to Pakistan issued a statement contradicting Suhrawardy. On his return to Karachi and hearing of the ambassador's statement, he requested a four-day foreign policy debate for the Assembly. Then he wrote a letter to President Dwight D. Eisenhower, informing him that the pro-American atmosphere he had just generated would perish if the United States government did not endorse his views on the use of arms against any aggressor. He received no reply. Suhrawardy, however, opened the foreign policy debate with a speech, supporting a pro-United States policy and sent another letter to President Eisenhower urging an immediate response and informing him that the foreign policy debate would last for only four days.

On the last day of the foreign policy debate he received the President's telegram, endorsing his interpretation, which he read to the Assembly. For the first time, the Assembly unanimously approved his foreign policy. The policy, however, was revoked by the United States government within two weeks of Suhrawardy's resignation in October 1957. The United States President, addressing the House of Representatives, mentioned that America would not tolerate the use of its arms against aggressors other than communist aggressors, otherwise the aid would be stopped.

Kashmir Dispute. Next to security of its borders, the Kashmir issue was Pakistan's primary problem with India. When India was partitioned on 14 August 1947 the ruling monarchs of each principality were offered options of either joining Pakistan or India, or even remaining independently sovereign. Kashmir, with its overwhelmingly Muslim population and being contiguous to Pakistan, was naturally expected to join Pakistan. But its Hindu ruler, Maharaja Hari Singh, against the wishes of his subjects, opted for India, and invited Indian troops into his state to repel tribal incursions from Pakistan. Thus, the Kashmir dispute was created and remains unsolved to this day.

Suhrawardy 'was genuinely anxious to reduce tensions between his country and India over Kashmir.'[313] He suggested stationing United Nations troops in Kashmir and instructed Pakistan's permanent representative to the United Nations to arrange for a debate to discuss the Kashmir question.[314] The resolution, which was presented at the end of the proceedings, received the positive support of all Security Council members, except the USSR who abstained on the first day, when the resolution was adopted, but voted against the operative clause on the following day. By a vote of 10-0, with Russia abstaining, the Security Council for the fifth time called for a plebiscite in Kashmir and challenged the right of Kashmir's puppet assembly to unite the state with India. Indians were disappointed by Russia's abstention, after Nikita Khrushchev had noisily proclaimed India's right to Kashmir—but, in the world of real politik, Russia was at that time trying to win Muslim friends in the Middle East. These United Nations votes were considered to be a great diplomatic victory for Pakistan. Suhrawardy sent a personal representative to the USSR to contact the Soviet government. Conceding a 'moral victory' to Pakistan, Nehru was 'deeply pained' by this acknowledgement.[315]

The success at the United Nations made Suhrawardy feel that he could counteract Nehru in the arena of international politics. He, therefore, made contact with governments of different countries, unmasking the real reason for Nehru's refusal to hold a plebiscite in Kashmir under United Nations auspices and defying international opinion, simply because the latter knew, that once a plebiscite was held in the state, its Muslim population would vote to join Muslim Pakistan and he would become a refugee in India.[316] Suhrawardy also convinced them that all bilateral talks in the past had failed to solve the Kashmir problem because of India's insincerity and, therefore, there was no further usefulness to be achieved by holding such talks. He confidently declared in a Paltan Maidan meeting in Dhaka that 70 of the 81 United Nations members would support Pakistan, while India would get only 11 votes, when the issue came up for discussion and voting at the next General Assembly sitting in September.[317] Thus, for the first time, a solution to the long-standing Kashmir problem was thought to be close at hand. In fact, both the domestic and the external policies of Pakistan started moving in a radical direction. The entire nation was resuscitated with new life and began to be spoken of with respect and admiration in the comity of nations.

RESIGNATION

At home 'Suhrawardy was looked upon as one who equalled Nehru in politics and diplomacy. Suhrawardy was certainly a greater parliamentarian and orator than Nehru and had equal experience in organizing politics in the country.'[318] Thus while Suhrawardy, at the peak of his reputation, was gaining international support on Kashmir and becoming a national leader, the reactionary forces represented by the strong West Pakistan-based business community and bureaucracy, including the President, were conspiring to oust him from power and to avoid a general election.[319] Welcoming President Iskander Mirza at the annual dinner of the Federation of the Chambers of Commerce and Industry in Karachi, the Federation President frontally attacked the economic policies of the Suhrawardy government. 'Our politicians,' he said, 'have made a mess of the situation and their parity politics have not only affected the political status of the country but also (have) had a serious impact on the economic life of the nation.... Parity in the political sphere may be a workable compromise but its application in economic planning without considering other important economic facts may lead us into blind alleys from where there may be no way out.'[320]

Suhrawardy had forced an agreement on the allocation of foreign exchange, based on parity between East and West Pakistan because, he claimed, no part of the country could be developed at the expense of the other.[321] But this angered and antagonized the business community of Karachi. His conflict with them came to a head when the commerce ministry, headed by a Bengali, proposed to set up a shipping corporation in the public sector for interwing coastal trade.[322]

The Prime Minister also soon clashed with his coalition colleagues. Although the President publicly backed Suhrawardy's stand on One Unit in West Pakistan, his Republican Party wanted to undo it. Foreign Minister Malik Feroz Khan Noon, the leader of the parliamentary Republican Party, declared in London that he and his party were honour bound to support a resolution for the break-up of One Unit; other members and ministers of the Republican Party did likewise. NAP leader, Khan Abdul Ghaffar Khan, who also opposed One Unit, began to receive tremendous popular acclaim in NWFP. G.M. Syed, also of the NAP from Sindh, began to act as if he had become the ruler of Pakistan and attacked Suhrawardy as a lightweight politician. He even held a meeting of secretariat officers, who emanated from Sindh, and assured them that West Pakistan would be demerged and they would all go back to Sindh. The Republicans even began scheming with the NAP and agreed to support any resolution moved in the central legislature to disintegrate One Unit.

This obviously placed Suhrawardy in a perfidious position. The Republican Party's connivance with NAP was directed against the Prime Minister personally, his stand on One Unit and on his foreign policy. It struck at the very roots of the coalition on which his ministry was based. Suhrawardy boldly opposed this attack because, he maintained, the undoing of One Unit would mean the undoing of the 1956 constitution, framed ten years after Pakistan's creation, upon which he based his efforts to introduce the first general elections in the country's history and thereby eliminate the entrenched leadership from the body politic of Pakistan.[323] Without doubt his stand on One Unit won him many Punjabi friends and the overwhelming popular support he received assured him of success in the country's first general election. But the vested interest groups had never wanted a Bengali to succeed. Therefore Suhrawardy's downfall was inevitable. The President, who was deeply involved in palace cliques and intrigues, sent for the Prime Minister on 10 October upon Suhrawardy's return to Karachi from a tour in West Pakistan, where he had campaigned to arouse public sentiment in favour of One Unit, and presented him with a letter from the Republicans, withdrawing their confidence in him and making contemptible charges of corruption against his ministry. But ultimately, it came down to the real motive, which was Suhrawardy's attitude towards the Republican Party on the One Unit issue, irrespective of the fact that the Republicans themselves had broken the coalition when they agreed to disintegrate One Unit against his advice.

Suhrawardy sent a letter to the President on the night of 10 October, advising him that constitutionally he had the right to demand a meeting of parliament and suggested that Iskander Mirza should convene a meeting on 24 October, where he would seek a vote of confidence. The Prime Minister's East Pakistani colleagues released this information to the press, against his direct wishes. The next morning the President read the news in the papers, refused to call a meeting of the legislature, and asked Suhrawardy to resign by 10:30 a.m. failing which he would dismiss him. Suhrawardy resigned, in deference to the President's wishes, to avoid the ignominy of dismissal, after remaining in power for only 13 months. Suhrawardy's resignation was so astonishing and so sudden that the entire nation was stunned. The students of the University of Karachi sarcastically put up a full-page advertisement in *Dawn,* the city's leading English daily, inviting applications for the most 'temporary post of Prime Minister of Pakistan' from those applicants who would be willing to get the boot without notice.[324]

The President and the Republicans, obviously, did not want Suhrawardy to test his strength in the legislature as this could have split their party and brought about a re-orientation of parties and a new coalition, and above all, would have made parliament the maker of ministries. The President spent six laborious days trying to create a workable coalition between the Muslim League and the Republican Party—which had been at daggers drawn, abusing each other in the most virulent terms, with Ismail Ibrahim Chundrigar of the Muslim League as the sixth Prime Minister, on the basic assurance that separate electorate would form the basis of the forthcoming general elections. This was an astonishing volte-face as the joint electorate system was a cardinal principle of the constitution of the Republican Party and the Muslim League, themselves, had consented to joint electorate at Murree.

One may, therefore, conclude, without resorting to a great deal of in-depth analysis, that the Muslim League toned down its opposition to the Republicans and the Republicans compromised their principles on the electorate issue, simply in order to keep Suhrawardy out of the Prime Ministership. The Muslim League justified its coalition with the Republican Party to its supporters by getting separate electorate accepted. The League's reason for insisting on separate electorate was, quite plainly, its propaganda value through which it could secure the support of many Muslim voters, by resurrecting the flames of religious fanaticism and communal distrust. To the Republican Party the question of electorates was not of much importance; one way or the other it was prepared to yield, as hardly any propaganda had been carried out in West Pakistan in favour of joint electorate and the Republican Party had neither roots nor an organization to do so. In any event, the electorate issue had no significance for West Pakistan where 98 per cent of the voters were Muslims. For the sake of remaining in power, the Republication Party was prepared to alienate East Pakistan, which was directly concerned with the problem.

To keep Suhrawardy out, the Republican Party agreed to coalesce with the Muslim League, giving it the Prime Ministership, but maintaining the whip hand with its membership of 24 to 22. However, this coalition, not easily achieved, was rendered possible by pressure from the President, who felt that the Muslim League was now the only party to which he could entrust his future return to office. The Muslim League government, however, began victimizing opponents in such a callous manner that the Republicans became frightened. Chundrigar called a meeting of the legislature for 28 November 1957 and categorically stated that if he could not put through separate electorates by that date, he would resign.[325] The Republicans felt that if they agreed to work with the Muslim League for separate electorates, their existence as a separate party would be at stake and they would eventually be absorbed into the League. This the President was pressing them to do. The rank and file of the Republican Party, however, felt that if they merged with the Muslim League they, individually, would be ostracised and ultimately effaced as the Muslim League would never forgive them for their earlier secession and assumption of political power. The Republican Party

Organizing Committee in Lahore held a meeting on 17 November, where it repudiated the action of the Republican leaders in coalescing with the Muslim League and passed a resolution that, before they agreed to separate electorates, they would proceed to East Pakistan to ascertain for themselves the majority view there.[326] Chundrigar, in spite of his categorical statement earlier, did not move the Electoral Bill on 28 November.

However, while parliament was in session, the Muslim League leaders of Karachi staged a demonstration outside the National Assembly, insulted Dr Khan Sahib and certain Republican members who were watching the demonstration, and smashed the windscreen of Suhrawardy's car with sticks and rocks. Amongst the demonstrators were a number of highly-strung youths who were demanding separate electorate as necessary to the existence of Pakistan and that joint electorate would cut at the very foundations of the ideology of Pakistan, was against the spirit of Islam, and would lead to Hindu domination. They further warned that anyone who preached joint electorate was a traitor to Pakistan and should be killed. Prime Minister Chundrigar addressed the demonstrators and told them that they had achieved their objectives and should disband.[327] The demonstration had frightened the Republican Party. The President, who had linked his destiny with the Muslim League, pressed hard upon the Republican Party to support separate electorates and the Muslim League Prime Minister, with his 11 members. The Republicans realized that they would not be able to form and sustain their own ministry in West Pakistan and the Muslim League would snatch it from them. Suhrawardy, however, promised them his party's support if they formed their ministry and broke away from the Muslim League, but made it clear that neither he, nor any Awami League member, would take office.

The meeting of the legislature had been adjourned until 11 December. By that time the Republican Party had decided to support joint electorate and Chundrigar felt compelled to resign, within two months of his assumption of power. However, the President, anxious to remain in power even after Chundrigar's resignation, commissioned him to form another ministry, hoping that he would be able to bring pressure on the Republicans to accept separate electorate. Finding, however, that the Republicans were in a recalcitrant mood and not prepared to meet his wishes — with time passing and his position in insisting on a Prime Minister who had no support making him look ridiculous — he reluctantly called upon the Republican leader, Feroz Khan Noon, to form a ministry, as the seventh Prime Minister of Pakistan. Noon had once been Governor of East Bengal and Pakistan's Foreign Minister in Suhrawardy's cabinet. He formed his Republican government on 16 December 1957, with Awami League's moral support, which had been given on the clear understanding that the country's general elections would be held as early as possible. The new Prime Minister announced mid-February 1959 as the last date for the overdue general elections.

MILITARY DICTATORSHIP

President Iskander Mirza again became alarmed at the prospect of general election, which for entirely personal reasons, he did not want. The irony is, as Suhrawardy stated on a number of occasions in later years, that the Awami League, in the likely event of them coming to power after the forthcoming general elections, had every intention of asking Iskander Mirza to retain the position of the Presidency, but with severely reduced powers.[328] Even then in an unprecedented move on 7 October 1958, he abrogated his own constitution and assumed total power. He dismissed the central and provincial governments and promulgated martial law throughout the country.[329] General Ayub Khan, the Commander-in-Chief of the Pakistan Army, was appointed as the Chief Martial Law Administrator (CMLA). The President declared: 'As for the traitors, I ask them to leave the country if they can, while the going is good.'[330] The first victim of his own declaration, however, was the President himself. Only 20 days later, on 27 October, CMLA Ayub Khan, in another coup, forced the President at pistol-point to resign and leave the country within 24 hours.[331] Thus ended the era of civil servants' coups and the rule of a master-intriguer, culminating in a military dictatorship that obliterated the last vestige of symbolic democracy.[332] Pakistan passed into an era of abysmal darkness.

When Suhrawardy was Prime Minister, he had confronted Ayub with the current rumour that the army were considering a coup. Ayub replied, 'Sir, if there is a coup, it will be over my dead body.'[333] Initially, Ayub claimed that he would retain power for only a short while, until the political climate was right to return the reins of power to a civilian government. Suhrawardy said at the time to friends that Ayub would retain power for ten years—he was right, almost to the day.[334]

In this way General Ayub Khan came to power. He had tasted it first, as the Defence Minister, under Mohammad Ali Bogra. Since then, visibly or invisibly, he had remained entwined in central politics.

EBDOed and Jailed

Assuming complete power, Ayub Khan banished all erstwhile politicians from the political scene for seven years, under the Elective Bodies Disqualification Order (EBDO) promulgated on 7 August 1959. Suhrawardy was placed under EBDO in July 1960. The matter did not end there. While banished from politics and solely engaged in his law practice, on 30 January 1962, Ayub Khan arrested him making no official charge, which would have necessitated a trial, but only on the allegation of anti-state activity one month prior to the enforcement of his one-man constitution on 1 March, which allowed him to rule Pakistan through 80,000 Basic Democrats. Suhrawardy had confirmed his arrest, when in the previous December at Lahore, on being privately approached by the President for his views on the proposed constitution, he advised him (since he believed the time was opportune for the return of democracy) to revive the 1956 constitution, since the grounds on which it was then abrogated, no longer existed.[335] The President feared Suhrawardy's opposition to his constitution and arrested him. He was seventy. His arrest was the most foolish act of the four years of Ayub's military administration. The entire student community of East Pakistan protested his arrest, universities closed down and strikes were called; all this was answered by mass arrests and political repression.

Suhrawardy, in a stern rejoinder to the government accusation justifying his arrest, wrote to President Ayub: 'You will pardon me if I fail to understand how you, Mr President, who have known to me at close quarters, should have paid the slightest attention to the false statements, insinuations and allegations which must have been made to you, challenging my patriotism. I do not refer to the 'reasons' of my detention, for these are so obviously and patently false that they could not have been the real reasons for the order of detention, and your mind must have been poisoned by other allegations. In your forthright statement to the Press the day after my arrest you gave reasons and made charges not one of which is to be found among the 'reasons' of my detention. Hence, it is quite clear that I have been arrested for reasons other than those supplied to me.... Perhaps, Mr President, you will forgive me if I were to submit that from your statement regarding myself it appears that the real reason for detaining me is an apprehension that my presence outside would interfere with the working of the constitution about to be launched, otherwise reference to this has no meaning in the statement in which you gave reasons for my detention (Appendix I).'

Suhrawardy asked the President: 'Say it, Mr President, with your hand on your heart, and then may Allah be our Judge, in this world or the next. For, if this is how you feel about it, it is not right that I should live.'

Recounting his contribution to the creation of Pakistan, he further told the President: 'Let me tell you, Mr President, what you do not know, that Pakistan is my life. I have, I believe, played a great part in bringing it into existence. Bengal was the only province—among the Muslim majority provinces—that gave a Muslim League ministry to the Quaid-i-Azam; Bengal was the pawn in his hand due to which the Congress accepted the partition of India. And to make Bengal accept the Muslim League, and align itself in the struggle for Pakistan, I had to work day and night, at the cost of my own living, health and safety.'

In May 1962, general elections were held in the country in accordance with the provisions of the new constitution that established a federal-termed unitary government and established a national assembly to be elected by 80,000 Basic Democrats. All political parties in East Pakistan boycotted the election, maintaining the return of true representatives impossible under the indirect Basic Democracy system. However, following the general election, martial law was lifted on 8 June. Sixteen days later, on 24 June, nine prominent leaders of East Pakistan demanded abrogation of the constitution and framing of a new one by representatives elected through universal adult franchise. The demand for Suhrawardy's release from jail also gained momentum. Finally, in submission to popular pressure, the President released him on 19 August after a detention in solitary confinement of six months and twenty days, which was the direct cause of the heart trouble he was soon to suffer and from which he never recovered.

Ironically, President Ayub's carefully presented self-assurance received a temporary setback, when, after having, unjustly, arrested Suhrawardy, fearing the latter's powerful opposition to the imposition of his pet constitution, he resorted to the ignominy of bargaining farcically with Suhrawardy's children for the release of their father.[336] Thus, on 19 August, in the middle of the afternoon, Suhrawardy's two children, Begum Sulaiman and Rashid Suhrawardy, who had just arrived in Pakistan from London for his school holidays, were contacted by the Foreign Minister, Mohammad Ali Bogra, and requested to urgently meet with him at the Foreign Minister's residence. Bogra, who hailed from East Pakistan, had not set foot in the province since Suhrawardy's arrest for fear of the hostile reception that would greet him. The proceedings that ensued once Begum Sulaiman and Rashid Suhrawardy arrived at the Minister's residence degenerated into a pure farce and it is difficult to appreciate that perhaps the fate of a nation and the life of a great political figure were involved. Bogra contacted President Ayub in Rawalpindi on the hotline and Ayub in his most authoritative tones informed the Suhrawardy children that he was prepared to release their father but demanded one small condition, that Suhrawardy must give an undertaking that he would not travel to East Pakistan until six months had elapsed. Using the Foreign Minister's car and escort, Begum Sulaiman and Rashid drove to Karachi jail where they met with their father and relayed the President's message. Suhrawardy's reaction was typical; he was not prepared to accept any conditions, of any kind. They returned to the Foreign Minister's residence, recontacted Ayub, communicated their father's response and the President, in slightly less authoritative tones, suggested three months as the time limit. They returned to the jail with the outriders and escort clearing a path through Karachi's dense traffic and populace and informed Suhrawardy of Ayub's compromise. 'No,' he said, 'no conditions. Tell him I'm quite happy here, editing my tapes and films and reading my books.' Back to Bogra's residence, phone-call to the President, message conveyed and, to everyone's disbelief, Ayub said, 'One month. Surely he cannot object to one month.'

Going through the same travel arrangements, as before, Ayub's new proposal was greeted with the same negative response. On returning to the Foreign Minister's residence the President was contacted once again and his bellow of '2 weeks, surely he will agree to 2 weeks' almost belied the need of a telephone. Returning to the jail with, by this time, a very confused police escort and outriders, both Begum Sulaiman and Rashid begged their father to accept this condition of Ayub's if only, as Rashid cheekily said, to save on petrol consumption. Ayub's new proposal was met with a roar of laughter from Suhrawardy and a shaking of his head at the fatuousness of the situation and with tears in his eyes from laughter, he said, 'Alright, tell him I will accept, since I have to go into hospital for a month, for a check-up, in any case.' So, in a manner that would have done justice to Feydeau farce Suhrawardy's solitary confinement of nearly 7 months came to an end.

A FALLEN WARRIOR OF DEMOCRACY

Suhrawardy, after his release from jail, visited Dhaka at the first opportunity, arriving on 16 September, and moved by the ovation he received at the airport, where the plane had to stop three-quarters of a mile from the airport building owing to the size of the crowd, asked his audience to stand solidly united and to assume the lead in the movement for the restoration of democracy in Pakistan. A life-long liberal democrat, Suhrawardy wasted no time in contacting all political parties opposed to Ayub Khan, persuaded them to attend a convention in Lahore and announced the formation of the National Democratic Front (NDF) on 5 October 1962.[337] The day the NDF was established fifty-four leaders signed the declaration, calling it a movement for the restoration of democracy in Pakistan. Suhrawardy opposed the reviving of political parties because, with divergent political programmes, he could predict disunity and mud-slinging among them, which would dissipate their energy and deviate their attention from the single goal of restoring democracy. He also opposed abrogation of the new constitution, which might create an administrative vacuum and would offer an unwanted opportunity to the government to prolong its undemocratic rule.

Along with the Front leaders Suhrawardy visited every corner of the country. The campaign for the restoration of democracy created such political fervour that it forced Ayub Khan to appoint a high-powered commission to investigate and report on the demand for the return of democracy, based on universal adult franchise, if the people wanted it. With his consent, too, the new parliament in its Dhaka session passed the Fundamental Rights Bill.

Just as the movement for the restoration of democracy got off the ground under the dynamic leadership of Shaheed Suhrawardy, providence stood in its way. A combination of three month's strenuous work and the debilitating effects of his long incarceration broke down his health and he suffered from two heart attacks on 3 and 12 January 1963, forcing him to enter hospital. It was during this time, on 6 January, that the President promulgated two new ordinances, forbidding all EBDOed politicians from associating themselves with any form of political activity, on pain of two years jail, fine, or both.[338] At the same time, the President assumed the power to reduce, completely absolve, or further extend the period of political restraint for a further six months. Without doubt, the ordinances were directed primarily at Suhrawardy, whose personal popularity, allied to the tumultuous support he and his movement received for democratization of the constitution, was now reaching mammoth proportions. From his hospital bed Suhrawardy responded angrily, denouncing the ordinances as the highest form of corruption and repression.[339] He further told the President that, in the eyes of the latter, the EBDOed politicians might appear vilified, but, in the esteem of the people, they still enjoyed some kind of respect.

However, Suhrawardy's doctor advised him to receive heart treatment abroad. On 19 March, Suhrawardy left for Beirut. After some improvement in his health, he went to London to recuperate at the home of his son, Rashid. From London he returned to Beirut in November and was planning to undergo an overdue hernia operation in Zurich. He planned to return home on 3 or 4 January 1964. While preparations were being made to accord him a grand reception on his return from treatment abroad, the news of his sudden death, in Beirut's Hotel Intercontinental, plunged the entire country into deep sorrow. Suhrawardy expired in his suite in the early hours of 5 December 1963, when only an operator of the hotel telephone exchange was present by his side. At 3:00 a.m. he had a sudden heart attack and, as he tried to contact one of his Lebanese friends on the telephone, the receiver fell from his hand. The operator got alarmed and rushed upstairs to see Suhrawardy lying on the floor unconscious. Medical help was called but it was too late as he breathed his last at 3:20 a.m. His mortal remains lie buried in the old High Court compound of Dhaka, alongside the graves of A.K. Fazlul Huq and Khwaja Nazimuddin.

The circumstances surrounding Suhrawardy's death are shrouded in mystery, which give rise to many people, including Sheikh Mujibur Rahman, believing that it was not a natural one. While there is no conclusive proof to this effect, two incidents occurred that lend potency to this controversy.[340] Shortly before Suhrawardy's death Zulfikar Ali Bhutto, who at the time was Foreign Minister of Pakistan and whose cruelty and ruthlessness, to be so transparently manifested within a decade, were already showing signs of growth, said to Francois Jabres, a mutual friend of the two men, 'Tell Suhrawardy not to try and return to Pakistan, otherwise I shall make sure personally that he never sets foot on its soil.' Whilst one was prepared to, at the time, ignore Bhutto's crude bombast as nothing more than the immature ranting of a dock-side bully, his comments were given extra import when a few days later a Central Intelligence Department officer, who was friendly with the Suhrawardy family, said to Begum Sulaiman, 'Tell your father to take great care of himself. The word is going round that they are out to get him.' Three days later he was dead.

Suhrawardy was probably intuitively aware of imminent death. This is evident from the letter he wrote on 29 November to Manik Mia, the Editor of Dhaka's leading Bengali daily, *The Dainik Ittefaq*: 'Of course, this is for you only. If I die, I shall be happy. There is no point in living. I am of no further use to anybody—and if of use to myself—then this life is not worth it.'[341] These words written only six days before his death speak eloquently of his cherished life-long goal of establishing the rule of law in Pakistan and of his dedication to the needs and comforts of his people. Of his stormy political career of forty-three years, he was in government for less than ten years—seven years in undivided Bengal as minister for Labour and Commerce, Civil Supplies, Finance and Prime Minister and two years in Pakistan as Law and Parliamentary Affairs Minister and later as Prime Minister; yet, whether in power or out of it, he was the people's leader and they stood by him. Gratefully Suhrawardy gave everything he had—his rare intellect, wealth, health and finally his life. In the creation of Pakistan he was second only to Jinnah but in the creation of a democratic opposition in Pakistan he was second to none.[342] His relentless struggle for the restoration of democracy in Pakistan is the greatest monument to his memory and a gift to Pakistan.

Mahatma Gandhi, while addressing a Muslim gathering, is purported to have once said: 'Jinnah, there is your statesman; Liaquat, there is your politician; Suhrawardy, there is your leader.'[343] There can be no better assessment of the three top men involved in the struggle for independence. Indeed Suhrawardy was a leader—a born leader of the masses destined to lead the teeming millions of his country. That the people's love for him was not false was proved countless times when they, in their hundreds and thousands, trudged through the muddy and dusty roads of Bengal, to have a glimpse of their beloved leader—a political Messiah—and to hear him as if he had 'brought them a new message of hope and liberty—a new panacea for the ills of the country.'[344]

During the general elections of 1937 and 1946, he travelled widely, employing all available means of transport—trains, steamers, boats, bullock carts, even walking for mile after mile and addressed twenty-five to thirty meetings a day, living on the most simple rations. The situation was exactly the same in 1954. Yet, in spite of the multiplicity of experiences gained from the stunning successes he achieved in the 1937 and 1946 elections, people are still astonished how he managed to organize the Jukto Front in barely a year, which inflicted the most crushing of defeats upon the ruling Muslim League in 1954, a party that he, himself, had helped to build, making it into the most potent springboard for the creation of Pakistan. Unfortunately, death seized him in 1963 before he was able to prepare the NDF in his final campaign to inflict a similar defeat upon the enemies of democracy.

Suhrawardy's political mentor, without doubt, was C.R. Das, a great son of Bengal. He tutored Suhrawardy and profoundly influenced him. 'The magnitude and greatness of their life-mission,' says Abul Mansur Ahmad, 'was on the same level. Chittaranjan's mission aimed to establish unity between the Hindus and the Muslims of India. If his mission had succeeded, India would not have been partitioned. Shaheed's mission was the unity of the two wings of Pakistan. The future will judge if the tragedy that had befallen India after Das's untimely and accidental death would, likewise, befall Pakistan.'[345] As with C.R. Das, Shaheed Suhrawardy also earned fabulous fees as a lawyer and similarly distributed most of what he earned on charity or donated it to his party. A few months before his death, Suhrawardy once told A.K. Brohi privately, 'Mr Brohi, I would like to close this chapter of my political struggle and die in peace, but I cannot let down the people of Pakistan who have reposed so much confidence upon me. Besides, I have to think about my only son. I have nothing to leave to my son—not even enough to enable him to prosecute his studies further.'[346] 'Truly,' says Abul Hashim, 'he died a magnificent pauper, receiving the burial of an emperor.'[347]

'Generally,' says Tofazzal Hossain, 'rich people forget and avoid their poor relatives. But it was different with Shaheed Suhrawardy. He searched them out, visited their cottages, never hesitated to have meals with them and helped them generously.'[348] He could mix with the common people—slum dwellers, workers, labourers and peasants to create confidence in them as easily as he trod among the statesmen of the world to explain Pakistan's bonafides.[349]

'While in Calcutta,' writes Sheikh Mujibur Rahman, 'I accidentally saw a black exercise book. It contained, among others, a list of pensioners. Suhrawardy paid them a total monthly pension of Rs3000. Among the pensioners, irrespective of religion, were old servants, barbers, labourers, some of the old writers and political workers.'[350] He also maintained a separate establishment at his house for poor but meritorious students. He arranged jobs for them when they had completed their studies. This was in keeping with his family tradition.

The facets of Shaheed Suhrawardy's character were multi-dimensional. As Ataur Rahman Khan describes, 'It was both mild and firm, cold and grim, simple and complex. The outside was firm and reserved, but the inside was tender-hearted and sweet. Whoever met him for the first time could feel surprised, or could even mistake him.'[351] Possessed of a towering personality, well beyond the reach of the common man, he never, however, kept him at a distance. He also possessed an inexhaustible fund of energy and worked, when in office, from eighteen to twenty hours a day. He never believed in political vindictiveness or attacked his political opponents. In politics he introduced the principles of tolerance and reason, often treating his enemies with a magnanimity sadly lacking in many of his contemporaries. There are numerous instances when he defended his opponents in the law courts without accepting a fee. 'But the remarkable feature of Suhrawardy's life,' says A.K. Brohi, 'consisted precisely in educating his detractors and went on his way supremely indifferent to the libel that his political opponents published against him.'[352] He never surrendered to threats or backed away from a fight, if he believed in the justice of his position. When, after Jinnah's death, fascism became manifest under Liaquat Ali Khan's leadership, one of his friends advised him to leave Pakistan for a while, he roared, 'Never! Tell them I accept their challenge on behalf of the people of Pakistan.'[353]

Suhrawardy was a 'great man with uncommon talent amounting very often to intellectual audacity which is an essential qualification of a statesman but a disqualification for a politician. He alone did his best and risked his popularity and politician's career in his attempts to stabilize Pakistan as a nation-state by building up the Pakistani nation. This was an uphill task. In this respect, Suhrawardy was the one leader amongst the leaders of Pakistan, next only to the Quaid-i-Azam, who really understood the spirit of Pakistan and acted up to that spirit. All his post-partition activities were directed toward this one objective.'[354]

'What he could not achieve by a life-long struggle,' observes A.K. Brohi, 'will be consummated by his death. And the fact that the people of Pakistan paid an unusually high tribute to his memory by receiving his earthly remains as they were flown into Pakistan with a kind of ovation and applause which few before him and still fewer after him will ever be privileged to receive, is a portent of things to come. In a strange way history, immediately after his death, has held a referendum and the verdict by the people of Pakistan, as I find it evidenced by the enormous crowds of people who have lifted up

their hands in solemn prayer for their dear-departed one, is un-
mistakable.'[355]

Suhrawardy was a bright star in the firmament of our national history.
'When the history of our times will be written by an unbiased historian of
the future,' continues A.K. Brohi, 'I have no doubt whatsoever that he would
assign to the late Mr Suhrawardy a place of high importance in the roll call
of national honour. He has undoubtedly left a mark on the pages of
our national history; both before and after the creation of Pakistan his
role, judged by any standard, would appear to be one of paramount
significance.'[356]

DEMOCRACY UNTRIED

It was Suhrawardy who, underscoring the necessity for a united and strong
Pakistan, had supported amalgamation of the four provinces of the West wing
called West Pakistan, convinced the East Pakistanis to forgo their
incontrovertible claim to their majority, accept parity as a state principle and
introduced the joint electorate system to unify the different religious sections
of the country.[357] Unfortunately, those who had opposed the very creation of
Pakistan, finally became its sole custodians after its creation, forcing
Suhrawardy to fight for the adoption of the people's fundamental rights, with
the same tenacity and dedication as he had fought for the freedom of his
people from British hegemony.

The task was uphill because, as he said time and again, democracy, which
alone could have saved the nation, was never given an opportunity to be tried
in Pakistan. In fact, Jinnah had mortally wounded it when he implanted
bureaucrats in the body politic of Pakistan, who, in their arrogance, staged
repeated successful coups; the first, when Ghulam Mohammad dismissed
Khwaja Nazimuddin; the second, also by him, when he dissolved the
National Assembly; and the third, when President Iskander Mirza and
General Ayub Khan jointly imposed martial law in the country.[358]

Democracy could hardly flourish in Pakistan with two diametrically
opposite peoples: the East Pakistanis believed in democracy, emanating from
the grassroot level, while the West Pakistanis distrusted it because they were
never permitted to practice it. Politics there centred around the whims and
caprices of big landlords; in East Pakistan, there was no landlord to threaten
them.

Thus, while the country as one mourned his death, bowed and, as a mark
of deep respect to his departed soul lowered its national flag to half-mast—
a rare honour to an opposition leader—still it could not save Pakistan.[359] His
death not only removed the main obstacle to Ayub's dictatorial regime but it
cut the only link that still bound the two distant provinces together.

Suhrawardy was the only leader who could speak the language of the common people from both wings and was admired equally by both. The unity that he had established for the restoration of democracy in Pakistan, as the only key to its survival, broke down when immediately after his death political parties were quickly revived in contravention to his final wishes, thus giving the President a heaven-sent opportunity to reject the Franchise Commission's report and to rule Pakistan dictatorially. With the last hope for the restoration of democracy in Pakistan thus destroyed, the fragmentation of Pakistan became inevitable. Suhrawardy echoed this in his memoirs and also in his letter to his son-in-law Ahmad Sulaiman: 'You see, as far as we leaders of the past generation are concerned we can only act constitutionally, and we have failed. The trouble is that an unconstitutional leadership will arise, which may destroy the country, and also sweep us away in the process.'[360]

The inevitable happened. The fourth coup, staged by the army alone, which supplanted the military oligarchy of General Ayub, gave the *coup de grace* to the concept of Pakistan, when the Government of General Agha Mohammad Yahya Khan refused to hand over power to the leader of the majority party, Sheikh Mujibur Rahman, who had been elected in the first general election held on the basis of universal adult franchise, in the twenty-five years of Pakistan's existence. In the wake of a country-wide uprising in 1969, General Yahya Khan assumed the reins of government.[361] He pursued a policy, which was to create devastating repercussions, resulting in what was best and worst for Pakistan. Thus, instead of boldly accepting the election result as the people's final verdict on their fate and going down in the pages of history as the second Quaid-i-Azam, he waged war against the majority of the people.[362] The war of liberation ended with the creation of two sovereign Muslim states, Bangladesh and Pakistan, in partial fulfillment of what the Lahore Resolution had envisaged in 1940. But it was not attained in peace.

PART II

Memoirs

MILITARY OLIGARCHY

The course of politics in Pakistan, ever since its creation on 14 August 1947, leads one irresistibly to the conclusion that it has been conditioned by the desire of those in real authority, the forces that actually determined the government policies and actions, to delay the introduction of democracy as long as possible and, just when it was on the verge of fruition and all steps had been taken to enable it to function, to suppress it altogether.

An Unholy Policy

The latest manifestation of such an unholy policy was the action of a constitutional president, viz., Major General Iskander Mirza and the Commander-in-Chief of the Army, General Mohammad Ayub Khan, who conspired to abrogate the constitution of 1956, which both had pledged to uphold, and to dismiss the ministers, dissolve the legislatures, suppress and ban all political parties and political activities, suspend civil liberties, and place the country under the combined rule of a President and a Chief Martial Law Administrator. Their strength was based on the existence of a standing army drawn not from the nation as a whole but from two well-defined preserves: Punjabis and Pathans. It was highly disciplined and brave and patriotic in its lower ranks, but was amenable to exploitation by its superior officers; it was an army equipped with arms, immeasurably superior to the puny strength of an unarmed civilian population, which could be used against the people when called upon. Most soldiers belonged to a stratum of society easily capable of indoctrination that as saviours of the nation they had been divinely charged with the noble duty of obliterating politics and politicians as amoral and pestilential.

This phase of military dictatorships and military saviours is in apparent conformity with the general world movement for supplanting and suppressing democracies (as democracies in their turn have supplanted oligarchies and kingships); and even where democracies have theoretically been restored in their ding-dong battle against such dictatorships, they have in fact never been free but have always been directed and controlled by the military, who, having once tasted blood, find it advantageous and necessary in their vested, as well as newly-acquired, interests to keep civilian power in subordination.

Military officers, high and low, were put in charge of important administrative civilian posts for which they were untrained and unfit and were even given judicial powers to try offences and pass severe sentences which were successively reviewed by several grades of the military hierarchy to the progressive disadvantage of the convicted. Not only retired but also active military personnel, high and low, and members of their families were rewarded with posts, lands, licences, permits and pecuniary advantages commensurate with their ranks, their influence or their family connections.

The military, therefore, are as a class interested in the continuance of a system so beneficial to them, and a body of disciplined personnel is thus ready and prepared to exert itself to the full to maintain its gains and privileges and to prevent a reversion to those bad old days when for a mere pittance its members could be called upon to endanger their lives to safeguard the independence and security of their motherland. Hence, experience shows, and illustrations are not wanting, that military dictatorships tend to perpetuate themselves, overtly or covertly.

FRUSTRATION AND FAILURE

It would be incorrect to state that in the short history of Pakistan attempts have not been made from time to time to give to the country a democratic government; but they have ended in frustration and failure.

THE FIRST CONSTITUENT ASSEMBLY

The members of the first Constituent Assembly created by the Independence Act of 1947 of the British parliament, which functioned both as the constitution-making body and as the central legislature of Pakistan, were elected by those pre-partition members of the provincial legislatures whose constituencies fell within Pakistan as it emerged after the Radcliffe Award. The representative character of the members of the Constituent Assembly was thus indirect. The existing provincial legislatures of Sindh and of the NWFP—the latter had become part of Pakistan as the result of a referendum—remained in tact; the provincial legislatures of Bengal and of the Punjab were split according to the areas allotted to India and Pakistan. Hence, the provincial representatives of the areas allotted to West Punjab formed the Legislature of West Punjab, and the provincial representatives of the areas allotted to East Bengal formed the Legislature of East Bengal.

The Radcliffe Award did great injustice to the Muslims of the Punjab and Bengal. In the Punjab it gave to India the Muslim majority district of Gurdaspur and, by means of a corridor, made a portion of Kashmir contiguous to India. Had this not been done the whole of Kashmir would have been contiguous to Pakistan, and the Hindu maharajah could not have acceded to India—this would have conflicted against both the principle of the religious complexion of the population and of total contiguity—or obtained the help of the Indian Army without India invading Pakistan. In Bengal the Award partitioned the Muslim majority district of Jessore, giving away to India (West Bengal) a portion predominantly Muslim; it also gave to West Bengal the entire Muslim majority district of Malda and did not even partition it although south Malda was overwhelmingly Muslim.[1] It gave to India some portions of the district of Sylhet which was initially a district of Assam. This area was preponderantly Muslim and Bengali, and a referendum had been held of the whole district to ascertain whether the people of the entire district wanted to go to Pakistan or to India. The referendum had been in favour of Pakistan.

MATCHLESS GENEROSITY OF EAST BENGAL

In spite of East Bengal having been so truncated, its population was larger than that of West Pakistan (56% to 44%). The members were elected to the Constituent Assembly in proportion to the population of the various provinces. East Bengal representatives were thus in a majority in the Constituent Assembly, but the Muslim members of the East Bengal Legislature, with matchless generosity and self-sacrifice, in the interest of Pakistan as a nation and Muslim politics as a whole and unmindful of their provincial or parochial interests, elected to the Pakistan Constituent Assembly a number of non-Bengali Muslims from the Congress dominated Muslim majority NWFP and the Muslim minority provinces of India, who had no chance of being elected by the legislatures of their own provinces, and whom the legislatures of the Muslim majority provinces of the NWFP, Punjab and Sindh refused to elect, in preference to their own nationals. Amongst such persons elected by the East Bengal Legislature were such Muslim League stalwarts as Nawabzada Liaquat Ali Khan, I.H. Quraishi, and Khan Abdul Qayyum Khan of NWFP and not less than five others of national importance. Hence in the Constituent Assembly, Bengalis as such were actually in a minority, but, being more politically conscious, tended to influence the deliberations of the assembly out of proportion to their actual numbers.

RELUCTANCE TO FRAME CONSTITUTION

Now it was contended that there could not be a properly constituted democratic central legislature of independent Pakistan until a new constitution had been framed by the Constituent Assembly and a general election held based on the new constitution. Until then Pakistan must continue to be governed under the Government of India Act of 1935 as adapted, and the Independence Act of 1947. Hence, the first obstacle to the election of a representative legislature as a pre-requisite for democracy and a democratic government was obviously the want of a new constitution of independent Pakistan.

Fascist Mentality. Nawabzada Liaquat Ali Khan, the first Prime Minister of Pakistan, was reluctant to frame a constitution early. He had been the secretary of the AIML which had embattled for Pakistan and inherited it when it was created. Thus, Quaid-i-Azam Mohammad Ali Jinnah, its President, took upon himself the office of Governor General of the Dominion of Pakistan, instead of Lord Louis Mountbatten who had at first been favoured as the Governor General of the dominions of both Pakistan and India, and further bestowed the prime ministership on its secretary.

The Muslim League had been the voice of the Muslim masses of India, as was proved in the 1946 election by its sweeping successes in Bengal and the Muslim minority provinces, and its substantial successes in Sindh and in the Punjab. With the creation of Pakistan this was the only political party of the Muslims in Pakistan; the Muslim members of the Indian National Congress, even though strong in the NWFP where they were known as the Red Shirts, and in Sindh, were submerged in Pakistan as a whole. The Congress Party in East Bengal was composed of Hindus. Liaquat Ali Khan wanted to preserve the PML as the only political party of the Muslims in spite of the fact that Jinnah in one of his very first speeches delivered after the creation of Pakistan had declared that henceforth the Muslim League would be one of several political parties in the country and not the sole Muslim party. Liaquat Ali Khan, however, felt that a new constitution and a fresh general election would bring into existence other political parties of Muslims which might challenge the supreme authority of the Muslim League. He was anxious to avoid this and to maintain control of the Muslim League as long as possible. This he perhaps considered was needed to consolidate Pakistan and, hence, there was no immediate hurry to frame the constitution and hold general elections. In his zeal for the Muslim League, however, he identified the party with the state and with the government, which was a Muslim League government, and maintained that anyone who opposed the Muslim League political party, and thus directly or indirectly his government, was a traitor to the state. This laid him open to the charge of fascism.

The Muslim League in its own turn became a blind supporter of the government. From a mass organization of Muslims it became a closed corporation, excluding from its membership all those who had some spirit of independence and liberty and an urge for democracy; it developed a fascist mentality; it divided amongst its privileged members all the perquisites of government such as foreign representation, import, route, car, bus, arms, revolver and other permits and licences, and foreign exchange and trading and industrial facilities; it thus created a group of monied men around it and built up a handsome party fund. It was mostly in West Pakistan that the perquisites were distributed. In East Bengal, later called East Pakistan, the Muslim League ran into somewhat heavy weather.

I had been instrumental in creating and organizing the party in the whole of Bengal and was known to the people as the architect of the Muslim League, but, owing to differences in political outlook, I found myself in opposition to the PML. The people of East Bengal, in general, were opposed to the official Muslim League. This did not include, of course, those who were beneficiaries of government largesse, for the same technique of distributing patronage and perquisites to the members of the official Muslim League—such as the monopoly to import cloth from India, or licences to export betel leaves (*pan*) to West Pakistan, or to import salt from West Pakistan or to operate on road or riverine routes (routine permits)—was adopted in East Bengal as well. But the quantum in East Bengal was small in comparison to the perquisites distributed in West Pakistan, leading to considerable capital formation and rapid industrial development in the latter region, although this was confined to the privileged few.

BPC Report Rejected. In spite of all his support to the Muslim League, however, Liaquat Ali Khan had to take some steps to produce a new constitution—India had produced one at an early stage—and a BPC drawn from representatives from the various provinces was created to establish the basis for one. The BPC had stormy and lengthy sessions. Many were the problems that had to be covered: the name of the state, whether Islamic or not, and the extent of the Islamic provisions. The number of representatives to be elected from the various provinces and tribal areas, whether their numbers should be in proportion to the population and whether the number to which East Bengal was entitled should be whittled down to equalize it with all the representatives of West Pakistan taken together (principle of parity), were critical issues. Should the electorate be joint or separate? Should the state be unitary or federal, unicameral or bicameral, and, if bicameral, what should be the number of representatives in each legislature from each of the provinces? Also, should there be one or several state or official languages?

There was never any question, however, that the constitution would be parliamentary, with a constitutional head of government, with a prime minister choosing his colleagues, and a cabinet system with joint responsibility. Elections would be by adult suffrage. There was a complete hold-up while a pseudo-religious body of learned *alims* or *ulemas* of various Muslim sects thrashed out what should be the contents of an Islamic constitution. Several reports were placed before the Constituent Assembly by the BPC which were rejected either by the East Pakistan or West Pakistan representatives. The reports were referred back from time to time for further consideration.

INTRIGUE AND CHICANERY

Meanwhile, there had been changes in the personnel of the central government even though the Muslim League policy of fascism continued unchanged, albeit with abating strength as opposition forces could no longer be suppressed. Jinnah died on 11 September 1948. Khwaja Nazimuddin, who at that time was Chief Minister of East Pakistan, was appointed on the recommendation of the Muslim League cabinet, as Governor General of the Dominion of Pakistan; Nawabzada Liaquat Ali Khan continued as Prime Minister. After the assassination of the latter on 16 October 1951, Khwaja Nazimuddin became Prime Minister. Ghulam Mohammad, the Finance Minister, was selected for the post of Governor General by the cabinet and was duly appointed by Her Majesty Queen Elizabeth II.

FREQUENT CHANGES IN GOVERNMENT

During the regimes of both Liaquat Ali Khan and Khwaja Nazimuddin the provincial ministries of West Pakistan were manipulated by the central government. There were frequent changes in the chief ministerships and in the cabinets of the various provinces to suit the interests of the Muslim League Party and of the central government, and the entire political atmosphere was vitiated by intrigue and chicanery.

In May 1953, for some reasons which are not clear (officially due to the delay in framing the constitution and unofficially to the suggestion to reduce the strength of the army by 30,000 and to various international forces necessitating closer ties with the Western democracies) Governor General Ghulam Mohammad dismissed Khwaja Nazimuddin in a dramatic manner by cutting off his telephone line and preventing his access to Queen Elizabeth. Khwaja Nazimuddin wanted not only to appeal to the Queen against his dismissal but also he wanted to exercise his right as a prime minister of one of the Dominions (and, hence, as one of her principal ministers), to demand the dismissal of Ghulam Mohammad from the Governor Generalship. It was significant (and demonstrated the venality and demoralization of the Muslim League) that the dismissal of Khwaja Nazimuddin, who was its President and also the Muslim League Prime Minister of Pakistan, had just exhibited that he had a sweeping majority in the legislature and should have been hailed with satisfaction, jubilation and approval by the Muslim League Party, but there was hardly one dissident voice at the time. Ghulam Mohammad sent for Mohammad Ali Chowdhury, subsequently better known as Bogra Mohammad Ali or Mohammad Ali of Bogra, (or even as Bogra from the United States where he was serving as Pakistan ambassador) and appointed him Prime Minister. The cabinet appeared to have continued as before, and the Muslim League members of the central legislature accepted the change without demur.

When Khwaja Nazimuddin, East Pakistan's Chief Minister, became the Governor General in 1948 his place was taken by Nurul Amin who continued in that post until 1954 when general elections were held to the provincial legislature. The legislature should have expired much earlier; it was kept alive and its life extended annually on one pretext or another by the central legislature. The central and the EPML governments were both afraid that if elections were held the Muslim League would be swept off the board and would lose the province. Actually, in the very early stages, one by-election had been held in which a stalwart of the Muslim League was defeated by a very young but on-coming worker of the opposition party (the Awami League). Thereafter, in spite of vacancies occurring from time to time, no further by-elections were held. By 1954 when general elections were held— these could no longer be avoided without the Muslim League being held up to unbearable contempt and ridicule—there were not less than 32 vacant seats in the East Pakistan Legislature; some of these had been lying empty for several years. When one contrasts this with the democratic conventions that prevailed during British times, when immediate steps were taken to hold by-elections and fill vacancies within three months, one can realize to what extent the Muslim League had taken to undemocratic ways just to retain itself in power and enjoy its privileges.

ELECTIONS TO WEST PAKISTAN LEGISLATURES RIGGED

Now, although there could not be—or at least so it was maintained—general elections to the central legislature, which was also a constituent assembly, without a new constitution, elections to provincial legislatures in West Pakistan were held as their life expired by efflux of time. These elections were rigged with a vengeance in the interests of the Muslim League. The

West Punjab elections were held in 1951 and although Sirdar Abdur Rab Nishtar, the Governor, asserted categorically, time and again, that the officials would be neutral, Liaquat Ali Khan held a different view. It cannot be controverted that government officials used all their influence and powers of persuasion and coercion on behalf of the candidates of the Muslim League. They canvassed for them, utilized government transport to convey them to the polls, and even went so far as to transfer votes from one ballot box to another and even to break open the ballot boxes of opposition candidates and to make false returns. The opponent parties were the Jinnah Awami Muslim League, of which I was the head, the Azad Pakistan party of Mian Iftikharuddin and the Jamaat-i-Islami. In spite of the terrible rigging my party won 32 seats, the Azad Pakistan Party, 2, and the Jamaat-i-Islami, probably 2, out of a total 175 seats.

Thereafter, elections were held in the NWFP, of which Khan Abdul Qayyum Khan was the Chief Minister, and he openly and flagrantly used all his powers of coercion, undue influence, and executive interference on behalf of the candidates selected by him. Although he was the President of the Provincial Muslim League, he even opposed the candidates who had been nominated by the central Muslim League High Command to the exclusion of his own nominees and succeeded through sheer brutality, force and chicanery in getting his own men returned. He threatened to arrest me if I set foot in the NWFP on behalf of my own party members. The NWFP elections were far worse than any hitherto witnessed in India or Pakistan. As, however, the resulting ministry supported the central Muslim League ministry, the high command overlooked the contumaciousness and seemed gratified at a result which after all had succeeded in smashing all opposition, even though by nefarious means.

Then elections were held in Bahawalpur; the chief architect on behalf of the Muslim League was Hasan Mahmud, and he rigged the elections adequately. Elections thereafter were held in Sindh; there was some rigging but nothing comparable to the others. There was little need of it in Sindh where the feudal landlords were strong and the popular movement was weak and could make little headway against the entrenched vested interests. The result of these elections was that there was no difference in the complexion of the legislatures. The same Muslim League governments and party were in power and the same kind of people had been returned, namely, those belonging to the feudal aristocracy, except in the NWFP where Khan Abdul Qayyum Khan had taken care to see that a large number of illiterates were elected so that no one in the legislature would ever be able to challenge his supremacy. The central Muslim League government supported all these misdeeds as its power was perpetuated in the provinces and in the centre.

NATIONAL ASSEMBLY DISSOLVED

After the dismissal of Khwaja Nazimuddin in May 1953, Bogra Mohammad Ali functioned as Prime Minister and leader of the Muslim League Party. He obtained the consent of the British government to declare Pakistan a republic under the new constitution which was expected to be introduced and was discussed in the Constituent Assembly in December 1954. But, again, there was a setback. It appears that in October 1954 determined attempts were made by Fazlur Rahman (commerce minister) and others to curtail the powers of the Governor General, and, it is said, to challenge the capacity and sanity of Ghulam Mohammad to continue as governor general. Ghulam Mohammad thereupon dismissed the ministers and dissolved the Constituent Assembly. To what extent Bogra Mohammad Ali, the Prime Minister, was involved in the conspiracy against Ghulam Mohammad was never made clear. Ghulam Mohammad suspected that he had knowledge of it, if not more. He maintained he had not. In any event he was given the benefit of the doubt and kept on as the nominated president of the Council of Ministers, but hardly as Prime Minister, and a fresh set of ministers was appointed. This included General Mohammad Ayub Khan, the Commander-in-Chief of the Army, as Minister of Defence, and Major General Iskander Mirza, who was brought back from East Bengal where he had been sent as Governor, as Minister of Interior.

I was lying ill in Zurich in 1954 after I had been successful in defeating the Muslim League in East Bengal in the provincial general election, which at long last had been held in March 1954. All the parties opposed to the Muslim League, namely, my party (which was the strongest), Fazlul Huq's KSP and Maulana Athar Ali's Nizam-i-Islam Party, formed themselves into a United Front. It was settled with Fazlul Huq that while I would support him for the Chief Ministership of East Bengal, he would support me and follow my guidance in central politics. At that time Maulana Bhashani was the provincial President of the Awami League. In spite of the tours, speeches, propaganda and personal contacts of Prime Minister Bogra Mohammad Ali in East Bengal, conducted with all paraphernalia in a very lavish and extravagant manner on behalf of the Muslim League and the grandeur and organization of government at the disposal of the Prime Minister, in spite of election meetings addressed by Miss Fatima Jinnah, who was specially brought to buttress the Muslim League, and in spite of canvassing by government officials, particularly the Inspector General of Police, Doha, on behalf of the candidates of the Muslim League, the Muslim League gained only nine out of 237 Muslim seats.[2] The brunt of selecting the candidates on behalf of the United Front and the task of addressing, organizing the meetings and carrying on propaganda and touring all the constituencies fell mainly on me. Maulana Bhashani and Fazlul Huq went where needed, the latter mainly where the members of his own party were candidates. I fell ill with amoebic dysentery in May 1954 and was taken to a Zurich hospital for treatment.

In spite of the signal victory of the opposition against the Muslim League whereby the existing members from East Bengal in the central legislature lost the slightest vestige of a claim to representative character, the central government refused to elect new members from the East Pakistan Legislature to the central legislature or to make any changes in the central ministry and ignored the defeat of the Muslim League as a matter not affecting the central government or its policy.

Section 92-A promulgated. After the election Fazlul Huq was appointed Chief Minister of East Pakistan on behalf of the United Front. With his usual emotionalism and want of balance when in the presence of an audience, he made a speech at a meeting in Calcutta which was calculated to draw the acclaim and plaudits of his Hindu-India audience. The newspapers reported him stating that he could not understand the *raison d'etre* of Pakistan and would bend his energies to bring the two parts of Bengal together. When the report was published, several meetings were held in East Bengal condemning him, including one presided over by Maulana Bhashani. The rift in the United Front had opened. The central government called him a traitor. He was dismissed from the Chief Ministership with all his ministers, the legislature was suspended and Section 92-A of the constitution, under which the Governor General took over the province and the Governor acted as his agent, was promulgated.

Colonel (later Major General) Iskander Mirza, the Defence Secretary, was sent as Governor and he promptly arrested and detained under the Public Safety Act (this provided for preventive detention without trial) a very large number, probably 3,000, of the workers of the United Front. These mostly belonged to the Awami League which was the predominant party. Some time later the central government took a decision to prosecute Fazlul Huq for treason but on his giving an assurance that he would retire from politics the proceedings were dropped.

LAW MINISTER TO AVOID DICTATORSHIP

Before I left for Zurich Ghulam Mohammad and Bogra Mohammad Ali saw me, and further sent emissaries to me when I was lying ill in Zurich, and requested that I join the central ministry when I recovered and returned to Pakistan. They felt that they needed some popular support for the central ministry and for that reason were even prepared to elect to the Constituent Assembly members from the newly-elected East Pakistan Legislature if I joined the cabinet. I returned to Pakistan on 5 December 1954 by which time the old Constituent Assembly had been dissolved. The old ministry had been dismissed and a new one set up. I was immediately contacted and bombarded by Ghulam Mohammad and Bogra Mohammad Ali to join the central ministry of what they called 'all talents'. They had already induced Dr Khan Sahib to join the cabinet. He had been the Congress Chief Minister of NWFP at the time of partition and had continued in that post until the referendum which allotted NWFP to Pakistan. He was also the brother of the Red Shirt Frontier leader, Khan Abdul Ghaffar Khan, but was, at the same time, a great personal friend of Iskander Mirza. Fazlul Huq's party in East Pakistan was represented by Abu Hossain Sarkar.

Ghulam Mohammad threatened that if I did not join the cabinet he would hand over the government to Commander-in-Chief Ayub Khan, then also Defence Minister, and the country would have a military dictatorship. I held out for over a fortnight. Partly wishing to avoid a military dictatorship in Pakistan and partly because Ghulam Mohammad promised that he would set up a constituent assembly and restore the constitution if I joined the ministry and took the matter in my hands, I consented to work as Law Minister with Bogra Mohammad Ali who was the appointed President of the Council of Ministers. He had been my Parliamentary Secretary in Bengal when I was a minister and my Finance Minister when I was Chief Minister of United Bengal.

My party did not like my joining the ministry but I thought the stakes were high, and I was anxious not only to avoid the evils of a military dictatorship but also to get the constitution restored. Tamizuddin Khan was already contesting in the High Court the validity of the dissolution of the Constituent Assembly. The various legal proceedings and the steps taken in the Law Ministry to meet the situation were interesting for the constitutional lawyer and we had to work overtime. The services of Diplock, QC, an eminent constitutional lawyer, were secured. In the end the Supreme Court advised that the Governor General should set up a new constitutional assembly on a pattern similar to the previous one and with the same powers. However, it gave him authority to alter the number of representatives and to establish quotas for the various provinces and regions as he thought best in the interests of the country.

Second Constituent Assembly. I had already decided to set up a constituent assembly in which East Bengal on the one hand and the provinces and regions of West Pakistan taken together on the other, would be equally represented. But, as the representation had been radically altered, we thought we could not name the new setup a constituent assembly. It differed from the one constituted by the Independence Act of 1947; therefore, the designation constituent convention seemed more suitable and less confusing. After the advice of the Supreme Court, however, we decided to call it a constituent assembly.

I consented to parity between East and West Pakistan in the interest of a better understanding between the East and West wings and to dissipate any feeling that East Pakistan would dominate over the West by virtue of its larger number if the representation was according to population, a feeling which had given rise to ugly incidents and walk-outs in the previous constituent assembly. I also hoped that provincial parties would give way to all-Pakistan political parties. Along with parity in representation, the policy of the government would be to achieve parity in all fields such as services, industrialisation development expenditure, foreign aid, central government allocations, and even in defence matters. But I had to convince East Bengal of the desirability of accepting parity. It was an uphill task. I was abused by Fazlul Huq as well as by Maulana Bhashani. But, for good or ill, I managed to carry the day in the party.

On 21 June 1955 fresh elections to the central legislature from the various provinces and constituent units were held and a new constituent assembly was brought into being. I again became a member of this after having been deprived of my membership in 1949. As the election was by the system of a single transferable vote, a large number of members of the United Front were elected from East Bengal. Only one member could be chosen by the members of the Muslim League in the East Pakistan Legislature from the provincial quota of 40 and Bogra Mohammad Ali was elected. Fazlur Rahman, who was also a member of the Muslim League, came in independently, having managed to get some votes from some independent members. It can be said, to the credit of the members of East Bengal, that they rarely, if ever, shifted their loyalties or betrayed their parties. The charge laid by the 1958 Martial Law regime that the members oscillated from party to party to suit their individual ends could not with any degree of honesty be levelled against members from East Bengal. This could, however, be applied to the feudal members of the West Pakistan Legislature, particularly when the contest was raging fast and furious between the Muslim League and the Republican parties.

The new Constituent Assembly was to meet on 7 July 1955 at Murree. On 6 July a dinner was held at Government House at which Nawab Gurmani, Interior Minister Major General Iskander Mirza, Defence Minister General Ayub Khan, Dr Khan Sahib and Chowdhury Mohammad Ali were present. It was decided that we should sit together and come to an agreement on the controversial points which were holding up the framing of the constitution. While the sessions of the Constituent Assembly were being held, negotiations proceeded side by side. On 13 July a 5-point agreement, signed by the leaders of the various parties, was negotiated. Bogra signed on behalf of the Muslim

League. Nawab Gurmani, Dr Khan Sahib and Chowdhury Mohammad Ali signed on behalf of West Pakistan. Fazlul Huq was to sign on behalf of East Pakistan, but Huq insisted on the signatures of Ataur Rahman Khan and Abul Mansur Ahmad. After they had signed, Nawab Gurmani undertook to take Fazlul Huq's signature and reported that he had done so.

The five negotiated points were:

1. West Pakistan was to be integrated into One Unit;
2. Each wing was to have full regional autonomy;
3. There would be parity between the two wings in all respects, not merely in representation;
4. Election would be through the medium of joint electorate; and
5. Bengali and Urdu would be the two state languages.

It was understood that Bogra Mohammad Ali would resign and I would be the next Prime Minister.

OFFER OF PRIME MINISTERSHIP SUBTLY UPSET

On 16 July 1955 Ghulam Mohammad returned to Karachi from London. On 5 August 1955 he was forced to take leave, on the grounds of illness and inability to carry on, and Major General Iskander Mirza took over as acting Governor General. On 7 August Chowdhury Mohammad Ali was elected as the leader of the Muslim League Party which decided that Bogra Mohammad Ali should resign and the Governor General be asked to appoint me as the Prime Minister. On the next day, Chowdhury Mohammad Ali announced that a coalition between the Muslim League and the Awami League had been established and a resolution passed to form a cabinet with myself as Prime Minister. The arrangements appeared to be so firm and official that BBC broadcast my name as the next Prime Minister. Ali came to me on behalf of the Muslim League Party after obtaining the consent of Governor General Iskander Mirza and formally offered me the Prime Ministership. We sat down to select the ministers of my new cabinet and for the division of portfolios. In this connection, he saw me several times.

However, Iskander Mirza, who had been forced to give his consent because the Muslim League had an overwhelming majority in the Constituent Assembly, was averse to my selection (he is reported to have said that I would be Prime Minister only over his dead body). This was perhaps because as a member of the cabinet I had not supported him wholeheartedly in August 1955 when he was selected as Governor General displacing Ghulam Mohammad. It may be recalled that, at that time, Iskander Mirza was also a member of the cabinet as Interior Minister, and the Commander-in-Chief Ayub Khan, a great friend and protagonist of his, was the Defence Minister.

These two induced Bogra Mohammad Ali to propose that Ghulam Mohammad was becoming incapable physically and mentally and that his orders could be understood only by his personal secretary. They suggested that a Medical Board should be appointed to report on his sanity unless he resigned. This he did with much weeping and wailing and bitterness. The cabinet was required to recommend his successor to Queen Elizabeth II. Commander-in-Chief Ayub Khan canvassed forcibly in favour of Iskander Mirza and it is well known that he was responsible for procuring the one vote which swung the election in the cabinet in favour of his nominee.

No sooner had the Muslim League decided, with Iskander Mirza's consent, that I should be Prime Minister than he started to undermine the decision. He sent agents to Fazlul Huq—whom only a few days ago he had denounced as a traitor—and offered him the post of Interior Minister with his party provided he support Chowdhury Mohammad Ali as Prime Minister. Fazlul Huq, seeing in this offer chances for his own rehabilitation to turn the tables on those who had called him a traitor and to return to politics in a cabinet post, accepted the position with alacrity although it had been agreed at the time the United Front was constituted in 1954 that he would support me in the centre. At the same time Iskander Mirza played upon the feelings of Chowdhury Mohammad Ali and offered him the Prime Ministership.

Iskander Mirza advanced a specious argument that a convention should be established that if the Governor General was from Bengal, I, another person from Bengal, should not become Prime Minister. The Prime Minister should be from West Pakistan. Iskander Mirza claimed that he was from Bengal as he was descended from Mir Jafar who had been made the Nawab Nazim (ruler) of Bengal by Lord Clive after Mir Jafar had betrayed Sirajuddowllah at Plassey. But Iskander Mirza had seen nothing of Murshidabad, the family seat, and his connection with Bengal and his claim to be considered a Bengali was less than tenuous. This was discarded by him when it suited his purpose at a later stage. He was probably born in Bombay, spent the whole of his life outside Bengal, and, after serving in the army for some time and being wounded in a skirmish with the Pathans, joined the political service and spent most of his professional life among the Pathans as a British political agent in the tribal areas. He spoke Pushto fluently and had learned the art of offering suitable inducements and of playing off one party against another.

Chowdhury Mohammad Ali, who himself had been the first to offer me the Prime Ministership, hesitated, but ultimately the temptation was too great for him. The Muslim League was canvassed to change its resolution and offer Chowdhury Mohammad Ali the Prime Ministership with Fazlul Huq as Minister of Interior. The personnel of the entire cabinet was changed. I resigned from the cabinet and became the Leader of the Opposition. I was permitted to keep the state house, which I had occupied as Law Minister, and which became the official residence of the Leader of the Opposition. Chowdhury Mohammad Ali established some parliamentary conventions; the chief one affecting me was an official recognition of the position of the Leader of the Opposition with a free house and phone, and consultations with the opposition as regards proceedings in Parliament. I am not certain whether the position also carried an allowance as a perquisite of the office. I never drew any nor had the slightest intention of doing so.

ONE UNIT AS A SOLID FRONT AGAINST EAST PAKISTAN

We now come to a very disturbed state of politics both in West and East Pakistan for which Iskander Mirza was largely, if not wholly, responsible.

One of the first tasks which Chowdhury Mohammad Ali attempted was to integrate all the provinces of West Pakistan into one.[3] It is regrettable that the idea, mooted by the British as a matter of administrative convenience, was revived as a result of distrust, suspicion and hostility to East Pakistan. It was believed that if West Pakistan could put up a solid front it would prevent East Pakistan from dominating the West which it might be able to do in spite of having surrendered its majority and accepting parity if any of the provinces of West Pakistan aligned with it. Provincial jealousies and hostilities in West Pakistan were so bitter that he thought this was more than a possibility. Indeed on previous occasions Khan Abdul Qayyum Khan of the NWFP had combined with Bengal representatives to oppose some of the proposals of the Punjabi group, and this had rankled deep in his mind as an act of betrayal of the interests of West Pakistan.

Chowdhury Mohammad Ali so managed that each of the provincial legislatures of West Pakistan passed resolutions almost unanimously in favour of integration. The resolution by the Sindh and by the provincial assembly, of which Ayub Khuhro was the Chief Minister, was obtained by threats, intimidation, and arrest of members and, in the NWFP where Sardar Abdur Rashid, a former Inspector General of Police, was Chief Minister, by making a false promise that Peshawar would be made the capital of West Pakistan. The One Unit Bill, as it was called, had a stormy passage through the Constituent Assembly.

Sardar Abdur Rashid of the NWFP, who had supported the resolution for integration into the provincial legislature but had been dismissed, produced a secret document authored and circulated by Mian Mumtaz Khan Daultana in which it was asserted that integration would ensure the domination of the Punjab not only in West Pakistan but in Pakistan as a whole; in order to camouflage this objective, it would be advisable to get the resolution for integration moved and supported by representatives of provinces and areas other than the Punjab. To secure the support of the minor provinces, Chowdhury Mohammad Ali induced the representatives of Punjab province proper to accept 40 per cent representation although its population vis-á-vis other areas entitled it to 56 per cent. Of course there were other areas outside Punjab proper in which Punjabis predominated and which could be trusted to return Punjabis to the provincial legislature. Sardar Abdur Rashid denounced integration vehemently.

I opposed integration on the ground that there had not been sufficient propaganda on its behalf, that the people had not consented to it, that the consent of the legislatures of the provinces other than that of the Punjab had been obtained by coercion and false promises and that there should be more propaganda to explain the implications and advantages to the people and to canvass their support before taking legislative action. For it could be argued that, administratively, it was desirable on account of the common rivers, the roads and the railway and irrigation systems and might perhaps also help to ease the bitterness and hostility which existed between Pathan and Punjabi, Sindhi and Punjabi, and Baluchi and Punjabi. At the same time, I stated that if once the provinces were integrated and an administration set up the scheme should be given a chance to function. An early breakup, which was possible in view of public opinion not having been canvassed, might lead to greater bitterness between the various racial groups in West Pakistan.

The bill for integration was duly passed in spite of vehement opposition. It was strongly supported by Dr Khan Sahib of the NWFP, though his brother Khan Abdul Ghaffar Khan, the Red Shirt leader, was dead opposed to it. In the course of my speech I warned Dr Khan Sahib not to be misled by the promises given by the Muslim League to appoint him as the first Chief Minister of West Pakistan as a guarantee of its good faith and intentions that the minor provinces would get a fair deal and would not be dominated by the Punjab. I said I was sure that the Muslim League would betray him in the end. As would be obvious, Dr Khan Sahib told me to mind my own business. Chowdhury Mohammad Ali, in his capacity as leader of the Muslim League Party and as Prime Minister, made this promise on the floor of the House.

A new West Pakistan Legislature was constituted by election by the members of the various defunct legislatures who were grouped into electoral colleges district-wise with special representation for Swat, Dir, Amb, the Balochistan states and the tribal areas. Dr Khan Sahib was appointed Chief Minister of West Pakistan with Nawab Mushtaq Hossain Gurmani as Governor.

After the passage of the One Unit Bill, Chowdhury Mohammad Ali addressed himself to the task of framing a constitution for Pakistan in a spirit of dedication, and the assistance of Sir Ivor Jennings, an eminent constitution expert from Cambridge, was secured for the purpose. The constitution was duly passed but was not promulgated until 23 March 1956. This, it was believed, was the date on which the basic Resolution which flowered into the demand for Pakistan had been passed at a session of the Muslim League in 1940. Pakistan became a Republic and Iskander Mirza, who till then had been Governor General, was elected president under the new constitution of 1956. Iskander Mirza was a very close personal friend of Dr Khan Sahib. It is one of his tragedies that after he had done whatever he could to maintain Dr Khan Sahib the two fell out a short time before Dr Khan Sahib was assassinated.

RELUCTANT CREATION OF THE REPUBLICAN PARTY

What I had forecast came to pass. The Muslim League Party in the new West Pakistan Legislature became restive. It claimed that as the vast majority of the members of the New West Pakistan Assembly were members of the Muslim League, having been elected by members whose own election as Muslim League candidates had been rigged in their favour, it was unjust that the Chief Minister of such an assembly should be a non-party man and a non-Muslim Leaguer, as Dr Khan Sahib manifestly was. Therefore, they demanded that he should resign or be dismissed from office and the leader of the Muslim League Party be appointed in his place.

The movement was led by Mian Mumtaz Khan Daultana, supported by Sardar Bahadur Khan, the younger brother of the Commander-in-Chief Ayub Khan. Sardar Bahadur Khan was the leader of the Muslim League Party in the West Pakistan Provincial Assembly and if the move succeeded he would naturally be the Chief Minister of the province. Chowdhury Mohammad Ali, the Prime Minister, pleaded with the Muslim League members not to press this demand as this would dishonour the assurances which he had given to Dr Khan Sahib on the floor of the House and on account of which he had won the latter's powerful support for the One Unit Bill which was the very foundation of the existence of the province. One of his arguments was that if Dr Khan Sahib was removed I would be proved right, and this would lower the prestige of the Muslim League and raise mine which would be most undesirable.

The West Pakistan Muslim Leaguers, however, were adamant and Dr Khan Sahib was reluctantly compelled to form a party of his own to save himself. This party was composed of those members of the Muslim League who felt that the bond given by Chowdhury Mohammad Ali should be honoured and that Dr Khan Sahib should be supported. The Muslim League Party thus split into two. The new party was called the Republican Party. It was generally understood that President Iskander Mirza had a hand in its creation in order to save Dr Khan Sahib. Incidentally, it provided President Iskander Mirza with a political party in West Pakistan which he would utilize as it suited his purpose. It happened, too, that most of its members had in the prepartition days been members of the Unionist Party which was composed mostly of feudal landlords who traditionally supported power. The first trial of strength came with the election of the Speaker. The Republican candidate won by the vote cast by the chairman. The Muslim League Party in the central legislature also split in two on the above lines.

THE MINORITY SARKAR MINISTRY

In East Pakistan President Iskander Mirza had been able to shatter the United Front further by making Fazlul Huq his Interior Minister. The party of Fazlul Huq, known as the KSP and which had no definite programme or principles but was in fact and deed the personal party of Fazlul Huq, became the President's party and acted according to his bidding. After Chowdhury Mohammad Ali became Prime Minister, Section 92-A was withdrawn from East Bengal and a nominee of Fazlul Huq, Abu Hossain Sarkar, was appointed Chief Minister. Sarkar's foothold was extremely precarious as the Awami League was in opposition. He managed to maintain himself by refusing to call a meeting of the legislature.

A budget session should have been called in March 1956 but by a special dispensation from Chowdhury Mohammad Ali this was delayed by three months. By mutual arrangement he was temporarily dismissed; the budget was certified by the Governor for three months and he was reappointed after a few days. When he did call the budget session ultimately, before the expiry of three months, he gave only four days for the discussion and the passing of the budget. This was clearly a farce and against all constitutional practice. In the British days four days used to be given for preliminary discussion and 15 days for considering the items in the budget. As no rules of procedure had been drawn up since the partition, Sarkar took advantage of the situation to give only four days for both. The Speaker, Abdul Hakim, refused to entertain the budget, possibly in conspiracy with Sarkar, and adjourned the House *sine die*. Sarkar was again dismissed temporarily. The legislature was again suspended, Section 92-A was imposed and the budget was certified by the Governor as before. This suited Fazlul Huq and Sarkar very well as by this means a meeting of the legislature was avoided and three days later Sarkar was again appointed Chief Minister. The intrigue and chicanery were so obvious that Chowdhury Mohammad Ali had for very shame to insist that Sarkar should get the budget passed by the end of August 1956. Sarkar, right till the end, refused to face a meeting of the legislature to get the budget passed. Even President Iskander Mirza could not save him further.

This crisis in East Pakistan coincided with that developing in West Pakistan between the Muslim Leaguers and the Republicans. The one led to a change of government in East Pakistan and the other to a change in the central government. It may be worthwhile mentioning that Sarkar adopted much the same expedient to secure support as Dr Khan Sahib had adopted in West Pakistan; the overnight creation of ministers and parliamentary secretaries *ad libitum* out of all proportion to administrative requirements. The only difference was that while Dr Khan Sahib faced the House until March 1957, Sarkar continually ran away from it.

PRIME MINISTER OF PAKISTAN

The situation in West Pakistan placed Chowdhury Mohammad Ali in a dilemma. He was the Prime Minister of the Muslim League Party which had now split in two, and he owed his office to Iskander Mirza. The latter now called upon him to leave the Muslim League and to join the Republican Party which after all had been formed to support the assurances which he, Chowdhury Mohammad Ali, had given to Dr Khan Sahib, and it would be anomalous if he continued to remain a member of the Muslim League which had betrayed him. But Chowdhury Mohammad Ali vacillated. Sometimes he thought he would join the Republican Party; at other times he felt he could not leave the Muslim League. Ultimately he decided to stick to the Muslim League. President Iskander Mirza in his turn decided to ask for his resignation or otherwise dismiss him. Having obtained his consent to resign, Iskander Mirza went straight to East Pakistan where I was at that time, took me on his plane, brought me back to Karachi, obtained the rather reluctant resignation of Chowdhury Mohammad Ali and appointed me Prime Minister on 12 September 1956. The Awami League was a minority in the central legislature. It had only 14 members. With seven Hindu members supporting me, I had a party of 21 members only, and the other 20 necessary to have a majority in the House, which was composed of 80 members, were mostly members of the Republican Party with some independents. On the whole, 47 to 50 members pledged me their support. The Muslim League and Fazlul Huq's party formed the opposition, and Chundrigar of the Muslim League was recognized as leader.

In East Pakistan, Sarkar had already resigned on 6 September 1956 and Ataur Rahman Khan, who was the leader of the Awami League Party in the provincial legislature, was appointed Chief Minister. In the central cabinet I appointed five ministers from East Pakistan and five from West Pakistan. Dr Khan Sahib continued as Chief Minister in West Pakistan.

In the West Pakistan Legislature there was a constant tussle going on between the Muslim League and the Republican Party; members were defecting and re-defecting and Dr Khan Sahib, as the head of the Republican Party and as Chief Minister, could only retain his position by appointing more and more ministers and deputy ministers and parliamentary secretaries from amongst those who could bring even one or two supporters. Their number grew out of all proportion to the needs of the administration and assumed the aspect of a political scandal. In spite of this he was unable to get his March 1957 budget passed and, at the last moment, advised the prorogation of the House. Section 92-A was promulgated and the budget was certified. When Dr Khan Sahib demanded he should be reinstated—Abu Hossain Sarkar had been reinstated twice by Chowdhury Mohammad Ali— I insisted that he should first prove to me that he had a majority in the House by signatures. He was unable to do so and I felt myself unable to reinstate him although my own existence as Prime Minister depended upon the support of the Republican Party in the central legislature. During my absence at the Commonwealth Prime Ministers' conference in London in January 1957, President Iskander Mirza had induced the Acting Prime Minister, Abul Mansur Ahmad, to reinstate the ministry. Sardar Abdur Rashid was appointed Chief Minister.

A group of ten persons who belonged to NAP became, practically, the arbiters between the Republicans and the Muslim League and apparently had the fate of West Pakistan and, possibly even of Pakistan, in their hands. If they voted for the Muslim League, Sardar Abdur Rashid would be defeated. If they voted for Sardar Abdur Rashid, he would be firmly established in power.

THE HARD CORE OF THE NAP

It may be useful here to consider how the party came to be formed and what was its background and policy (although the diversion is likely to be long and may take us into a review of the political conditions and of the parties in West and East Pakistan).

In the first Constituent Assembly, which was also the central legislature or parliament, there were, amongst the members of the opposition, two stalwarts: Mian Iftikharuddin, leader of the Azad Pakistan Party, and Khan Abdul Ghaffar Khan, leader of the Red Shirts. Mian Iftikharuddin had influential newspapers at his command (*The Pakistan Times* in English and *The Imroze* in Urdu) which carried on pro-communist, pro-socialist and anti-capitalist propaganda and gave laudatory accounts of the progress being achieved by the communist regimes in Russia and in the Muslim Republics of the USSR and in China. Faiz Ahmad Faiz, one of the greatest of living Urdu poets, of progressive tendencies and with a reputation of being a communist, was their editor.

Before partition, sometime in March 1947, Mian Iftikharuddin was the first person to court jail on behalf of the Muslim League in support of the Pakistan movement against the Unionist government of the Punjab which was led by Malik Khizr Hayat Khan and had the support of the Sikhs and the Hindus. His example led other Muslims to defy the Unionist government non-violently and a large number of important people, including the Khan of Mamdot, Mian Mumtaz Daultana, and, if I am not mistaken, Begum Shahnawaz, were sent to prison. Mian Iftikharuddin therefore was counted as a Pakistani patriot in spite of his pro-Russian leanings. He was very wealthy, had great personal charm and was a man of transparent honesty and courage, but he had not been able to create a political party of reasonable dimensions. On account of his progressive attitude he was supported by communists, fellow travellers and pro-communist labourers. In the 1951 general elections to the Punjab Provincial Legislature he was successful in bringing in only two members of his party, viz., himself and the financier of his newspapers. In the central assembly he was the sole representative of his party.

Khan Abdul Ghaffar Khan was a Congressman and as such had opposed the Pakistan movement and the referendum which led to NWFP becoming part of Pakistan. He had a powerful, non-violent organization called the Red Shirts and was known as the Frontier Gandhi. As a member of the Pakistan central parliament he asserted that although he had been opposed to the concept of Pakistan, he had accepted it after its creation and, after NWFP became part of Pakistan, he was a loyal Pakistani. But he demanded that a region which should be called Pathanistan (or Pakhtunistan) in which Pathans were the predominant population should be created as an autonomous province of Pakistan. The boundaries of this province were never defined but would apparently include—

- the areas of the NWFP where the Pathans had settled and tribal groups predominated;
- some districts of the Punjab where Pushtu was the language of the majority; and
- the northern portion of Balochistan which was also Pathan in race and language and had links with the Pathans on the other side of the border in Afghanistan as, incidentally, had nearly all the Pathan tribes.

It is generally conceded that the Pathans are more politically advanced than any of the other peoples (viz., Punjabis and Sindhis) of West Pakistan. The latter, in such areas as have earned the unenviable distinction of being considered criminal, can well be called elemental and rather rough (some might call it crude) in their social relationships. In these areas the peasantry is dominated by the local feudal landlords and feels tied to them by bonds of loyalty which force them to make forays on the territories of neighbouring landlords chiefly to lift cattle and women. Robberies, murders, crimes against women and family feuds are common. There is little or no political consciousness. By reason of their social outlawries their feudal lords are under the thumb of the smallest village police official and have to obey implicitly the local authorities of law and order with whom they are in close contact. The peasantry, however, in spite of these disabilities, are fine, upstanding men and, when not tainted by the criminal impetus from outside, lead a fairly normal existence punctuated by the normal village faction fights.

Of the two, the Punjabi peasant is better off, and the Sindhi peasant, known as *hari,* is an economically crushed creature whose body and soul appear to have been sold to his landlord. In the urban areas, in the Punjab particularly, there are many educational, technical, medical, agricultural and cultural institutions of a high order which have created a body of well-educated and well-equipped men capable of taking part in the administration of the country and in the various facets of national activity. Feudal aristocracy is fast becoming attuned to the norms of civilized society, and the peasantry under the impact of struggle for independence and of political parties is fast developing political consciousness. Unfortunately, in Sindh the progress is slow in spite of the brave efforts of the government and educationists; and feudal aristocracy still wields considerable influence complicated with a species of pseudo-religious, sectarian fanaticism peculiar to the province.

The Pathans on the other hand have a tradition of liberty. In the tribal areas they waged constant war against the British which could only be temporarily quelled by sheer bribery and by personal contacts and agreements with the *maliks* (chiefs) of the tribes. In settled areas the people have imbibed the anti-British Congress doctrine of independence and have thus developed an organization and political consciousness of a high order. Much of the desire for an autonomous province was the result of a fear that the Punjabis would dominate the central government to the detriment of non-Punjabi regions. The Pathanistan movement received strong support from the Pathans of the settled areas and, in spite of the heavy subsidies paid to the tribal *maliks* by the Pakistan government, from the tribal areas as well. However, it received a setback when Afghanistan began to support the movement and thus gave an opportunity to the Pakistan government and Pakistanis generally, including many Pathan themselves, to assert that it was secessionist with the ultimate objective of amalgamating the Pathan areas of Pakistan with those of Afghanistan. The support given by India to the movement, not only by propaganda but through agents and funds, gave further strength to the argument that the movement was meant to disintegrate Pakistan.

Afghanistan claimed that it had a large number of Pathans within its boundaries although in fact the major portion of the Pathans were in Pakistan. It also claimed that it was the natural sovereign of the Pathans: had not the Afghans conquered the northern areas of India? It encouraged and financed the Pathanistan or Pakhtunistan movement, carried on hostile propaganda against Pakistan, which led to attacks on the Pakistan Embassy and the Consulates at Kabul and Jalalabad, and demanded through its radio that the Pathans should be given independence. Khan Abdul Ghaffar Khan, on the other hand, asserted that he had nothing to do with this propaganda from Afghanistan. It was embarrassing him greatly, and the autonomous province of Pakhtunistan which he visualized was to remain an integral part of Pakistan. The Pakistan government, however, asserted that in fact this was a secessionist movement because Abdul Ghaffar Khan had been against the creation of Pakistan; he was a Congressman who had sympathies and links with India which was encouraging and supporting the Pakhtunistan movement. It further asserted that Abdul Ghaffar Khan had personally been in touch with Kabul through the Faqir of Ipi and that he was a traitor and could not be believed. He formed a very important part of the opposition in the assembly until his detention without trial under the Public Safety Act.

There were other well-known leaders, mostly outside the assembly, like Abdus Samad Khan Achakzai of Balochistan, Shaikh Abdul Majid Sindhi, and G.M. Syed of Sindh and others, many of whom had been Congressmen and had opposed the creation of Pakistan, who now found themselves in opposition to the Muslim League government. These men subsequently formed the hard core and were the top leaders of the NAP in the country when it ultimately was established.

MAJOR CONTRIBUTION

I must now digress further to say something about my party in Pakistan since it has great bearing on the creation of the NAP. This necessarily compels me most reluctantly to give at least a brief outline of my political activities, a matter which I have avoided discussing all along, and which the rulers of Pakistan, particularly those of West Pakistan, know little about or knowing, would like to ignore. By a peculiar combination of circumstances I, too, found myself in opposition to the Muslim League government of Liaquat Ali Khan, although it appeared to many that I had made a major contribution in the establishment of Pakistan.

While wordy warfare raged on the division of India into Pakistan and Indian Union or Bharat, as the latter chose to designate itself officially, general elections were held throughout India in 1946 on the issue of partition.

The creation of Pakistan was at stake. At that time the Muslims were divided into two main camps. One was the AIML, a purely Muslim organization, captained by Mohammad Ali Jinnah; the other, the Indian National Congress, was a non-communal organization with a preponderance of Hindu members which was guided by Mahatma Gandhi. Jinnah himself had once been an important member of the Congress but had left it owing to ideological differences.

The Muslims had long before begun to realize that they were being excluded from participation in the administration and in the advantages of office. There also seemed to be ingrained substantial irreconcilable differences between Hindus and Muslims in outlook, in pattern of behaviour in religious rites and in customs and practices which led to frequent communal bloody conflicts. There was also considerable disparity in the economic condition of the two communities. Generally speaking, the Muslims were the labourers and peasants, the hewers of wood and the drawers of water, and this difference, coupled perhaps with the feeling that not so long ago the Muslims were the rulers of the country, was as responsible for the feeling of disparateness as the religious and social incompatibilities.

With the possibility of Home Rule and later independence being granted to India, the Muslims felt that unless they came to an understanding with the Hindus, who formed the major portion of the population of India, they would be crushed by the mill-stone of the Hindu majority. The Congress, although a non-communal organization and having many Muslim members of eminence such as Mohammad Ali Jinnah himself, did not command the confidence of the resurgent Muslims. To avoid bickerings which were retarding progress, the Muslim League and the Congress came to an agreement at Lucknow in 1916 (the Lucknow Pact of 1916) by which the Hindus agreed to separate electorate for the Muslims. But the Muslims had to give up some seats in the Muslim majority provinces to which they would have been entitled by virtue of their population in return for some weightage in Muslim representation in the Muslim minority provinces. The Government of India Act of 1919, which introduced diarchy as a step towards Home Rule, was based on this agreement.

In some regions, not very extensive, such as the NWFP and Sindh, the Muslims had a considerable majority; in Bengal and the Punjab their majority was very much less (56% as against 44%), in Assam the Muslims were 40 per cent, in the United Provinces 18 per cent and, in other parts of India, they were in a hopeless minority. The end of the First World War saw the partition of Turkey and the rise of the Khilafat movement in India led by the two brothers, Maulana Mohammad Ali and Maulana Showkat Ali. This was a Muslim mass movement, as distinct from the Muslim League, which at best was a middle class movement of the aristocracy and the intelligentsia.

Mahatma Gandhi, who had only a few years earlier returned to India, was able, by cooperating with the Khilafat movement, to transform the Indian National Congress itself into a mass movement and bring the Hindus and Muslims together in a common upheaval against British rule. He no doubt hoped and believed that by this means he would be able to weld the Hindus and the Muslims together for the attainment of self-government, after which the differences between the two communities would be ironed out. His programme of civil disobedience did not appeal to Jinnah and he left the Congress. In spite of a tremendous upsurge of unity, the differences between Hindus and Muslims—of which the Calcutta riots of 1926 were a manifestation—soon made their appearance and demanded a solution. Many were the attempts to settle them and many were the conferences held to adjust the conflicting rights of the two communities, but they resulted in failure. Ultimately, the AIML, claiming to be the spokesman of the Muslims of India, proclaimed at its session in Lahore in 1940 that the Muslims of India were not a community in India but a separate nation and demanded that the contiguous regions of India mainly inhabited by them should be made autonomous. The League in essence demanded the partition of India.

The elections of 1946 were understood to determine whether the Muslims were in favour of the partition of India and the creation of two independent states, Pakistan and Bharat. If they wanted partition they would vote for the candidates of the Muslim League; if they wanted India to remain integral, they would vote for the Muslim candidates set up by the Congress, or, in the Punjab, for the Muslim candidates set up by the Unionist Party, which, being composed of Muslims, Sikhs and Hindus, was also against the partition of India. It was easy to ascertain Muslim opinion as the voting was compartmental and the Muslims voted for Muslims only. It would be natural to expect that the Muslims of the Muslim majority areas would vote for the Muslim League, as they stood to gain by the partition, and that the Muslims of the Muslim minority provinces would vote for Muslim Congress candidates and against the partition, as the Muslims of these areas would be left totally stranded by partition and at the mercy of the Hindu majority. But these Muslims were led to expect that their rights would be safeguarded by special provisions. Moreover, large areas of India, particularly the entire provinces of the Punjab and of Bengal and possibly Assam, were expected to form part of Pakistan. With their fairly considerable Hindu population it was confidently hoped that the existence of the latter in the midst of a major Muslim population would guarantee fair treatment to the Muslims of India as *quid pro quo* for fair treatment to them.

Jinnah also maintained that Pakistan would be the homeland, not only of the Muslims of the Muslim majority areas but of all the 100 million Muslims of India. Strange as it may appear (this will always remain to the credit of the unfortunate Muslims of the Muslim minority provinces and an abiding proof of their dignity, their courage and their spirit of self-sacrifice who were unhappily and unfortunately forgotten by the Muslims of the Muslim majority areas who reaped the most advantages from Pakistan), these minority Muslims returned Muslim League candidates almost one hundred per cent with the fullest knowledge that with the creation of Pakistan they would be left derelict and defenceless in India at the mercy of a hostile Hindu majority who would never forgive them for having voted for Pakistan.

In the NWFP, however, with its 85 per cent Muslim majority, the Muslim voters returned a majority of Congress members who formed a Congress ministry under, I believe, Dr Khan Sahib. In Sindh (75% Muslim) about 50 per cent were thus returned with the result that Sindh, too, had a Congress ministry until the murder of its Chief Minister Allahbux after which a Muslim League ministry under Sir Ghulam Hussain Hedayetullah was formed. In the Punjab where the proportion of Muslims to non-Muslims was practically the same as in Bengal (56–44%), the votes were divided between the Unionist and the Muslim League candidates and a Unionist ministry with Malik Sir Khizr Hayat Khan Tiwana was installed. Of the Muslim majority provinces, Bengal alone returned an overwhelming number of Muslim League members, and a Muslim League ministry, with myself as Chief Minister, took office.

The brunt of all elections in Bengal on behalf of the Muslim League had fallen upon me in my capacity as secretary of the Bengal branch of the AIML since 1937. Entering politics in 1920 I became a member of the Bengal Legislative Assembly and joined the Khilafat organization and was the secretary of the Calcutta Khilafat Committee for a number of years. In the initial stages I was loosely associated with the Congress and was the Deputy Mayor of Calcutta with Deshbandhu C.R. Das as Mayor. He was the greatest Bengali, may I say Indian, scarcely less in stature than Mahatma Gandhi, I have ever had the good fortune to know. He was endowed with wide vision, he was wholly non-communal, generous to a fault, courageous and capable of unparalleled self-sacrifice. His intellectual attainments and keen insight were of the highest order. As an advocate he commanded fabulous fees which he laid at the feet of his country. Towards the end of his days he renounced his profession, devoted himself to politics and the service of his country and died a pauper overwhelmed with debts. I believe with many that had he lived he would have been able to guide the destiny of India along channels that would have eliminated the causes of conflict and bitterness, which had bedevilled the relationship between Hindus and Muslims, which, for want of a just solution, led to the partition of India and the creation of Pakistan.

Deshbandhu died in 1925 and J.M. Sengupta succeeded him as Mayor; I continued as Deputy Mayor. In May 1926 there was a communal riot in Calcutta of unprecedented violence because Hindus insisted on playing music before a mosque; this was strongly resented by Muslims. The Hindus demanded I should not help the oppressed Muslims, who were only 22 per cent of the population and were being victimized and oppressed by the Hindu police, even with legal and moral assistance. Their insistence was so vehement and unfair that I was forced to the conclusion that the talk of Hindu-Muslim unity was a myth and that the Hindus wanted nothing but complete surrender from the Muslims as the price of unity. A Unity Conference at Simla, presided over by the Maharajah of Alwar, was convened to consider the various causes of conflict between Hindus and Muslims in the light of the Calcutta happenings. It was here for the first time that I came in close contact with Jinnah. The conference ended in failure. It appeared to me that the only hope for Muslims was to stand on their own legs and look after their own separate interests if they wanted to survive and progress.

I organized a large number of labour unions and employees unions, some communal and some general, such as seamen, railway employees, jute and cotton mill labourers, rickshaw pullers, hackney carriage and buffalo cart drivers and *khansamas* (butlers) and at one time had as many as 36 trade unions as members of a Chamber of Labour I had founded to oppose the communist labour organizations (I paraded a blue flag in opposition to the Red.). I opposed the Nehru Report of 1928 which advocated joint electorate with reservation of seats for Muslims and gave evidence before the Round Table Conference in 1933 on behalf of the All-India Muslim Conference headed by His Highness The Aga Khan.

With the promulgation of the Government of India Act of 1935, I founded a party which I called the Independent Muslim Party to fight the elections in Bengal and started organizing the Muslims based on a membership fee of two annas. I set up a vast network of committees throughout Bengal and selected my candidates. About this time Jinnah returned to India from London, where he had practically settled down and was practising before the Privy Council, took charge of the Muslim League and turned it into a mass organization with a membership fee of two annas as well. At his request and after great hesitation and considerable deliberation, I consented to merge my organization with the AIML with myself as the secretary of the Bengal Provincial branch. I had thereafter to organize all the elections on behalf of the Muslim League in that capacity down to the general elections of 1946 on which the fate of Pakistan depended.

The opposition in the 1946 elections to the Muslim League, and hence to the creation of Pakistan, was led by Fazlul Huq with his KSP. His attitude needs a little explanation. He was a remarkable man with a remarkable career. Born in 1873, he became one of the best known and best beloved leaders of Bengal with his long connection with the East Bengal countryside and its people. A man of acutely active intelligence, colossal memory, great erudition and a deep insight into human character and mass psychology, he swayed the emotions and captured the imagination of the people of Bengal with his remarkable gift of oratory and fluency of language. He had great personal charm, which subdued his most rabid opponents when they confronted him. He was associated with the Muslim League from its inception in 1906. He was in the forefront of Muslim politics and participated in the talks at Lucknow which led to the pact of 1916 between the Congress and the Muslim League. After the Reforms of 1919 he was the Education Minister in the Bengal cabinet of Sir Surendranath Banerjee and established the Government Islamia College in Calcutta which enabled a large number of Muslim students, who could not get admission into other colleges, to pursue their higher studies. This greatly enhanced his reputation, prestige and popularity.

In the 1937 elections, the first after the Act of 1935 which abolished diarchy, Fazlul Huq contested the elections as chief of the KPP against the Muslim League, and I had the unfortunate duty of contesting his party. He personally won two seats, defeating Khwaja Nazimuddin in one; I, too, won two seats and relinquished my safest seat in favour of Khwaja Nazimuddin who thus, through a by-election, became a member of the legislature.[4] The KPP won 36 seats as against 39 captured by the Muslim League.[5] To prevent Fazlul Huq from falling into the clutches of the Hindus, with whom he had started negotiations, the Muslim League Party in its turn offered to support him for the Chief Ministership in coalition with his party. He thus became the Chief Minister of Bengal with the backing of a strong Muslim block. His renewed contacts with the Muslim League led him to attend the crucial Lahore session of the AIML in 1940 where he was entrusted with the honour of moving the Lahore Resolution. In 1941 he disobeyed the mandate of the Muslim League regarding the membership of the Defence Council and was considered guilty of using intemperate language towards Jinnah. The Muslim League ministers resigned from his cabinet on 7 December 1941, and he formed a new ministry in coalition with the Hindu Mahasabha. He resigned in 1943 and contested the 1946 election as the KPP leader.

MUSLIM LEAGUE VICTORY IN 1946

The Muslim League in Bengal swept the polls in the 1946 election. Out of 119 Muslim seats in a House of 250 members, 114 were captured by the Muslim League and Fazlul Huq was able to secure only five for himself, his relations and his party. Four members selected from special constituencies joined the Muslim League Party. Fazlul Huq joined the Congress opposition. As I had done the main chore of bringing the Muslim League to power, the party elected me Chief Minister of United Bengal in preference to Khwaja

Nazimuddin who contested me for the leadership. As we have seen, Bengal was the only Muslim majority province in which a Muslim League ministry came into power.

A Muslim League convention was held at Delhi in April 1946. I attended it with a large contingent of members of the legislature. I was received at the railway station by Jinnah and was given the honour of moving the main resolution at the convention. My tenure of office in Bengal, however, was extremely troubled as the Hindus could not tolerate a strong and stable Muslim League government in power when we were nearing independence and the fate of India was under discussion. On 16 August 1946 which the Muslim League High Command had designated Direct Action Day and which thousands of Muslims of Calcutta observed by attending a public and wholly peaceful meeting, the Hindus, who appeared to have been well-prepared, attacked the Muslims who were taken wholly by surprise. Later the riots spread to some of the districts of West Bengal which had an overwhelmingly preponderant Hindu population. I had my hands full quelling these disturbances. The Hindus were frustrated in their endeavours to massacre the Muslims which they seemed to have planned at the instance of their militant co-religionists of northern India and they bid their time.

The Calcutta riots had repercussions in the Muslim majority district of Noakhali in East Bengal. During the Calcutta riots the Hindus had invaded Muslim mosques and killed the congregation at their prayers, including the *imams* and *muezzins* who came from the district of Noakhali. In revenge, the Muslims of Noakhali burned a number of Hindu villages, about 282 people were killed and four women were abducted of whom three were subsequently restored. *The Amrita Bazaar Patrika* and other Congress papers flashed a statement by the secretary of the Bengal Provincial Committee that 50,000 Hindus had been killed and numberless women abducted. Excited by such reports, the Hindus massacred and humiliated the Muslims in Garmukhteswar in the United Provinces and throughout the province of Bihar where they are believed to have killed as many as 100,000 Muslims—men, women and children—with unbelievable savagery. The Hindu mobs in Bihar roamed the countryside for four days, killing, burning, looting, raping, mutilating, in the apparently justified belief that the Government of Bihar and the Hindu police were behind them and would not hinder them. Only the arrival of a company of British soldiers brought the riots under control.

It will remain to the credit of Pandit Jawaharlal Nehru that he had the courage to face a howling Hindu mob in Bihar and order them to stop rioting; otherwise he would have them shot. He was at that time the Prime Minister of India. In spite of advice to the contrary from Khwaja Nazimuddin, I gave assistance and asylum in Bengal to Muslims that had fled Bihar.[6] This exasperated the Hindus still more but they could do little as long as I was in power.

The partition of India, and with it Bengal, was scheduled for 15 August 1947. From the beginning of August the Hindus started a planned campaign of murder and arson against the Muslim localities in Calcutta. Muslim officers, including the Muslim police, had left or were leaving for East Bengal, leaving behind a police force practically 100 per cent Hindu; the Muslim armed police, whom I had recruited from the Punjab to the local police force and without whom the Calcutta riots would never have been brought under control, also left for East Bengal. The British armed forces in Calcutta had been replaced by Hindus who now believed that they had a clear field to massacre the Muslims.

I had come to Karachi on 6 or 7 August to attend a meeting of the Working Committee of the Muslim League, but I was keeping in touch with the situation in Bengal which was rapidly deteriorating. I felt that the Muslims of Calcutta and of some districts in West Bengal were in great danger as the Hindus were now determined to wipe them out if they could or to drive them away. I thought that my place should be with them, and I felt it my duty to decline the very generous offer of Jinnah who wanted to appoint me as Roving Ambassador and his personal representative to acquaint the governments all over the world with the *raison d'etre* of Pakistan. He even asked me not to return to Calcutta but to hand over charge from Karachi to the Shadow Hindu Chief Minister, P.C. Ghosh, who was to become the Chief Minister of West Bengal after partition. I communicated the offer to Liaquat Ali Khan who said he would have jumped at it had Jinnah made it to him. I told him that the post was scarcely suitable for him as he was sure to be made the Prime Minister of Pakistan. In reply I was astonished to hear from him, and this was as late as 9 August, that Jinnah had not yet spoken one word to him about the Prime Ministership.

COMMUNAL HARMONY

After the Working Committee meeting I took the plane to Calcutta and received reports of how locality after locality inhabited by Muslims were being attacked and the Muslims were being massacred in a planned manner with the help of the Hindu police who were firing on Muslims who defended themselves. I went straight to Mahatma Gandhi, who was living in Sodhpore in the outskirts of Calcutta, and asked him to use his influence to stop the massacres. I had laid on a train for him to proceed to Noakhali and urged him to postpone his visit. I spoke to him for more than two hours and placed before him the entire picture, pointing out that it was his duty to stay and stop the massacre and work for communal harmony if he believed in justice and humanity. If he wanted the minorities in India and Pakistan to exist, if he wanted peace between Pakistan and India, he must stay. I felt that if the Muslims of Calcutta and environs were massacred or driven away there would be repercussions in East Bengal and that the Hindus there would be similarly treated. There were about four times as many Hindus in East Bengal as Muslims in West Bengal: As many amongst the former were well-to-do, very large landholders, money lenders, businessmen, traders, doctors, professors, and teachers, while the latter were generally poor and landless. The result would be that the Muslims of Bihar, Assam and the United Provinces certainly, and elsewhere probably, would be slaughtered or driven out to make room for the refugees. There would be a terrible holocaust all over the country.

PEACE MISSION IN INDIA

During all this discourse Gandhi barely interrupted me and listened to all I had to say. Ultimately, and indeed with grave nobility as he realized what a hard, difficult and dangerous task was ahead of him, he agreed to do all he could provided that I stayed and worked with him in one of the worst-affected localities, Belliaghatta. Immediately I consented to do so, but he insisted that as my life would be in danger, I should take the permission of my father and daughter. The next day I came to stay with him in a somewhat dilapidated building lent by the Muslim owners and participated in the most astonishing meetings, almost beyond belief and far exceeding anything I had hoped for or could have visualized. We held meetings in locality after locality. In form they were public prayer meetings which he had initiated and which were normally attended by some of his Hindu devotees. But their character had changed entirely, and after the customary chants and invocations they were addressed both by him and myself. They were a mixed gathering of men and women, Hindu and Muslim, who attended in hundreds of thousands in complete friendship and mutual understanding. The atmosphere was entirely metamorphosed; instead of bitterness and hatred and murder and rapine, communal harmony was established, although not without some attacks on my person in the beginning, which, fortunately for me, failed to find their target.

15 August was celebrated with great eclat and Hindus and Muslims, who had arrayed against each other for a year, now exchanged visits—men, women and children—with fruits and presents. In fact, a miracle appeared to have been wrought; peace, as if by magic, reigned in troubled Bengal and we were saved that terrible and savage blood bath in which the Punjab, the Sikh states of the Punjab, the states of Alwar and Bharatpur and the city of

Delhi were wallowing. There was an unhappy, but fortunately minor, recurrence at Belliaghatta which spread to a few parts of Calcutta on 3 September. This was precipitated by the Hindu Mahasabha whose volunteers went so far as to launch a vicious attack on Gandhiji himself. Mahatma Gandhi undertook a fast unto death. He would not break it, even though perilously near breakdown, until I assured him that I was satisfied—for it was my personal satisfaction that he insisted on—that the Hindus were really penitent and that the government and the police had taken adequate steps to prevent any further recurrence. It showed the greatness of his heart and his magnanimous spirit that at every meeting, preaching the doctrine of communal harmony, he gave the credit for the new spirit of brotherhood and toleration to me and said he would not have been able to achieve anything had I not been by his side.

Having established peace in Bengal—for what he achieved in Calcutta had its beneficent repercussions throughout Bengal—he went to Delhi where the Muslims were being ruthlessly and systematically massacred. He told me I need not accompany him since that would be beyond our agreement but that he would be glad if I were to do so. I followed him. I was kept in touch with the communal situation by the Jamiat-i-Ulema-i-Hind, a deputation of which saw me and the Mahatma daily, and whose secretary, Maulana Hafizur Rahman, left no stone unturned to look after the cause of the unfortunate Muslims. Gandhiji often listened to my requests and, I believe, I was able to make some slight contribution to get the Delhi mosques cleared of Sikh refugees for which Gandhiji again had to undertake a fast.

Similarly, I think, I contributed a little to the safety of the Muslims in Delhi, Rewari, Gurgaon and other places near Delhi which I visited. I witnessed the caravans of Muslim, Sikh and Hindu refugees fleeing from East and West Punjab and was able to visit the camps of the Muslim refugees and discuss their welfare and safety with District Magistrates in Jullundur and Ambala Divisions, particularly in Hoshiarpur, Jullundur, Qadian, Panipat, and Karnal. I was able also to induce Mahatma Gandhi to convince the Indian cabinet to hand over more than Rs500 million payable to Pakistan under an agreement which Sirdar Patel had refused to surrender on the ostensible grounds that the money would be used in the Kashmir campaign. I brought to Gandhiji's notice the report of the massacre of Muslim Officers and their families by the Dogra troops when they were actually leaving Srinagar for Pakistan under safe conduct, a report authenticated by Shaikh Abdullah. He suggested as a solution of the Kashmir problem that the Maharajah should accede both to Pakistan and to India. I conveyed this suggestion to Chowdhury Zafrullah Khan who was on his way to the United Nations to answer the Indian complaint. Unfortunately, this suggestion did not find acceptance with the Pakistan government.

While staying with Mahatma Gandhi I busied myself drawing up a charter of minority rights which would be useful for the Muslims in India and for the Hindus in Pakistan.[7] During this period I was travelling continuously between Delhi, Lahore, Karachi and Calcutta. After discussing the matter with Mahatma Gandhi I approached Jinnah for his opinion and approval. His immediate reaction was that I should get the acceptance of the Indian leaders. Mahatmaji agreed to my draft as did Pandit Nehru and Sirdar Patel. When I again saw Jinnah he wanted the written acceptance of Mahatma Gandhi before he would consider it, although he agreed that such a charter would be a useful document. Mahatma Gandhi thereupon endorsed my draft which, to the best of my recollection, was to the effect that he agreed with the draft, though he considered it somewhat prolix, but doubted that Jinnah sincerely meant to abide by it.

I made the mistake of showing the endorsement of Gandhiji to Jinnah who flared upon seeing it; he refused to consider the document and handed it back to me. The next day Jinnah wanted the document back and said he wanted particularly to see the endorsement of Mahatma Gandhi. I could see that if Jinnah had the document in his possession he would work himself up into a tearing rage and start another feud with Mahatma Gandhi which would destroy all hope of any agreement on this important issue and might further complicate matters between India and Pakistan and increase the tension that already existed between the two leaders. I begged leave of Jinnah not to hand over the document to him and left Karachi. For this Jinnah never forgave me.

In addition to his previous offer, Jinnah had been kind enough to offer me successively the Refugee Ministry, Permanent Representative for Pakistan in the United Nations, Ambassador to the countries of the Middle East and even the Defence Ministry. I had to decline all these offers as I felt that my immediate mission was to make all possible effort to establish communal harmony between Hindus and Muslims in Pakistan and India. Moreover, when I had induced Mahatma Gandhi to work for communal harmony in Calcutta he had made a request that I should not accept any ministry, whether offered by India or Pakistan, for at least one year, a request to which I gladly acceded.

Mahatma Gandhi was assassinated on 30 January 1948 by a member of the RSS, a savagely militant and murderous Hindu organization, on the grounds that he was helping Muslims unduly and betraying Hindu interests. According to the assailant I was second on the list and Pandit Nehru third. I was watching with increasing anxiety the growing bitterness between the Hindus and Muslims in India and Pakistan as an aftermath of the partition. For the Punjab, where the holocaust had been terrible and refugees were streaming from one side to the other, an agreement was arrived at between

Liaquat Ali Khan and Sirdar Patel for a total interchange of all Muslims on the one hand and all Sikhs and Hindus on the other, between East and West Punjab. But in other parts of India Muslims were the victims of sporadic attacks and were seeking refuge in Pakistan in large numbers.

Except for some stray disturbances in the beginning, as took place in both countries, it must be said to the credit of Pakistan that after the dust had settled and issues had become clearer, there were no communal conflicts in Pakistan and no justification for the exodus of Hindus. At the same time no special efforts were being made by the central government to encourage them to stay, which I thought should have been done in the interests of the Muslims in India. A half-hearted attempt in this direction was made by inviting Acharya Kripalani, the secretary of the All-India Congress Committee, to come to Sindh and request the Hindus not to flee as they were doing for no rhyme or reason. Publicly he exhorted them to stay, but it is reliably learnt that privately he told them that it would be safer for them to leave and it was stupid to stay. As a result a large number of Hindus left Karachi and Sindh. There are now only a few left in West Pakistan, concentrated mostly in one or two districts of Sindh.

PEACE MISSION IN EAST BENGAL

East Bengal had a very large Hindu population. Amongst them were wealthy landlords and money-lenders, government servants, merchants, traders, shopkeepers, artisans, agriculturists, and landless labourers. In addition, all the important professions such as doctors, teachers, professors and lawyers were Hindu. With the departure of the 'officer class' who opted for India, the wealthier and the educated class began gradually to leave East Bengal. This created panic among the less fortunate Hindus; the exodus was increasing in volume, and I felt that it had to be checked in the interests of Pakistan and for the sake of the Muslims of India, even if we were callous enough to forget the interests of the Hindus of East Bengal and the call of humanity. Young and spirited Bengali Hindus were establishing Gandhi *ashrams* in various parts of Calcutta with which I associated myself with the objective of promoting communal harmony, the Hindus guaranteeing the safety of the Muslims as a social and political obligation. Similarly, while Hindu leaders only could adequately influence the Hindus in India, it was up to the Muslims to influence their co-religionists in Pakistan.

With this idea I started a communal harmony movement in East Bengal. I have to record with regret that Khwaja Nazimuddin, the Chief Minister, and his ministers considered that there was no point in the Hindus staying in East Bengal and no attempt should be made to restrain them from leaving. Indeed one influential minister believed seriously that they should be expelled, little realizing how disastrous it would be for the Muslims of West Bengal and beyond if there was a general Hindu exodus. Khwaja Nazimuddin was also of the opinion that the bitterness between Hindus and Muslims was so great that the Muslims of East Bengal would reject the movement for communal harmony and that the Hindus would do likewise as they were not likely to believe my bonafides and my mission would end in failure. It is gratifying that his view proved to be wrong. Muslims once more gave evidence of that generosity and toleration of which I knew they were capable.

The meetings which I held throughout East Bengal were most enthusiastically attended both by Hindus and Muslims in unprecedentedly large numbers. The mission was a complete success and Muslims everywhere solemnly promised to live in peace and harmony with their Hindu neighbours and to protect them from harm. They lived up to their promise. The Hindus promised not to leave. The unprecedented success of my mission perturbed Khwaja Nazimuddin and his ministers so much that he served on me an order expelling me from East Bengal just as I was leaving Dhaka to attend a communal harmony meeting in the countryside.[8] This made it impossible for me to take up residence in East Bengal for which I was preparing. Nevertheless, the seeds I had sown and the organization I had left behind continued to grow and function, and the exodus of Hindus which had again commenced when I was expelled was stopped. Today there is still a large number of Hindus in East Pakistan, living in peace and comfort; this is an object lesson to India, where, it is reported, there have already been 520 communal riots in all of which Muslims have suffered as against three in Pakistan.

UNSEATED IN THE ASSEMBLY

Although living in Calcutta I was a member of the Constituent Assembly of Pakistan. As no nationality law had been promulgated, I could still be a member of the Pakistan Constituent Assembly in Karachi while staying in Calcutta. I differed from the policy of the Pakistan government on certain fundamental issues and found myself in the opposition. I felt that government should give firm assurances to the minorities and should encourage them to stay and look after their safety and welfare instead of regarding them with suspicion and distrust and alarming them by charging them with disloyalty. According to me they had every right to be treated on a par with the Muslims as integral nationals of Pakistan. Such a policy would contribute substantially to the safety of the Muslims of India. Secondly, I was opposed to the theory of Liaquat Ali Khan that the Muslim League should be the one and only political party in the country for Muslims and that any Muslim who opposed it, or opposed the policies of his Muslim League government, was a traitor to the state. I felt that in a democratic country there must be as much room for opposition as for pro-government activities. Political parties must be allowed to grow and function and democratic conventions must be followed.

To deprive me of my seat in the Constituent Assembly, a law was passed in 1948 under which a member who had not become a permanent resident of some part of Pakistan and resided there for at least six months could lose his membership if the Speaker of the House so desired, although no nationality law had been passed until then. One of my friends in East Bengal immediately transferred his property to my name to meet the requirements of the law, but I was prevented by *force majeure* from entering East Bengal and settling there. As long as the Quaid-i-Azam, who was also the Speaker of the Constituent Assembly, was alive no steps were taken to unseat me. However, after his death and no sooner I publicly declared that I was definitely planning to settle permanently in West Pakistan on and from 5 March 1949 than Liaquat Ali Khan induced the Speaker, Moulvi Tamizuddin Khan, to terminate my membership in the Constituent Assembly on 26 February 1949.[9]

MOVEMENT FOR DEMOCRACY

After coming to West Pakistan I decided to organize a political party to be called the Awami Muslim League, a suggestion I had already made to several of my friends. Its doors would be open to all Muslim Pakistani nationals so that once more we could have a mass Muslim organization like the old Muslim League of Jinnah. Liaquat Ali Khan reacted by calling me a traitor, an agent of India and various other opprobrious names unworthy of himself—and threatened to 'crush all opposition under his heel.'[10] Be it said to the credit of the Muslims of Pakistan that many rose to the occasion and accepted the challenge, and his fulminations did more to establish my party and create an opposition party in the country than any effort on my part could have achieved.

CREATION OF OPPOSITION

In West Pakistan the work was no doubt uphill, but it was facilitated to some extent by the fact that the official Muslim League, also called the Pocket Muslim League, had excluded a number of important and influential people from its membership, even detaining them without trial under the Public Safety Laws for daring to challenge the policies of government.

In East Pakistan the Awami Muslim League found ready acceptance, for, after all, the Muslims of East Pakistan knew me very well; I had worked in Bengal for more than a generation and had spent twelve agonizing years among them in organizing the Muslim League. The Awami Muslim League obviously had no members in the Constituent Assembly; this had been created in 1949 and was just a field opposition. The first contest came in 1951 when the general elections for the provincial legislature of West Punjab were held. I merged my organization with one that the Nawab of Mamdot had created, which he called the Jinnah Muslim League, and we set up candidates on behalf of the Jinnah Awami Muslim League. It was actually due to the father of the present Nawab, Nawab Iftikhar Ali Khan, that Jinnah had found a footing in the Punjab before partition and he had a major contribution in whatever success the Muslim League had in the Punjab. The Nawab was the first Chief Minister of West Punjab after the partition, but, owing to disputes with one of his ministers, Mian Mohammad Mumtaz Khan Daultana, who supplanted him as Chief Minister and captured the Muslim League of the province, he found himself excluded from the official Muslim League and had perforce to organize his own party. Although the Punjab elections of 1951 were the very first occasion when our strength was put to the test, our party obtained successes which may well be called substantial if we take into consideration that the government used all its resources and mechanisms to defeat the opponents of the Muslim League.

The elections gave me an opportunity to acquaint the people of the Punjab with my policy as I was the chief of the party and its principal speaker, and I availed myself of the occasion to visit practically all the constituencies of the Punjab, including places which had never been visited before by any of the leaders of the province. After some time the Nawab of Mamdot and I parted company with regret as he felt that there was no possibility of defeating the Muslim League for the next twenty years, and he could hardly be called upon to jeopardize his future and that of his children by remaining in a hopeless opposition and to be deprived of the various allotments, permits and largesses which were being distributed by the Muslim League government to its supporters. The Nawab of Mamdot happened to be the biggest landholder in united Punjab, but as his property was all in East Punjab he had to leave everything behind when he migrated. He naturally felt that he was entitled to some of the perquisites of government patronage that were being distributed to undeserving persons and from which he was excluded because he was in the opposition.

With his secession, my party regained its original name of Awami Muslim League from which I later dropped the label 'Muslim' because I considered that the people were getting used to the idea of a common citizenship with the Hindus, and that it was necessary for the strength and development of

Pakistan that all its citizens should cooperate with each other from a common political platform irrespective of religion. I thus opened the doors of the party to non-Muslims should they choose to join. I looked forward to the day when separate electorate would be considered an anachronism and would be displaced by joint electorate when Hindus and Muslims would be able to vote for a common candidate, a conception bitterly opposed by the Muslim League.

Thereafter, elections were held in the NWFP from which I was excluded, in Bahawalpur where I was able to get some members of my party returned and in Sindh where I found it difficult to make any headway against the entrenched feudal landlords. These elections, however, furnished me with an opportunity to tour the provinces, address meetings, form branches of my party and secure adherents and to acquaint myself with local conditions and become known to the people.

In East Bengal the Awami League was making great strides. I had nominated Maulana Bhashani as President of the East Bengal Awami League. I had met him in Sirajganj as long ago as 1931 when I was distributing relief to people suffering from the devastations of floods in North Bengal. He was a powerful speaker—a real demagogue—and his speeches and similes had mass appeal. The Awami League was organized from the bottom with union, thana, subdivision, district and provincial committees along the lines on which I had organized the Muslim League—which in most places became the Awami League with all its members, lock, stock and barrel.

MILITARY ALLIANCES TO DEFEND DEMOCRACY

In the first half of 1954 Pakistan entered an alliance with the United States and signed a Mutual Defence Aid agreement. Pakistan agreed, in return for military aid, to maintain a high standard of military strength both for its own defence and for the defence of the free world and to maintain peace in the area. It also became a member of two military pacts—the Baghdad Pact and the SEATO—and received massive military and economic aid in ever growing volume from the United States and substantial donations from Commonwealth countries.

Pakistan had not received its share of either civil or military equipment from India after partition and had to build up everything from scratch. Further, it was tragic that the area that fell to its lot was underdeveloped— economically poor with barely any industry. It had a splendid army of brave soldiers but practically no equipment. Its need for development and its military weakness in the immediate neighbourhood of a hostile India (with its 15 munition and military equipment factories and factories for cars, trucks, aircraft, steel and general industrial potential) necessitated its approach to powers that could sympathize with it and whose political outlook it shared.

The passion for democracy and for the rule of law and justice that the people had inherited as a result of long years of British training and education and their aversion to any form of authoritarianism and dictatorship negating all liberties—coupled with an unconscious bias in favour of the British who granted us independence and had built up an excellent administrative, judicial and military machine—inclined us towards the Western pattern of democracy. The antipathy of Muslims to any concept which might loosely be termed as anti-God or anti-religious as a policy of the state, the regimentation of the people and subordination of the individual to paramount needs of the state as defined by the communist party were abhorrent. The frequent purges, executions and massacres for political reasons, the concentration camps, the brain-washings, the farcical trials of alleged foreign spies and local patriots and similar factors impelled us readily to accept alliances and agreements based on which the United States supplied us with military equipment and appurtenances, which, with our meagre resources, we would never have been able to purchase or manufacture. We thus became capable of defending ourselves and preventing infiltration of communist and subversive elements.

These agreements and alliances also helped us to establish links, common ties and development projects with other countries. There were also joint military exercises and a concerted policy to prevent communist infiltration and subversion. In due course we were provided with funds and assistance of various kinds by the United States and other friendly and Commonwealth countries which helped us to establish industries to make us self-sufficient in various fields, develop our internal resources and sustain our economy and our budgetary provisions. I have little doubt that all this flood of assistance was prompted by the much derided Baghdad Pact (later called CENTO after the withdrawal of Iraq) and the SEATO, which gave a practical demonstration of the ability of non-communist states to meet in a defensive alliance and save themselves from communist infiltration. In spite of the fact that the USSR and its satellites had entered into an offensive and defensive agreement known as the Warsaw Pact—so tight that any member, such as Hungary, attempting to resign from it was crushed by Soviet forces—and in spite of the fact that a similar alliance existed between the USSR and China, the communist countries took strong objection to these military pacts, though they were defensive and of doubtful military utility in a real crisis, arguing that military pacts as such encouraged war and militancy and were detrimental to world peace.

The United States when supplying arms to Pakistan had made it a condition that they could only be used for defensive purposes against communist aggression. Russia considered itself the target of the Baghdad

Pact; China made the same charge as regards SEATO. India made the Baghdad Pact an excuse for getting out of its commitments, solemnly made before the United Nations, as regards Kashmir. Even Pakistan felt itself unable to appreciate the practical value of the limitation imposed by the USA. After all, said Pakistan—and I made this clear when the Baghdad Pact meeting was held at Karachi under my presidentship—we could hardly separate American and non-American arms in case we were attacked by India. We would have to save ourselves.[11] In any event, who could say that Indian aggression, if it ever happened, would not be communist or communist-inspired aggression in view of the hostility of the communist powers to Pakistan and India's flirtation with China and Russia and its patronizing acceptance of American aid (as an unwanted charity forced down its unwilling throat by the United States with the sinister motive to keep it non-aligned).[12]

It can thus be seen that these alliances were strongly resented by the communist powers and by India and provided an easy weapon in the hands of domestic pro-communist elements to attack the Government of Pakistan. The opposition, at that time the Awami League which was the strongest of the opposition parties, took advantage of this and it became difficult to differentiate the pro-communist elements from non-or even anti-communist opposition. After I left the ministry in 1955, Maulana Bhashani had a clear field before him. He was clearly in touch with communists and fellow travellers; he had been invited and had attended several peace conferences outside the country which were promoted by communists. He had been made much of, his followers and admirers flattering his vanity by comparing him to Mao Tse-tung. It will always remain a mystery why the United States did not promote peace conferences but left it to the USSR and the communist parties to do so. This gave an image to the world that while the latter wanted world peace the USA and other democracies of the Western pattern were warmongers. The opposition elements in Pakistan propagated that American aid, military and civil, was being disbursed to popularize the fascist regime of the Muslim League, which was backed by the bureaucracy, the military, feudal elements and industrial magnates, and to arm it against the people.

The United States and the foreign policy of Pakistan were made special targets, and Maulana Bhashani was able to gather round him a number of young men—students, communists, fellow travellers and genuine patriots. At the time impressionable young leaders like Sheikh Mujibur Rahman and political thinkers like Toffazal Hossain, better known as Manik Mia, the editor of the most influential and most widely circulated Bengali daily in East Pakistan, supported the opposition view. Being myself in the opposition I could do little to counteract this propaganda, but, on the score of foreign policy, I warned the people to be careful and not be carried away by sentiment. The opposition knew little of the needs and requirements of Pakistan, and we were scarcely in a position to criticize foreign policy since it had never been bipartisan and the country had never been taken into confidence.

Government did little to help itself. It did little to meet the challenge of the opposition, which it ignored and probably did not take seriously since it came from East Bengal, for the policies of the central government in all fields had been conditioned by the needs, requirements and sentiments of West Pakistan. Indeed it would not be far wrong to say that the picture of Pakistan projected to the world was that of West Pakistan alone, and even the aid-giving countries accepted it as such with East Pakistan trailing far behind. It is significant that the visits of foreign potentates conducted by the central government were confined to a tour of the show places of West Pakistan only. Government did so little to explain its foreign policy that it gave the general impression that it was ashamed or could not justify it. In the matter of economic assistance it published with utmost reluctance, without any graceful acknowledgement, scraps of news of assistance from foreign sources which gave no indication of the massive aid it was receiving from friendly countries, particularly from the USA. In fact, it did little to counteract the pro-communist, anti-West and anti-American propaganda.

When I became Prime Minister on 12 September 1956, I felt that one of my first duties would be to change the political atmosphere in Pakistan in order to earn the support of the people on which alone I could justify my existence in office. My first speech on the subject was addressed to the students of Dhaka University in one of their residential halls.[13] I had before me a hostile audience, but little by little, by reasoned arguments, I was able to win their support by the time I had finished my speech. Sheikh Mujibur Rahman, one of my star organizers whose claim to prominence was because he was a good field worker in touch with both the workers and the leaders throughout the province, and Tofazzal Hossain whose powerful pen swayed mass opinion through the Bengali daily, *The Ittefaq,* accepted my views and supported me. Thereafter, I toured the province and obtained mass approval. Bhashani remained unconvinced. He promoted with great eclat an Indo-Pakistan cultural gathering at a village called Kagmari in the district of Tangail, which lasted for several days, and there we came to grips.[14] At two successive meetings of the Awami League Council, where he fondly believed he would be successful, I obtained 800 votes to his 35. For a long time he was uncertain what to do.

THE NAP BLACKMAILS

West Pakistan opposition leaders such as Khan Abdul Ghaffar Khan, Shaikh Abdul Majid Sindhi and G.M. Syed, had approached me earlier to lead them and were prepared to join the Awami League. I, however, felt that I could not accept their offer at the moment as the antecedents of many were likely to be a great handicap to the party which I was building up as a mass organization of tried pro-Pakistani elements. These gentlemen now found in the defection of Maulana Bhashani an opportunity to offer him the presidentship of their party, which henceforth came to be called the NAP and drew its adherents in West Pakistan mostly from the erstwhile Muslim members of the Indian National Congress and in both East and West Pakistan from communists, fellow travellers and uncompromising anti-Americans. It took on the shape of an all-Pakistan party. It had no members to represent it in the East Pakistan Assembly and only one in the central assembly, but ten members in the West Pakistan Legislature formed themselves into a parliamentary group of the NAP which had one immediate aim: to disintegrate the One Unit. They took advantage of the rivalry, to which I have referred earlier, between the Muslim League and the Republican Party. The Muslim League approached the NAP and offered to vote for the disintegration of One Unit if it in turn voted with the Muslim League against the Republican ministry which their joint votes could defeat. Sardar Bahadur Khan, the parliamentary leader of the Muslim League, and Qazi Isa, secretary of the organization, signed on behalf of the Muslim League.

With this valuable weapon in hand the Muslim League approached the Republican Party for what it could offer, for they realized that the mere defeat of the Republican ministry in the provincial legislature and the passage of a resolution against One Unit would not solve the problem. The ultimate solution rested with the central parliament where the Republican Party held the strings. The Republican Party offered not only to vote in the provincial legislature for the disintegration of One Unit but also to get it passed in the central legislature. Sardar Abdul Rashid signed a disintegration promise on behalf of the Republican Party. Both of them offered to the NAP *ad lib* representation in the provincial ministry. The Republican Party was confident it would corner me and force me to side with it. To my misfortune, I refused to be bullied; I considered that this method of bargaining with the One Unit scheme, as a pawn in the game of power politics, was debasing politics and democracy. After all it was these self-same parties, headed by Mian Mumtaz Khan Daultana and Dr Khan Sahib, who had pushed the scheme through. Moreover, the NAP had been anathema to both of them until they started to play this game and to be blackmailed in their lust for power.

As the two major, significant parties in West Pakistan had become so demoralized as to give up all their principles, I thought it my duty to approach the people directly to obtain their reactions and received a thundering response. I made it as soft as I could against the Republican Party ministry, appealing to it to retrace its steps and not to be blackmailed by the members of the NAP which merely numbered ten persons. Dr Khan Sahib, who at that time was President of the Republican Party, resented my attitude which he no doubt considered went against the interests of his party. He also received from interested persons very exaggerated, garbled reports of my speeches which annoyed him still more. The Republican Party in solemn conclave also passed a resolution against Nawab Mushtaq Hussain Gurmani, the Governor of West Pakistan, for allegedly conspiring with the Muslim League against the Republican ministry. In my opinion this was against the ethics of his office and I called upon him to resign. In his place I appointed Akhtar Hussain, a senior civilian with an excellent record of service and an enviable reputation for level headedness who was highly thought of by his colleagues.

RESIGNATION

At the instance of Dr Khan Sahib, President Iskander Mirza demanded my resignation, but at the same time he asked me to see him the next day when he would try to adjust the differences. As I had no intention of forsaking my principles and yielding to blackmail, I demanded that President Iskander Mirza should convene a meeting of parliament where I believed I would obtain a vote of confidence. Angered by the fact, as he told me later, that he came to know of this demand of mine from the morning papers which was brought to his notice by Dr Khan Sahib before he had opened my letter and before he had time to consider it and perhaps make some adjustments, President Mirza refused to call a meeting of parliament. Relying upon an article in the constitution of 1956 whereby the President was given the power to dismiss a minister if he thought that minister had lost the confidence of the majority of the members of the House, he called upon me to resign. Otherwise, he would dismiss me. I resigned, partly to avoid the humiliation of a dismissal and partly to demonstrate that Pakistan was not lacking in ministers who could give up their office for the sake of their principles. Iskander Mirza asked me to continue until he could appoint a successor. Meanwhile, he sent me some offers of reconciliation through the Pir Sahib of Manoki Sharif; but six days later he accepted my resignation and appointed Chundrigar, the leader of the Muslim League Party, as Prime Minister. The Republican Party supported this move.

Electorate Issue. When I had assumed office in September 1956, I had asserted in my very first statement that a cardinal item of my policy was that I was determined to have general elections at the earliest opportunity. Many of my friends at that time told me that I had sounded the death-knell of my ministry, for those in real power, who could pull all civil, administrative, military, feudal, financial and vested interest strings, would see to it that general elections were never held and democracy never permitted to function. I solved one difficult problem to my satisfaction, namely, that of securing public approval of my foreign policy when public opinion was going all the other way. For the first time there had been an open and frank debate in parliament with all cards on the table. For the first time the country had been taken into confidence, and the country and the parliament had endorsed it. Now there remained the problem of general elections. The constitution had given the power to appoint the Chief Election Commissioner to the President. The cabinet had the greatest difficulty in persuading the gentleman appointed to expedite the arrangements and to force the pace to the extent I desired, in spite of my clearing away for him obstacle after obstacle. But there was one matter of principle which also had to be resolved and without which the electoral rolls could not be properly and formally prepared: the issue of joint or separate electorate.

The elections to the central and provincial legislatures under the Government of India Act of 1935 had been held based on separate electorates, as had all the general provincial elections in Pakistan. This was only an expedient for the legislatures, for in Bengal at least elections to the local bodies such as union boards, municipalities, district boards and district school boards, were all held on the basis of joint electorate. I had been an uncompromising protagonist of separate electorates when the Muslims were fighting for their rights in the united India, and it was necessary they should be represented by members of their own choice. But, after the creation of Pakistan, there was no such need on the part of the vast majority Muslim population of Pakistan. If anyone had the right to ask for separate electorates or special representation it would be the Hindus. But they gave up this right and preferred the system of joint electorate, finding in it a better avenue of cooperation with the Muslims and a better method of securing the goodwill of the majority community and, through such cooperation and goodwill, safeguarding their interests and their safety.

I maintained that in order to create a sound Pakistani nation in which all elements of society could cooperate for a common national purpose, the joint electorate was essential. The Muslim League, however, insisted on maintaining the system of separate electorates, asserting that it was an essential part of Islam. To the Muslim League the creation of Pakistani nationhood was of little consequence; they were more concerned with capturing the support of the Muslim masses by appealing to their fanatical sentiments. The Jamaat-i-Islami attempted to show that joint electorate would be against Muslim interests in Bengal. Its arguments and figures were proven to be fallacious and were contradicted by the results of joint electorate in the local bodies. Before finally framing the relevant clause in the constitution, Chowdhury Mohammad Ali, the Prime Minister, had sought the views of the two legislatures. The East Pakistan Legislature voted overwhelmingly and, perhaps, solidly, in favour of joint electorate; the West Pakistan Legislature voted overwhelmingly in favour of separate electorate. The constitution, as finally framed, left it to the provincial legislatures to settle the form of the electorates in their own region.

I was able to induce the central parliament to alter that clause in the constitution and accept joint electorate for both wings. This avoided the determination of the number of several communal compartments and the number of representatives from each community, the delimitation of constituencies for each community, the preparation of separate electoral rolls, and the arrangement for separate election booths. Instead we had one electoral roll for each territorial constituency. This also settled a very controversial religious problem which had already cost several lives in West Pakistan, particularly in Lahore and Multan; whether the Ahmadis, also called Qadianis, were Muslims or not. A large section of the Muslims held that they were not and, hence, should not be allowed to be registered in the Muslim electoral rolls. It was maintained that they should be treated as non-Muslims, and if government desired to give special representation they could have their own electoral roll similar to other non-Muslim minorities under the separate electorate system. The Ahmadis, however, claimed that they were Muslims and should be treated as such and should be entered in the Muslim electoral roll. This controversy led to serious riots and loss of many lives, and martial law had to be imposed in Lahore. Joint electorate, which visualized a single roster of Muslims and non-Muslims and in which there was no reservation of seats for any community, obviously solved the political implications of this very dangerous religious controversy.

My views on joint electorate were supported strongly by President Iskander Mirza and I knew that Commander-in-Chief Ayub Khan was also in favour. Electoral rolls were accordingly prepared. However, no sooner had Chundrigar assumed the office of Prime Minister on 18 October 1957 than he ordered the electoral rolls to be split, with all its complications, on the basis of separate electorate: he stated that he would have the constitution amended accordingly by a certain date or he would resign.[15] In the beginning the Republican Party supported me on the question of joint electorate. President Iskander Mirza supported Chundrigar's demand for separate electorate, and, as some would put it, pulled the strings in favour of the

Muslim League Prime Minister. The Muslim League, however, was not content to let matters rest here and tried to encroach on the provincial preserves of the West Pakistan Republican government.

The agreement between the Muslim League and the Republican Party in the centre failed to reproduce itself in the province. The Republican Party sought a way out of the impasse by proposing that it would send a fact-finding committee to East Pakistan to ascertain at first hand the view of the people in general and what was most beneficial to their interests. Chundrigar postponed the date of his threatened resignation. The tour undertaken by the committee was the signal for rival demonstrations and several minor clashes between the proponents of the two views in East Bengal. In the end the Republican Party gave its opinion in favour of joint electorate and refused to support Chundrigar. It would not be far from wrong to conjecture that its policy, however welcome to me, was conditioned by considerations to its own advantage. Chundrigar resigned on 11 December 1957.

President Iskander Mirza accepted Chundrigar's resignation and again commissioned him to form a ministry in the hope that he would be able, through subtle manipulations, to get sufficient support for Chundrigar from the Republican Party which he apparently was prepared to liquidate in favour of the Muslim League. As the Republican Party had supported joint electorate, I promised to support it with my members and supporters but made it clear that I would not accept any office for myself or for any member of my party.

The Republican Party and my party remained firm in spite of the attempts of President Iskander Mirza to wean away members from the Republican Party. Chundrigar failed to constitute a ministry which would command the support of the House and resigned again. Malik Feroz Khan Noon, who had been designated as leader by the Republican Party and the Awami League, was appointed as Prime Minister. The electoral rolls, which had been scrapped by Chundrigar's arbitrary executive order, had again to be prepared. General elections which I had hoped would be held in March 1957—and according to the Election Commission should be held by March 1958—had again to be postponed. This suited those elements which did not want a general election. Arrangements were finally made by the Election Commission to hold the elections in February–March 1959.

Over Emphasizing Religion in Politics

The political parties got ready to address the constituencies. The Muslim League Party, captained by Khan Abdul Qayyum Khan of the NWFP, apparently made the capture of power its main policy and threatened that rivers of blood would flow if it did not succeed in the West Pakistan

Legislature and in the central parliament. The constitution of 1956 had re-named Pakistan as the Islamic Republic of Pakistan; there were references to the Quran and Sunnah in several places in the text; there were special provisions to see that the laws that would be enacted and had been enacted were in conformity with these two origins of Muslim Law. Nevertheless, the Muslim League lost no opportunity to arouse fanaticism and champion the cause of Islam as the surest and easiest way of getting support from the Muslims of West Pakistan, and its propaganda was so full of blood and thunder and potential for violence that other non-fanatical parties were finding it increasingly difficult to hold meetings peacefully. The central government, which could have taken steps to curb such threats of violence, refrained from doing so.

The main aim of the Republican Party appeared to be to resist the Muslim League and prevent the success of such parties as might challenge the privileged position of the landlords and introduce land reforms. There was no need for land reforms in East Pakistan; in fact, if any changes were to be made in the land laws there, they could be in the reverse direction so as to not totally obliterate the middle class. In West Pakistan, however, the landlords were well entrenched and powerful; hence, the demand for land reforms was becoming increasingly insistent, and the Republican Party, composed mostly of unprogressive feudal landlords, was hard put to it to stem the tide. The Republican government in West Pakistan transferred and manipulated the civil servants in a manner calculated to ensure that the votes were cast in favour of the party. It even stooped to transferring the inspecting school staff and *patwaries* (Land Revenue) and irrigation water-rate assessment officers, a class carrying enormous influence with the agriculturists. This became such a scandal that I had to request President Iskander Mirza to take steps to stop such corruption. I warned him that the country had been waiting for this general election ever since the foundation of Pakistan and had pinned on it all hopes for its future progress. I further predicted that there would be a serious cataclysm if the elections were not fair and free and that nothing short of marital law would be able to tide over the crisis.

The Jamaat-i-Islami was all out for an Islamic constitution of its own conception. Its founder, Maulana Abul Ala Maudoodi, however, attempted to demonstrate that all the modern conceptions of democracy and welfare states were in accordance with Islamic precepts. He suffered from the disability of having opposed the concept of Pakistan, of declaring that the Kashmir War—if that conflict could be so called—was not a jihad, and from the fact that his organization was itself believed to be authoritarian. Hence, although the Jamaat-i-Islam was a well-knit, disciplined party, its appeal was limited to a rather fanatical circle and would have indeed reached the saturation point but for the repressive tactics of President Ayub at that time which seemed bound to increase its popularity. There was some time earlier a rift in the party which, to an extent, tarnished its reputation. Its pretensions that its members were pure, God-fearing, and pious (*Swaleh*) and non-members were not, and that anyone becoming a member—for instance when the head thought he would be a successful candidate on behalf of the party—became at once invested with all these excellent qualities, aroused justifiable criticism. In spite of its attractive Islamic appeal, there were those who kept away from it because of the belief that it was dangerous to make politics subservient to religion, not because of any inherent inconsistencies, but because the contents of religion were open to different interpretations.

In Islam there were several sects, the principal ones being Sunnis, Shiahs and Ahle Hadeeth; in the same sect there were differing schools of thought, such as *Deobandi* and *Brelvi*. Matters were further complicated by the existence of the Qadianis or Ahmadis who claimed to be the only true Muslims. These were considered by some other Muslims as heretics and apostates and not Muslims at all. Each sect and sub-sect held very strongly to its beliefs, and the peace of the state, particularly in West Pakistan, was marred by sanguinary riots. The problem, therefore, was whose interpretation was to prevail? If it was to be that of the majority community, namely, the Sunnis of the Hanafi sect, then of which school? And why not the interpretation of others who held to their own views as rigidly? Whereas there could be compromises in politics, there could not be any in religious beliefs. Hence, many thought that it was dangerous to over emphasize religion in politics, since, as new cultural, social, political and economic conditions emerged, solutions in Islam could be found only through analogy with possible divergent interpretations.

The NAP appeared to have faded out after its failure to bring about the disintegration of the One Unit in West Pakistan. It had many members who were quite influential in their constituencies but who had no organization. It had not declared its election programme.

The Awami League suggested the concept of a Pakistani nation, non-communal in outlook and based on joint electorate. It supported land reforms in West Pakistan of a fairly drastic nature and clean politics. I objected to Islam being injected into the business of canvassing for votes, which should have been based on reason, logic and argument and on sound political sense and not on fanaticism. To my mind, the main motive of the parties who appealed to the people in the name of Islam was to exploit the sentiment of the masses. That it caused apprehension in the minds of non-Muslims or amongst the minority sects, and that their appeals aroused religious fanaticism with its possibilities of mischief in a country torn with religious and sectarian prejudices, was, to them, beside the point so long as they got votes.

To my mind Islam should have been kept above the conflict of political parties as a sacred trust to which all Muslims, to whichever party they belonged, were wedded. Surely, in a country where the vast majority of the population was Muslim, those grand principles of the Islamic faith enshrined in the Quran and taught and observed by the Prophet, based on justice, truth, toleration, charity in the broadest sense and social welfare, could not but be accepted and promoted. Islam had taught that it was the duty of the ruler to provide everyone with food, shelter, clothing, education, medical treatment and the means to earn an honest livelihood. Social welfare was a cardinal maxim; these were the true concepts of an Islamic state, and surely emphasis on these was more justifiable than general platitudes and vague insistence on Islam and such a programme should earn the support of all citizens, irrespective of religion. On the other hand, insistence on Islam placed the Hindus, particularly of East Pakistan, in a most unenviable position. At the same time, the militant section of the Hindus of India was furnished with a weapon which they could utilize to justify the Hinduisation of India and the treatment of Muslims as a subject race of second class citizens if and when they were so minded in retaliation for the aggressive Islamisation of Pakistan and the treatment of Hindus as a subject race.

AWAMI LEAGUE SUPPORT TO REPUBLICANS

Hitherto, I had been supporting the government of Malik Feroz Khan Noon without allowing my party to take office. For some reason which I could not fathom, his insistence that we should take office became embarrassingly frequent. I warned him that he would run into danger and should be satisfied with our support. How could he, I argued, expect his ministers to relinquish some of their important portfolios without which it was not possible for my party to accept office? It would be a sheer insult to East Pakistan if its ministers were allotted minor portfolios—if there was no equitable division. He, however, promised that he would see to it that the portfolios were divided fairly and prevailed upon me to consent to members of my party accepting ministries. As I had expected, he could not prevail upon his Republican ministers to relinquish any major portfolios and could allot only minor ones to the ministers of my party.

President Iskander Mirza was also pressing me to allow my party to take office, even while he was making arrangements to dismiss the ministers and to impose martial law—while the troops were getting into position to take over the government. The ministers of my party felt they had been betrayed by the Prime Minister. They resigned from the ministry before assuming office but without detracting from the support which I had promised to the ministry of Malik Feroz Khan Noon. It shows how hard pressed were

President Iskander Mirza and Commander-in-Chief General Ayub Khan to find plausible reasons for such drastic measures as abrogation of the constitution and the imposition of martial law that they cited the resignation of the ministers of East Pakistan as one of the causes justifying their action.

MIRZA'S TANGLED MAZE OF POLITICS FAVOURING REVOLUTION

In East Pakistan a shameful incident had happened within the precincts of the legislature. The Deputy Speaker was so severely assaulted with chairs and other missiles by certain members that he was led away bleeding and with internal injuries from which he subsequently succumbed. When General Iskander Mirza appointed Fazlul Huq as his Interior Minister in 1955, he adopted Huq's KSP as his own, pampered and flattered it, met its members secretly, and utilized it to suit his own ends. Before I took office as Prime Minister this party was in power in East Pakistan with Abu Hossain Sarkar, Huq's nominee, as Chief Minister. Sarkar resigned as he found himself unable to face the House and to get his budget passed. Ataur Rahman Khan of the Awami League was made Chief Minister a few days before I was appointed Prime Minister. Such a tangled maze of politics had President Iskander Mirza created that while his party in the West, the Republican Party, supported me, his party in the East, namely, the KSP, opposed me in the centre and formed the opposition to the Awami League ministry in East Pakistan. Some time before the incident took place, it appeared that President Iskander Mirza was already contemplating getting rid of Malik Feroz Khan Noon and creating a contretemps in East Pakistan. The day previous to the assault the Speaker of the Provincial Assembly, who was a supporter of the KSP, was charged by the Government of Ataur Rahman Khan with partiality and with irresponsible behaviour. There was an uproarious scene between the opposing factions and the Speaker withdrew from the Assembly. The supporters of the government insisted that he should not be allowed to occupy the chair again. Actually he came the next day to his room in the assembly but made no attempt to proceed to the chamber. In his stead the Deputy Speaker presided.

The provincial government had information the previous evening that the KSP members of the legislature had vowed that they would commit violence on the person of the Deputy Speaker if he came to occupy the chair and would not on any account permit him to do so. In the face of this threat the government had either to resign or accept the challenge. There was one other alternative, namely, that the Governor be directed by the President to take action under Article 193 and take charge of the provincial government as agent of the President.[16]

I happened to be in Dhaka at the time and tried but failed to get in touch with the President, who was in Karachi, although the leaders of the KSP were able to get him on the telephone easily. I got in touch with the Prime Minister, also in Karachi, who said that Article 193 could not even be considered and that the challenge to violence had to be faced; otherwise there would be an end to all civilized democratic government. The provincial minister ordered the police, under the personal command of the Inspector General of Police, to be ready to rush into the assembly chamber at the first sign of violence but at the same time he cautioned its supporters to be absolutely quiet and not meet violence with violence lest they be held responsible for any abusive acts within the House. No sooner, however, had the Deputy Speaker entered the assembly than some opposition members started to throw chairs and whatever other missiles they could lay their hands upon at him. To his misfortune, instead of surrounding him, the guards gave way and left him open to the hail of missiles. The police also did not rush in as had been planned. They came a little later after the Deputy Speaker had been severely wounded. The supporters of the government, who would under other circumstances have rushed forward and prevented the opposition from committing the assault, sat silent expecting every moment that the police would rush in to the rescue of the Deputy Speaker. This was a most unfortunate event as the Deputy Speaker succumbed to his injuries.

I am regretfully constrained to state that whether President Iskander Mirza did or did not visualize the occurrence in its entirety, the opposition party would never have dared to act so brutally and savagely, so fearlessly and without restraint, if it had not felt that it had the backing of the President. It is believed that he desired deliberately to create some situation in East Pakistan which might supply him with arguments for the ultimate abrogation of the constitution, which he had already decided on some time ago and for which he had made all arrangements.

OCTOBER REVOLUTION

In preparation for the forthcoming general elections to be held in February–March 1959, I had laid on a huge programme of meetings beginning from October 1958 and for the next five months in both parts of Pakistan. I had held two meetings, one in Quetta about the time that the Khan of Kalat had been taken into custody under the orders of the Government of Malik Feroz Khan Noon and another in Jacobabad in Sindh. Both of these were successful far beyond my expectations. Then the news reached me that the constitution had been abrogated, the President had taken over the country, the ministry had been dismissed, the legislature dissolved and martial law had been imposed.

On 7 October 1958 a proclamation was issued by President Iskander Mirza purporting to justify his drastic action and recounting the ills from which the country was suffering. It contained many of the political ills I had myself referred to in the course of my speeches, but the complete strangulation of democracy was hardly the remedy. In fact, the answer lay in establishing true and unfettered democracy within the confines of law and order. Politicians and political parties and even politics as a philosophy were roundly abused as having been responsible for all the ills of Pakistan, and it was declared that democracy had failed in Pakistan, although, as a matter of fact, democracy had never been given a chance to function.

There had not been a general election of parliament since the inception of Pakistan. Neither had there been a government which could enjoy the confidence of elected representatives of the people and which could have effectively countered any unconstitutional interference and intrigue on the part of the head of the state or the military.

Press conferences were held by President Iskander Mirza which the CMLA, General Ayub Khan, also attended. The President boasted of how it had been planned and that the necessary military moves were in progress for three weeks. The CMLA said that 'plans for the coup had been ready for some time, but it was the President's decision when to put them into action.'

After attempting to justify the coup de'tat, which they glorified as a revolution, President Iskander Mirza stated that he had no intention of prolonging unduly the state of martial law, that he would restore democracy, duly controlled, as soon as possible, and that he would get in touch with reliable politicians.

It was later learned reliably that the President resorted to this coup procedure to get rid of Malik Feroz Khan Noon in the centre and induct in his place Nawab Muzaffar Ali Qizilbash, who was at that time the Chief Minister of West Pakistan and belonged to the Republican Party.

The President was anxious, even during my tenure of office, to install this man as Deputy Prime Minister. He was immediately contradicted to his face by the CMLA who asserted with vehemence that on no account would they have anything to do with politicians and there was no intention whatsoever of restoring democracy 'until the mess had been cleared up.' This conflict occurred at two press conferences; thus it was clear that it would not be long before the two separated.

SECOND OCTOBER REVOLUTION

What exactly took place between the two heads of the revolution is not known. Rumour, based somewhat on substantial facts, has it that President

Iskander Mirza found it desirable to eliminate CMLA General Ayub Khan. Through an Air Force Officer, subsequently promoted, he approached the new Commander-in-Chief, General Musa, to take steps accordingly.[17] Unfortunately for President Iskander Mirza, the steps he was going to take were also known to his very immediate entourage, and the CMLA was kept secretly informed of developments. Under the circumstances, the President was never in a position to strike. Before he could take any other step, the CMLA on 27 October 1958 dramatically sent four of his top generals with drawn revolvers to procure the President's instant resignation.[18] The President and his wife were arrested, whisked off to Quetta and then magnanimously deported to London after suffering considerable humiliation. General Mohammad Ayub Khan assumed the office of the President as well as of the CMLA. Ex-President Iskander Mirza was allowed to draw his pension as a retired ex-Army officer in addition to Rs2,000 per month allowable to past governors general or presidents. It is said that drastic steps were not taken against him due to the intervention of Langley, the United States' Ambassador in Pakistan, who was very friendly with Iskander Mirza.

27 October, therefore, marks the beginning of a second 'glorious' October Revolution.

REFORMS WITH LITTLE BEARING ON DEMOCRACY

The Revolution was the beginning of certain changes which are hardly worth mentioning as they have little bearing on the history of democracy in Pakistan other than a statement by President Ayub Khan that he would introduce democracy in the country in a form which the people would be able to understand and which would be 'in conformity with the genius of the people.' The President confessed that he knew little of the problems of the country and appointed committee after committee and commission after commission to advise him on various problems. Little came of these commissions.

An important change, meant to brighten up the administration and make it more efficient and expeditious, was the introduction of a new system under which Section Officers replaced Assistant Secretaries. This neither decreased the cost of the administration, as it was expected to do, nor increased its efficiency; rather it created more confusion. Files became untraceable and many papers were lost.

An Education Commission produced a report which strung together the advanced educational system of wealthier countries. The President supported it with all fervour, but it was so resented by the students, the teachers and the guardians that it had to be scrapped. Its partial and tentative execution threw the educational system into such a state of confusion that it led to continuous strikes and demonstrations by the student community.

One of the items of reform was to purge the civil service of incompetent or dishonest elements from top to bottom. Officers, whose own work was being scrutinized by superior committees, were appointed to examine the work of their subordinates, and who, while reporting against their subordinate officers, were themselves dismissed for incompetence or dishonesty. It was obvious that little justice could be done under such circumstances and that many officers were victimized. It is true that some officers, who could not quite make the grade and were protected from removal by the Civil Service Rules, were dismissed from service, as were some officers suspected of dishonesty against whom normally nothing could be proved. It is equally true that quite a number of incompetent and suspect officers continued in service and were promoted in their turn. The discrimination appeared to be largely due to party factions in the Service, and the party who had the confidence of the President obviously won good efficiency ratings. No one, not even the top secretaries, had the courage to pass orders which required discretion. Files were passed from hand to hand. No one was prepared to take responsibility until it was made worth his while. There were, of course, a few honourable exceptions. But administrative efficiency definitely collapsed and corruption became rampant in all grades on a scale unprecedented and unimaginable. Bribes were taken and favours conferred openly and brazenly with no fear of consequences. The anti-Corruption Department was utilized for political purposes or to prevent insignificant small fry from stealing petty cash—just sufficient activity to justify its existence.

Action was taken against politicians. At first, in March 1959, an order, shortly called the Public Offices Disqualification Order (PODO), was passed levelled against those who had committed misconduct in the discharge of their public duties. This order provided for impartial judicial tribunals and gave facilities to any member of the public to register complaints. This would have left the door open for the prosecution of those who enjoyed official favours. No action was taken by the government to frame rules or appoint any tribunal on the grounds that it was considering how the procedure could be simplified and disposal expedited. Seeing that, in spite of the lapse of several months, no tribunal was even appointed, this was exposed as nothing more than a lame excuse. This order was replaced by an Elective Bodies Disqualification Order (EBDO) under which the government alone could initiate proceedings, thus paving the ground for protecting its favourites on the one hand and for political victimization of opponents on the other. Under this order tribunals were not independent and, in spite of the appointment of a judge as the chairman, were dominated by the military member. Under EBDO selected politicians were prosecuted for orders passed by them when in office on the grounds of corruption, nepotism or misconduct. The latter term was left purposely vague and undefined.

Tribunals were appointed for the centre and for the two provinces. They were each presided over by a judge. Another member was a retired government officer. The third and most important member was the military representative who actually swayed the proceedings and whose opinion, invariably in favour of the prosecution, carried the day. The politicians who were so charged were allowed access to the previous files such as were placed before them—but they could not take full notes: in fact they were not given enough time or opportunity to do so. Neither could they be defended by any lawyer. There was no trial if they agreed to the prescribed penalty. Those who contested ran the risk of being called upon to reimburse the state for any monetary loss which their orders were alleged to have caused. Most of the people preferred to agree to the prescribed penalty to avoid the mental and physical harassment of defending themselves, for which they were ill-equipped, at a trial the result of which was a foregone conclusion. A few had the temerity to contest the proceeding, and I believe that only one such person was exculpated after tremendous harassment and expense. The penalty imposed on those who did not contest the charges, or who were found guilty as a result of the contested proceedings, was that they were deprived of the right to contest an election to any representative body until 31 December 1966.

For short, such persons are called EBDOed. On the whole the charges were petty and frivolous and fade into nothingness when compared with the conduct of the existing rules. The same penalty was made applicable to all who had been detained without trial under the Public Safety Acts at any time and for any period by any of the past governments. Some, whose deeds were worthy of condemnation on every other score, were accorded the seal of approval in respect of the Public Safety Acts. A subsequent ordinance relieved persons who had been detained for six weeks or less from the mischief of the penalty in order to enable a particular favourite of the President to contest an election.

An apparently creditable piece of legislation was that known as the land reforms. The claim made by the Martial Law regime that land reform would not have been possible under a democratic regime does not appear to be based on any sound premise. It is true that in West Pakistan it was not expected that in the forthcoming elections the major landholders, who had an enormous—though dwindling—influence over their tenants, would be returned. The Republican government of West Pakistan was leaving no stone unturned to help them. The Jamaat-i-Islami was believed to support the landlords and had denounced expropriation of private property as un-Islamic. The Muslim League was vague concerning the issue. The Awami League in

West Pakistan had a programme of land reform which was very definite and fairly drastic and which appealed to the intelligentsia, the middle class, the petty landholders, the peasants and to agricultural labourers. With every possibility of my party sweeping the elections in East Pakistan, it was highly probable that, with the addition of the few seats which I expected to capture in West Pakistan (I placed my hopes as high as 30%) and aided by some successful candidates of the NAP and progressive members of the Muslim League, we would have been able successfully to launch land reform if the general elections had been held. Land reforms under the Martial Law regime left substantial areas of land with the landlords.

It was well understood for some time past that land reform was inevitable in West Pakistan, and one of the main provisions would be the fixation of the maximum quantity of land which a landlord would be permitted to hold. Many of the major landlords had, with considerable foresight, distributed their lands amongst their relatives and reliable tenants. So, while the property actually remained entire, each individual was, on paper, the owner of lands below the permissible maximum. Refugee landlords had been allotted a maximum of 36,000 units, the area depending upon the productivity of the land. As a rule, 36,000 units represented 500 acres of canal-irrigated land or 1,000 to 1,200 acres of unirrigated land. This was the standard adopted by the Martial Law regime for the land reform. However, over and above this a landlord was permitted to distribute up to 18,000 units to dependents or to hold the land for orchards. Furthermore, lands which had been granted to special landlords for raising cattle and for horse breeding—and these were quite substantial—were exempted.

On the whole, it is estimated that the amount of surplus agricultural lands taken over by the government and capable of cultivation was probably not more than a negligible area of 750,000 acres. The major portion of the lands surrendered by the landlords was barren, uncultivable, useless and undistributable. Actually 2,350,000 acres were resumed. Of this 400,000 acres were unfit for cultivation; 1,200,000 acres were cultivable waste, waterlogged, saline and eroded land and 750,000 acres were cultivable. Of the latter only 420,000 acres were actually cultivated.

The irrigation works which had been commenced during earlier political regimes were now completed and a vast amount of virgin land, mostly in Sindh, was brought under cultivation. Under a law passed in 'the bad old days' no one could be allotted these lands unless he was already entered in the revenue records of Sindh as a landholder. A pliable and amiable feudal landlord of Sindh was induced to distribute small areas of his land to his military friends to get their names entered in the Revenue Records as Sindhi agriculturists. This paved the way for the creation of new absentee landlords who could not hold lands to the maximum extent permissible by the land reform. President Ayub Khan, of district Hazara in West Punjab, became a fortunate owner of such land in Sindh. The very fertile areas were earmarked for high military officers and fortunate members of their families, mostly around the Fouji (army) Sugar Mills. Most of the generals and officers in the lower echelons had lands allotted to them on easy terms according to their position in the Army. Substantial chunks of land were set apart for ex-Army personnel who were formed into cooperative associations and were given facilities and funds for cultivation. Certain other plots were set apart for people from the Pathan tribal areas where there was considerable dearth of cultivable land. A negligible quantity of land was given to some settlers from far away East Pakistan. Later, after three years of hard trying, the latter, finding these lands unproductive and uncultivable, abandoned them. It is understood that they were allotted some better land to which they were not given title; the Sindhis refused to give it to them.

On the whole, the allotments were such that the Sindhis resented that so much of their land should have been handed over to non-Sindhis rather than to landless Sindhis. This resentment found expression in a unanimous demand in Sindh for the breakup of One Unit which had made such exploitation possible.

The problem of the Indus Basin and the dispute with India regarding the rivers irrigating West Pakistan were settled by the Martial Law administration by giving up all claims to the waters of three rivers, namely, the Sutlej, the Beas and the Ravi and by being satisfied with the Indus, the Jhelum and the Chenab, the last being subject to the needs and requirements of Kashmir. To make up for the lost water dams and link canals had to be constructed at considerable cost to feed the irrigation canals hitherto supplied by the three Indian rivers. The World Bank and friendly countries stepped in to pay the cost as India refused to bear any except an unreasonably infinitesimal portion.[19] The cost estimates, based on which monies were promised, were far short of the requirements, and within a year or two it was found that the contributions would have to be more than doubled. This was a matter of life and death for West Pakistan, but it was equally a matter of other people's money. Later, Pakistan was called upon to abandon one of the dams (the Tarbela), which was an essential part of the scheme and without which the scheme would be a continuing financial drain.

It was understood that this agreement was brought about by the good offices of the United States. The general reaction of the people of West Pakistan was that such an agreement could easily have been effected much earlier and on better terms and reflected no credit whatsoever to the Martial Law government. This was actually one step in the policy of the United States to get rid of some of the causes of contention between India and Pakistan. Far from Pakistan benefitting by it, it made further expansion of its irrigation system impossible and, to say the least, placed the existing economy of West Pakistan in considerable jeopardy. Some of the link canals that began to function became waterlogged and threw out of cultivation large areas on both banks. It is feared that other large link canals, for which substantial tracts of cultivated land have already been appropriated and which are under construction, will, when they begin to function, waterlog and throw more lands out of cultivation thus creating new problems of reclamation.

One of the first steps taken by the Martial Law administration was to remove the federal capital from Karachi to Islamabad, an area contiguous to Rawalpindi. This had been endorsed by a clause in the constitution promulgated by the President. Until such time as Islamabad became capable of functioning, Rawalpindi was to serve as the temporary federal capital. The argument in favour of such an unnecessary, wasteful, extravagant and luxury scheme was that Karachi has an enervating climate and that work can be better done in the cool atmosphere of Islamabad. Further, the capital should not be situated where the government could be influenced by public opinion but should be removed far away from the mercantile community to prevent its coordination with the civil administration. None of these arguments were valid other than that the capital would be impervious to popular opinion and would be the centre of unhindered intrigues and capricious policies. Karachi has an equable climate, with all the advantages of the sea, and is hot and uncomfortable for only a month or two at the most, whereas Islamabad, like Rawalpindi, is extremely hot in summer and extremely cold in winter, so much so that employees from East Pakistan find it totally unbearable. Many who were transferred to Rawalpindi without adequate accommodation or clothing suffered grievously and a few are believed to have succumbed to pneumonia in the first winter. The merchants were not prevented from contaminating the officers; they found it much easier to approach them in the cloistered shelter of Rawalpindi, the interim capital.

President Field Marshal Ayub Khan exposed one of the real reasons for the move in a speech made at the opening of the Rawal Dam, constructed at considerable expense to supply drinking water to Islamabad and Rawalpindi. In effect, he said, 'Why am I being blamed for shifting the capital from Karachi to Islamabad; would not one like to have the capital near the place where one had spent thirty-five years of one's experience?' (Rawalpindi is the headquarters of the Pakistan army, with a very large group of officers and men with full military equipment.) This was a sound argument, indeed, to justify the shifting of capitals from place to place according to where the reigning President had spent the best part of his life.

The popular opinion, of course, was that the capital was shifted so that the President might keep a watch on the army and, at the same time, keep the civilian administration and the ministry constantly under threat of army pressure. Even a full-fledged parliamentary democracy with its headquarters at Islamabad contiguous to Rawalpindi can scarcely be expected to function freely, unhindered by army interference or influence or surveillance. It need hardly be said that the removal of the capital was resented throughout Pakistan—even by the intelligentsia of the Punjab, where some support for it could have been expected as it enhanced the prestige of that province. It was a luxury which Pakistan could not afford—an expensive whim at the expense of development and social welfare projects and detrimental to the interests of the country. East Pakistan was uncompromisingly hostile to the move regarding it as a measure to perpetuate military domination.

A commission was appointed, presided over by an eminent retired judge of the Supreme Court, to recommend to the President the contents of the future constitution. The commission examined a large number of people and toured the entire country. I regret that I could not accede to their request to submit my views to them as I was certain that its recommendations would not be accepted, and what would finally be promulgated would be the views of the President himself. After the commission submitted its report it was allegedly studied by a cabinet committee. After this, it was scrutinized by President Ayub Khan and a constitution was published by him on 2 February 1962 which became fully operative on 8 June 1962, the day chosen by the central legislature under the new constitution to meet at Rawalpindi for its first sitting.

Martial Law was lifted. The constitution as promulgated differed widely from the recommendations of the Constitution Commission and was on the lines which the President laid down in several of his speeches, even while the Constitution Commission was trying to assess conditions in the country. The President said: 'We must have indirect elections through the Basic Democrats and not direct elections through adult franchise; even if the Constitution Commission recommends direct elections to the parliament the cabinet would never agree.' Again, 'We must have the presidential form of government, in which the President is really powerful.' The President also interpreted certain provisions in the constitution as 'checks and balances' to prevent parliament from interfering in matters pertaining to the administration.

Even in the law-making sphere, the executive should be allowed considerable freedom to implement the law. In only one matter did he alter his views which, from the very inception, were impractical and gave no consideration to the distance separating East and West Pakistan. He was against the federal system and provincial assemblies, which, he said, would lead to confusion and more disintegration. He accepted a nominal federal structure but gave no powers to the legislatures, central or provincial, and provincial autonomy existed only in name. Most of the important functions were handled by semi-autonomous institutions, controlled, in practice, by the centre. The President took the fullest responsibility for the final product because of his wide experience, extensive knowledge, unerring wisdom—and his contacts with, and deep insight into, the character of the people of Pakistan. Because it did away with parliamentary democracy, he called it the 'presidential' form of government; but, in effect, it reserved to the President the powers of a dictator.

With the introduction of martial law, military tribunals were appointed throughout the country to try cases of corruption, smuggling, black-marketing and other offences. Some of these were newly created by Martial Law regulations; others were brought within the jurisdiction of the tribunals. These tribunals were empowered to impose very drastic penalties. These could be reviewed by a higher Martial Law authority which had the power to reduce the fine and the period of imprisonment. Further review by a still higher Martial Law authority was possible and penalties could be reduced still further or remitted altogether. This appellate or revisionary power was exercised on suitable occasions for suitable reasons. For a time there was a definite curb on anti-social activities, but this was a passing phase and corruption and nepotism reached astronomical dimensions in all echelons of the service. Some persons in authority were credited with misdeeds before which those ascribed to previous politicians paled into insignificance; the worst of the latter category could claim to be angels of purity in comparison to the present strata.

A very important effect of certain of the revolution's reforms was to denigrate lawyers and judges. Lawyers were the pet aversion of the President and he lost no opportunity to abuse them. They were the dregs of the community whose sole interest was in fleecing their clients, delaying and distorting the course of justice and in misleading judges. If he had it in his power he would have eliminated them altogether, and he did bar them from appearing before the Basic Democrat tribunals, summary Martial Law courts, and EBDO tribunals. He showed his distrust for the judiciary by passing ordinance after ordinance which prevented administrative orders from being legally called into question in any court of law, whether it be the High Court or even the Supreme Court. Several amendments were made in the Civil and Criminal Procedure Codes which so tangled the administration of justice that they necessarily had to be revised.

One of the most promising schemes jointly worked out by the Pakistan government and the Ford Foundation was the setting up of pilot schemes in both East and West Pakistan which were called the Pakistan Agricultural Academy.[20] In East Pakistan the headquarters were in Comilla and its director was one of the finest officers in the Civil Service—with administrative ability, imagination and a spirit of understanding. I understand that he was later appointed Vice President of the Planning Commission. The Ford

Foundation helped the Academy in a very big way meeting all capital expenses for tubewells, seed farms, small irrigation projects and similar other works. The scheme was enormously good for the areas where it was being worked, proving that the villager—if he is rightly guided and if matters are properly explained to him and his confidence is secured—understands how best he can improve his standard of living.

The scheme was based on cooperative farming. Not only did agricultural production increase; the members were also able to deposit their savings in their own bank and establish rural industries. After the third year of the five-year project the Academy was in a position to advise what kind of an organization should be set up and the nature of the training which should be imparted to officers responsible for managing the details of village programmes, which, properly handled, can be of enormous benefit to the country. This scheme should be substantially supported; it will pay more dividends than schemes which only serve to make the rich richer and the poor poorer. In the Academy in East Pakistan, apart from a few experts maintained by the Ford Foundation, there were some dedicated Peace Corps volunteers whose knowledge, advice and labour helped enormously to make this scheme a success. There was no question in my mind that agriculture and its development in all its phases should form the most important branch of planning.

DEMORALIZATION OF THE CIVIL SERVICE

The Martial Law or the Revolutionary regime utilized to the full the government machinery to advance its own special interests, and the successor government, hardly different from its predecessor, did the same. It had been a tradition that the Indian Civil Service was not allowed to meddle in politics. But in the course of the struggle for Pakistan, there is little doubt that some Muslim members of the Service did try to influence the Muslim masses to vote for the Muslim League and Pakistan and that some Hindu members of the Service did likewise in favour of the Congress. The tradition received a severe jolt which the importance of the issues appeared to justify in the eyes of the officers. Fortunately, the Muslim officers were few and there were none such in Bengal or in the Muslim minority provinces where there was no such need: hence, the departure from tradition was limited to the area which subsequently became West Pakistan.[21] After Pakistan the Services went back to perform their duties of administration and, indeed, did so with an ardour and selflessness without which the newly created state would have been submerged. Unfortunately, however, the Muslim League ministry that was enthroned in Pakistan—and which had already tossed out many provincial ministries in West Pakistan to further its own ends—utilized the

government officials and machinery in the provincial elections that were held
between 1951 and 1953. After the elections the Services again went back to
their duties, but the Martial Law regime used them so mercilessly and
demoralized them so utterly that it will take an age before they can be purged
from the contamination. Even the officers of East Pakistan, who had, but for
a few well-known, venal exceptions, kept themselves aloof from party
politics, were impressed to advance the political interests of the Revolutionary
regime to the detriment of their legitimate administrative duties.

All the officers throughout the country conducted propaganda on behalf
of the Revolution, and the district officers and their subordinates had to
address meeting after meeting in which their main theme was abusing
previous regimes and the politicians and the leaders of the people. In the
worst days of their demoralization, their association with politics had never
been so close and thick as this, and no political regime would have dared to
use them in the above manner. They were utilized to pass resolutions in
various tiers of the Basic Democracy to support the policies of the
government as if they had popular acclaim behind them. They generally
associated themselves with the politics of the new regime rather than attend
to their own duties. Indeed, the officers were hardly at their posts and were
busy most of the time in furthering the interests of the Revolutionary regime
with the result that the district administration, so necessary for the welfare
of the country, went to pieces.

For the first time also Governors, who by tradition had hitherto remained
neutral and non-political, entered the political arena and that, too, with a
vengeance. The close liaison between the Governor of West Pakistan and the
President and the various violent or coercive repressive measures that were
taken to support the cause of the President were no secret. East Pakistan has
also had its share. The first Governor to be appointed after the Revolution
was former Inspector General of Police, Zakir Hussain, who discharged his
duties of repression with diligence and fervour. He had to make way for
General Azam Khan and was compensated by being promoted as Minister
of Interior. General Azam Khan, as a fairly successful Minister of Refugees,
had earned some popularity for himself in West Pakistan which the President
could not tolerate. He was appointed Governor of East Pakistan in spite of
his protests. General Azam Khan became a controversial figure. His first
speeches in East Pakistan had the threatening undercurrent of martial law
but, stung by the hapless condition of the people of East Pakistan—their
poverty, their distress, their fortitude in the midst of calamities and the
manner in which they had been neglected—he acted with considerable energy
and vehemence. He addressed several meetings and made several promises.
Unfortunately, he was not able to fulfill those promises, because he was not

backed by the central government and adequate funds were not placed in his hands.

Although there was massive favourable propaganda at the time that General Azam Khan became very popular with the masses in East Pakistan, it was true only to a limited extent. Nobody ever doubted his honesty and sincerity and his desire to help the people. But there were doubts regarding his capacity and his ability when the people found that he too easily made promises which he could not keep. However, after my arrest and detention on 30 January 1962 in Karachi, the pendulum swung definitely in his favour. The agitation for my release, particularly among the students and the younger generation, developed into insulting and mildly violent demonstrations when the President visited Dhaka soon after my arrest. It is believed that General Azam Khan objected to my arrest, which the President and the Minister of Interior had decided upon among themselves, as he felt that he should have been consulted as governor of the province most affected. It is further believed that he refused to order firing on the students, although he was commanded to do so, or to take punitive action against them. He was removed from office and received, at the time of leaving East Pakistan, the greatest ovation that any person from West Pakistan, official or otherwise, had ever received.

After General Azam Khan had been removed, G.M. Faruque was appointed Governor. Faruque had a brilliant record of service in the field of development as the head of the Pakistan Industrial Development Corporation (PIDC) and the Water and Power Development Authority (WAPDA). As Governor he immediately addressed himself to the task of development in East Pakistan. He discovered what we had known all along: that the development of East Pakistan had been sorely neglected. But all his plans regarding development of roads, river and railway communications; development of power stations and electrical energy; development of large and small industries and development of agriculture, forestry and fisheries needed financial support which was not forthcoming.

Demonstrations of students were held in Dhaka and throughout East Pakistan against the educational reforms of the military regime which, ignoring the economic condition of the people, imposed burdens which they were unable to bear. Although these demonstrations were peaceful something seemed to have gone wrong somewhere and the East Pakistan Rifles and the armed police were called out to obstruct the students. Unfortunately, there were collisions and some students were killed.

A very serious situation was developing which could only be met either by wise statesmanship or by wholesale repression. Ghulam Faruque chose the first course and obtained by telephone the sanction of the President who was at that time in London. Later he was taken to task for not resorting to repression. But the real reason for his forced resignation was that he refused to associate himself and his office with the political party which the President had created, viz. the Muslim League (Convention) and which the President wanted in every manner possible, open or covert, fair or foul, to be supported by the Governor, who was expected to tour the province on its behalf. Faruque refused to do so and he had to submit his resignation.

Abdul Monem Khan, a central minister, was appointed Governor. After that the Governor appeared to have no work other than to hold meetings, canvass for the political party of the President and organize it with the help of government servants. Also, the ministers who had been appointed by the President and were not responsible to the legislature were mainly employed in boosting the President, holding meetings all over the country, canvassing for the presidential party (Muslim League Convention), watching that government officers also carried on political propaganda utilizing all paraphernalia and facilities of the government. They also canvassed for the presidential party candidate during the by-elections to the central and provincial legislatures by bringing pressure to bear on Basic Democrat voters. The ministers did little administrative work; they were not permitted to interfere with orders of the secretaries and were, in fact, public relations officers of the President.

ASTRONOMICAL WASTE OF PUBLIC FUNDS

Never before had so much public money been spent by any regime on propaganda in its own defence or for its own publicity.

Soon after the Revolution, the President undertook a propaganda tour in East and West Pakistan on special trains which were designated, seriously, 'Pak Jamhooriat' (Pakistan democracy, or 'holy' democracy, if the work 'Pak' is not meant to be an abbreviation of Pakistan). On this tour, apart from his entourage, he was accompanied by journalists, indigenous and foreign, who were right royally entertained. The important ones who broadcast to the world the wonderful popularity of the Martial Law regime were loaded with presents. The further expense for the spate of literature produced by the Bureau of National Reconstruction to justify and extol the Second 'Glorious' Revolution, for subvention to newspapers or to pay advertisement charges to foreign newspapers to publish glowing accounts of the Revolutionary regime, reached fantastic proportions. The radio was pressed into service; the country was flooded with speakers and singers. Film and dramatic groups roamed the country, and all cinemas were compelled to exhibit the propaganda films of government—all this at the cost of the public exchequer.

If we now take into account the pay of the government officials of the permanent service who put aside their administrative work to devote themselves to carrying on propaganda in favour of the government in power, and the cost involved in the tours of and the time spent by the President, the governors and the hordes of ministers and parliamentary secretaries paid from public revenues, one perhaps will be able to conceive of the astronomical waste of public funds. No political party would have dared to spend for its own propaganda an infinitesimal fraction of the money which the Martial Law regime spent to popularize itself or to support the President and his political party.

AYUB'S ISLAMIZATION PROGRAMME QUESTIONED

While in the beginning the Revolutionary regime was against the exploitation of Islam for political purposes, the President, in a desperate endeavour to capture the popular imagination and secure some support, started laying stress on Islam as a way of life and exhorting people to abide by its eternal principles (Vaguely it is true, without reference to its content or concepts but enough to appeal to religious sentiments which only too easily give way to fanaticism.). There was a period when there was hardly any presidential speech in which he did not exploit Islam. One is led to recall that one of the first acts of the Revolutionary regime was to change the name of the country from the 'Islamic Republic of Pakistan' of the constitution of 1956 to 'Pakistan'. But this mood could not override the temptation to acquire easy popularity. He apparently thought it would be enough if, in the course of his speeches, he repeatedly made reference to the word 'Islam' or the Islamic way of life, or the Islamic spirit. He little realized that one day he would not be able to stem the flood he was releasing and would himself have to call upon others who were taking a leaf out of his own book.

In his constitution of 1962 he attempted to make a compromise. This constitution was largely plagiarized from the constitution of 1956 except in the most essential matter: that whereas the latter is based on the parliamentary system, that of 1962 was a pseudo-presidential form and was in essence an irresponsible dictatorship. The constitution of 1956 had made five references to the Quran and Sunnah as the basis of Islam; that of 1962 deleted all these references. In the constitution of 1956 a body was visualized that would be set up within a year to recommend how the existing laws could be brought into conformity with the injunctions of the Quran and Sunnah. Such a body was actually set up. It consisted of *ulema* (scholars or priests trained in traditional Muslim religion) and laymen and was presided over by a retired judge of the Supreme Court. The report to which objection was taken by the principal *alim* member (a person learned in religious lore) was never published. It has been kept secret and has been shelved.

In the 1962 constitution provision was made for an Advisory Council of Islamic Ideology (ACII) to advise the legislature when anyone objected to a projected piece of legislation on religious grounds or whether it disregards, violates or is otherwise not in accord with the Principles of Law Making (non-justiciable fundamental rights) or did not offend the injunctions of Islam. He presumably thought that people would accept this compromise. But once having started to exploit Islam, he found it difficult to resist the extreme demands of those who could speak on the subject with greater authority. He later declared that he was prepared to restore the previous name and all the deleted reference to the Quran and Sunnah, to refer all proposals for legislation to the ACII and ask them to revise all existing laws to conform to the 'Islamic spirit'.

I was left wondering how this could be practical, but so he is alleged to have spoken at a meeting reported in the *Pakistan Times* on 1 May 1963. The speech was worth a perusal on this score. After referring to India and the arms buildup—and between vitriolic and abusive references to politicians—he referred to four ideals, the first being that 'we must live as Muslims which we can only do if we make full use of our intelligence.' (The other three were equally naive and hardly worth mentioning.) He refuted the charge that Islam was being tampered with, and said, 'The present setup is motivated, governed and inspired by Islam only. We are paying more and more attention toward recreating the true Islamic spirit, which (so he defines Islam) is that of harmony, concord and sweetness.' 'In the field of legislation all laws have to be referred to the ACII before their enactment. The existing laws of the country are also being submitted to the Advisory Council for bringing them in conformity with the spirit of Islam'—whatever this may mean. Of course, neither was done. Can political exploitation of Islam go further? This furnished one more instance of how he resiled from the principles of the 'Glorious' Revolution.

But the harvest was not yet over. The question of what is or is not Islamic can be very controversial, and it is difficult to discover whose decision or interpretation was to be considered final. The constitution visualized that:

- the Islamic Research Institute, already functioning, would collect all data and submit its view to the ACII;
- this Council's opinion may differ and shall send its own views to the legislature;
- the legislature in its turn might have its own views on the subject and could override the view of the Council and legislate accordingly;
- the President who is entitled to differ may do so and have his own view. According to the Political Parties Act passed in July 1962, no political

party whose objectives were in conflict with Islamic ideology would be allowed to function;

- this vital Islamic question was to be decided by the Supreme Court; and
- the *ulema*, with their own view, set up their own body which, they claimed, must be the final authority and a guide to the people.

Later, the nation had to reap the whirlwind. This involvement with Islam brought controversial doctrines to the fore. Two clashes between important schools of thought among the Sunni *ulemas* and their followers, viz. the *Deobandi* (from the madrasahs of Deoband in India), and the *Brelvi* (or Bareilly), ended in several murders. The smouldering fires between the Shiahs and the Sunnis once again burst into flame and led to serious clashes marked with the utmost savagery in a remote village in Sindh and in the sophisticated capital city of Lahore. Once fanaticism had been encouraged — and for this the President must be held responsible — no one knew what turn it would take. The old controversy between Ahmadis (Qadianis) and the others could easily have been raked up. Already one of the Moulvis, who had, through sheer flattery and opportunism, worked his way into the confidence of the President and was a member of the ACII, was demanding that separate electorates must once again be restored as a cardinal tenet of Islam and the Minister of Law echoed it as a matter which still was not decided. The end was not in sight, although the Revolution declared itself unequivocally in favour of joint electorate, and all the elections held by it such as the elections of Basic Democrats, of the President and of members of all the legislatures were on that basis.

AMERICAN AID IGNORES EAST PAKISTAN

As was to be expected, the Revolutionary regime and the factual military dictatorship suppressed all of the various liberties and freedoms associated with democracy. All political parties were banned, meetings and speeches were forbidden, labour movements were strictly controlled and strikes were declared illegal, criticism of the government was penalized with 14 years rigorous imprisonment and the press was regimented. The Bureau of National Reconstruction was extremely active in distributing handouts which alone the press were permitted to publish. The Chief Secretary of the East Pakistan government established an innovation of periodical meetings with the press and softened the blow of repression by persuasion.

The only paper that had the courage occasionally to register a mild dissertation, which adversely reflected on aspects of the administration, was a Bengal daily called the *Ittefaq*, issued in Dhaka, with a growing circulation.

Its editor, Tofazzal Hossain (Manik Mia), stood out as one of the best political thinkers in East Pakistan and exercised tremendous influence not only through his writings but also through his personality. At first, before I became Prime Minister, he was severely antagonistic to the United States. Later, however, he developed a better sense of proportion and, although critical of the United States in many of its world policies—to which greater publicity was given to distorted versions than to actual facts—he generally appreciated the assistance which Pakistan received and the goodwill of the American people. What further inclined him towards the Western democracies was his growing antagonism and dread—and one may even put it as high as hatred—of communism which he considered incompatible with the freedoms associated with the concept of democracy. His attitude in the end appeared to be that if communism is the alternative, let us have the Americans and Western democracy. Let us at the same time, however, not slavishly applaud everything American.

When the United States helps the government of a country to suppress democracy, whether it is aware of it or not, then where do we go? This is a problem which confronts popular and democratic movements in several countries, and the answer to it appears to have eluded everyone, including the United States. How far can the theory go that the United States, by its economic and military aid, helps the people of a country and not the government? The aid has to be given to and through the government which is in power. The United States can, at best, advise the government as how the aid is to be spent and that only in general terms. Advice may be rejected; anything more, such as conditions of aid, will be tantamount to interfering with the internal administration of the country and an encroachment on its sovereignty.

The United States is helpless if the aid helps to boost the government and suppress national, popular, and democratic forces. Sometimes the United States dare not stop the aid, however oppressive the government may be (provided the government is anti-communist, neutral, or not actually communist; exceptions are, of course, those governments which are pro-communist or communist), lest it be charged with giving aid with political strings and lest the stoppage of aid throws the country into the lap of communism. The aid, therefore, can well be utilized for purposes for which it was not meant. It can even be wasted. How far this practice is justified for a country that claims to be the shadow-bearer of democracy is the problem. It is not appreciated wholly by the national element which considers that the United States should insist, as a condition of aid, that democracy be restored and that it should not bolster personal and oppressive regimes—although, of course, it should not stop aid. If the United States does not do so it is helping very directly the dictatorship and is helping to suppress democratic elements.

Manik Mia resented strongly—and in this, undoubtedly, he was voicing the opinion of East Pakistan—that American aid was being given to the central government with the fullest knowledge that it was being almost exclusively utilized for West Pakistan and that East Pakistan was being ignored by the United States. On one occasion, American Ambassador McConaughy, while speaking to some pressmen in East Pakistan, seemed to indicate that the United States would be glad to assist East Pakistan's development. This was objected to at once by the West Pakistan papers, with a unanimity which was presumably guided by the secret hand of the central authorities, on the grounds that it was no business of the United States to see how its aid was spent and that the speech of the ambassador was tantamount to interference in the internal affairs of Pakistan. Strangely enough, the secretary of the NAP in East Pakistan, Mahmud Ali, also came out with a similar criticism, presumably because he thought it was a good opportunity to fulminate against the United States and stand out at the same time as a shining patriot interested in the integrity of Pakistan, its honour and independence. Manik Mia, however, boldly supported the American ambassador, and the views which he expressed were adopted by the Bar Library (the Lawyers' Association) of the Dhaka High Court and throughout the province. Some time later Manik Mia was prosecuted by the Martial Law regime for alleged criticism of the administrative policies of the regime, but, owing to the ineptitude of the prosecuting authorities, he was acquitted.

EAST PAKISTAN PRESS STRANGULATED

But this did not satisfy the government. Manik Mia had been demanding for a considerable time that the press in East Pakistan should be treated the same as the press in West Pakistan in the matter of government advertisements which should be distributed to the papers according to their circulation. He objected to the policy followed by the Martial Law regime which patronized papers that supported the government, although their circulation was much less than that of the *Ittefaq* and, in some cases, practically negligible, by giving them government advertisements in large doses. Further, rates given to the press in East Pakistan were ridiculously low. As an example, whereas Rs23 per inch were given to the English daily *Dawn* and Rs16 per inch to the Urdu daily *Jang*, both of West Pakistan, only Rs4.50 per inch was given to *Ittefaq*. After a great deal of difficulty he managed to get the rate increased slightly—perhaps to about Rs6 per inch which would have, to some extent, enabled the papers in East Pakistan to pay the working journalists the higher wages which government had fixed by ordinance. It would almost appear that this measure was taken to close down East Pakistan papers, for, much as they would have liked to pay the higher wages, they were unable to discharge the burden without sufficient advertisements and had to close down or lower their standards.

But while on the one hand the government increased the rate, it ordered on the other that the four main papers of East Pakistan, namely, *The Ittefaq* (with a circulation of 30,000 and increasing daily), *The Sangbad, The Pakistan Observer* and another paper which had the temerity to differ from government in some of its policies, should be deprived of all advertisements by government or government-controlled authorities. Advertisements were given to a new government (Muslim League Convention) paper, *The Jehal*, and to pro-government papers like *The Azad, The Morning News* and *The Eastern Examiner*, the last belonging to the Minister of Information with a nominal circulation of 200. The regulations stopping advertisements appear to have been issued by the President himself before the constitution of 1962 was in force; but the actual order was issued by the Ministry of Information after ministers had been appointed, though this was denied by the latter.

This extremely unjust, perverse and discriminatory order was justified by the President with the remark that surely government should distribute patronage to those whom it could trust, and it did not trust the papers which criticized it. Consequently, the government was justified in not contracting business with them—as they were not his trusted agents—and in distributing government advertisements to those that supported him. Some would call this policy a sheer case of bribery and corruption, having nothing whatsoever to do with the purpose for which advertisements are given by clients to newspapers, namely, to inform the public. Such open declaration of patronage cannot but result in the demoralization of the press and its subservience to government. Incidentally, Manik Mia promoted an English views weekly called the *Dhaka Times* which contained fairly well-documented articles on the conditions in East Pakistan.

A FACADE OF DEMOCRACY

I now come to a very important measure introduced by the President. This was highly controversial, propagated throughout the world by paid agencies as a measure of profound wisdom and unrivalled utility for a benighted and errant country like Pakistan—applicable to people who needed to be guided and controlled while maintaining a facade of democracy—which may have misled well-intentioned democratic countries. I refer to the system of Basic Democracy on which the President laid great stress and which he considered to be an inspired scheme which for the first time would enable the masses to be associated with policy and administration so much so that they, themselves, might become the government.

The originator of this system is believed to have been Brigadier F.R. Khan, the first Director of the Bureau of National Reconstruction, who was probably responsible for all the constructive steps which were taken under President Ayub Khan and who inspired his policies. When Brigadier Khan became influential he had to be demoted and was ultimately removed from service. His fall was precipitated by some charges which he had brought against one of the Field Marshal's favourite ministers whom he considered unworthy of his high office.

The system of Basic Democracy was meant to serve a dual purpose: to put up a facade of democracy and thus appease friendly foreign powers that baulked at military dictatorships, and, at the same time, provide the President with a ready-made party of non-officials who might be useful to him in his political manoeuvres to perpetuate his power but who would at the same time have no political label.

The system seems to have been inspired by the pattern of the lowest form of rural self-governing institutions in Bengal known as union boards. In Bengal, a number of villages were grouped into a union, the average number of such villages per union being about fifteen and the average population about 12,000. Each union was divided into three wards and each ward elected two persons as a plural constituency. These six members, with the addition of three nominated by government, formed the Union Board which elected its own chairman. The nominated members, instead of being helpful, acted as government agents, and the Awami League government of Ataur Rahman Khan decided to do away with the system of nominations. Nine members were now elected from the three wards, and the chairman and the vice-chairman of the Union Board were elected directly by all voters of the union, thus making a board of eleven members, all elected.

The Union Board had certain local functions such as maintenance of the rural police known as *chowkidars,* village communications, minor development works and assistance to village educational institutions. The income from the taxes levied by them was usually insufficient to meet these requirements, but, ultimately, the lid was taken off the maximum tax they could impose. The chairman of the Union Board was generally a person who commanded the confidence of the people, though not necessarily so. In West Pakistan there does not seem to have been any such elected rural institution. There were certain village *panchayats* but these were social institutions rather than self-governing bodies.

Under the system of Basic Democracies a unit was created out of a collection of villages with a population of 1,500 people in East Pakistan and 1,000 in West Pakistan which was empowered to elect one representative. A combination of ten such units constituted a union council. Five persons were nominated by government to each of these councils. These fifteen persons elected their own chairman. There was a similar system for the cities; the combination of units was called a union committee. This was the lowest tier of Basic Democracy.

Theoretically, there were 4,000 such councils and committees and, hence, 40,000 elected Basic Democrats in each province. As a matter of fact, however, the constituencies were delimited in a haphazard manner and the figures are an approximation.

The tier above the Union Council and the Union Committee was a Thana (police station) Council in East Pakistan and Tehsil (subdivision) Council in West Pakistan; members were all the elected chairmen of union councils and union committees within its area and an equal number of persons nominated by government. The subdivisional or tehsil officer was chairman. They had no specific functions and were solely for supervisory or control purposes. The tier above it, namely, the third tier, was the District Council, presided over by the District Officer, known as the Deputy Commissioner. This council was composed of an equal number of officials and non-officials, all of whom were nominated by government. One-fourth of them were re-elected chairmen of the lowest tier. Above this was the Division Council—or the fourth tier—with a similar composition of officials and non-officials, wholly nominated by government, with powers of control but no function. At the apex was the Provincial Development Advisory Council, presided over by the Governor of the province. Of course, all were nominated; half were official and half nominated non-official. One-sixth of the total membership was from re-elected chairmen.

The system was announced when the people were psychologically benumbed by the promulgation of Martial Law, and the election of Basic Democrats—as the elected members of the union councils and committees were called—was held at a time when the local officers were all-powerful and domineering as a result of Martial Law and were unrestrained by public opinion. The old electoral rolls were utilized, but it was announced that the appropriate local officer had the discretion to delete the name of any voter from the list or reject the candidature of any person considered undesirable on account of his previous political affiliation or activities. Such a person could be deprived of his membership even after election. A long list of the grounds of disqualification and removal was published. Political parties had been outlawed; no one could even refer to them, except, of course, to abuse and revile them. No one who was not on the voter list of a constituency could stand for that constituency; hence, there could be no challenge from outside the area to a local boss.

These humiliating conditions—along with Martial Law in full and oppressive operation—prevented persons with self-respect from offering themselves for election, and, although no doubt some people of position and respectability did offer themselves and were elected, the majority of those elected were persons who could never have dreamt of being successful in any fair and free election. Many of them had a record of previous convictions or were under the surveillance of the police of dangerous characters or were police agents and informers. In many constituencies there were no candidates. In many, the local officers were hard put to find people to stand, and the elections were uncontested; in others where there was a contest hardly any votes were cast and people had to be driven to the polls. But obviously also, with such a limited number of voters to approach some constituencies had a plethora of candidates. Persons elected under such conditions could hardly be considered to be representatives of the people; the most that could be expected is that they would dutifully carry out the injunctions of the local officers and support the President.

Apart, however, from the special features of the election, the system of such small narrow constituencies could not be expected to return persons of position and respectability who generally commanded influence over a large area. Such limited constituency tended to return the local rough or bully, who, by virtue of his antecedents, is always under the influence of the police. In West Pakistan such people were assisted by tribal, sectarian, caste, family or feudal connections. The system, instead of being an improvement on the Union Board of Bengal as a representative institution, was definitely a retrograde measure, further vitiated by the addition of nominated members.

The scheme was a logical outcome of the political theory of the Martial Law revolution, namely, distrust of the people and contempt for their intelligence, their integrity and their capacity to think rationally. This was explained fully and brutally in a small pamphlet issued by government. The objective clearly was to create a handpicked group of people who would be pampered, flattered, bribed and corrupted, bullied and intimidated by government officials as the occasion required who would be ready at hand to support every move of government and yet could be presented to the world as true representatives of the people; they would, in due time, form the electoral body for the legislature, when they would be set up and, for the President, when he chose to offer himself for election.

The intelligentsia disfranchised. The system had the further merit of depriving the educated section of the people from the right to vote at general elections for the legislature. As the process of education—not in the sense of literacy, according to this valuable treatise, but in the sense of creating a national outlook and consciousness which did not exist—would take a long time, which the President put at between 20 and 25 years, the system would be a permanent feature of Pakistan. And, thus, it was incorporated in the constitution promulgated by the President in 1962. The country was put back to 1882, and the years of political education, representative institutions, struggles and achievements since then may be considered as if they had never been.

The theory underlying the scheme was that whereas a Pakistan villager could understand the interests of his village, he was incapable of the concept that his country too required good management; in so many words, 'he has no national consciousness or awareness.' Hence, intensive education to make him aware of his self-interest before elections could be held on a national basis was necessary; otherwise, if he had to choose between individuals, whose merits and demerits were unknown to him, there would be a competition between candidates in the employment of dishonest methods. Probably there had never been in any country such a scathing denunciation of its own people by its rulers and such utter ignorance and want of understanding. Obviously the originators of Martial Law chose to ignore the fact—for it cannot be imagined that they were not aware of it—that elections through political parties are the best means of educating the people, for these parties have to justify their existence on principles and programmes and must be careful in selecting candidates under pain of losing the support and the votes of the electors if undesirable persons are nominated. Indeed, the competition in dishonesty is most likely to occur in the absence of political parties; this was amply proved and recognized when elections under the constitution of 1962 were held. There was no justification whatsoever for this insult to the people of Pakistan.

In East Pakistan the people had shown an advanced degree of political consciousness and judgement which had been demonstrated in election after election. In West Pakistan the feudal aristocracy and the needs of the British to recruit its Indian army from that region had no doubt prevented the development of a sound political consciousness.[22] But the general ignorance was being rapidly dissipated under the stress of the propaganda conducted by rival political parties, and the provincial elections held after the partition had proved that the people had the capacity to judge between rival candidates and parties if the government left them alone. After all, it is the self-same people, later condemned as being incapable of looking beyond the confines of their village, who helped to create Pakistan with an awakened political consciousness.

A general cry for abolition. The scheme claimed to transfer power to the people, the executive officers acting merely as agents of the various tiers or as officers-in-council. Under the scheme union councils and committees were to be entrusted with functions under the following categories: administrative or municipal, judicial, police, development and, above all, national reconstruction, the last term being so vague in connotation as capable of being debased to exploitation. After their creation, these bodies seem to have been neglected until the time approached for them to be exploited. After due flattery and subtle suggestions that they, in fact, were the government, they were vested with powers of taxation under twenty-nine different heads. The chairmen were to assist revenue officials in the collection of taxes, assist the administration and carry out orders given to them. They were charged to prepare a fairly heavy budget, to tax the people in various ways and use the money so obtained for development purposes. The budget had to be sanctioned by the executive officer, usually the tehsil or the subdivisional officer, who would return it if he was of the opinion that sufficient taxes had not been levied.

Obviously the system was no plain sailing for the union committees. The conditions of the rural people, particularly in East Pakistan, were such that they were not capable of standing the strain of further taxation; in fact their condition was so wretched that they had hardly enough to eat or to clothe themselves, let alone look after their health or the education of their children. Taxes, therefore, though levied, could not be collected, and where collected they made the institutions so unpopular that there was a general cry for the abolition of the system which did no good to anybody other than the President and, generally speaking, the chairmen. It had succeeded neither in setting up honest representatives nor in associating them with the administration of the government.

Malversation of development funds. The chairman of the Union Council received the proceeds of the taxes which he was expected to spend on schemes sanctioned by the executive officer. The general opinion was that the money found its way into his pocket in various ways. He was in charge of the execution of development works and was given the privilege of certifying the expenses without submitting vouchers or audit; more often than not the wealth of the chairman increased substantially and mysteriously. This placed him and his members at the mercy of the officials. This was amply demonstrated in some by-elections to the legislature when chairmen were forced to vote for the government candidates (of the President's party) on pain of being prosecuted for malversation of development funds, so amply placed at their disposal, if they dared to do otherwise. Of course, apart from this, the local officials had such power and influence over them that it was only the brave that could withstand their pressure; but there were some brave men amongst them, which gave some hope, however feeble, for the future emancipation of the country. There were, no doubt, cases where these committees were able to do valuable work, particularly when their self-help projects were supported by substantial grants on a scale which no previous government could have conceived for want of resources and which was rendered possible by the massive aid given by the United States to the Martial Law regime and its successor dictatorship.

Apart from the power of taxation, the chairmen had been given other powers which contributed to their wealth. Power under Family Laws Ordinance to register and certify marriages and divorces and reconcile parties, power to try civil and criminal cases of limited jurisdiction (against the recommendations of the Law Commission) and power to issue nationality certificates to persons proposing to transfer property, a power obviously susceptible to considerable abuse.

During John Bell's tenure of office as head of the United States International Cooperation Agency (ICA), a programme for village aid had been planned and village communities profited greatly by the scheme. Many social service workers in various parts of East Pakistan even approached me to see that the village aid programme was extended to their area and promised to implement it to the satisfaction of the ICA. For some reasons unknown, the ICA—which later became the United States Agency for International Development (USAID)—decided to abandon the scheme which lost its identity, its purpose and its usefulness. Under this scheme lavish grants were made to district councils for distribution to the primary tiers in rural development.

Condemned beyond reprieve. After being put in a proper frame of mind, the elected section of the Basic Democrats of the lowest tier were called upon to cast their votes for or against the President, when martial law was in full swing and when anyone who criticized the government was liable to rigorous imprisonment for 14 years. The President was the only living candidate, the other candidate being a black box to receive negative votes. Surprisingly enough, a fair proportion of votes, in both provinces—more in East Pakistan than in West Pakistan—were cast against him, although under the circumstances it would not have caused any comment had he received 99.99 per cent of the vote. The President laid down that voting in his favour would carry the following implications:

- Confidence in him;
- Conferment on him of the power to frame a new constitution for the country according to his liking;
- Continuance as President without any further election for a period which he would himself determine in his own discretion for himself after the promulgation of the constitution.

Although the Constitution Commission had suggested that elections to the legislature should be direct, based on adult franchise and joint electorate, the President in his wisdom ordained, as everyone knew he would, that the Basic

Democrats would form the electoral body. That is to say, that while he accepted the principle of joint electorate, he discarded that of direct election. Accordingly, after the publication of the constitution in February 1962, the Basic Democrats were further utilized to vote for members of the central and provincial legislatures. The average number of voters on the electoral rolls for one seat in the central legislature was 500 and in the provincial legislatures, 250. In some constituencies there were as many as 30 candidates who hoped to be successful if they could get together the few votes of their immediate friends. This was hailed by the regimented press as a great victory for democracy. The President, till then a staunch opponent of political parties, all of which had been banned, forbade candidates from taking their stand on political affiliations and exhorted the Basic Democrats to vote honestly for the candidate they considered best fitted to represent them. No candidate was allowed to address a meeting on his own. The Basic Democrats of a constituency were collected together by the authorities, and the candidates were called upon to address them and answer questions. Some flattered the Basic Democrats as the backbone of the country and true representatives of the people, promising to fight for the continuance of the system; others insisted on Islam and a Islamic constitution; others boldly stated that if they were elected they would champion the cause of democracy.

These principles, however, had little to do with the actual elections, especially in the feudal areas and in the cities of West Pakistan where there had sprung up a new class of extremely wealthy industrialists and permit holders. The extent of corruption to which the Basic Democrats lent themselves was unprecedented. It was a natural consequence of the small number of voters on the electoral roll and condemned beyond reprieve the Basic Democrats system as an electorate. The elections were held while I was in detention under the Public Safety Act.

In East Pakistan, some erstwhile members of the defunct Awami League, who could have refused to do so as a protest against my detention, did stand; a number were returned thus forming the nucleus of an opposition party in the National Assembly which the President had not visualized. Compared to the corruption in West Pakistan, that in East Pakistan was negligible, one of the obvious reasons being that the candidates did not have the resources. Except in the tribal areas of West Pakistan, the officials as a rule did not press for any candidate. Later in the National Assembly the opposition party grew in numbers until the difference between the government party and the opposition party was almost nominal, a state of affairs which the President had never conceived possible when he promulgated the constitution.

DISPARITY IN CAPITAL DEVELOPMENT

The First Five-year Plan was to terminate in 1960 and the Planning Commission set to work on the Second Five-year Plan. Each of the provinces had its own planning commission and sent up schemes for the consideration of the centre. In East Pakistan the Planning Commission was assisted by experts provided by the United Nations, Harvard University and the Ford Foundation, and their cooperation with local officers was extremely fruitful. But the final planning had to be made by the centre and this is where the snag came in. Unfortunately for East Pakistan, the most important departments of the central government were in the hands of West Pakistan civilian officers such as the Planning Commission itself, the Finance Department, the Industries Department, the Commerce Department and the various financing institutions, e.g. the Pakistan Industrial Credit and Investment Corporation (PICIC), the Pakistan Industrial Finance Corporation (PIFCO), agricultural credit institutions and banks.

There had been phenomenal growth of industrial concerns in West Pakistan which had been assisted by liberal allowances for depreciation and tax holidays. Licenses for establishing industries were freely given. Textile mills in particular made fabulous profits. It is estimated that these made sufficient profits in a year or 18 months to pay off the entire capital cost at the obvious expense of the consumer. Foreign exchange for the licenses and permits was provided by government at the official rate of exchange—in the free international market the value of the Pakistani rupee was much lower; the fortunate recipients, thus, also received a subsidy of at least 50 per cent. Similarly, liberal licenses were given to commercial magnates to import consumer goods, machinery, and spares. Thus, the foundations were laid in West Pakistan for a capacity for capital development.

Unhappily the industrialists and importers of East Pakistan were not so well treated and licenses were refused on the slightest pretext. The government operated on the theory that Pakistan, although divided, had only one economy. Foreign exchange was pooled and permission to set up an industry in East Pakistan, which had already been set up in the West, was refused. East Pakistan had to be content with setting up jute mills, which could not be set up in West Pakistan; two paper mills which could utilize the local bamboos and soft wood trees for pulp; a sugar mill; a fertilizer factory; and with little else. East Pakistan, thus, had to buy goods produced in West Pakistan at prices higher than if it had imported the goods. The theory of one economy and no parallel industries and niggardly and restricted licenses put an effective stop to the growth of industry and the capacity for capital formation in East Pakistan.

During the one year I was in office we tried to rectify this discrimination to some extent though vehemently opposed by the bureaucratic elements, and we divided the foreign exchange available for industries between Karachi, which received 15 per cent, and West Pakistan and East Pakistan which divided the balance of 85 per cent equally and left it to the provinces to issue licenses. We disproved the theory that capital was shy in East Pakistan as applicants began to pour in; licenses were snapped up and industries were quickly established. The policy was abandoned after I left and, for years thereafter, hardly any new licenses were issued.

East Pakistan suffered from another disability, namely, that it could not utilize funds allotted to it for development within the financial year thus allowing it to lapse. East Pakistan pointed out time and again that it received its allotment at a late stage in the financial year which ended on 31 March, and, the dry season being short, it was impossible for it to utilize the money unless it came well in advance. It pleaded that it be allowed to change its financial year so as to end on 30 June. No attention was paid to its pleadings and the central government held that East Pakistan was incapable of spending funds for development and had no absorbing capacity. As a result, the theory of parity, which was supposed to run through the entire gamut of governmental activities according to the constitution, was practically a dead letter.

Allotments outside the plan for West Pakistan. In its first draft of the Second Five-year Plan the central Planning Commission set apart a little over Rs4,000 million for East Pakistan and Rs9,000 million for West Pakistan. The allocation by the Planning Commission was deeply resented by the planners of East Pakistan who had formulated schemes which could have absorbed more than Rs9,000 million. The United Nations experts protested to the Planning Commission, and also pointed out that politically it would be very unwise to have such a large difference. They also impressed upon the Planning Commission to take courage and plan the Second Five-year Plan on a grander scale and boldly ask for more aid. As a result of this protest and advice, the Planning Commission increased the allotment to East Pakistan to about Rs8,600 million and West Pakistan to about Rs10,000 million, making it clear at the same time that it did not expect that East Pakistan would be able to spend the money as it did not have sufficient absorbing capacity. Thus a large sum of money was allotted to East Pakistan for development. But the comparative parity of allotment in the Second Five-year Plan was completely upset by allotments outside the Plan. Some countries agreed to give loans to Pakistan for establishment of industries, the benefit of which mostly went to West Pakistan. Apart from this, the Indus Basin scheme, with its estimated expenditure of US$1,800 million, was also outside the Plan. Then there were further expenditures outside the plan which may have run into US$1,000 million for reclaiming waterlogged and saline lands in West Pakistan which were going out of cultivation.

There can be no doubt that both the Indus Basin scheme and the scheme to reclaim waterlogged lands were essential for the economy of West Pakistan; nobody can begrudge that essential expenditure. At the same time, East Pakistan had its own pressing problems for which no schemes were framed and no allotments made. East Pakistan's floods were becoming progressively and annually more and more destructive. The people of East Pakistan considered that the central government should have made efforts to prepare plans for flood control there; friendly countries should have been approached by the central government as for the Indus Basin scheme and for the anti-waterlogging and salinity scheme, inasmuch as East Pakistan could not do so directly. It was believed that Chowdhury Mohammad Ali had advised that this problem of East Pakistan should be postponed for consideration until funds had been secured for West Pakistan, lest by placing too many problems the funds for West Pakistan might be retarded.

During my tenure of office as Prime Minister I had requested the United States to be good enough to send a team of experts to suggest schemes for flood control. General Krugg was sent out with a team and he made certain valuable suggestions which were laid aside with my demission from office. Some schemes of flood control were later prepared by the East Pakistan WAPDA, and I am told they were vetted by some international experts. These, however, were determined to be very expensive and, although East Pakistan WAPDA had been allotted about Rs400 million, far more than any previous allotments, the amount available for flood control schemes hardly touched the fringe of the problem

EAST PAKISTAN PROGRESSIVELY IMPOVERISHED

Some time in October 1961 the President appointed a finance commission for the purpose of revising the Raisman Award, according to which a portion of the central income arising from export duties from jute and cotton and from income and sales taxes was allotted to the provinces. This commission was composed of representatives, including economists, from East Pakistan, West Pakistan and the centre. The East Pakistan economists, who were members of the Finance Commission, demonstrated how East Pakistan had been progressively impoverished since the establishment of Pakistan and demonstrated how the per capita income in East Pakistan—at one time higher than that of West Pakistan—had declined while the cost of living had increased. East Pakistan had also been deprived of its fair share of foreign exchange. They suggested that East Pakistan should be permitted to pursue an economic policy which would be to its benefit and to utilize the foreign exchange earned by it.

However, various loans had been taken by the Pakistan government and spent in West Pakistan and the time was fast approaching for their repayment and amortisation. Since the foreign exchange earnings of West Pakistan were not sufficient to meet the necessary payments the future foreign exchange earned by East Pakistan was to be used for the purpose. The reports of the economists of East Pakistan on this subject deserve perusal and study, but they have been kept out of circulation.

GRIEVANCES OF EAST PAKISTAN

Perhaps it may be useful here to set out in outline some of the grievances of East Pakistan on this score. As these assumed greater and greater importance, the view of East Pakistan was that the basic differences could not be solved by the mere allocation of larger funds for development.

The money spent for defence purposes and on the army, which was a central expenditure, was obviously provided by both wings, but it was estimated that 98 per cent of the money was spent in West Pakistan or for West Pakistan personnel. Hence, there was a constant drain of funds from East Pakistan without any return and consequent progressive impoverishment of the province. The theory used to justify this disparity (that the protection of East Pakistan lay in West Pakistan and that if East Pakistan was ever attacked by India, West Pakistan would attack India in turn) appeared to be far-fetched, as there seemed no likelihood that Pakistan would ever be in a position to take the offensive against India.

Many attempts were made from time to time from general headquarters to enlist more soldiers from East Bengal. Although quite a number of Bengalis were recruited during the two World Wars and were disbanded, the recruitment officers from the West could find no one in East Pakistan to conform to their standards. Even I, when Prime Minister and Defence Minister, could not induce Commander-in-Chief General Ayub Khan to raise some battalions in East Pakistan or to militarize the Ansars. Steps were taken to show that something was being done, but there was always a lag, an excuse and an ultimate retreat. In 1961, the centenary of the Bengal Regiment was celebrated. This Regiment was composed of 2,000 soldiers only and a battalion or two was proposed to be added as a great concession to Bengali sentiment. This could not have been effective until 1965. The following figures, from the army list in 1958, convey some idea of the actual state of affairs:

	East Pakistan	West Pakistan
Lieutenant Generals	0	3
Major Generals	0	20
Brigadiers	1	34
Colonels	1	49
Lieutenant Colonels	2	198
Majors	10	590
Air Force Officers	60	640
Naval Officers	7	598
Total	81	2,132

Apart from the income and increased opportunities for employment to people of West Pakistan, the existence of the army led to general economic activity in the manufacture of commodities, sale of consumer goods and buoyancy in general market conditions.

Similarly, as would appear from the civil side of the central budget, there was an annual drain from East Pakistan to West Pakistan. The special expenditures of the centre on the federal capital, on the frontier tribes and on refugees and rehabilitation were all in the West as were the major portions of that spent on central educational, health and medical institutions and roads. On the capital expenditure side, the amount spent in East Pakistan was approximately half the amount spent in West Pakistan. In the Foreign affairs section, there were hardly any East Pakistanis. For instance, in the Pakistan High Commission in London, out of 30 officers, 3 were from East Pakistan and out of 450 rank and file, 20 were from East Pakistan.

Another grievance was that the foreign exchange of East Pakistan was utilized to bolster the economy of West Pakistan and was increasingly reserved for that purpose. This was one of the main reasons for the demand for a separate economy for East Pakistan.

Up to about 1953–1954 exports were about equal; but East Pakistan earned more foreign exchange after that time. All along, the imports to East Pakistan were about one-third of the total; in 1959–1960, the first year of Martial Law, they were one-fourth. It was calculated that between 1947 and 1961, East Pakistan transferred to West Pakistan Rs4,730 million. If we take into account that East Pakistan received credit for her foreign exchange at the official rate and importers, whether of machines or consumer goods, derived the advantage of the open market rate, the West Pakistani importers got a further benefit of about Rs2,638 additional millions.

I have also referred to the poor allotment made to East Pakistan on the theory of shy capital, parallel industry and want of power of absorption. East Pakistan therefore had to buy cloth from West Pakistan, as well as cement, and was not even permitted to develop its rubber industry, such as production of cycle and motor tyres, although the imported raw material was cheaper in East Pakistan than in the West. Later, after East Pakistan had awakened to the accumulated injustices it had to suffer at the hands of the central West Pakistani administration—who were the virtual rulers of Pakistan—money was specially allotted to enable industries to be established in East Pakistan. Unfortunately, it came too late; the resources of Bengali would-be-industrialists had been exhausted in fruitless endeavours and there was insufficient capital formation. As an example, licenses were issued to establish 24 textile mills. Each of these was limited to 12,500 spindles and 250, 200 or 180 looms, although it is recognized that 25,000 spindles and 500 looms is an economic unit. Twenty-two of these 24 licenses in effect sold their licenses to West Pakistani industrialists. Jute and sugar mills were later set up through EPIDC. East Pakistan could be properly industrialized only through the public sector.

The policy of President Ayub's government, that the remedy was not to give to East Pakistan the benefit of the foreign exchange earned by it but to industrialize it by investing the capital of West Pakistan, increased the imbalance further. The industry was built by the foreign exchange of East Pakistan, but the profits were transferred to Karachi; the salary earners were from West Pakistan. Even giving to East Pakistan a larger share in the development expenditure would only have been of marginal benefit.

In the services also, particularly in the senior grades, there were hardly any East Pakistanis. Most of the East Pakistani officers working in the centre were returned home, and indications were that it would be several decades—if ever—before parity in the central services would be reached. The following figures illustrate the point.

	East Pakistan	West Pakistan
Secretaries	0	19
Joint Secretaries	7	39
Deputy Secretaries	24	102
Under Secretaries	88	675
President's Secretaries	3	69
Total	122	904

All establishments of the central government operating in East Pakistan were manned by West Pakistanis. And, in matters of grants-in-aid to the revenue budget by the central government, East Pakistan received Rs213 million whereas West Pakistan and Karachi received Rs467 million between 1947 and 1959.

The educational facilities in East Pakistan were extremely poor. Most of the private schools were staffed with Hindu teachers and they left after partition. No special effort was made to fill the gap. The following will perhaps illustrate the situation. Out of sixty-two or so colleges in West Pakistan, all were government institutions or financed by government. Out of a similar number in East Pakistan, six were government colleges and the rest were private institutions with meagre resources. How could an East Pakistani boy hope to succeed in competition under these circumstances? Moreover, it should be remembered that East Pakistan had no big landlords, and the boys generally came from poor families. It transpired that to get a degree or division an East Pakistani student had to secure a higher percentage of marks than his counterpart in West Pakistan; the result was that an East Pakistani student of the same standard as his West Pakistan counterpart got a lower division, and the percentage of failures was higher.

Owing to industries not having been established and the import and export trade being mostly in the hands of West Pakistan commercial magnates, there was no capital formation and hence there was need for far greater government support in the East than in the West. Indeed the view in East Pakistan was that to make up for the leeway, the PIDC should itself embark on industrial ventures or participate in private enterprise in a big way; and it should not sell out to private parties thereafter.

The railways of East Pakistan were neglected for many years. This is a long story, but the result was that the railway workshops that East Pakistan inherited were not maintained, the track had deteriorated dangerously, the wagons were dilapidated, the passenger coaches would rock and roll and rattle and jump and were positively dangerous and the rolling stock was insufficient for goods as well as for passengers. It was also believed that East Pakistan had to pay to the centre on capital account, not on the basis of the assets received by East Pakistan, but in proportion to population for the total assets. The railway system in West Pakistan was another world compared to that in East Pakistan. Loans taken for railways were divided between the two wings according to the mileage and not according to needs. The division came, but there was not much advantage to be had unless East Pakistan railways were helped specially to make up the leeway. Hardly any new lines had been laid. No attempt was made to double the railway line to Chittagong.

There was hardly any expenditure on the improvement of road communications. At first it was proposed to take this in hand, but suddenly it was discovered by the central government that East Pakistan had large rivers: therefore, river communications should be improved with the result that neither road nor river communications were taken in hand. There was enormous demand for improvement of road communication, particularly in

North Bengal. River communications deteriorated and many important channels silted up, isolating many places. A fleet of extra dredgers was necessary. Just before independence there were 16,425 miles of roads of which 5,706 were high-type motorable roads. By 1960 there were 9,672 miles of such high-type roads of which 8,772 miles were in West Pakistan and 900 miles in East Pakistan.

Hardly anything had been done to develop power although from time to time there were several schemes under active consideration. Except for a small thermal power station at Bheramara in Kushtia, North Bengal had no power station; Governor Faruque even suggested that we should put up an atomic power station in that area. Although gas of very good quality and unlimited in quantity was discovered in the Sylhet area, only a fraction was being utilized for a fertilizer factory. There should be research on its optimum use. There was a proposal to pipe it to Chittagong for the steel factory, which may possibly be wasteful, and perhaps to Dhaka to run the electric power station or for domestic use. German chemical engineers suggested that the gas is so good and pure that it could be utilized for petrochemical industries, but this was delayed although such an industry in East Pakistan had a better chance of competing in the world market than one in West Pakistan based on the comparatively impure Sui gas.

The Karnafuli electric power project made little progress until the Americans stepped in to complete it. But to prevent the water from flooding the upper reaches which possibly would have invaded Indian territory, the dam was not made high enough for it to supply the quantum of electricity for which it was planned, viz. 120,000 KW. At low water it was not able to produce more than 40,000 KW. Only two out of three generators had been installed by 1962; both were temporarily out of commission owing to some defect and, in any event, only one could be used during the low-water period. Moreover, the price of electricity was far too high and placed the East Pakistan industrialists at a disadvantage. Hence, instead of using the electricity next door for the production of steel, furnaces that would use the oil expected to be produced by the proposed refinery or the gas from Sylhet were being alternatively considered.

The PIDC installed a steel plant based on the open hearth furnace which is antiquated and expensive to work. The Japanese sold one of their outdated plants against their loan. Such a plant could be purchased for a song, indeed for scrap value, if tenders had been invited. Instead of producing rails or steel sheets, corrugated or otherwise, for which there was a demand in East Pakistan, the steel mill proposed to produce structural steel which was already being produced in more than adequate quantities by industrialists who established steel rolling mills under licence from government. As the PIDC would be able to import billets more cheaply, it would be competing against the industrialists of East Pakistan driving them out of the market. It was obvious that it should confine itself to producing only such articles that were not being produced by private industry. It would also be saving more foreign exchange by doing so.

The Ganges-Kobadak Project was limping, but was nearing completion. The people in East Pakistan were not used to purchasing water and it was reported that the sale price of water was placed so high that the agriculturalists were unable to purchase it. A proposal was made by East Pakistan WAPDA to reduce the price, but the capital cost would have to be written off.

Another cause of complaint was that grants and aid were utilized mostly in West Pakistan. It was on one occasion calculated that 88 per cent of the American aid was spent in West Pakistan and only 12 per cent in the East. If the aid from all the countries was calculated, 95 per cent had been spent in West Pakistan and 5 per cent in the East.

The removal of the capital from Karachi to Islamabad had also been deeply resented. When Karachi was administered by the central government as the capital of Pakistan all expenditure on government buildings and improvement works came from the central funds. The people of East Pakistan, therefore, resented the removal of the capital without consulting them and could see no reason why West Pakistan should get the benefit of what had already been spent and what further would be spent. They also objected to the removal of the capital to a place near the military General Headquarters; moreover the climate there was so extreme, both in summer and winter, that East Pakistanis found it extremely difficult to bear and many asked to be transferred elsewhere. The fact that Dhaka had been designated as the subsidiary or second capital and the legislative centre, where according to President Ayub's own constitution all meetings of parliament were to be held, was not considered a sufficient recompense. It was more in the nature of a hoax. It is worth noting that only 300 acres were allotted for the subsidiary capital of Pakistan—and you were not permitted to laugh at it. The town planners insisted that they could not manage under 1,000 acres, which in itself was a miserably niggardly demand, but they were asked to carry on with 300 acres with hopes of more in the future. With some ulterior design hidden from the common folk, a parliament building under another name was also being constructed at Islamabad. East Pakistan retaliated with a demand that the administrative capital of Pakistan should be shifted to Dhaka.

New jetties were built in the Chittagong port, but there were no improvement in the wharves, sheds or sidings, or in railway communications to and from Chittagong. This most important port, which supplied the eastern and northern portions of East Pakistan, had only one single-track railway line to bear the traffic. No wonder that the movement was slow, even when wagons were available (which owing to a shortage was rare). The port was so cluttered with goods that it took weeks for a consignment to be cleared, and it occasionally happened that as many as 28 ships were standing to outside the bar waiting for their turn to discharge cargo. It was well known that demurrage charges of ships were high, and it was not surprising, therefore, that the people of East Pakistan had to pay high prices for their imported articles. As large ships could not cross the bar at Chittagong, goods had to be removed from ships at the outer anchorage by lighters. The lighterage charges, with double unloading and loading, were added to the price. The United States at one time added 40 per cent surcharge on freight to compensate for the difficulties in the handling of cargo and for demurrage charges. This was withdrawn but apparently temporarily. The government placed such colossal orders for importation of cement that the Chittagong and Khulna ports could not handle the cargo. The Khulna anchorage, too, could have been developed and alternative and better sites were found, but no steps were taken to use them.

There was enormous scope for the development of forests and marine, river and tank fisheries. East Pakistan could become a rich and prosperous country if special attention were paid to these two matters, at least. It goes without saying that they have been neglected. Agriculture, which is the mainstay of the country, had been sorely neglected. Greater production could lead to all round prosperity, strengthen internal resources and lead to greater and sustained development. There was a need for greater and continuous research. The price of jute needed support. All the assurances of government ended in tall talk.

I have referred to the above matters to demonstrate that there was no justification for the argument that East Pakistan was not able to use monies that might be allotted to it for development and that it had no absorptive capacity. The President advanced this particular argument himself to justify the disparity in the allotments, although he paid lip service to the principle of parity, enshrined in the constitution. Holding these views the President could hardly have been expected to introduce any drastic changes in the pattern of development.

The report submitted by the members from East Pakistan of the Finance Commission was countered by their opposite numbers in West Pakistan. The centre produced its own report. The award dealing with allocation of revenues to the provinces from central revenue was altered to the extent that East Pakistan was allotted Rs110 million and West Pakistan Rs40 million and there the matter rested. The reports of the Finance Commission were kept a dark secret.

COURAGEOUS OPPOSITION IN WEST PAKISTAN

While my arrest, which was followed by the arrest of several of the local leaders throughout East Pakistan—both Manik Mia and Mujibur Rahman were arrested within a few days—brought to the surface in East Pakistan the smouldering discontent and opposition to the Martial Law regime, instances of courageous opposition were not wanting in West Pakistan. The NWFP resented vehemently the continued detention of the aging and ailing Khan Abdul Ghaffar Khan and relays of Pathans marched to the court of the Magistrate and protested against the Martial Law regime. They were duly arrested. But as more and more offered themselves, government stopped arresting them. Instead it began to victimize the prominent Pathan leaders, detained them without trial, confiscated their properties and even resorted to whipping. The action taken by the regime left a scar which found expression in a demand for the disintegration of One Unit and the establishment or restoration of democracy and a democratic constitution, which was hardly mitigated by returning a portion of their confiscated properties to some of the leaders.

In Balochistan, the situation deteriorated considerably. The arrest, detention and deposition of the Khan of Kalat aroused the tribal chiefs to well-nigh rebellion. Balochistan was considered a backward area and government maintained order through the tribal chiefs who administered according to tribal customs and through the tribal jirgas. With the spread of political education, however, the tribes were beginning to resent the authority of their chiefs; they were expecting and demanding to be brought into line with the advanced areas of Pakistan, to abolish the jirga system and the Frontier Crimes Regulations, and to establish democratic institutions. The arrest of the Khan of Kalat, however, brought the two groups—the chiefs and the people—together for a common purpose. A group of militant Baluchis took to the hills and started guerrilla warfare against government forces.

The details were best known to the active participants. What I set forth below was gathered from the statements made by the Baluchi leaders themselves in the National Assembly as well as from their public speeches in Quetta and Karachi. It appeared that the Major General in charge of the Pakistan army called upon the Baluchi chief. Sirdar Nauroz Khan, who was conducting the guerrilla war to surrender his arms, promising on the Quran that there would be no reprisals. Sirdar Nauroz Khan came down from the hills and saw him personally; after both swore on the Quran he called upon his followers to surrender their arms. They accordingly did so, but they were arrested and some of them were tried. Seven were hanged and seven were sentenced to life imprisonment. When the son of Nauroz Khan was being taken to the gallows, he hung the Quran around his neck and refused to remove it declaring that actually it was not he who was being hanged, but the Quran. It was further alleged that many were placed in a concentration camp where the prisoners were crucified and tortured in ways that do not bear repeating. Balochistan was thus seething with discontent. The government deposed some of the Sirdars and prosecuted one of the members of the National Assembly. It also released the Khan of Kalat in the hope it would appease the Baluchis. However, while the senior tribal chiefs still continued to be members of the Shai (King's) jirga and the smaller jirgas, the younger members of their clans were not pacified.

PAKISTAN'S FUTURE AT STAKE

It had to be said with regret, for the future of Pakistan was at stake, that never had there been such discontent against any regime—never had the fissiparous tendencies so come to the surface. Instead of promoting national unity and national integration, which the Revolution proclaimed as its aim—impliedly and even implicitly recognizing that they did not exist in Pakistan—the regime fanned the smouldering ember of regional antagonisms to a conflagration almost beyond control. East Pakistan, rightly or wrongly, considered it had been and was being exploited by West Pakistan, whereas in West Pakistan, the NWFP, Balochistan, Sindh and Karachi—and even some parts of Bahawalpur—demanded provincial autonomy and the disintegration of One Unit. Even the people of Punjab were beginning to realize that they could not live in peace and in comfort with hostile neighbours. What was the solution? To some of us, the solution rested with the real leaders of all the areas—real leaders, not those brought to the fore by the mishandling of the electorate—getting together in a spirit of national cohesion (which still inspired them in spite of the abuses showered on them by the President) and finding an amicable solution based on justice to all peoples and all regions of Pakistan. In short, we needed a democratic constitution and the establishment of real democracy as a permanent solution.

It had been seen that the first act of the Revolutionary regime was to declare all political parties illegal, to confiscate their property and to ban all political activities. The country was plastered with a spate of abuse and vilification of politicians of the previous political regimes and of politics as a philosophy. The leaders of the country who had been at some time or the other responsible for its administration were picked out and charged with various acts of malfeasance, misfeasance and non-feasance. Brought before and convicted by the EBDO tribunals, they were debarred from seeking election from any electoral body until December 1966 and, obviously, therefore, were deprived of voting rights. But such is the perversity of the stupid people of Pakistan, who are so easily deluded by false propaganda and have no political education and no national consciousness, that the prestige of the politicians rose in inverse proportion to the virulence of the vilification. Few wavered in their loyalties to the parties to which they had belonged, however defunct and obliterated, except that amorphous class of opportunists who hang around government officials and are specially amenable to government influence.

While political parties were banned—it was a sin and a crime to refer to them—the President was busy laying foundations of his own while sterilizing all else. His first step was to deliver speeches from special trains and at public meetings. At first they were well attended and people came to see the new head of the state. But the glamour disappeared soon enough, and the meetings became thinner and thinner while his vituperations progressively grew in volume and intensity, until the Press and Information Department had to disown some of the expressions he had used and which had been duly taped and were published in the press. These tapes were, of course, subsequently edited. It is on record that at a meeting in the stadium in Dhaka, the audience rose to leave as soon as he started speaking, but they were forced to stay when they found the egresses closed against them. The scheme of Basic Democrats, who were elected under peculiar circumstances while martial law was in full swing and people had hardly realized what had struck them, was to provide him with a party which could be and was utilized by him to strengthen his personal political ambitions and status.

Suhrawardy Arrested

After the report of the Constitution Commission was presented, the promulgation of a constitution could hardly be postponed any longer. But the constitution had to be such as would place unrestricted power in the hands of the President and reduce the legislatures to farcical institutions without powers; the ministers were to serve merely as agents for carrying on propaganda to extol the President. It was pitiful to see the ministers wandering from place to place with no powers either to direct the policy of their departments or to administer them—with no aim or objective but to flatter the President personally and thus justify their selection and keep their offices. Before the constitution was introduced, however, soundings were taken as regards possible reactions. According to a Martial Law regulation any criticism of government was punishable with rigorous imprisonment for 14 years, and meetings were forbidden. The politicians were silent. The President had no misgivings regarding West Pakistan; they could be curbed, marshalled and brought into line; he was not so certain as regards East Pakistan.

Unfortunately for me, wherever his agents made enquiries they were met with one reply, namely, that they were awaiting my reactions. This would have been considered naturally if the President had known anything of the politics of East Pakistan. He did not in spite of the fact that he had for some time served as General Officer Commanding of the forces stationed in that region. I had worked there for several decades, and people had confidence in me; this had been enhanced, rather than reduced, during my tenure of office as Prime Minister. I had established the Muslim League throughout the province since 1936 and, similarly, the Awami League after 1949. The President was given the impression that I had been busy as a bee establishing cells throughout the province to obstruct his constitution and was waiting to act as soon as the constitution would be promulgated.

In fact, I had not been anywhere except Dhaka and Chittagong and that only for the purpose of my profession as advocate and there was nothing further from my thoughts than to obstruct the constitution. His director of the Intelligence Branch, the closest confidant of the President on the internal situation in the country, sounded my opinion through an American friend of mine. Unfortunately, I did not conceal my views but advised that it would be wiser for him to adopt the 1956 constitution and proceed from there rather than promulgate a new one which was bound to be controversial. He understood from this that I would obstruct his constitution and accordingly arrested me in Karachi where I had gone in connection with a case on 30 January 1962. He was advised that my alleged popularity was a myth and that if I was arrested there would be no commotion, particularly if he announced at the same time that under the Second Five-year Plan unprecedented financial resources, such as had never been dreamt of by previous governments, had been allotted to East Pakistan. This would certainly, according to his way of thinking, prove his own bonafides and concern for East Pakistan, and, in short, would act as a bribe which would prevent any movement in my favour.

To justify my arrest, a communique was issued by the government charging me with subversive activities, and the President gave a press conference in which he charged me with treason against Pakistan and suggested that I was planning the secession of East Pakistan and the disintegration of West Pakistan. Normally, direct allegations are not made by government when any person is detained without trial as a preventive measure. According to law the detenu must be given an opportunity to apply to the courts where the sufficiency of the grounds for his detention as supplied to him may be considered; the course of justice is bound to be defiled if the President, or the government, insists from beforehand that the charges stand proven and the detenu is guilty. Some friends of mine moved a *habeas corpus* petition in the High Court without consulting me. The High

Court admitted the petition for hearing, although an ordinance had been passed debarring courts from entertaining such a petition. There was, however, a loophole in the ordinance. But, before the petition could come up for final hearing, the President passed another ordinance plugging that loophole and absolutely deprived the courts of jurisdiction to hear any petition challenging preventive detention on any ground whatsoever.

The charges against me were obviously untrue and those who had been in contact with me knew that they were untrue. In the first place, I had studiously avoided involving myself in internal politics and when I had been asked for my opinion or advice on any political matter I had asked my friends to act as they thought best. During the Martial Law regime East Pakistan was no doubt growing very restive. With its highly developed political consciousness it resented military dictatorship and wanted an early return to democracy. Over and above this, it was becoming more and more aware that it had been treated with grave injustice in matters economic, and that its development had been retarded for the benefit of West Pakistan. There was no doubt a feeling among the intelligentsia that there was no hope for any political or economic redress as long as the administration, both civil and military, was in the hands of West Pakistan; the only salvation for East Pakistan was for economic independence and democracy.

In the beginning East Pakistan was attuned to accept federation if the administration of most of the subjects were transferred to the provinces. Later, it felt that this was not sufficient to secure the interests of East Pakistan and that nothing short of provincial autonomy, with as little interference from the centre as possible—and only then in the very important fields of defence and currency—would suffice. However, the issues of defence and currency could be made so wide and comprehensive that they could cover and impinge on all activities of government. The idea of confederation was then mooted as the only possible solution that would avoid separation. I had been approached by those who were thinking on the above line, as well as by the students and others among the younger generation, and I had put my foot down on all talk which might loosen the ties between East and West Pakistan. I held the view that East and West Pakistan must work together for the salvation of the country. The most practical solution was to get together people of good will, honesty and patriotism of both wings who would try to understand each other's problems and would work out a policy which would do justice to all regions of Pakistan.

Students of Dhaka University knew that the charges against me were false and when the President, on the heels of my arrest, came to East Pakistan with certain important ambassadors who were to witness his acumen and his victory he was met with hostile demonstrations. A permanent arch with the inscription 'Ayub Gate' was burnt down. All posters carrying his picture were torn down from the walls and trampled upon. Foreign Minister Manzur Qadir, whose duty, apparently, was to go around and explain the policies of the President, was roughly handled and was saved from serious injury by the intervention of the Vice Chancellor.[23] It is a matter of gratification to me that few, if any, believed the charges brought against me by the President, and I was undeservedly elevated to the position of a hero and a martyr.

ONE-MAN CONSTITUTION IMPOSED

The President announced his constitution on 2 February 1962. He declared emphatically that he would have no political parties under any circumstances. He stated that he, solely, was responsible for the constitution which was the product of his wisdom, his wide experience, his careful consideration and scrutiny and his contacts with the people of Pakistan. Of course, he thanked the Constitution Commission—while rejecting even its semi-democratic recommendations—and his cabinet which was supposed to have reviewed the recommendations. A central legislature of 156 members (of whom six were to be ladies, three from each province) and two provincial legislatures of 155 members (each inclusive of five lady members) were to be elected by the Basic Democrats. There was not to be any further election for the position of President. Most of the administrative clauses of the 1956 constitution were incorporated with some vital differences. The nomenclature of the state was changed from the 'Islamic Republic of Pakistan' to the 'Republic of Pakistan'. All references to the Quran and Sunnah were deleted, the ACII was maintained (Article 199–206), but its function limited to advising on whether a proposed law violated or was otherwise not in accordance with the principles of law-making (Article 6). Fundamental rights, defined and made justiciable in the 1956 constitution, which were called 'Principles of Law-making' and served as a guide to the legislatures, had been rendered non-justiciable—Article 6(2).

It is interesting to note that Foreign Minister Manzur Qadir echoed the arguments of the President who justified this departure by citing the example of the constitution of England, without realizing that the latter is unwritten and not codified.

The cabinet system was abolished. Ministers were to be appointed by the President, according to his wish, from amongst the members of the national legislature or from outside (Article 33). Those appointed from among the members were to lose their seats—Article 25(2). There was provision for appointment of parliamentary secretaries from amongst the members by the President (Article 35), but they would not lose their seats (Article 120). The President was to certify the budget ending 30 June (the financial year had been altered to end on 30 June instead of 31 March). This would form the basis for future budgets and no objections were entertained (Article 235). Budget carrying equal provisions for up to an increase of 10 per cent (Article 40) would be non-votable for all time to come, but the legislature was empowered to vote on new taxes. Islamabad, a large tract of land with an area of not less than 200 square miles—Article 211(2)—near Rawalpindi, the general headquarters of the Pakistan army, was made the administrative capital and the principal seat of government (Article 211). Karachi was reduced to provincial status.

In order to soften the inevitable opposition to such a fantastic display of personal whim and dictatorial power which involved the country in much useless expenditure it could ill afford, Dhaka, the capital of East Pakistan, became the second capital and the principal seat of the National Assembly where all sessions of the central legislature were to be held—Article 211(3) and (5). The area for the time being was to be 300 acres. Amendment to the constitution was made practically impossible without the cooperation of the President; the amendment would first have to be passed by not less than two-thirds (104) of the members—Article 209(1). If the President did not agree, then a three-fourths majority of the total (117) was necessary—Article 291(4). The President still had recourse to referendum to Basic Democrats concerning whether a bill should be assented to or not or, finally, he could dissolve the legislature and order fresh elections, including for that of the President.

Provision was made for impeachment of the President with conditions that made such a step impossible. Not only was it necessary that three-fourths of the total number of members must vote for the motion—Article 13(6), but if less than half of the total voted for the motion then all would lose their seats—Article 13(1) and (7). An innovation was made in the distribution of subjects to the centre and the provinces. In the Government of India Act of 1935, produced after very great care and as the result of considerable administrative and political experience, there were three lists of subjects; one exclusively operable by the centre; one called the concurrent list, operable both by the centre and the provinces, with overriding powers to the centre; and another with subjects exclusively within the jurisdiction of the provinces. In the 1962 constitution there was only one list of subjects under the exclusive jurisdiction of the centre (Article 131). All others were to be provincial subjects. This, in fact, was a snare and a delusion. It was meant to give the impression that the provinces were masters in their own houses and that the new constitution had decentralized powers. Actually the most important clause in the 1935 constitution, reproduced in 1956, was that the centre had no power to interfere in matters on the provincial list. This provision had been deleted from the 1962 document. Furthermore, powers were given to the centre to interfere in the provincial administration in the name of planning and coordination, the security of Pakistan (including economic and financial stability) and the achievement of uniformity—Article 131(2).

There was a peculiar clause that not more than three persons, exclusive of the President, could stand for the Presidency. If more stood, then a joint sitting of the national and provincial assemblies would select three candidates. Apparently, each member was to have three votes. Hence, if the President had a majority in the legislatures, as was likely considering the Basic Democrat representatives and those from the ex-princely states, the tribal areas, and the parliamentary secretaries, he could always set up three from amongst his own friends and relatives, get them selected, and then by getting them to withdraw their candidature discreetly, get himself returned without a contest.

The constitution had a mixed reception. In East Pakistan no person of prominence or otherwise, except one, welcomed it—excluding, of course, a very few district Basic Democracy councils. In West Pakistan some ran to the President to congratulate him and deputations were organized for the purpose. A prominent learned Moulvi (an *alim* and *maulana*) was the first to run. He received his prize by being appointed to the ACII. He praised the constitution as being truly Islamic and according to the tenets of Islam. The change in name, the deletion of the Quran and Sunnah and of the clause to bring all laws into conformity with the injunctions of Islam, were discreetly ignored. Had not the President provided for the ACII (so had the 1956 constitution, with wider powers—but forget it!), had he not made usury illegal (but so had 1956), had he not said that drinking of wine should be moderated as a principle (the stupid constitution of 1956 made prohibition its goal)? And then Islam believed in the absolution of the ruler and not democracy; hence, his constitution was Islamic and conformed to the genius of the people. Scores of people suddenly discovered what was the genius of the people—the constitution expressed it so wonderfully. The Basic Democracy councils were enthusiastic.

Maulana Maudoodi had the temerity to criticize it, and some papers inadvertently published his criticisms. He was sternly warned by Foreign Minister Manzur Qadir, who reminded him and everyone else that Martial Law was still in operation; anyone criticizing the constitution was liable to go to prison for 14 years. The papers were duly warned. Manzur Qadir ran from one Bar association to another meeting groups of the intelligentsia, and everywhere he was met with hostile criticism and sarcastic remarks. But, they obviously did not find publicity.

THE PRESIDENT RESILED FROM HIS PET THEORIES

With publicity all in one direction, it is not at all surprising that the President should begin to imagine that he was divinely inspired and had been sent to Pakistan as its Saviour. Later, it must indeed have been a great blow to resile from all his pet theories, from all the pillars of his Revolutionary government, from every single principle he advocated, save one, and have to seek the support of the ignorant, deluded mass whom he had hitherto despised, mistrusted and condemned. The only principle to which he still clinged was the absolutism of his power which enabled him to build up a huge fortune for himself and members of his family, complete with the elimination of possible rivals and contestants.

Owing to my arrest many members of my party thought it proper to boycott the elections. Some, as I have stated earlier, did stand and were elected. Most of the candidates who offered themselves for election belonged to the defunct Muslim League Party. The Jamaat-i-Islami in West Pakistan also contested the elections, but, of course, without the label.

The central legislature met on 8 June 1962 on which day Martial Law was lifted. One of the first difficulties which the President had to face was to find ministers from amongst the members of the legislature and invite them to accept office and relinquish their membership at the same time. To satisfy them he issued an order amending that section of the constitution and resiling from his previous stand. He purported to act under a clause in the constitution which gave him power to amend the constitution by an order to remove difficulties that may arise in bringing the constitution or any provision of the constitution into operation—Article 224(3). To my mind it was clear that his order was not covered by the enabling clause and was unconstitutional, without jurisdiction and would be declared illegal if challenged in a court. The East Pakistan High Court declared the order to be illegal in a proceeding to which two of the ministers were parties. Although it was an order of general significance the Speaker of the National Assembly, Tamizuddin Khan, allowed the other ministers, who were not parties to the proceedings, to vote as members. The Supreme Court upheld the order of the East Pakistan High Court and all such ministers as were members of the legislature lost their seats.

Although in his own opening speech before the National Assembly the President inveighed against political parties, there was an immediate demand for a bill to permit political parties to exist. Such a bill was passed, although the President tried hard to limit their number to two or three. There was only one restriction: political parties formed with the object of propagating any opinion in any manner prejudicial to (sic) Islamic ideology would be declared illegal and this would be decided by the Supreme Court. All persons who were automatically EBDOed because they had been arrested under the Public Safety Act could become members of political parties except for those who had been charged and who either accepted the penalty imposed and did not contest the charges or who contested them and were found guilty.

It would be obvious to any person brought up to respect the rule of law that it is against all fundamental rights and principles of legislation and is unconscionable to impose a subsequent penalty or disqualification on a guilty person which was not contemplated at the time that he was found guilty. As it is, EBDO itself was an *ex-post facto* law, and persons were condemned subsequently for acts which carried no penalties at the time of their commission and this law even determined the extent of penalty that could be imposed. The Political Parties Act, however, did not forbid guilty persons from giving expression to their political views, although they could not be members of any political party. A further disability was imposed by Ordinance 1 of 1963 which made it penal for a person placed under EBDO to indulge in any form of political activity.

Taking note of the fact that there was considerable discontent in the country over elections of the Basic Democrats and by the Basic Democrats and that the intelligentsia had been practically disfranchised, the President appointed a franchise commission with Akhtar Hussain, one-time Governor of West Pakistan—also previously a Central Minister and Chief Election Commissioner—as its chairman. He submitted a unanimous report to the effect that the elections to the legislatures should be joint and by adult franchise. A minority report by him and one other member advised that the election of the President should be through Basic Democrats. Obviously, he had no alternative inasmuch as the President had made the Basic Democrats his own special contribution to political philosophy, and he was on no account prepared to give them up as an electoral body.

Nevertheless, it was clear to the President that the time was fast approaching when he would have to resile from all his pet theories and would have to enter the political field openly. He knew that, therefore, he must promote a political party of his own.

SUHRAWARDY'S RELEASE DEMANDED

After Martial Law was lifted, meetings were held all over Pakistan demanding that I should be released. In Karachi a meeting of all parties—believed to have been attended by about 200,000 people—was held demanding my release. Khan Abdul Qayyum Khan addressed the meeting in very strong terms, and he was supported by Chowdhury Khaliquzzaman and representatives of the Muslim League, the NAP, the Awami League and the Jamaat-i-Islami parties. During the Martial Law regime Khan Abdul Qayyum

Khan had been arrested for a statement derogatory to the President and was tried by a military tribunal and convicted. I appeared on his behalf before the Martial Law court, although I had not yet recovered from an attack of double pneumonia. Khan Abdul Qayyum Khan after that was always kind enough to acknowledge that although he belonged to an opposite party and had indeed prevented me from entering the NWFP on a previous occasion, I had at some risk to myself come to his assistance.

Unfortunately, the Khan was not able to bear the pain and restrictions of imprisonment, and he tendered an apology to the President and was released. However, after Martial Law was lifted he made several speeches in my support. The last speech he made was in Lahore, after which he was again arrested. The President had asked the Governor of West Pakistan to arrest him. The Governor was well disposed towards the Khan and did not want to do so. Instead, he took a guarantee from him that he would not address the meeting in Lahore. The Khan was, however, pushed by his followers to such an extent that the felt compelled to attend the meeting, at which he was alleged to have made remarks about certain sections of the military who wanted him to intervene on a certain occasion. He was accordingly arrested. Later, exasperated presumably by his detention, he declared that he was in error in having made a political speech as he had been EBDOed but that he was pressed to attend the meeting against his will and regretted the statements he had made. He apologized and stated that he would henceforth refrain from public speeches and other political activities. He was released. It was doubtful if he would ever be able to secure again the confidence of the people or of his party.

In East Pakistan a colossal meeting was held in Dhaka in a place devoted to public meetings which was popularly known as the Paltan Maidan and later as the Outer Stadium. The meeting demanded my immediate release.

Since my arrest the President had been trying to impress on the people of East Pakistan how generous he had been to that province. He took advantage of the larger allocation in the Second Five-year Plan to substantiate his assertion. It was not everyone who knew that the first allotment to East Pakistan was poor and that it was increased at the instance of the United Nations experts. The President had nothing to do with it. The second plan itself had been conceived on a much larger scale and with more money made possible by unprecedented and lavish contributions by the United States. To answer the charge that parity had not been observed, he resorted to the theory that East Pakistan was not capable of absorbing more, and that the loans and the allotments for the Indus River Basin and for waterlogging and salinity prevention should not be taken into account as they were outside the plan. But then he had no answer as to why there was no plan, no aid and no allotment to control the East Pakistan floods.

Moreover, people remembered that in the first days of the Revolution the President had spoken sneeringly of East Pakistan, stating that the people were beggars who had been drawing heavily on the central funds and that they were not returning the loans or paying their rents on the plea of natural calamities. He, therefore, considered it necessary to collect the rents and dues through the 'certificate procedure' where the demand had to be met at once. Movables such as cattle, ploughs, and household utensils could be attached and sold at auction. People remembered that they had had to sell their lands and all their possessions and became paupers and landless labourers due to his harsh measures and were not prepared to give him credit for the generosity he was claiming. Moreover, when they looked into the matter they found that though allotments had been made, they were not being spent and the schemes were being shelved even in the third year of the plan. The imperative necessity of placating East Pakistan fortunately resulted in the schemes being expedited, and it later was easier to get a license for an industry in East Pakistan than in the West, even though ultimately all was for the benefit of western capitalists. In spite of comparisons made by the President to show that previous regimes had not done as much as he had done, East Pakistan refused to be placated or bribed and demanded my release.

It was said that the President was prepared to release me. His special adviser, General Burki, saw me on his behalf while I was in jail. I told him quite clearly that I wanted nothing for myself; all that I wanted was that he should provide a democratic constitution. The East Pakistan ministers, however, who had been appointed by the President (I regret to say that other than Bogra Mohammad Ali who had been appointed as Foreign Minister, the other East Pakistan ministers had been involved in criminal cases) advised him very strongly not to release me, as they would have no place at all if this was done. Fazlul Qadir Chowdhury, who on one occasion had been convicted as a receiver of stolen property, and for whom I was successful in obtaining an acquittal from the Supreme Court on technical grounds, told the President that he wielded tremendous influence in East Pakistan and that he would turn the tide in favour of the President. Before the parliament closed its session, he went to Dhaka boasting loudly at the airport that he would show that others could also hold meetings at the Paltan Maidan and at other places as he desired.[24] When he arrived in Chittagong by train, he was met by a hostile crowd, composed largely of students and young men, who were severely beaten up by the police. His public meeting was also rudely disturbed, and he found that he could not hold a public meeting anywhere in East Pakistan, let alone the Paltan Maidan, although he announced his programme time and again.

Khan Abdus Sabur Khan, one of his ministers, then took up the cudgel on behalf of the President. This gentleman had been convicted by a military tribunal to one year rigorous imprisonment and a substantial fine. The prison term had subsequently been reduced to four months which he had duly served. He fared no better. Neither did another minister, Waheeduzzaman, who had been saved from prosecution in Calcutta by the partition and against whom inquiries were pending in East Pakistan for certain defalcations. Bogra Mohammad Ali was then ordered to proceed to East Pakistan, but as he did not want to risk his reputation he advised the President to release me first and refused to go until I was released. He saw me while I was in detention and suggested some conditions which were not of any great significance; I refused to accept any conditions whatsoever or give any assurances. He had to cancel his reservations for East Pakistan time and again. He went there after I was released on 19 August 1962 and was able to get a hearing when he arrived in Dhaka.[25]

THE NINE SIGNATORIES

In East Pakistan a manifesto was prepared to which all the defunct parties contributed and which was signed by such leaders as were available on the spot.[26] This became known as the 'Nine Leaders Statement' and assumed considerable importance. The basis of the statement was that no single person had the right to frame the constitution of a country, that it could only be framed by representatives of the people elected for the purpose and that, therefore, an election should be held on the basis of adult franchise and a constituent assembly created for the express purpose of framing a constitution for Pakistan. As regards political parties, they were of the opinion that none of them should be revived, or any new ones created, inasmuch as under the constitution of 1962 there was no room for political activity which could only be usefully undertaken in a free atmosphere. The legislature had no powers at all; all were concentrated in the hands of the President. Too many restrictions had been placed in the path of political parties. The real leaders of the people had been debarred from joining them and, hence, all should cooperate in the main task of establishing democracy first. The signatories left it vague whether the form of the government should be presidential or parliamentary. They considered the presidential form unsuitable for the country because those many institutions and conventions had not been developed which could make the presidential form democratic. Meetings were held throughout East Pakistan supporting this statement, and it found an echo in West Pakistan as well.

It might be useful here to say a few words about the nine signatories and one or two others who met for consultation. Nurul Amin had been the Chief

Minister of East Pakistan for nearly six years (1948–1954) and was the President of the East Pakistan Muslim League. The demand that political parties should not be revived in the absence of leaders who had been EBDOed or arrested and in the absence of a proper climate was so insistent on the part of those in East Pakistan who could think politically that Nurul Amin felt that he had no alternative but to fall in line with this view if he wanted to safeguard his political future. He was offered the governorship of East Pakistan which he refused. He was also offered one of the two posts of Special Adviser to the President under the constitution, the other being held by General Burki from West Pakistan. This he also refused.

Abu Hossain Sarkar, the President of the KSP, represented that party after the death of Fazlul Huq, although it was practically moribund and had ceased to have even that tenuous political basis which had been supplied by the leadership of Huq. Another member of the KSP, Hamidul Huq Choudhury, who had been a minister both in East Pakistan and in the centre, and had at one time been prosecuted under PRODA, was found guilty and disqualified, was one of the signatories. He somewhat resented that I should be acknowledged as spokesman on behalf of East Pakistan and tried unsuccessfully to induce the others to accept the theory of collective leadership. There were two other members of the KSP amongst the signatories: Syed Azizul Huq, a nephew of Fazlul Huq, and S. M. Solaiman, its secretary. Ataur Rahman Khan and Sheikh Mujibur Rahman signed on behalf of the Awami League. Shah Azizur Rahman, secretary of the East Pakistan Muslim League, joined the group. Pir Mohsenuddin signed the statement as a member of the Nizam-i-Islam Party, although this party had not committed itself to non-revival theory and had ceased to have any political significance. Mahmud Ali, secretary of the East Pakistan NAP signed on behalf of that party. Latterly, Maulana Abdur Rashid Tarkabagish, the last President of the East Pakistan Awami League before the Revolution, also took part in the discussion as also did Yusuf Ali Chowdhury, alias Mohan Mia of the KSP.

DEMOCRATIZATION OF THE CONSTITUTION

I addressed colossal meetings in most of the district towns of East Pakistan and in a few subdivisional towns on behalf of the NDF. I was debarred by the Political Parties Act of 1962 from being a member of a political party, but, according to my reading, the EBDOed politicians were not prohibited from holding political opinions and giving expression to them.[27] Khan Abdul Qayyum Khan seemed to hold a different view after his arrest, and Mian Mumtaz Khan Daultana, who at one time was in constant touch with

President Ayub, was equally circumspect. The reason why I took the line of exhibiting this large and solid volume of public opinion was to impress upon the President that East Pakistan was unanimously behind the movement and the demand for democracy. According to the constitution it was well-nigh impossible to get a single article amended unless the President agreed. I wanted him to take notice of the feeling in East Pakistan on the point and agree to the democratization of the constitution by suitable amendments.

The President reacted by declaring that he had, in fact, given a democratic constitution and was a great protagonist of democracy. For the consumption of the people of East Pakistan he asserted—and reiterated and constantly and vehemently repeated—that since he had done more for East Pakistan than anyone had ever done before and had allotted large sums of money for its development, he, therefore, must be supported in whatever he did. But the politically conscious people of East Pakistan, who did not quite forget his earlier denunciations and contempt for East Pakistan and its people and leaders, were not to be bribed by such largesse. They gave credit for this to the inevitable march of time and to the more elaborate Second Five-year Plan, with its chequered history, and not to any special springs of generosity. Neither he nor his ministers could get a hearing or address a meeting in East Pakistan.

In West Pakistan his tirades against the mounting demand for democracy grew in bitterness with choice barracks-room expletives. His spokesmen threatened that Martial Law would be reimposed if the movement gained ground. But he soon realized that some crumbs had to be thrown, some promises had to be made and even some strings might have to be loosened. To keep his existing powers and emoluments intact and guarantee another tenure of office for himself, he had to keep the press bribed and muzzled and every public figure who could effectively lead an opposition inoperative and politically disabled. He exploited his promises, high sounding but signifying nothing, as indicative for him to keep the central legislature or parliament in hand. He had taken all measures to produce a legislature which would be submissive and controlled and yet he found himself confronted—to his immense surprise—by an opposition almost as numerous as the government party. It was led by his own brother, Sardar Bahadur Khan.

The majority of those who supported the government were either ministers, parliamentary secretaries, office holders, nominees of deputy commissioners and political agents or members subject to police pressure. There were some outside these categories who were kept within the fold by keeping some ministerships and parliamentary secretaryships vacant and dangling. Against those who refused to be tempted, other means were employed. For instance, an opposition member from West Pakistan had the supply of irrigation water for his lands cut off, and could only get it restored by promising the Governor of West Pakistan to support the central government. Another member who had to pay to the cooperative bank was vigórously proceeded against for the realization of his dues; these measures were suddenly relaxed when he similarly succumbed. Investigations were started against the brother of a lady member in connection with a factory; when she came over to the government side the fortunate brother got some money permits for machinery. A few could stand out. One person preferred to relinquish 1,500 acres of very rich, fertile, valuable land near Layallpur city—he used this as a stud farm and could have kept it under the Land Reform laws—rather than go to the government side. Bribery and cajolery, coercion, intimidation and threats fouled what little apparent independence and self-respect was left to the members; the tragedy was that the President himself was the principal player in the game.

President Ayub insisted that he was a great protagonist of democracy—a great change after his denunciation of the intelligence and integrity of the people of Pakistan which he described at such length in his pamphlet on Basic Democracy—and supported his claim by pointing to many measures undertaken by him. These measures may be examined seriatim to see to what extent his claim was justified.

AYUB'S MEASURES EXAMINED

The measures were described by him as follows:
1. He promulgated a democratic constitution when he could have continued uncontrolled martial law.
2. He himself invented the institution of Basic Democracy, wherein the representatives are elected through adult franchise.
3. He took a mandate from the country through the Basic Democrats by a referendum according to democratic practice which—
   • amounted to a vote of confidence in him;
   • gave him authorization to frame a constitution for the country according to his wishes; and
   • continued him in office after the 'commencement' of the constitution without further elections, as the first President under the constitution, for a period which it was left to him to determine.
4. To advise him on the content of the future constitution, he set up a constitution commission presided over by a retired judge of the Supreme Court.
5. He fixed the initial period of his post-constitution presidency at three years and two months only from the 'commencement' of the constitution on 8 June 1962. He could easily have fixed it for five or ten years or any period, however long.

6. He provided for election to the presidency at three years and two months and ever after (and will himself contest for the office).

7. He provided for elections to the legislatures before the expiry of 1965, their life being three years only from the date of their first sitting. The central legislature sat on 8 June 1962.

8. To determine what should be the electorate for the office of president and for the legislatures, he appointed a franchise commission to advise him.

9. He provided for impeachment of the President in the constitution.

10. He allowed political parties to function.

11. He was prepared to recognize fundamental rights and made them justiciable.

Let us consider these claims serially.

The constitution. The constitution, brought into force on 8 June 1962, was, in fact, no constitution at all. The President had supreme powers to override it by declaring an emergency. It could not possibly be called democratic; it was merely a cloak for uncontrolled, dictatorial power of the President. The legislatures were powerless instruments of his will, and the ministers appointed by him were not responsible to them. Further the legislatures had no power over budgets. The constitution was designed to perpetuate his powers and his position as President. He could hardly have continued martial law further without blackening his face in international circles from which Pakistan was receiving aid and before which he had to justify, at least morally, why it should not be lifted when after four years of uncontrolled power he had achieved so little.

Moreover, he, with President Iskander Mirza, the other author of the Revolution, had given a solemn promise four years before, when he was abrogating the constitution and imposing martial law, that the country would be made democratic as soon as possible. What could be more conveniently misleading than to put up the semblance of a constitution to satisfy the criticism of the democratic powers? As a first step towards the fulfilment of the promise, a constitution commission was appointed only to have even its semi-democratic proposals rejected. Considerable time was spent in examining and re-examining the report, but time passed and the publication of the constitution could not be delayed indefinitely.

Basic Democrats. It might appear strange at first sight that a military dictatorship, so firmly rooted in power, should have introduced a system which appeared on the surface to be democratic; but, in essence, there was no democratic decentralization. The basic institution was no democracy at all in the absence of political parties or political idealism; it had no real power. Control was centralized in the hands of the bureaucracy whose power was consolidated through the hierarchical system of councils subject to surveillance and control at every level. Its principal function was to support the President in the name of the people. The circumstances under which this system, with its distrust for the people and contempt for their intelligence, capacity and outlook, was introduced have been elaborated above.

The elections were held when Martial Law was in full swing and when people were still numb from its impact, especially from the spate of regulations and orders having the force of law—which created new offences daily and prescribed direct penalties out of all proportion to the supposed crime—and threatened the people with rigorous imprisonment for 14 years for criticizing the regime. Deputy commissioners and returning officers were empowered to erase from the voters' list the name of any voter or to reject the nomination paper of any candidate (and even to cancel his election) whom they considered politically undesirable or disqualified on any of several grounds. Thus, persons with self-respect normally kept aloof from the elections; only a few participated. In many places, no nomination papers were filed and people were cajoled, impressed and coerced by the authorities to stand as candidates. Hardly any votes were cast in many places. It is said that there were Basic Democrats who were returned to office by their own solitary vote. Voters came from such a limited circle that family, tribal, religious, or sectarian considerations; special powers such as those of a lambarder (an honorary tax collector in West Pakistan) vested in the candidate; petty landowners; village touts (brokers dealing in shady transactions and often acting as intermediaries between criminals and the authorities); unscrupulous police agents; goondas or gangsters who terrorized the neighbourhood and were listed as bad characters in the police records, determined the elections.

With such material, it was obvious that there would be dishonesty and corruption. During both the elections for the chairmanships of the union councils or committees and for the legislatures (the same Basic Democrats voted for the central as well as the provincial seats), votes were sold to the highest bidders. They were neither responsive to political parties nor swayed by patriotic considerations. Never indeed had Pakistan witnessed such wholesale demoralization and corruption during elections as during President Ayub Khan's Martial Law and its successor regime. The President created the institution of Basic Democracy to provide a personal following for himself—at first outside political parties and later as an ingredient of the Muslim League (Convention)—and he loaded them with favours, especially just previous to calling upon them to give him a vote of confidence. They were given powers to levy taxes on a large number of items. From the funds so raised the chairmen were given a remuneration of Rs400 a month and a paid secretary. After sundry other expenses, the chairmen, in consultation with their subdivisional officers, were required to spend the balance—supplemented by a munificent allotment of Rs300 million—on local development projects with neither supervision nor audit of accounts. They were given minor criminal and civil powers.

This experiment had been tried long before during the British regime and abandoned, because the union boards and union courts were influenced by local party factions and were liable to partisanship and corruption although their members were of better quality and more representative of the people than Basic Democrats. They were empowered to certify that sellers and purchasers of property were Pakistani nationals, an item which proved to be a handsome source of income for the chairmen. They became registrars of births, deaths, marriages and divorces and were empowered to effect reconciliation between a divorced couple or to register a divorce in the absence of reconciliation. They were given sundry other powers, which they turned to their advantage. The institution, far from being democratic, was not even representative of the people though elected as above. It was designed to support the President when required and to provide him with a closed forum to pass resolutions as directed by district authorities and where the President and ministers could express their views without danger of adverse comment. It has been recognized even by the Franchise Commission that the system has bred corruption on an extensive scale.

The mandate. A vote by the Basic democrats, such as above, could by no manner or means be accepted as a mandate of the country. The terms of the mandate were prescribed by the President himself to suit his interests. They were three in number, and one may give him credit that there were not more since he could have obtained the votes under all circumstances irrespective of the terms of the mandate. In fact, the voters had no choice, and it was not possible to agitate against the terms of the mandate without courting the danger of rigorous imprisonment for 14 years. The votes were taken when Martial Law was in full swing; the voters were taken to the polls by government officers who provided them with conveyance. The votes were cast against the dumb 'black box'. Surprisingly enough—and this shows that in the bosom of some Basic Democrats lurked such opposition to the regime and distrust of the President that it transcended the fear of official reprisals—a fairly large number of votes were cast against President Ayub, although one could have reasonably expected, if he was at all popular, to see one hundred per cent votes in his favour. He won against the dumb 'black box' by a substantial margin; the result could not have been otherwise.

The Constitution Commission. A constitution commission was set up as a result of the mandate; its main recommendations were not accepted. Of course, the Commission was profusely thanked for its honest labours. The recommendations were examined by a cabinet committee, and the President himself, thereafter, produced a constitution, for which he assumed the fullest and sole responsibility as the author thereof as the unique product of his wisdom and experience. That constitution is in conformity with the opinions which he expressed from time to time as his personal views even when the Commission was gathering opinions and was deliberating. Where then was the justification for appointing the Commission?

The term of the Presidency. The President claimed that with the mandate of the country, via the Basic Democrats, in his favour, he could have fixed his own terms as the first President for a longer period than three years and sixty days, but his democratic instincts stood in the way. But the real reason for his apparent moderation and self-sacrifice was that he wanted the next elections to be held before the EBDOed politicians were unmuzzled, that is to say, before December 1966. Hence, the elections of the President, the Basic Democrats, and the legislatures had to be done before that date. Such was his fear of the EBDOed politicians that in addition to the explicit disability imposed by the EBDO, namely, disqualification from standing for any elected body until December 1966, many other disabilities had been imposed on the EBDOed by subsequent legislation, namely, by the Political Parties Act of 1962 and by Ordinance I of 1963 (subsequently passed into law) which prevented them from indulging in any political activity whatsoever. The President limited the period of his unelected and automatic presidentship to three years and sixty days, not as a result of any democratic urge, but to ensure his own return, should he fail to eliminate his rivals and get returned without a contest.

Election to Presidency. He opened the presidentship for election, and proposed to offer himself for election as a true democrat. This sounds much better than the actual reality. He cleverly managed to eliminate possible rivals and EBDOed all influential politicians who could have posed a danger to him by preventing them from standing for any elected body or from influencing elections as they could not indulge in any political activity whatsoever. He emasculated political parties and threatened to take action against newspapers which were critical of his regime, and thus he stifled all opposition.

Secondly, he inserted a peculiar clause in the constitution according to which no more than three persons could stand for the presidentship. If there were more than three candidates (exclusive of the President himself who would be the fourth), a joint session of the central and the two provincial legislatures would select three of those who filed nomination papers. Under those circumstances, the President could put up at least three nominal candidates and, in the joint session of the legislatures where he would have a huge majority, he could easily get his three nominees selected. They could subsequently discreetly withdraw and leave him uncontested. Thirdly, if by some mischance or miscalculation, there was a contest, there would be no danger to his own election by his pet, pampered, controlled and corrupt Basic Democrats who formed the electoral college under the constitution (Article 165). He saw to it that election of the President was not by adult franchise; this required an amendment of the constitution. There were more than 40,000 Basic Democrats in each province (Article 155). This number could apparently be increased to any number by executive order.

He suggested that the number of such units—known as electoral units— should be increased from 80,000 to 120,000 (60,000 in each wing); this was accepted by the Franchise Commission. This would decrease still further the number of voters in each primary unit and increase the chances of the wrong type of people being elected—those subject to bribery and corruption. Incidentally, it would place on the public exchequer an additional burden and on the poor people of Pakistan, additional local taxation.

Provisions for election to legislatures. He was careful to provide in the constitution that the legislatures and the Basic Democrats were elected before the disability on the EBDOed expired, that is, before December 1966. The terms of the Basic Democrats were to expire in October 1964, the legislature in June 1965 and of the President on 6 August 1965.

Franchise Commission. A franchise commission was constituted by the President to advise on the formation of an electoral college for the office of President and for the legislatures. It was well known that he had advised the commission that he would not be able to resist the demand for adult franchise for elections to the legislature, but the President's own election, particularly in his case, should be by Basic Democrats as he could not be expected to canvass crores of voters. The chairman of the Franchise Commission, Akhtar Hussain, and a provincial minister, Hassan Ali Chowdhury, uncle of the deceased Mohammad Ali of Bogra, recommended accordingly. The President then appeared to have second thoughts on adult franchise and wanted to have the election to the legislatures by the electoral colleges of Basic Democrats. In any event, the electorate, whichever it might be, adult population or Basic Democrats, could not elect persons disqualified by EBDO, and, as the political parties were emasculated, there was considerable confusion in the political arena. Moreover, the suggestions of the Franchise Commission as regards the election to the office of President were such that, if accepted, the election would not be plain sailing for him. Hence, he did not accept the report.

One other danger was looming which was bound to cause considerable agitation and which might give him an excuse for postponing the elections and having another coup d'etat. Hitherto, the President had taken joint electorate, which he, personally, had always favoured for granted. The Basic Democrats were elected by a joint electorate; his own vote of confidence as well as elections to the legislatures were conducted under the same system. Now, apparently fishing for the support of fanatical Muslims and of political elements which relied for success on religious and communal passions who insisted that separate electorate was an accepted Islamic concept and not a political contrivance, and that a joint electorate was repugnant to Islamic ideology, he gradually insinuated through his Law Minister that he might revert to separate electorates. By this he hoped to create a rift in the opposition, to divide the Hindus and Muslims of East Pakistan once more and reduce the number of Muslim representatives from East Pakistan. East Pakistan would undoubtedly revolt against such a proposal. Incidentally, it could take so long to resolve the problem that it would not be possible to have the elections within the time prescribed by President Ayub's constitution. Hence, another revolution and another coup could become the obvious result. This could also help to shelve the recommendations of the Franchise Commission which were very inconvenient for the President. Some prominent leaders of the Muslim League (Council), however, who at one time had pressed for separate electorate on the grounds that it was predicated by the spirit of Islam—and more because it gave their party with its communal tendencies a better chance in the elections—accepted joint electorate. Hopefully, this might induce the President to desist from the very mischievous manoeuvre of reverting to separate electorate.

It appeared that the opposition in the national parliament was prepared to accept the proposals of the Franchise Commission. Government placed the report before the National Assembly just a quarter of an hour before the close of the session held in early 1963 in order to stifle all discussion and have the report referred—without ascertaining the views of the members—to a select committee in which it would have a majority. It could, therefore, push its own views on the nature of the elections and throw overboard the report of the Franchise Commission. The government should, obviously, have placed a franchise bill before the House which would have given some indication of its views. The opposition rightly objected to such foul, unparliamentary, undemocratic tactics, and, it was reported, created uproarious scenes.

A few of the recommendations—all based on joint electorate—which the President found inconvenient and which diminished his chances of success appeared to be as follows:

First, the Franchise Commission exploded the President's arguments advanced in favour of indirect elections. The members argued that even though the average voter was illiterate, he could appreciate national interests and could cast his vote with understanding and a sense of responsibility using proper judgement regarding the merits of a candidate given proof of their sagacity and integrity. Certain vested interests and a section of the intelligentsia did not agree with this concept, but the Franchise Commission held, in common with the Simon Commission and the Indian Franchise Commission, that literacy is not a test of wisdom, character or political ability and does not imply that the individual is incapable of casting an independent vote. It further pointed out that elections through the Basic Democrats electorate—the members of which were elected indirectly—were marked by bribery and corruption, while adult franchise would promote political education and the development of parties based on sound political ideology. After further explaining that political parties help to crystallize and mobilize public opinion, the Commission recommended that elections to the legislatures should be through adult franchise. This would require amendment of the constitution and, hence, the cooperation of the President. It, however, warned that political propaganda must not degenerate into a campaign of hatred, misrepresentation and inflamed passions, and candidates who encouraged this should be disqualified.

Second, it recommended that the election of the President should also be through adult franchise, but certain special circumstances existed which appeared to favour election through Basic Democrats provided that the number could be increased from 80,000 to 120,000 and multi-member constituencies were permitted where necessitated by circumstances. Third, if its general recommendation that the President should be elected through universal adult franchise based on joint electorate was not accepted and the election was held through Basic Democrats instead, it recommended:

- That Article 167 of the constitution which limited presidential candidates to three (by selection by a joint session of all the legislatures) should be repealed.
- If that was not accepted, then the selection should be by the members of the new legislatures, elected through universal adult suffrage, and that each member should have only one vote and not three.
- That the election of Basic Democrats should be after the selection had been made so that the voters of the Basic Democrats could know the identity of Presidential candidates; and
- To enable this, the office of the present President should be extended by two months.

It was clear that if the proposals of the Franchise Commission were accepted, then all the dreams of the President that he would utilize the existing legislatures to select his three candidates by bloc-voting and, after their withdrawal, he would return uncontested to office would be frustrated. But the main proposal which frightened the President was adult franchise for elections to the legislature; this could have far-reaching consequences. It might even become possible to amend the constitution, and democratize it accordingly, which he could not tolerate. Moreover, a legislature in which he did not have a majority might not support his political proposals. This explains why the President did not place a Franchise Bill before the House, why he did not expose his views and why he flung the report at the House at the last moment. The constitution could not be amended and all would be well. In any event, his own re-election was secure as long as Basic Democrats, then or in the future, formed the electoral college.

Impeachment of the President. The provisions for impeachment of the President make the constitution a farce. Three-fourths of the total number of members were required for a successful issue. This would be impossible to obtain in the face of the array of parliamentary secretaries, tribal representatives—who are mostly nominees of deputy commissioners; representatives of Swat, Dir, and Chitral; the erstwhile princely houses and feudal landlords; and postulants for office, permits and licenses. Further, if, after the President had been given time to organize his forces and influence (he would get between 14 and 30 days), the proponents of the motion (who must be one-third of the total number of members) could not muster half of the members of the central legislature in favour of the motion, they would all lose their seats in the legislature. Who could be expected to take the risk under such circumstances? The clause was wholly illusory.

'He allowed political parties to function.' He did indeed, but with such restrictions that, to use the words of Miss Fatima Jinnah, they were emasculated—all but his own. To him political parties were anathema, and he held them responsible for all the ills of the people. He, later, not only joined a political party but promoted it himself; he brought it into being, vigorously canvassed for it and mobilized the governors, the ministers, the parliamentary secretaries and government servants to do so also. He extended to it all the patronage of government—licenses, permits, contracts, and expenditure of development funds, through the favour of deputy commissioners. As an excuse for his volte-face, he stated that the people he had to work with and the ministers and parliamentary secretaries and the members of the legislatures who had been elected on a non-political basis by the non-political Basic Democrats, refused to listen to his wise advice and his words of reason. He was, therefore, forced to agree to a Political Parties Act, which was passed on 15 July 1962.

The President had advised strongly that not more than two or three political parties should be allowed to function, but his advisers could not see eye to eye with him even on this minor point. But parties likely to command public confidence had been properly emasculated. No EBDOed person could become a member. A political party could not act in a manner prejudicial to the (sic) Islamic ideology or the integrity and security of Pakistan. On both counts, wide loopholes were left for the government to harass political parties he did not want to exist and if the central government decided that a particular political party was guilty of either transgression, the matter could be referred to the Supreme Court whose decision would be final.

A political party was defined as a body of individuals or an association of persons setting up an organizational structure or collecting funds or owning properties with the object of propagating political opinions, or indulging in any other political activities. By a further ordinance dated 6 January 1963—subsequently enacted into law—the definition of political parties was enlarged with the intention of making the NDF a political party and thus debarring the EBDOed politicians from participation with it. The NDF was, in essence, a movement which did not have an organizational structure and did not collect funds or own property. It was not a body of individuals or an association of persons. According to the new definition a political party included a group or combination of persons who were operating for the purpose of propagating political opinions or indulging in any other political activity. It was still to be decided if the NDF was indeed a group or a combination of persons at all.

Actually the movement took the form of meetings arranged by local workers in various parts of the country on the platform of which leaders of various defunct or revived political parties appeared as it suited their convenience in order to advocate a democratic constitution for the country. The NDF, therefore, instead of being a group or combination of persons was a movement supported by an amorphous gathering of millions and millions of people who believed in democracy. By another clause, an EBDOed person was debarred from 'associating himself with the activities of a political party (as so defined and enlarged), and further debarred from association with the activities of another person similarly debarred, that is, another EBDOed.' If he did so he was punishable with imprisonment for two years or with fine or with both. Further, if, in the opinion of the government, an EBDOed person was indulging in or likely to indulge in any political activity he could be ordered for a period of six months—extendable by another period of six months—to refrain from addressing any meeting, including a press conference, or issuing any statement of a political nature to the press. Contravention was punishable with imprisonment for two years or with fine or with both.

Fundamental rights. President Ayub Khan said he was prepared to recognize fundamental rights and to make them justiciable as a concession to democracy. In his constitution he more or less incorporated the fundamental rights as classified in the constitution of 1956. However, they were not fundamental and justiciable but were merely guides so that legislatures would not encroach on them. The legislatures, therefore, were paramount. Even if they did pass infringing legislation, such legislation could not be challenged in a court of law as being incompetent. He justified this on the grounds that in the English constitution parliament is supreme and its enactments cannot be challenged in a court of law as being unconstitutional. However, he ignored the fact that the English constitution is unwritten. The President stated that he was prepared to recognize as fundamental rights the Principles of Legislation set out in the constitution of 1956 and make them justiciable but only if they are subject to the existing laws and ordinances which make the fundamental rights nugatory and lifeless. The opposition in the National Assembly objected to the constitution being amended in the above form, and, as government needed a two-thirds majority to carry its amendments, it promised in return for the requisite support to exclude some of the minor pieces of legislation as governing fundamental rights. We may be certain that the concessions will be illusory, and the opposition is not likely to support the government and provide it with its majority unless laws which nullify fundamental rights are excluded.

OBSTRUCTIONS TO HOLDING PUBLIC MEETING

After my triumphant and successful meetings in East Pakistan I went to Lahore in West Pakistan where I was received enthusiastically. It was with difficulty that I escaped the overwhelming enthusiasm of the crowd, and I took refuge in the nearest car which I could find. Unable to tolerate the growing volume of support on my behalf, the government resorted to obstruction, intimidation and violence. A great supporter of authority, A.M. Quraishi—a shady character with a murky past who was proud of his associations with the underworld—got together a number of trucks, each with a few roughs (*goondas*) holding *lathis* (staves).[28] Each had little black pennants fluttering from its top; this was meant to be a black flag demonstration. The roughs did not get off their trucks, apparently overawed by the huge crowd that had come to welcome me. The police permitted the crowd to follow me up to a certain point. When the people were turning back, they suddenly fell upon them with *lathis* and beat them mercilessly. The assault was an obvious manoeuvre to demonstrate that government took exception to my reception and would obstruct such manifestations in my favour. *Dawn,* a pro-government, pro-Ayub English daily with wide circulation and heavily patronized by the government with advertisements at maximum rates and believed normally to be its spokesman in policy matters, carried (inadvertently perhaps) pictures of the reception, the trucks with the black pennants and the police assault. After the incident the black flag trucks paraded the city in triumph. Such licensed and registered trucks are not permitted to convey people or parade the streets without special permission from the police. There was no doubt that the government of West Pakistan and the central government were on the warpath.

From this time onwards I was not given any peace in West Pakistan. It would have been far wiser on my part to have had a meeting in Karachi immediately after my release when I would certainly have carried the city by storm. I thought, however, that it would have been unfair to the people of East Pakistan, who had actually started a sound political movement to secure my release, if I held a public meeting in West Pakistan first, where I would be called upon to give my views before meeting the people of East Pakistan. The political thinking in West Pakistan undoubtedly differed in material particulars from that in East Pakistan. It was confused, and a substantial number of people preferred traditionally to support the government in power and reap whatever benefits they could harvest by such support. In other words, they had developed an opportunist mentality. My view had always been that in order to keep the two wings together and promote national unity and integration, something more was necessary than that the majority of the population in both wings was predominantly Muslim, facilely described as the link of Islam. It was necessary also to have economic justice and economic development for all the regions and peoples of Pakistan. But, above all, the political outlook in both wings should be identical and as harmonious as possible. In view of the differences in the historical background of the two wings this was extremely difficult to obtain; still, endeavours had to be made in that direction. Otherwise political integration would be impossible and the two wings would fall apart. This integration could, in my opinion, be achieved through democratic processes only.

In West Pakistan the following parties were well established: the Muslim League, the Awami League, the Jamaat-i-Islami and the NAP. Chowdhury Mohammad Ali was also endeavouring to organize the Nizam-i-Islam Party and to make it an all-Pakistan organization. After his resignation from the Prime Ministership in 1956 he started a party which he called the Tehrik-i-Islam Party. He was not successful and for a little while joined the Jamaat-i-Islami and, later, the Nizam-i-Islam. He had a stalwart lieutenant in Mian Abdul Bari, a member of the National Assembly; but the strength of the party was his own personality. It had hardly any members or organization or influence in the country. The Awami League and the NAP decided on non-revival theory until democracy was established. The Jamaat-i-Islami Party went into swift action and once more re-established its organization.

LEAGUE CONVENTION WITH A BAD START

The Muslim League also was anxious to revive itself and was encouraged by the President to do so who saw in its power-hunting traditions ultimate support for himself. The members of this defunct League had stood for election to the primary Basic Democracy units and to the legislatures from the Basic Democrats electorate. Many prominent members of the Muslim League had welcomed the Martial Law regime and had rushed to congratulate the President on the constitution he had promulgated. He had every reason to be satisfied with the docility of the party, although it was as defunct as the others. After the promulgation of the constitution, however, on 8 June 1962, there had been a disturbance in the trend of support when its members, led by its President, Khan Abdul Qayyum Khan, joined the other parties in demanding my release from preventive detention. The Vice-President of the organization, Maulana Muhammad Akram Khan, was induced to call a meeting of the council of the Muslim League at Dhaka.

Apparently the inner coterie of political advisers of the President had second thoughts and feared that an organization not entirely under their control might also demand democracy, condemn the constitution and embarrass the President. In any event, they considered that East Pakistan was certainly not the proper venue for a meeting of the Muslim League. Suddenly, with no explanation, Maulana Mohammad Akram Khan cancelled the meeting and refused to give reasons for his precipitous and strange conduct. The central ministers and central parliamentary secretaries then met in Rawalpindi, the seat of the government, and decided to call a convention of the Muslim League in Karachi. The convention was to consist of 700 members, 350 from each wing, and Chowdhury Khaliquzzaman was to preside. Although a reception committee had been formed in Karachi, the invitations were issued from Rawalpindi to persons who were considered to be thoroughly reliable. Members from East Pakistan were provided with free passage (all except one, according to his own statement) and the payment of the fare was guaranteed by the Defence Department which was directly administered by the President. Under the constitution the Defence Minister had to be a Lieutenant General or higher and who could be better and safer than the Field Marshal President himself? To make up for the shortfall in East Pakistan representation, the clerical staff in Rawalpindi coming from East Pakistan were given leave to attend the convention. The expenses of all the delegates from both wings were met by the reception committee and by all accounts they had a very enjoyable time in West Pakistan. The meeting of the convention was held in the Fish Aquarium in Karachi. Apparently there was a direct telephone line from there to the presidential palace as he seemed to be in touch with the proceedings. One member from East Pakistan made a somewhat intemperate speech. The President, by phone, wanted to have him arrested and brought before him, but before that could be done he was discreetly put on a plane for East Pakistan.

In spite of the members having been hand-picked, the meeting was stormy from the beginning with the people from East Pakistan shouting for the release of Khan Abdul Qayyum Khan, demanding that a resolution for his release should first be passed before proceeding to business. All the ministers adorned the stage behind the proceedings. A contingent from the NWFP had been brought to the convention by Khan Habibullah Khan, one of the central ministers, and they were most vociferous in their condemnation of Qayyum Khan. Mian Mumtaz Daultana had also sent some of his followers and friends to the convention chief amongst them being Chattha and Kirmani. Kirmani was roughly handled by the pro-government party for demanding the release of Qayyum Khan and was forced to sit down. An objection was raised that this was not a convention of the Muslim League, so the assembly was designated as a 'Convention of Muslim Leaguers'. After recognizing that the presidential form of government was in accordance with the genius of the people of Pakistan and that nothing better than the constitution which had been promulgated could be conceived, it was resolved that the Muslim League should be organized from the bottom. Chief organizers were appointed for the centre and for East and West Pakistan.

The second session of the convention was a public session held in the Polo Ground next to the presidential palace. Karachi had become practically a city of Muslim refugees and displaced persons from India. Its pre-partition population of 350,000 Hindus and Muslims had been swollen by a Muslim population, mostly refugees, of more than 2 million. These refugees were staunch supporters of the Muslim League in India and many had to quit India on that account. It was expected, therefore, that the public meeting of the convention would be a grand success, particularly as only a few days earlier in Karachi, Qayyum Khan had, in an address at a meeting attended by about 200,000 people, requested my release. Very grand preparations were made, with *shamianas* (pavilions), carpets, flower pots, glittering neon tubelights, microphones and loudspeakers stretching into the far distance, to cater to a vast audience. Unfortunately, not more than 4,000 people attended, inclusive of the delegates.

A group of students first clamoured for attention, demanding that their resolution protesting the proposals of the Education Commission which had been appointed by the President, should be passed first. As the organizers of the convention demurred, the students clambered onto the platform, held their meeting, passed their protest resolution, and left. After they left not more than 1,500 people remained. Even then the meeting was not allowed to proceed peaceably, and the audience was such that objections were heard every time somebody alluded to the meeting as one of the Muslim League. There was considerable disturbance until a Moulvi from East Pakistan prayed to Allah to give guidance to the audience so that they might sit down peacefully and allow the meeting to proceed. One-half responded and the other did not, whereupon the Moulvi proceeded further to pray to Allah to give guidance to the other half, too. Ultimately, some well-known roughs, whose services had been engaged for the occasion, mauled the people who were disturbing the meeting; the convention then proceeded calmly to transact its business with 600 in attendance. The farcical meeting could be judged from the fact that when the meeting had settled down Fazlul Qadir Chowdhury shouted into the microphone: how could a handful of people hope to disturb this vast throng of 50,000 which he saw before him. This was meant for the consumption of the President next door at the presidential palace at the other end of the microphone. The Muslim League (Convention) had a bad start indeed.

There was, however, little doubt that the Muslim League (Convention) was in a position to set up some kind of an organization. Evidence supplied at the convention had shown that financial and other support would be provided through government patronage; influence and coercion by government officials, governors and ministers; public funds supplemented by a forced levy of substantial dimensions from industrial millionaires; voluntary contributions from the myriads of sycophants, hangers-on, worshippers of power and social and political hopefuls; licence and permit seekers and from would-be industrialists and magnates. There was bound to be set up a network of organizers, committees and members, at least on paper. Whether it would be able to withstand the strain of an election based on adult franchise was a different matter. That the President himself, who was canvassing for the party personally and holding meetings all over Pakistan, had doubts regarding the strength and popularity of his party was proved by the fact that he did not dare to take the risk of basing the next election to the legislatures or for the presidency on adult franchise.

The Main Revolutionary Principle Abandoned

This convention was organized by the President and ministers soon after the Political Parties Act was passed in July 1962 and, in spite of the President expressing a benevolent aloofness, few had any doubts that in fact this was the party the President would foster, patronize, utilize, join, canvass for, and ultimately assume the leadership of. The ministers pretended to be nothing other than ordinary members; the President pretended he had no interest in it other than an academic one, namely, that he would like to see it organized from the bottom as all parties should be. When Chowdhury Khaliquzzaman, the chief organizer, offered him the presidentship he reiterated firmly that he would not join any political party. A few days before he actually joined the party he gave a solemn assurance to the Raja Sahib of Mahmudabad, who had been one of the staunchest pillars of the AIML before partition, that he had no intention of joining the Muslim League (Convention). Since then he had worn himself thin addressing public meetings in West Pakistan and issuing statements exhorting the public to join the organization. The main revolutionary principle that the work of the state could best be carried out without political parties had been abandoned.

In view of the creation of what may be considered a government-sponsored Muslim League (picturesquely defined as the Pocket Muslim League), Mian Mumtaz Khan Daultana thought that the time had come to revive the Muslim League organization as it existed before the Martial Law regime. He believed that if he did not do so, the members of the defunct Muslim League would migrate toward the Muslim League (Convention) and would not be able to hold out against the blandishments offered by the government-sponsored organization. He did not agree with my contention that the Muslim League (Convention) would not make any headway with the masses or the intelligentsia and that only those who wanted to flatter the President and pretended to accept his constitution and dictatorship would join it. In his opinion, the members in West Pakistan were not developed enough politically for sound critical analysis and could be easily misled by appearances, particularly if backed by inducements. I also pointed out to him another grave anomaly. In East Pakistan the NDF was working on the basis of non-revival of parties, and already the East Pakistan Muslim League had refused to revive itself and had joined the NDF. I could not possibly let down Nurul Amin, who had gallantly refused the glamorous posts that had been offered him. Hence, it would not be possible for me to give to the revived Muslim League any place in the NDF organization in East Pakistan, although I could do so in West Pakistan. Daultana understood and agreed to abide by my solution.

One of the surviving joint or assistant secretaries of the Muslim League convened a meeting of the council of the Muslim League in Dhaka. Mian Daultana held a preliminary meeting of the West Pakistan Muslim League council in Lahore and went to Dhaka with a strong contingent of about 85 members. A meeting was held there which, as far as I can remember, was presided over by Maulana Mohammad Akram Khan. Khwaja Nazimuddin was elected President of the revived Muslim League (Council). The council meeting was very sparsely attended by East Pakistan members and many who did attend actually belonged to the non-revivalist group. The latter had attended to induce the organization to cooperate with the NDF if five or six conditions they had tabulated were accepted. The conditions were easily acceptable as they laid down certain basic principles of a democratic constitution and I accepted them.

Khwaja Nazimuddin started his campaign by addressing a meeting at the Paltan Maidan in Dhaka. The meeting was thinly attended; in East Pakistan generally his meetings were not successful. In West Pakistan, however, his meetings were all well attended, according to West Pakistan standards, and the Government of West Pakistan did not at first consider it worth while to disturb them. His reception at the Lahore railway station was very enthusiastic and a tremendous success. He made an effort to organize the Muslim League (Council) from the bottom, but there were persistent rumours that he might coalesce or cooperate with the Muslim League (Convention). These rumours were thrown up from time to time, probably by the government party, to create confusion in the ranks of the Muslim League (Council). Cooperation between the two, or their unification, scarcely seemed possible in view of the strong line that he took in his speeches that there was no room for cooperation until the conditions for the restoration of unadulterated democracy had been fulfilled.

REPEATED OBSTRUCTIONS TO HOLDING PUBLIC MEETING

I was advised to start my campaign in West Pakistan with a meeting in Lahore which was the nerve-centre of the political life of West Pakistan. I had hoped that Mahmud Ali Qasuri, secretary of the NAP, would be able to preside over the meeting. Apart from being a brilliant advocate he had a tremendous personality and always championed, particularly in the law courts, the cause of persons opposed by the government. His misfortune was that although he himself was not a communist, his chief advisers and workers were believed to be uncompromising leftists.[29] Since there were objections to his presidency as the NAP was still not well received in the Punjab and was suspected of being anti-national, I was forced to take the chair. The meeting was very well attended by Lahore standards, but it was disturbed by groups of young men speaking from two corners under the protection of the police. I, however, controlled the situation and these two very small groups of 25 and 15 persons found refuge in the police station next door. My next meeting was at Lyallpur. There the government definitely and openly organized disturbances. There were two groups of hooligans who kept shouting all the time. They were provided with intoxicants by the police officers at the meeting ground itself. Ultimately, they were driven off by the crowd that had come to hear me and the meeting ended peacefully.

My next meeting was to be held at Gujranwalla, a city where I had held very large meetings and where my party was specially popular. At the railway station I was accorded the usual tumultuous reception, but while being led to the car somebody shot at me and the bullet lodged in the thigh of the person to my right who was accompanying me. Some students carrying black flags (little strips of black cloth mounted on poles) and shouting the slogan 'Mian Sahib, Zindabad' were present but discreetly kept their distance. These students were brought by the police and subsequently led by the Police Inspector himself towards the house where I was resting. They were driven off before they could reach their destination in spite of the exhortations of the police who were pushing them on.

While I was attending a garden party given in my honour that evening several leaders from Lahore, including Sheikh Mujibur Rahman from East Pakistan, rushed in with great agitation. They had heard that a shot had been fired at me, and they insisted that I should not attend the public meeting. I insisted that I would do so, however, and the matter was left for future consideration. At night I went to a house adjacent to the meeting place from where I was to proceed to the meeting. On the way we noticed that a number of police trucks had brought bullies and roughs from villages and that about 400 of them, armed with iron-shod *lathis*, were lurking in the dark between the road and the railway line near the place of the meeting. It was clear that government was determined to prevent me from addressing the meeting and was willing to resort to violence on a large-scale. Mahmud Ali Qasuri, Nawabzada Nasrullah Khan, Mujibur Rahman, Khwaja Rafiq and many others who had come from Lahore to see me went to the meeting first.[30] It was the biggest gathering that had ever been seen in Gujranwalla. When they appeared on the stage and announced that the public meeting would not be held on account of the preparations that had been made to attack it, some roughs who were seated in front and were armed with sodawater bottles (a particularly dangerous missile which bursts when it hits the target) began pelting them on the stage. There was no doubt that the government was determined to prevent me from holding public meeting in West Pakistan. Under pressure from my friends, I decided to postpone meetings in the province until the government gave its assurance that it would not organize hostile demonstration to disturb them. The government refused to give any such assurance.

Thereafter, I held another series of spectacular meetings in East Pakistan in those district headquarters which I had not covered on the previous occasion and in a few important subdivisional headquarters. The leaders of the various non-revived parties appeared on the same platform amidst great enthusiasm. It appeared that the people were getting attuned to the idea of a grand united effort in which and through which the various parties would unite their differences. In speech after speech the leaders of all the parties elevated me to the position of spokesman for Pakistan and leader of the movement and pledged me their support.

BHASHANI'S DOUBLE-DEALING

This apparently did not suit the NAP, which felt that its leader Maulana Bhashani, who was in detention, was being relegated to the background. He had been arrested in 1958 soon after the revolution on 7 October. For some time he had been placed in solitary confinement and had passed an uncomfortable time, but, on his representation, he was given more comfortable quarters. The President decided to release him on 6 October 1959 on condition that he would be confined to his village at Kagmari in Tangail district in East Pakistan and would not address any public meetings. Maulana Bhashani felt that he was bound to be approached by people, and he knew that if he said anything at all the government might victimize him again alleging that he had violated the condition. He, therefore, at his own suggestion, was confined to a bungalow in Dhaka where his family lived with him but where he was well-guarded and was not permitted to see anyone except his lawyer and the doctors who were placed at his disposal. From the material point of view, he was fairly well-lodged and he was given an allowance. He is believed to have written letters to the President which were very flattering. Unfortunately, there does not seem to have been any agitation for his release. He and his party and friends took it very ill that there had been no movement during the year he was confined, while, later, there was much commotion for my release immediately after I was arrested on 30 January 1962.

The spectacular meetings held by the NDF in East Pakistan had brought other leaders to the fore and Maulana Bhashani was advised by the underground to stage a come-back by undertaking a fast which he called 'unto death', allegedly depriving himself of food and water. He was then removed to a hospital where he stayed for nine days. The NAP workers tried to arouse enthusiasm for his release amongst the students, the young men and the members of the public, but failed. We, however, held public meetings demanding not only his release but also that of Khan Abdul Qayyum Khan and other detenus. We saw him in hospital every day. There was no visible change in his condition, which was ascribed to his remarkable vitality. He spoke volubly day in and day out with his guards, his doctors and his visitors with such energy that people began to doubt whether he was actually fasting. With a simplicity which was the surest sign of a decaying but credulous mind which refused to believe that anyone could be guilty of such gross imposture, i believed he was fasting. However, I, too, began to have suspicions when, even on the eighth day, I found he was as vigorous and voluble as ever and his arms were as full and rounded as when he entered the hospital. It was ascertained that one of the doctors in attendance, who was a communist, fed him surreptitiously. The President was duly informed and he decided not to release him for 18 days and thus to exhibit plainly to the people of Pakistan what a fraud he was and to destroy his prestige forever. But, he was advised by his knowledgeable entourage and the East Pakistan organizers of the Muslim League (Convention) not to delay the release and not to denigrate him further as he could prove very useful in counteracting my influence and becoming a thorn in the side of the NDF.

Maulana Bhashani was released on 9 May. Like Mahatma Gandhi had done before him, he insisted on taking the first (public) sip of liquid at my hands, loyally supported by several of his devoted young leftist followers. After his release he gave a press conference, a marvellous achievement for a man who claimed that he had denied food and water for nine days. He then went on a voyage on the River Jamuna in a country-boat to recuperate according to his usual custom. He addressed some river bank meetings which were not well attended. His Paltan Maidan meeting also was not spectacular. I am afraid that it took some time to live down the rumour that he was not genuine.

At a meeting in Chittagong, which was probably the first after his complete recuperation, he made a speech in which he attacked the previous regimes and the political leaders with no less vehemence than President Ayub and praised the President for his perspicacity in overthrowing them; however, he took the precaution to plead for democracy at the same time. Apparently his followers could see the danger to their party if he continued to take the above line and must have warned him not to do so, for after that he changed his tactics and declared that he was prepared to support me and the NDF movement for democracy. But it was not easy to overlook his speech at Chittagong which showed his innermost feelings and the real trend of his mind and policies. In this manner Maulana Bhashani fulfilled his obligation to the President and any understanding he may have reached with him.

Moreover, in spite of his alleged support to the NDF he insisted in all speeches on his 16-point programme — or seven points, or five points — as the price of his cooperation. Many of them were controversial. He thus was able to undermine the objective to secure joint action by all parties. As the NAP had not yet been revived and he could not hold public meetings in its name, he called meetings of a non-existent Krishak Samity to propagate his views and helped the President considerably in creating confusion — if not an actual rift — in the NDF, thus sabotaging the movement. Maulana Bhashani stated that he was prepared to cooperate with any party, including that of President Ayub, which accepted his five-point programme which appeared to be as follows:

1. release all political prisoners;
2. adopt an independent, neutral foreign policy and withdraw from SEATO and CENTO;

3. provide for provincial autonomy;
4. establish full democracy; and
5. give full sovereignty to parliament, which includes justiciability of fundamental rights, adult franchise and full control of the budget.

Maulana Bhashani refused, however, to commit himself on the acceptability of President Ayub's constitution. He had a 3-hour conference with the President during which the release of political prisoners was discussed.[31] However, a few days previously he had stated that he would not meet the President unless the latter convened a joint meeting of the leaders of all parties and that he intended to meet the Governor of West Pakistan only on the subject of the release of all political prisoners.

A meeting of the high command of the NAP was held in Dhaka where the above points were further elaborated with the addition of the disintegration of One Unit in West Pakistan. Bhashani expressed the hope that there might be cooperation with other parties on a minimum programme. Immediately after the meeting, he announced that mass demonstrations to press for the demands should be held on 15 December and if Section 144 was imposed it should be defied. This point had not been raised at the meeting of the high command of the NAP which had defined the limits of the struggle for their programme as being conducted within the law and constitution. Bhashani's declaration took his lieutenants by surprise. Mahmudul Huq Usmani said that the matter had not been discussed before, but as Bhashani had said it, demonstration should be held. Mahmud Ali seemed to have resented this action of Bhashani which, he said, had not been passed by the NAP high command. This went against the resolution to remain within the bounds of law and which appeared to show that Bhashani transcended the party. Thereafter, the papers carried the news that Bhashani was to lead a cultural delegation to China on behalf of the Government of Pakistan. Much later, Bhashani contradicted this; he said that he was not being sent by the Government of Pakistan but had been invited by the Chinese government to attend their Independence Day celebration along with several NAP leaders. He could not accompany the members of the delegation to China as he was admitted to Jinnah Hospital suffering from a cold. However, he recovered sufficiently a few days later to go with his legal and medical advisers to participate in the celebration of 1 October. During his illness he was visited by several people, the most significant being Aziz Ahmed, the Foreign Secretary of the Government of Pakistan.

PRESIDENT'S ENMITY AND VENGEANCE

After Maulana Bhashani was released I held a few more meetings in East Pakistan and decided to return to West Pakistan. I hoped that after even government newspapers had criticized the West Pakistan government for violently obstructing me and preventing me from speaking in public that the government had changed its attitude. A meeting was announced, to be held at Patel Park in Karachi. Section 144 of the Criminal Procedure Code, which forbade meetings, was imposed on the plea that arms aid to India by the United States and the United Kingdom had created a dangerous tension. Rather than defying the ban I postponed the meeting for a fortnight during which the order was withdrawn. We received the impression that the government had relented and was prepared to allow my meeting to be held. Z.H. Lari, chief of the Muslim League (Council) in Karachi, was designated to preside; Mahmudul Huq Usmani of the NAP was to conduct the proceedings. Reports began to pour in that the government was arranging to disturb this meeting as well and that the police proposed to utilize some dangerous Pathan elements at Keamari for the purpose. These came to the meeting place in trucks escorted by a police officer. The Additional District Magistrate (ADM) and the local police station were informed; they promised to see that no disturbances took place. The ADM, however, made himself scarce when the meeting began. Just as I was leaving my house to attend the meeting, I was warned by a messenger not to go as some *goondas* had violently attacked the people on the dais. It appeared that the Pathans, who had been engaged by the police, interrupted Usmani while he was speaking. They marched up to the platform with *lathis* and revolvers, attacked some of the people on the dais with knives, slashed the *pandal* (the *shamiana* or pavillion), broke the microphones and carried three tape recorders away in triumph on lorries along with the microphones and other furnishings from the stage. The police, lurking just on the fringe, looked on benevolently. The attack and destruction lasted for nearly 20 minutes. After the hooligans had left, shouting slogans and dancing on the trucks and waving the microphones in triumph, while they paraded the streets of Karachi with police permission, the ADM and the police arrived from the nearby police station.

The Government of West Pakistan had not budged from its programme that come what may it would not allow me to hold a public meeting. It had no objection to anyone else holding a meeting, not even to Khwaja Nazimuddin who held meetings after the Muslim League (Council) had been formed and who was asserting that dictatorship must end and democracy be established. Unfortunately for me I appeared to be the sole target of the enmity and vengeance of the President who was good enough to raise me, undeservedly, to the rank of chief opponent, though I lay crushed, bruised and battered—abused by the President and humiliated by the EBDO conviction which had missed its mark. Instead of marring my reputation, it had raised me in the esteem of the people. This, I suppose, he could not bear.

It was necessary, however, to show the President that West Pakistan also demanded democracy. Meetings were arranged for me in Sindh but wherever a meeting was announced, Section 144 was imposed and the meeting was banned. As an alternative, it was thought desirable that some significant leaders might meet and draft a declaration supporting the movement for democracy. Accordingly, a group got together in the house of Mahmud Ali Qasuri at Lahore; a statement on the above lines was prepared and signed by me and by the leaders of the Jamaat-i-Islami (Maulana Maudoodi and Maulana Tufail Ahmad), the Awami League (Nawabzada Nasrullah and others), the NAP (Mahmud Ali Qasuri and others from the Punjab, Balochistan and NWFP) and some independents such as Chowdhury Fazal Ellahi, Yusuf Khattack and Colonel Abid Hossain. A representative contingent of all the non-revived parties of East Pakistan which had participated in the discussion and the drafting also signed. To my mind it was a signal triumph. Maulana Maudoodi, to my surprise and admiration—for it demonstrated his acumen for practical politics—did not insist on exploiting Islam, and all agreed that the first and foremost necessity was democracy. Hence, they agreed to the One-Point Programme. It was agreed that a convention would be held in due course to discuss the methods to obtain our objectives. The Muslim League (Council) was then in the process of formation. I knew that Daultana agreed with my programme and I was content with the League, until he was driven out by Khan Abdul Qayyum Khan, and with the Muslim League representatives from East Pakistan.

ALTERNATIVES SUGGESTED TO SAVE PAKISTAN

In addition to the election of a fresh constituent assembly to frame a fresh constitution, as suggested in the statement of the 'Nine Leaders', one may conceive of several other methods by which Pakistan could have had the benefit of a democratic constitution. The President could have amended the constitution of 1962 by substituting for it the 1956 constitution or by amending the clauses at variance with the latter. The 1956 constitution, with all its frailties which needed rectification, had still the merit that it was the result of the combined effort of all the members of a constituent assembly which had been elected on the basis laid down by the fundamental Independence Act of 1947 by which Pakistan was created, namely, by the members of the provincial legislatures who had themselves been elected by adult suffrage. These substitutions or amendments he could well have accepted, for after all, he had resiled one by one from the pillars any hypotheses on which he had based his own special constitution—which he had evolved as a result of his transcendent wisdom and wide experience and contacts.

A few examples will illustrate this. Through his ministers he vigorously exploited the amendment to the constitution (that he had made by an order under Article 224 and which was later declared illegal by the Supreme Court) which allowed ministers drawn from the legislatures to retain their seats as an inspirational synthesis of the presidential and parliamentary forms of government. He agreed to the existence of political parties, although he had trenchantly and abusively denounced them as the primary cause of the ruination of the state. He abandoned his insistence that the law should not permit more than two or three political parties, if any at all. More than that, he himself brought into existence the institution of Basic Democracy to serve his own political ends. It formed the nucleus of his own political party which he started immediately after the Political Parties Act was passed. He exploited Islam in such an unmerciful manner that it defied competition and tried to ingratiate himself with people whom he had hitherto denounced as nincompoops and despised as ignorants. He was even prepared to reconsider the basis of elections to the legislature, viz. to substitute the Basic Democrat Electoral College for adult franchise and to give the legislatures some powers over expenditures as long as those of his own household, increased by him several-fold just before the promulgation of the constitution, were not disturbed (By contrast, the Indian President reduced his own emoluments including his household budget, to an unimaginably low figure.).

As a further concession to civilization, he appeared ready to make fundamental rights justiciable, as if this would revolutionize the constitution, and would meet the growing demand for democracy—and further demonstrate that he was a real democrat—although time and again he, personally, and Manzur Qadir, his lawyer-Foreign Minister and chief exponent of his policy, had maintained strenuously that judges are misled by lawyers and should not be given the right to interpret whether fundamental rights had been violated by the legislatures or not. Of course, when the official bill was published it was found that these fundamental rights were made subject to laws and ordinances which had violated every single one of them. Such eyewash was rightly rejected by the opposition, and, as a two-thirds majority is necessary to pass amendments to the constitution, the bill, as proposed by the government, could not be enacted. The President obviously blamed the opposition for this impasse. Could he not, therefore, when he must have realized that his defences were crumbling, have given up those dictatorial powers he had reserved for himself and serve as a constitutional head of state with a parliamentary form of government—that is to say, adopt the 1956 constitution? This appeared the most logical thing to do.

Another alternative could have been to have fresh elections to the legislatures as soon as possible based on adult franchise. A central legislature so elected could set about democratizing the constitution. If the constitution was suitably amended so as to empower an elected legislature to amend it by majority vote so much the better. But, in any event, it was fairly certain that such an elected legislature would be able to provide the two-thirds majority required even if the elections were not fair and free (as no one would expect them to be after the manner in which the President utilized for his own benefit the government, civil and military resources at his command) and even if the entire machinery of the government was utilized to back the party of the President. Therefore, the President could see to it that the legislatures were elected by the Basic Democrats and not by adult suffrage.

Another possibility was that of a constitution agreed to by the leaders of public opinion at a Round Table Conference. The President argued that it is possible to have democracy with a presidential form of government. The 'Nine Leaders' of East Pakistan had in their statement shown an inclination for the parliamentary form but were prepared to consider an alternative. My personal view was that the people would not be able to follow the intricacies of such a combination. Democracy with a presidential system needs many institutional organizations with definite powers with which the people of Pakistan were not familiar. Moreover, the constitution did not provide for a presidential form of government; it was a misnomer to call it so. It was, in fact, a presidential dictatorship without checks and balances. The people understand the simple British parliamentary system which, until Martial Law, had been taken for granted in Pakistan. But, if the President desired to explore the possibilities of a synthesis, it would be necessary to consult the leaders of public opinion at a Round Table Conference.

But these are only methods—ways and means. The fundamental proposition was that we must have a democratic constitution, and all of us must work together to achieve this objective even though there were several political parties—revived and non-revived—with adherents who have not wavered from their loyalties. Each party had its own programme that might differ from those of others in basic ideas, in outlook, in ideology and in emphasis.

Apart from the fact that it would be surely impossible to evolve a programme which would satisfy all the demands of all the parties, there seemed to be no point in having a political system which was, in effect, a dictatorship. Hence, our programme could be limited to one point only: establishment of democracy, alternatively called democratization of the constitution, as a realistic concession to the latter's existence and to the possibility, however theoretical, of effecting amendments.

PARTY INTERESTS PREDOMINATE

My difficulties started with West Pakistan. I spoke at several conferences to most representative gatherings of the leaders drawn from all parties of Sindh, Balochistan and the NWFP where I was confronted with an insistent demand that the movement which I was inaugurating, and which I proposed to call the NDF, should have the disintegration of the One Unit in West Pakistan as part of its programme. Otherwise, they said, they were not interested in the establishment of democracy if it resulted in their continued subservience to Punjabi domination. I had the greatest difficulty in persuading them to give up the demand; I succeeded only by threatening to withdraw from the movement. Politically, I said, it would be unwise to support the invalidation of One Unit as it would give a handle immediately to the President to say that the NDF aimed at the disintegration of Pakistan and was made up of anti-nationals. Our energies would be dissipated trying to meet this allegation. Secondly, this would encourage each party to insist on its own party programme as a precedent condition and make confusion even more confounded. East Pakistan, as such, had several grievances which it would then insist be considered. Thirdly, we would not be able to put up a joint front. Basically we had to trust the people of Pakistan, their representatives and their combined wisdom and integrity to ensure justice to all people and all regions of Pakistan, and we were obligated to leave this problem to be tackled by them under a democratic constitution in a democratic manner.

In East Pakistan the NAP created difficulties. It seemed bent on taking advantage of every opportunity to push itself. Although it had accepted the non-revival theory, it held separate meetings of its own party members and organized its workers. One of their top groups led by Haji Danesh (of Dinajpur) and Mohiuddin (of Barisal)—and composed of several leftists who, to say the least, were in touch with the underground communist—showed me a 16-point programme and demanded I should accept it as the price for their cooperation. I explained the situation to them as best I could, but they were obviously drawing their inspiration from elsewhere. They were even prepared to sabotage Mahmud Ali, their secretary and representative, who was cooperating with the NDF. In the end they agreed to cooperate for the time being, finding they had no alternative, while they mentally reserved to themselves the opportunity to advance the interests of their own particular party. This attitude often brought them into conflict with Awami League workers who organized and met the expenses of the public meetings and who resented the NAP workers aggressively capturing the microphones and raising their own party slogans. This possibility did not have much effect on the morale of the people of East Pakistan and their adherence to the One-Point Programme, but it did leave open the possibilities of a schism in the future in the ranks of the NDF. Mahmud Ali found it difficult to control the members of this party.

As part of my effort to have a democratic constitution I maintained that East and West Pakistan must work in cooperation with each other, otherwise there was little hope to achieve our objective through constitutional means. There could be no national unity, no national integration, no common purposes, no national consciousness and no sense of interdependence in an abiding sense unless we had democracy. And, in the struggle for democracy, togetherness was absolutely essential. I felt that the common people of both wings wanted the dictatorship to end.

SEPARATION INEVITABLE

Before I came to the scene, there was a growing feeling that the separation of the two wings was inevitable. On 2 September 1962, the President told the press in Dhaka that if East Pakistan so wanted, it had every right to separate, but his advice to it was not to do so as it might be engulfed by India. My thesis and my propaganda succeeded in halting the movement and in creating a sense of national unity, but it incidentally strengthened the hold of President Ayub over East Pakistan. I certainly was able to dispel the feeling of bitterness and hatred which East Pakistan was beginning to entertain towards West Pakistan on the grounds of exploitation, neglect, discriminatory treatment and a host of other reasons, not the least of which was the military domination of West Pakistan. This was a cause of disappointment to many who believed that the inevitable separation was fast approaching and this would solve all the problems of East Pakistan. I, however, felt that based as the separation would be on hatred and antagonism, the ultimate consequences would probably be nothing short of disaster.

APPEALS TO PRESIDENT AYUB

The problem now before me was to give some shape and continuity to the NDF movement (it could not be called an organization) and its propaganda. In East Pakistan, when I toured the province the representatives and spokesmen of all parties appeared together on the same platform and made a united demand for a democratic constitution. I ascribed the tremendous response we got from all sections of the people to the hope in their hearts that the nation as a whole was striving for one great goal—that there was unity amongst the leaders and the parties and that such unity was bound to achieve its objectives. They were hoping against hope that the problems of East Pakistan—its poverty, its wretchedness, its starvation and its nakedness—were nearing solution. It was sad and moving, though heartening, to see persons, old and young, trudging for miles just to have a glimpse of me as if I had brought to them a new message of hope and liberty—a new panacea for the ills of the country. My speeches took the shape of appeals, appeals and further appeals to President Ayub to respond to the people's demands without a background of threats or unconstitutional action. But how long can a people live in a state of increasing hopelessness when their demands are so urgent and definitive and their appeals fall on barren soil, unwatered by the rain of mercy or understanding and hardened by greed and covetousness and lust for power?

A constitutional movement takes a long time to bear fruit and may not bear fruit at all when confronted with a selfish, conscienceless regime; it may collapse through the sheer inertia of continued and prolonged failure. An unconstitutional revolutionary movement either succeeds or fails; there is no period of hopeless expectations. East Pakistan was left wondering whether the constitutional turn I had given to the movement, which resulted in suppressing that fire of bitterness which perhaps would have led to excesses, had not made the struggle ineffective—doomed to failure.

LAST EFFORTS TO STAND UNITED

Towards the end, I set up in East Pakistan a committee consisting of two representatives from each of the Muslim League, the Awami League, the KSP and the NAP and one from the Nizam-i-Islam Party, to organize unity committees in districts and subdivisions as branches of the NDF and to keep alive the demand for democracy. I did not include in it any representative from the Muslim League (Council), confining myself to groups that had refused to revive themselves. Similarly, I did not take any representative from the Jamaat-i-Islam; I did not know if this committee had done any work.

If Nurul Amin has allowed the Muslim League (Council) to organize itself, instead of calling upon the Muslim Leaguers not to jump too soon, he has certainly weakened the chances for a united effort. For though Khwaja Nazimuddin appears to be all for democracy, he is more concerned with the phantasamagoria of the Muslim League (Council) sweeping the board in the next general election, even if the Basic Democrats form the electoral college for the legislature. As regards the by-elections for the seats rendered vacant by members who have become ministers, Khwaja Nazimuddin boasted immediately that he would capture all the seats without having any concept of the material of which the Basic Democrats were made and of the advantages which a dictator's government possessed. Even if all the parties combine to set up the best candidates, irrespective of parties against the Muslim League (Convention) or the President's party, chances of success are exceedingly slim; in fact, they are nil. Even then some funds would be necessary, though it would be impossible to match the resources of the President and of the government. Then there is the fissure between the Awami League and the NAP, and the speeches and activities of Bhashani must have tended to increase the differences.

The Awami League is getting restive. It is not worried about the Muslim League (Convention) but it finds that the Muslim League (Council) is taking away the adherents of Nurul Amin. It finds that the NAP is holding its separate group meetings all the time and is secretly organizing itself while maintaining a facade of non-revival stance. The KSP has no political urge, but Hamidul Huq Choudhury would like to utilize it for his own aggrandisement if he could. There is some danger of the Awami League losing ground through sheer inactivity and the curb I have placed on it. Mujibur Rahman, in particular, is fretting very strongly. He is prepared to accept the objective of democracy for Pakistan as the sole issue. He also feels that since, for the time being at least, I am the only person who can mobilize the masses in East Pakistan and capture their imagination, it is advisable to work under my umbrella. But he has doubts that national unity and national integration will solve the problems of East Pakistan. He is not interested in the field of foreign politics as he does not believe that any foreign country should become deeply committed here; East Pakistan must work out its own destiny. Hence, there is no point seeking foreign political involvement. But he is vitally interested in seeing that the Awami League is not destroyed or overwhelmed either by the opportunist, Muslim League (Council) organization, whose main objective is to capture power for the benefit of its own clan, or the NAP with its strong leftist tendencies and contacts and its reliance on the unstable elements of the community. He is unable to take any steps in my absence other than trying to keep the party together and prevent it from disintegrating in despair. He believes that the party should be revived and organized properly, as others are doing secretly or openly, and the younger generation should be prevented from straying into the communist camp. He feels that we are losing valuable time and opportunity.

Among some of the workers of the Awami League, the KSP and even the Muslim League, there is a feeling that we should have a new democratic party to meet the new challenges, and it may be called the National Democratic Party. Such a party would be a regular political party and would require a definite programme which cannot be confined to the single objective of establishing democracy. The programme of such a party would be a welfare and secular state with cultural and provincial autonomy for the various peoples and the provinces of Pakistan. But there are bound to be differences over the programme and the leadership which would need long and patient deliberation and a spirit of self-sacrifice.

In neither East nor in West Pakistan will the Jamaat-i-Islami, the Nizam-i-Islam or the Muslim League join a new party. In East Pakistan remains the non-revivalist Muslim League, the KSP, the NAP and the Awami League. The first requisite is not a minimum programme sufficient for cooperation for a given objective—which is enough for a joint front, Rather, a common and a wider programme for the party that will, at the same time, satisfy all the elements is necessary. Then one has to find a leader acceptable to all— and office bearers. If the Awami League is reasonable, cooperative and self-sacrificing, the non-revivalist Muslim League, which has temporarily lost much of its importance, and the KSP, which after the death of Fazlul Huq has no anchorage, will cooperate with the Awami League (barring Hamidul Huq Choudhury) in the new party. But the NAP will not until it gets its foreign policy programme accepted. This will not be in the interests of Pakistan, at least at present.

This is exactly what Ayub wants, as he will then pose before the Western World as their one and only mainstay and supporter, while the people— foolish, stupid and excitable—cannot be trusted. Hence, the Western powers should not insist on reversion to democracy but should leave him in power and position as the only stable and sane element in the country with no ostensible alternative leader of similar sanity in the offing. It is well known that he himself incited the people through his agents, official and non-official, to demand leaving CENTO and SEATO (which, in fact, is neither here nor there, except as a significant symbol) and, after manufacturing demonstrations, let them down in the legislature. Never has there been witnessed such a blatant case of supreme authority conspiring against his own people, making fools of them in the international sphere for the sake of his own aggrandisement.

And Bhashani is playing into President Ayub's hands. As regards the leadership of the new party, Bhashani will claim it; and after the manner in which he has behaved I cannot see how the Awami League will accept him. Neither do I see the non-revivalist Muslim League accepting the leadership of Bhashani or of Mujibur Rahman, nor Bhashani accepting that of Nurul Amin, or Hamidul Huq Choudhury, or even of Mujibur Rahman.

In West Pakistan we are left with the Awami League, the NAP, the Republicans, may be a few Muslim Leaguers who are disgusted with both sections of the Muslim League and some independents. The chances are that the leftist elements and the NAP will swamp the party and control the leadership if unable to capture it for itself. It must not be overlooked that the anti-One Unit feeling is rampant among all sections in Sindh, Balochistan, NWFP and Karachi, and this gives strength to the NAP and enhances its chances of leadership. It is only in the heart of the Punjab that this sentiment is anathema, but the valour which Mahmud Ali Qasuri has consistently shown in opposing the government at every turn must have helped to moderate the opposition to the NAP. The programme will be leftist to accommodate the NAP and there will be the same divergence regarding foreign policy. The Republicans will not join with Bhashani at its head and certainly the few Muslim Leaguers and independents, who would have joined had I been there, will not join. It would appear that the conclusion is that the NDF, to be successful, might be formed without the NAP. This is very unbecoming, but this decision has been forced on us by the double-dealing of Bhashani and his contacts with President Ayub on the one hand and the underground on the other.

I feel that the time is not ripe for a new line of work or a new party; neither is there any urgency for this. It is doubtful if the revival of the Muslim League (Council) or of the NAP is going to carry them far, though this has certainly destroyed the semblance of unity and—what is worse—has created factional rivalries and divergent objectives where unity of action was most necessary. It is more than possible that if the Awami League does not revive itself and continues to work single-mindedly without any thought of future aggrandisement, the triumph of democracy will be its triumph and it will be the Awami League or a new party of non-revivalists with the Awami League leaders, workers and organizers in the forefront, who will capture the confidence of the people.

In West Pakistan, those who had signed the joint declaration for democracy at Lahore urged that steps should be taken to call a convention. A joint convention of East and West Pakistan appeared to be impractical for the time being. After consultation, it seemed advisable to promote a conference with four representatives from each of the political groups in West Pakistan plus others whom I might invite to make the conference as representative as possible the better to work out a detailed programme for a convention in West Pakistan. I accordingly issued an invitation to the Awami League, the Jamaat-i-Islami, the Muslim League (Council), the NAP, the Republicans (who had met and decided not to revive themselves for the time being), some representatives from Sindh and Balochistan and a stalwart, self-less courageous leader, Maulana Abdul Sattar Khan Niazi. At first I chose Lahore as the venue for the conference. Then, to suit the majority, I shifted it to Karachi and fixed 26 and 27 January 1963 for the meeting. Only non-EBDOed persons were to be nominated by the parties, that is to say, only those who could be members of political parties. The EBDOed politicians, for example, Daultana of the Punjab, Ayub Khuhro, Qazi Fazlullah (from Sindh), and others of that category whom I might select, were to form an advisory group to guide the activities of the NDF. After the invitations were issued, I had a heart attack on 3 January 1963 and was removed to the Jinnah Hospital. This developed into a regular thrombosis on 11 January; after this

I was forbidden to speak, read papers, meet people or take any interest in what was going on outside.

FURTHER DISABILITY ON POLITICIANS

On 6 January 1963, two ordinances were promulgated by the President. In one he enlarged the definition of political parties to include unorganized movements (such as the NDF) so that the EBDOed politicians could not be even parties to a movement and placed a still further disability on them in order to prevent them from taking part in politics altogether or to associate with each other. The other ordinance gave power to the President, irrespective of any application made to him, to withdraw the disability imposed on such of the EBDOed as he deemed fit, that is, to remit their penalties. In a short statement that I made before the thrombosis overtook me, I objected to this direct form of corruption and intimidation; other politicians and newspapers followed suit. It may be stated at once that the first ordinance was placed before the National Assembly and passed, although it imposed a fresh disability on the EBDOed not contemplated at the time of conviction. The second ordinance was withdrawn and lapsed as even the National Assembly could not swallow this blatant form of corruption. The grounds given for the withdrawal, which was essentially a defeat for the government, was that inasmuch as the President had the power to remit penalties, there was no need for an ordinance to give him that power.

For a long time there was a controversy whether Khan Abdul Qayyum Khan had applied for pardon or not. He applied for the penalty to be remitted on the grounds that his conviction under EBDO was in respect of the same charges which had once been considered by Governor General Ghulam Mohammad for the purpose of taking proceedings against him under PODO (a predecessor of EBDO) and which had been dropped as unproved. Hence the EBDO conviction was bad in law. There was also a strong rumour that the President intended to pardon Qayyum Khan and then put him in charge of the Muslim League (Convention). Such rumours contributed to the destruction of the prestige which Qayyum Khan once enjoyed. The government also announced that 21 persons had applied for pardon, but it did not divulge names. All this created such a stink that the government did not dare to place the ordinance before the legislature for confirmation and it lapsed. The President did not have the courage to remit the penalty of anyone and take him into his fold.

The result of the first ordinance was that the EBDOed politicians who were to have attended the NDF conference on 26 and 27 January, which was meant to lay down the steps for calling a convention, could not attend the session. The meeting was held at Lakham House in Karachi.[32] It was a closed conference but was not a secret meeting. It ran into difficulties from the start. According to my arrangement with Daultana, I had invited the Muslim League (Council) to participate in West Pakistan with the NDF movement but had excluded it from the East Pakistan committee where I was working with the non-revivalist Muslim League. Khwaja Nazimuddin took exception to this and sent instructions to Sardar Bahadur Khan, his General Secretary, who was a member of the conference, to withdraw. It needed all the persuasive ability of Mian Daultana, who had promised on his honour to cooperate with the NDF to the extent of leaving the Muslim League if need be, to induce Sardar Bahadur Khan to continue to participate. The result of Khwaja Nazimuddin's action was that the operative portion was watered down to the 'appointment of a committee of ten to consider the possibilities of future cooperative action'—or something as evasive. At this conference, a resolution was placed for discussion. The operative portions, which came last, were emasculated (as above). The first portion was a criticism of the Martial Law regime, its unnecessary imposition and its failings—also those of the successor government then functioning. It was wholly unnecessary for the purposes for which this conference had been convened. Its advantage lay in the unanimity of the condemnation of the revolution. It was passed after considerable discussion and after several amendments and was signed by the 26 or 27 members present. A few of the invitees who could not attend had by telegram expressed their cooperation with the conference and had agreed to abide by its directives in anticipation. As it turned out, the directives were not worthy of consideration.

The government took exception to the wording of the resolution and registered a case under Section 124A and 153 (sedition against government established by law) against the signatories. Enquiries were started. The questions were directed towards implicating Mian Mumtaz Daultana and me. Subsequently ten of the signatories were picked out for prosecution. The selection was based on the alleged extent of their participation in drafting the resolution, although every one of those who signed was responsible for the final draft in equal measure. It spoke volumes that Sardar Bahadur Khan, the brother of the President, was not one of the accused, although he was the principal representative on behalf of the Muslim League and was the leader of the opposition in parliament.

The following persons were prosecuted; Maulana Mian Tufail Ahmad and Choudhury Ghulam Mohammad of the Jamaat-i-Islami; Nawabzada Nasrullah Khan and Khwaja Mohammad Rafiq of the Awami League; Mian Mahmud Ali Qasuri, Mahmudul Huq Usmani and Shaikh Abdul Majid Sindhi of the NAP: Z.H. Lari of the Muslim League and Maulana Abdul Sattar Khan Niazi and Sardar Ataullah Khan Mengal of Balochistan. Applications were made for bail and opposed by the government. The matter went up to the

Chief Justice of the West Pakistan High Court in Lahore. Justice Manzur Qadir ordered bail provided that the accused gave an undertaking that they would not make similar statements while free on bail. The judges of the West Pakistan High Court in Karachi passed a similar order in the case of Lari. Every one of the accused refused this conditional bail except Justice Lari who took up the defense that he should not be prosecuted as he was not present at the end when the resolution was finally drafted. The Supreme Court reversed the order of Justice Manzur Qadir on the grounds that the Criminal Procedure Code did not warrant the imposition of a condition and released all the accused on bail. A special magistrate was appointed to try the case. The reputation of Justice Lari, who as a judge of the High Court had shown considerable legal acumen and independence, suffered a serious setback, and there were a number of demonstrations against him.

POLITICAL LIFE AT A STANDSTILL

Public political life today is at a standstill in Pakistan. The Muslim League (Council) and the Jamaat-i-Islami are trying to organize themselves but are in a vacuum. The Awami League does not know what to do and is awaiting my return. The last ordinance forbidding EBDOed politicians who still command influence with the people to indulge in any kind of political activity or utterance seems to have succeeded, restricting and dulling the edge of the agitation for democracy. It is a matter for serious consideration as to what scope for further activity is left to them. Bhashani is continuing to undermine the NDF. It is reported that the President came in for a considerable amount of criticism in the central legislature when the budget was under discussion, and there has been some sniggering over the Christine Keeler affair and her statements that she and the President played in the swimming pool, when the President, husky and virile, pulled her by the leg and down she went. But the main matter of importance is that the President has now openly joined the Muslim League (Convention) and is touring the country and holding public meetings, calling upon the people to join his organization—and he has a clear field.

In spite of all his attempts to run down the previous politicians, abusing and vilifying them, sterilizing their political activities by EBDO proceedings, they have risen higher and higher in the esteem of the people. He has had to suppress them altogether in order to give himself a chance. Having entered the political field, he can now become a target for the opposition. But who will dare to bell the cat, furnished so well with claws? He has reaped great advantage from exploiting anti-American sentiment. He stands as a champion of Pakistan in danger as a result of the arms aid to India, a matter which has caused genuine, widespread alarm in Pakistan. But this is counterbalanced by the opposition and the contempt for his various acts of nepotism and corruption which can no longer remain concealed—though his minions are trying hard to justify them. He has all the cards in his possession. He is now a wealthy landowner, with vast estates and orchards and urban property, and has amassed enormous wealth. His sons, who were his ADCs, resigned from the army and are the wealthy possessors of licenses and industrial enterprises; all his relations have received a share—including his brother, Sardar Bahadur Khan, the leader of the opposition—for all of which, of course, justification is surely forthcoming. Apart from his personal wealth and that of his family, amassed since he became President, he has all the resources of the government at his disposal including an unlimited amount of secret service funds shoved away in odd corners. In addition to these advantages, he has shown great cunning in removing all political rivals from the field and emasculating political parties and other worthwhile opposition. Time would also appear to be on his side as it is difficult for opposing parties to keep on struggling against odds; personal and political differences can be laid aside for a time, but these are bound to obtrude and weaken the opposition.

As matters stand, however, his own unpopularity—and that of his regime—outstandingly outweighs all the advantages with which he has clothed himself. If the election of the President is to be by adult suffrage, he will have no chance of being returned to office unless he is able to manipulate the parliament so as to exclude all contestants except three of his friends who would retire from the contest. If the election of the President will be through a new batch of Basic Democrats (who will be elected in October 1964) and there are contestants who do not collude with him, he will jeopardize his position even then. But, while he himself is very unpopular, much will depend on the opposition being able to select a rival candidate. The EBDOed being out of the field, few are left. Any speculation on possible candidates may put them in danger. The President is today morally and politically a pitiable figure, but with abundant financial resources he appears to be a mighty colossus.

If the opposition can fix on a person, the chances of President Ayub would appear to be slim. There are three weapons in his hands:

- elimination of opponents through parliament where he has a majority;
- maintaining the Basic Democrats as the electoral body; and
- utilization of government officers, intimidation, coercion, bribery and corruption.

The last will not be necessary if he succeeds in eliminating opponents through parliament and will only moderately be required in the case of Basic

Democrats if he has an opponent. But with all that, he will find it difficult if the election of the President is by adult suffrage. In spite of all his efforts and expenditure, he will not be able to make any serious impression on East Pakistan. In West Pakistan he will have some sections of the Punjab and the tribal areas of the Pathans and a few big landowners of Sindh with him, but it is doubtful if these will be enough to carry him. But he may yet try a new gimmick. Finally, he has the army to play with and those whom he has enriched at the expense of the nation. Much will depend upon the extent to which the present central legislature, dominated as it is by President Ayub, accepts the recommendations of the Franchise Commission.[33]

Mass Upheaval in East Pakistan Feared

By all accounts there is general political stagnation and the question remains how it can be ended. The general theory is that when constitutional avenues are blocked, people find a way to adopt unconstitutional measures—in short, a revolution. Whether such a revolution is possible in view of the tremendous disparity between the armed forces and the people is doubtful. One contingency which we were probably approaching was the mass upheaval in East Pakistan against West Pakistan which would have included the army, the West Pakistan industrialists and even the non-Bengali refugee element. This would have led to bloody riots and murders and would have been based on sheer hatred. I have succeeded in stemming this, but we have yet to see if it is entirely extinguished. If not, desperation may once more light the smouldering fires and destroy me in the process as well.

Appendix I

Suhrawardy's letter to President Ayub Khan

Mr President,

I was arrested on the 30th January 1962, and have since been detained under the Security of Pakistan Act 1952, in the central jail at Karachi. On the 5th February 1962, I received the 'reasons' for my detention. They are so vague and indefinite that is impossible to make any representation regarding them other than a denial, and a reference to my past services as proof of their untruth. Nevertheless, though a representation is impossible, I feel that I am entitled to address you....

You will pardon me if I fail to understand how you, Mr President, who have known me at close quarters, should have paid the slightest attention to the false statements, insinuations and allegations which must have been made to you, challenging my patriotism. I do not refer to the 'reasons' of my detention, for these are so obviously and patently false that they could not have been the real reasons for the order of detention, and your mind must have been poisoned by other allegations. In your forthright statement to the Press the day after my arrest you gave reasons and made charges not one of which is to be found among the 'reasons' of my detention. Hence, it is quite clear that I have been arrested for reasons other than those supplied to me.

I propose to show how these 'reasons' are obviously unsubstantial.

Take the first 'reason'. 'Ever since the inception of Pakistan and particularly during the last three years, you have been associating with anti-Pakistan elements, both within and outside the country.'

I do not know whether I have to answer for my actions before I became Law Minister and later Prime Minister. I have never heard from you one word challenging my patriotism when we were working together. If you only knew, you would have realized how by staying behind in India immediately after the partition, I saved Bengal from the catastrophe which led to much bloodshed in the Punjab, with which you are very familiar. Indeed, if Bengal had also become an arena of such murders, no Muslim would have been allowed to live in India and a wholesale trek of Muslims to Pakistan might well have created an impossible situation for Pakistan. Now, as regards the last three years, the insinuation is absolutely false. For one, I have avoided associating with anyone on the political plane—and have refused to discuss Pakistan politics in any form. Let me first take 'outside the country'. In the absence of any particulars how can I answer it. The only occasion I have been away from the country since the Revolution was last year between the 13th July and the 13th November. When I left I had made up my mind that I was not going to meet any political element and, if I did, never to discuss matters relating to Pakistan. And I stuck to this. I wonder if permission was given to me to go out in order that a charge, such as the above, could be levelled against me, which I am unable, by the very fact that I met human beings outside the country to controvert my evidence. Incidentally, who are the anti-Pakistan elements I met; not surely your Ambassadors. I can state with confidence that I did not see a single person who could be considered an anti-Pakistani element. In any event association by itself with such alleged persons is no reason or ground and nothing which affects the security or defence of Pakistan.

Now as regards 'within the country', again I fail to understand what are the anti-Pakistan elements and who they are. It ought not to be difficult to specify them. Does this refer to Pakistanis? I have not had one word, let alone association with any anti-Pakistani element who is a Pakistani. How can anyone who is a Muslim, who loves Muslims, whose greatest anxiety is the safety of the Muslims we have left behind in India, ever think of placing East Pakistan, with its innocent Muslim population, who have loaded me with trust, and I hope, love, in the thrall of Hindu India. Or, do you mean secession? I never heard this until after I had returned from my tour abroad, and then only from a statement of yours that there was some such idea somewhere. *For Muslims Pakistan is one and indivisible.* It is for this we risked our lives and have grown old. Both must remain together. East Pakistan stands in the greatest danger of being overwhelmed and destroyed and annexed by police action, if it secedes. This is my reaction to any suggestion of secession. Again, I say, we must stay together and our safety is in cooperation with West Pakistan.

In order that West Pakistan did not have any cause of grievance arising out of its minority representation. I induced East Pakistan to accept parity. Although this has been insisted in previous reports, nobody could induce East Pakistan to accept parity to give up a political right cherished in all democratic countries, on which today the principle of self-determination itself is based with all its angularities. I, however, thought that cooperation with West Pakistan was essential for the existence and progress of Pakistan, and that the principle of parity could get rid of the provincial complex, and we would have common political parties in both wings instead of forming ourselves into provincial groups. And I toured East Pakistan (I was Law Minister then) and spoke to the people at countless meetings and induced them to endorse the principle of parity. It was on this principle that the

Constituent Assembly was elected for the first time in 1955 (when I was Law Minister).

I was called a traitor to East Pakistan, and I was told I was selling East Pakistan, but I held my ground and won for the sake of an integrated Pakistan. And do you think I could have been a party to secession? Alas! Mr President, by keeping me under detention with such terrible charges against me, you have destroyed my utility. I did not and never wanted and do not want any office or representation. I could have helped, if ever the occasion arose and my words would have proved useful to point out how necessary it was that the two wings must remain together, and that we must get rid of provincial feelings.

Mr President, may I respectfully point out that what has so often been repeated by my calumniators, and by repetition seems to have acquired some force, need not have been uttered by you. Pakistan was created as the homeland for the Muslims of India, and it was with this faith that we fought. We, in Bengal, and particularly the Muslims of West Bengal, suffered grievous annihilation at the hands of the Hindus, and we got Pakistan. Pakistan was our country; not an asylum for us. We had the right to come and we came. Yes, we came to our country, a country we had helped in creating. When the Nationality Act was passed here and there was no question of remaining a Pakistani national with residence in India, I chose to come here. I would beg you to recall that I was a member of the Constituent Assembly of Pakistan all the time until February 1949; there could be no question of any asylum for me in Pakistan, and it was only after I had declared that I was coming to settle in Pakistan and was moving definitely on the 5th March 1949 that it was left to Mr Tamizuddin Khan to remove me from my membership at the instance of the Muslim League ministry on the 26th February 1949, I think something which the Quaid-i-Azam would not do. So, do you still think that I sought asylum? *Of course, I am a refugee; so was the Quaid-i-Azam and so was Liaquat Ali Khan—so are millions of others, who have come to their home, guaranteed by the Quaid-i-Azam.*

Perhaps, Mr President, you will forgive me if I were to submit that from your statement regarding myself it appeared that the real reason for detaining me is an apprehension that my presence outside would interfere with the working of the constitution about to be launched, otherwise reference to this has no meaning in the statement in which you gave reasons for my detention. You might at least have assured yourself regarding this before taking action against me. It is axiomatic that the constitution that you are believed to be promulgating cannot be received enthusiastically by me, but surely this is not a sufficient ground for a detention. Probably 99 per cent of the people of Pakistan would feel, as I would do, whatever may appear in print.

Normally, we call communists and fellow travellers (real and not faked) anti-Pakistani. During these three years I have not contacted or been in touch—let alone associated—with any such person. If foreigners are meant, is the list confined to diplomats or does it include non-diplomats? Again, it would not be difficult to specify them. I believe I do not know a single non-diplomat, who is anti-Pakistani, and who belongs to a country commonly considered anti-Pakistan. If diplomats are meant, I have not associated with any anti-Pakistan element. I may have met those connected with countries normally considered anti-Pakistan on social occasions like many other Pakistanis; but this is no association such as is presumably insinuated in the first 'reason'. I claim that my patriotism is above suspicion and cannot be tarnished by any such contact.

I have noted with great pain, that you are alleged to have said in Dhaka (what is not to be found among the 'reasons'): 'It was not beyond him (ie, myself) to accept monetary assistance from those who are hostile to Pakistan.' Pardon me, Mr President, what possible justification have you for making such a serious charge; what kind of false and dirty reports must have been placed before you to induce you to make such a statement. This is one of the most damnable statements that can be made against anybody; and what chance has such a person of contradicting it, except by invoking your sense of justice and fairplay.

I may be a poor man, Mr President, and poor men are easily kicked about; but I have never stooped to such filthy activities. My only consolation is that such a statement will not be believed—by anyone in Pakistan or outside, except by those who wish to believe it. What you said to the Press clearly shows that my detention is based on false 'reasons'. Such a definite charge or reason, as you have made and which can be proved or disproved, does not form part of the 'reasons' of detention which have been supplied to me.

I will have occasion to refer to other statements of yours later, if they have not been dealt with, when dealing with the 'reasons'. Indeed, Mr President, what you have stated in interview, as being the reasons for my detention, are quite outside the 'reasons' for my detention supplied to me, as I have pointed out before.

Paragraph 2. I have been misusing my personal influence and friendship in attempting to alienate the sympathies of some countries friendly to Pakistan.

I feel flattered that I am told that I have some personal influence. This, under the present regime, does not exist. 'Friendship': I wonder whom this refers to. Apparently this refers again to some unnamed diplomat and diplomats of countries friendly to Pakistan. In the first place, I have never had any illusions out of office; anyone can be friends of any foreign diplomat or they can have feelings of friendship for anyone outside office. They are more concerned to be on good terms with the government in power, and are prone to misunderstand others out of office. Secondly, will one of them dare to say—unless he wishes to flatter you—that I have breathed or thought, or insinuated one word or sentiment against Pakistan, or said anything which may alienate the sympathies of friendly countries from Pakistan. Whenever I have had occasion to say anything about Pakistan to anybody—and such occasions have been rare indeed—I have impressed upon them the absolute desirability of helping Pakistan more and more so that it may be independent of outside help.

Let me tell you, Mr President, what you do not know, that Pakistan is my life. I have, I believe, played a great part in bringing it into existence. Bengal was the only province—among the Muslim majority provinces—that gave Muslim League ministry to the Quaid-i-Azam; Bengal was the pawn in his hand due to which the Congress accepted the partition of India. And to make Bengal accept the Muslim League, and align itself in the struggle for Pakistan, I had to work day and night, at the cost of my own living, health and safety.

I was the Secretary of the Bengal Provincial Muslim League and the entire work fell on my shoulders. I received some help from some local leaders, within the ambit of their own local influence; even then I had to go to the remotest villages and speak to the Muslims; I had to travel long distances on country conveyance and on dusty roads, or on country boats; stay where I could find a shelter, eat what I could eat; arguing, inducing and begging for Pakistan. I have been stoned and nearly killed. I have braved the spears of the fanatical army of my opponents, and all for Pakistan; when others sat back, reaped and have since reaped the fruit of my labours. And I succeeded in converting the country to the Muslim League ideology, and aligned it in favour of Pakistan. You would not know this, Mr President, on this side of the subcontinent. All this meant constant endeavours for years—ten years of the best portion of a life spent in toil and heartbreak, and then came the victory of 1946. To charge me that I would say anything that may alienate the sympathies of the friendly countries is, pardon me, Mr President, a damnable lie. I wish all those friendly countries would align themselves more openly with us, and come to our help whenever occasion required.

Third item. I am alleged in the course of the last three years to have openly aligned myself with elements outside the country who are opposed to the various reforms carried out by the present regime.

This, again, is very vague. This charge smacks of the question—'When did you last beat your wife?' It takes for granted some alignment—and if not open, then secret, which I deny as vehemently at this alleged open alignment. And, now, what are these elements opposed to the various reforms. Again, this too is vague for me to reply to.

This charge is frankly so meaningless that I am beginning to wonder if it does not refer to the Revolution itself—not to the reforms of the present regime, but to the present regime as a reform. This, of course, is not the charge; and I am sure you will allow that it is permissible to have different views regarding the Revolution. Some constitutionalists hold that there were sufficient powers in the constitution of 1956 to have undertaken all that the Revolution has done without abrogating it.

My view has always been that whatever might or might not be the justification, once a military regime has been established, and the military authorities have taken control, they must have a full run and must have the fullest opportunities to serve the country as best as they can, until in God's good time democracy is established in the country. It would be foolish to deny that the country as a whole would like to revert to democracy and you, yourself, Mr President, realizing this have promised the country to lead them to it. I am not disposed to deny that I, too, wish it—and it is totally immaterial if I am associated with it or not. But my inclination towards democracy is vastly a different matter from openly or secretly aligning myself with elements, etc. As a matter of fact, I do not approve of many reforms which the present regime has carried out; and which it had been able to do by virtue of the plenary powers it possesses—reforms of such a nature that no democratic government would have been able to pass them without much travail and struggle and much passage of time, unless it was accorded similar plenary powers.

Fourth. I am charged with having insidiously set up cells in various cities of both East and West Pakistan where I am alleged to carry on propaganda against the achievements of the present regime. What phantasmagorial imagination has conceived this: in the first place, brought up in the legal and constitutional tradition, and following particularly the constitution tradition of the Quaid-i-Azam, I cannot do anything or have done anything underground or underhand.

I have neither the capacity nor the ability nor the machinery, nor the knowledge or experience of how to set up cells. When you banned political parties, that was the end of my party and of all organizations. It is true that people cannot cease to be politically minded by merely banning of parties, and it can be taken for granted that as a rule people have some nostalgia for the parties to which they belonged. But, as political parties go, your fiat was enough for me; and my party stood abolished; and all the leaders ceased to exist as such. It is absolutely ridiculous that I should have set up cells in various cities. In the course of my legal practice, I have been only to Karachi (where I live permanently), Lahore, Dhaka and Chittagong. I have been invited by my friends and clients to visit them in their homes in various cities, where now free from politics, they wanted to entertain me, but I have refused to go. Not because I never conceived that, if visited them, I would be charged with 'setting up cells' — such a fantastic idea and the thought that anyone in this world would be found to entertain it never entered my mind. I did not do so, as I had little time in the midst of my work and was not interested; and was not inclined to take the trouble and was purposely avoiding contacts as far as possible. Had I been interested in the aforesaid cells, those visits would have been useful if I only knew how to set up cells; I ask where I have set up cells?

Fifth. There were two parts to this 'reason'.

First part. I am charged with having consistently (Please note the word consistently) preached hatred and contempt against the regime to my followers and colleagues of the now banned Awami League. Please may I ask why should I do so? 'Hatred and contempt' are strong words; and strong words are needed to breed hatred and contempt. In a Court of Law, the penal section has been quoted in the 'reason'; the whole context has to be taken into consideration with meticulous care, before there can be any such finding. Scraps of statements have been rejected as insufficient. Can any evidence be offered to this? On the face of it, the charge is ridiculous. I do not deny that some friends and colleagues of mine of the now banned Awami League have seen me mostly in connection with cases against them. But why should I preach hatred and contempt to them? Where was the occasion and what the purpose? Need I deny this fantastic charge? Have I become insane that I should indulge in such futility? Those who see me in court do not think so.

2nd part. I have been holding out promises to interests affected by the reform. In God's name, where? What are these interests which have been affected by reforms I want to undo. The only interest I can think of which the reforms have affected are the landlords of West Pakistan. I wonder, Mr President, if you are aware that 'land reforms' of a stricter nature was in the forefront of the programme of the Awami League; and if you are aware of what I did for the tenants of Bengal, to ensure them their rights, and my constant struggle against the landlords. The charge is so general that I can only reply to what I consider it means. Can any of your agents, or those sitting in their offices let me know where and to which landlord I have ever promised, etc, etc. And what circumstances?

Sixth. The charge is that even up to this date I have remained unreconciled to the concept of Pakistan. Mr President, you, who have worked with me particularly when I was Prime Minister, do you believe it? What I have done for the concept of Pakistan and what I have suffered, I alone know and alone can I say? I referred very briefly to what I did for Pakistan and its concept. I even might like to take you back to the speech I made at the last Muslim League Convention at Delhi: *Pakistan is my very life,* and to make this fifth charge against me speak of some cess-pools in your administrative machinery, which have not been brought to your notice.

Seventh. Reads: 'By unjustified criticism of the foreign policy of this country in the formulation of which policy you (I) played a leading role, you are (I am) causing serious embarrassment to the present government.' I am grateful to the authorities that they have been gracious enough to admit that I played a leading role in the formulation of the foreign policy of Pakistan.

Foreign policy is for the government of the day to formulate, to amend and to apply according to circumstances.

And now, Mr President, permit me, having dealt with the 'reasons' to refer to your own statement which you made to the press, which give reasons for my detention which are different from the charges and the reasons supplied to me. These reasons given by you must be the real reasons for my detention, for you have uttered them. Presumably, the reasons supplied to me have been manufactured in the office....

In the first portion of your statement you stated that I aimed at the disruption of East Pakistan first and then the rest of the country. What does the meaning 'disruption of East Pakistan mean? Was I trying to split it into groups? Or in conjunction with your statement that it was not beyond me to accept monetary assistance from those who are hostile to Pakistan, and that there were people to act as my agents with the sole object of disrupting East Pakistan, it probably means that I was receiving money from India in order to join up East Pakistan with India. Say it, Mr President, with your hand on your heart, and then may Allah be our Judge, in this world or the next. For if this is how you feel about, it is not right that I should live. If you know that I have no place in Hindu India, or Hindu Bengal nothing would please them more than to see me dead, and a sacrifice to the dagger of a Godse. To even conceive the idea of joining Hindu Bengal or Hindu India, is not merely a treason to Pakistan, but to the Muslims as a whole. It is nothing but tantamounts to offering so many victims for sacrifice. Do you think I cannot see it? I see much more clearly, than many, the rising tide of militant Hinduism in India which is placing the Muslims of India in grave danger of annihilation.

Appendix II

Rashid Suhrawardy's letter to the Provisional Government of Bangladesh, supporting the liberation movement made in response to Begum Akhter Sulaiman's statement*

London
7 October 1971

My sympathy and full support were with the liberation movement of the people of Bangladesh as soon as I learned of the genocide committed by the army of West Pakistan. Not being in politics I did not think a statement from me personally was necessary but since it has become apparent that the image and memory of my beloved father, Mr Huseyn Shaheed Suhrawardy, are being sought to be tarnished by one member of my immediate family by her recent statements I felt it incumbent upon me to speak out.

I would like to express in unequivocal terms that I wish the liberation movement of the people of Bangladesh all success. They have been economically exploited and politically dominated by West Pakistan for the past twenty-four years and they have now been forced to take up arms to resist the genocide and other heinous crimes that have been and are being perpetrated by the West Pakistan army.

I have no doubt in my mind that the brave freedom fighters will succeed in achieving full independence by ejecting the invading army.

I eagerly look forward to going to Bangladesh in the near future, to see that in an independent, sovereign republic people of all faiths and political affiliations are living in peace and harmony.

I also convey my greetings to the Government of Bangladesh, the members of which were all colleagues of my father and who were great objects of his affection.

---

* This was in response to Begum Akhter Sulaiman's statement made in June 1971 where an attempt to tarnish Suhrawardy's image was made just to support the Pakistan government action, committing genocide and East Pakistan.

Appendix III

The Resolution by Huseyn Shaheed Suhrawardy, Prime Minister of Bengal, moved at the Delhi Convention of Legislators on 9 April 1946.

'Whereas in this vast subcontinent of India a hundred million Muslims are adherents of a faith which regulates every department of their life—educational, social, economic and political—whose code is not confined merely to spiritual doctrines and tenets, or rituals and ceremonies, and which stands in sharp contrast to the exclusive nature of the Hindu *dharma* and philosophy which has fostered and maintained a rigid caste system for thousands of years, resulting in the degradation of sixty million human beings to the position of untouchables, creation of unnatural barriers between man and man and superimposition of social and economic inequalities on a large body of the people of the country, and which threatens to reduce Muslims, Christians and other minorities to the status of irredeemable helots, socially and economically;

'Whereas the Hindu caste system is a direct negation of nationalism, equality, democracy and all the noble ideals that Islam stands for;

'Whereas different historical backgrounds, traditions, cultures, social and economic orders of the Hindus and the Muslims made impossible the evolution of a single Indian nation inspired by common aspirations and ideals and whereas after centuries they still remain two distinct major nations;

Whereas soon after the introduction by the British of the policy of setting up political institutions in India on lines of Western democracies based on majority rule which means that the majority of the nation or society could impose its will on the minority of the other nation or society in spite of their opposition as amply demonstrated during the two and half years' regime of Congress government in the Hindu majority provinces under the Government of India Act 1935, when the Muslims were subjected to untold harassments and oppressions as a result of which they were convinced of the futility and ineffectiveness of the so-called safeguards provided in the constitution and in the Instruments of Instructions to the governors and were driven to the irresistible conclusion that in a United India Federation, if established, the Muslims, even in Muslim majority provinces, could meet with no better fate and their rights and interests could never be adequately protected against the perpetual Hindu majority at the centre;

'Whereas the Muslims are convinced that with a view to saving Muslim India from the domination of the Hindus and in order to afford them full scope to develop themselves according to their genius, it is necessary to constitute a sovereign, independent state comprising Bengal and Assam in the North-East zone and the Punjab, North-West Frontier Province, Sindh and Balochistan in the North-West zone;

'This convention of the Muslim League legislators of India, central and provincial, after careful consideration, hereby declares that the Muslim nation will never submit to any constitution for a United India and will never participate in any single constitution-making machinery set up for the purpose, and any formula devised by the British government for transferring power from the British to the peoples of India, which does not conform to the following just and equitable principles calculated to maintain internal peace and tranquillity in the country, will not contribute to the solution of the Indian problem:

- That the zones comprising Bengal and Assam in the North-East and the Punjab, the North-West Frontier Province, Sindh and Balochistan in the North-West of India, namely, the Pakistan zones, where the Muslims are a dominant majority, be constituted into one sovereign independent state and that an unequivocal undertaking be given to implement the establishment of Pakistan without delay.
- That two separate constitution-making bodies be set up by the peoples of Pakistan and Hindustan for the purpose of framing their respective constitutions.
- That the minorities in Pakistan and Hindustan be provided with safeguards on the line of the All-India Muslim League Resolution passed on 23 March 1940 at Lahore.
- That the acceptance of the Muslim League demand for Pakistan and its implementation without delay are the *sine qua non* for the Muslim League cooperation and participation in the formation of an Interim Government at the centre.
- This convention further emphatically declares that any attempt to impose a constitution on a United India basis or to force any interim arrangement at the centre, contrary to the Muslim demand, will leave the Muslims no alternative but to resist such imposition by all possible means for their survival and national existence.'

Notes

PART I: LIFE AND WORK

1. Ahsan, Raghib[a], *Jiban noy, itihash* (Life not, history), Ittefaq: Suhrawardy ed. (First ed.), edited by Tofazzal Hossain (Manik Mia), March 1964, New Nation Printing Press, 1 R. K. Mission Road, Dhaka, p. 17.
2. Sheikh Abu Najib Suhrawardy (1167 AC) is also regarded as the founder of the Suhrawardy Order of Saints. See *Obaidullah Al-Obaidi Suhrawardy,* Pakistan Publications, October 1970, Karachi, 1970, p. 1.
3. Ahsan[a], op. cit., p. 17.
4. Ibid.
5. The Suhrawardia Order was among the four principal orders of saints preaching Islam in the subcontinent: The other three orders were: Quaderia, Chistia and Nakshbandia-Mojaddedia.
6. Ahsan[a], op. cit., p. 17.
7. Ibid.
8. Ibid.
9. Ibid.
10. Ibid.
11. Ibid.
12. *Reminiscences of Gour and Pandua.* Quoted *in* Ahsan[a], op. cit., p. 17.
13. Ahsan[a], op. cit., p. 17.
14. Ibid.
15. *Maulana Obaidullah al-Obaidi Suhrawardy,* op. cit., pp. 5–11.
16. Ibid.
17. A copy of this article is available in the Asiatic Society Library, Dhaka.
18. Aziz, K.K., *Ameer Ali: his life and work,* Publishers United Ltd., Lahore, 1968, p. 543.
19. *Makhazul Ulum* or the Sources of Science. The Dhaka University Library preserves a copy of this book.
20. *Maulana Obaidullah al-Obaidi Suhrawardy,* op. cit., p. 5.
21. Ibid., p. 3.
22. Haq, Enamul (ed.), *Nawab-Bahadur Abdul Latif* (His writings and related documents), Samudra Prokashani, Dhaka, 1968, pp. 215–6.
23. *Maulana Obaidullah al-Obaidi Suhrawardy,* op. cit., p. 4.
24. Ibid.
25. The Mohammadan Anglo-Arabic College eventually became the Muslim University of Aligarh.
26. *Maulana Obaidullah al-Obaidi Suhrawardy,* op. cit., p. 5.
27. *Nawab Abdul Latif,* Pakistan Publications, February 1970, Karachi, pp. 11–14; Haq, op. cit., p. 79.
28. *Syed Ameer Ali,* Pakistan Publications, Karachi, February 1970, pp. 3–8; Aziz, op. cit., p. 567.
29. Qayyum, M.A., *Dhaka Muslim suhrit samiti* (Dhaka Mohammadan Friends Association), Mah-e-Nau (Bengali monthly), Pakistan Publications, Dhaka, April 1967, p. 17; Ali, S.M., *Maulana Obaidullah al-Obaidi,* Mah-e-Nau (Bengali monthly), Pakistan Publications, Dhaka, July 1967, p. 7.

30. The President of the association was Moulvi Himmat Ali. Moulvi Abdul Majid was appointed as secretary; Himayet Uddin and Moulvi Zahidur Rahman were joint secretaries. See Ali, op. cit., pp. 6–7.

31. Qayyum, op. cit., p. 31.

32. Ibid., pp. 31–34.

33. Ibid.

34. Ibid.

35. Ahmed, Nuruddin, *Amader itihasher joigyotam protinidhi marhum Shaheed Suhrawardy* (Huseyn Shaheed Suhrawardy: the fittest representative of our history), Ittefaq: Suhrawardy ed., op. cit., pp. 159–160.

36. Ibid., p. 159.

37. Ahsan[a], op. cit., p. 18; Ahmed, N., op. cit., p. 159.

38. Ibid.

39. Ibid.

40. Ahmed, N., op. cit., pp. 159–60.

41. *Majidia* was an insignia given to those who made an outstanding contribution to the Ottoman Empire. The insignia was established in 1852 by Sultan Abdul Aziz in honour of Sultan Abdul Majid.

42. Ahsan[a], op. cit., p. 18.

43. Ahmed, N., op. cit., p. 160.

44. Ahsan[a], op. cit., 18.

45. Ibid.

46. Ibid.

47. Fazal, Abul, *Suhrawardy prosonghe* (In Suhrawardy context), Ittefaq: Suhrawardy ed., op. cit., p. 133.

48. Ahsan[a], op. cit., p. 19.

49. Ahmad, K.[a], *Banglar jatio jagoron o Suhrawardy* (National renaissance of Bengal and Suhrawardy), Ittefaq: Suhrawardy ed., op. cit., p. 147.

50. Ibid.

51. Ahsan[a], op. cit., p. 19.

52. Ibid.

53. The Swaraj party was founded over differences among the Indian National Congress leaders on the question of council entry through 1924 elections to continue the struggle for freedom from inside the legislatures. C.R. Das was opposed, among others, by Dr Rajendra Prasad and Rajagopalachari. This divided the Congress into supporters of pro-changers and non-changers, the latter adhering to the direct action programme of Mahatma Gandhi. C.R. Das, with support from Hakim Ajmal Khan and Pandit Nehru, formed the Swaraj Party in 1923. See Azad, Maulana Abul Kalam, *India wins freedom,* Orient Longmans, Calcutta, 1960, pp. 20–21.

54. Fazal, op. cit., 133.

55. Ahsan[a], op. cit., p. 19.

56. Mujibur[a] Rahman, Sheikh, *Netake jamon dekhecchi* (As I saw my leader), Ittefaq: Suhrawardy ed, op. cit., p. 146. Sheikh Mujibur Rahman was the closest political disciple of Shaheed Suhrawardy. He became the president of the Awami League after Suhrawardy's death, when the party was revived, fought the 1970 election on his six-point programme and won a resounding victory. On refusal to hand over power by the centre, he led a non-violent movement and was arrested. The civil war that followed won victory and freedom for his province and he became its President (also Prime Minister). He was assassinated in a coup on 15 August 1975.

57. See Part II of this book, Memoirs, p. 102.

58. Rajpal wrote this book drawing instances from the life of the holy prophet of Islam against the evils of polygamy. The book gravely wounded the feelings of the Muslims and the

author was prosecuted in the Lahore High Court. But Justice Kunwar Daleep Singh acquitted him opening the floodgate of mischief and violence throughout the subcontinent, much greater than the Hindu-Muslim quarrels over cow slaughter and playing music before mosques. For details see Noman, Mohammad, *Muslim India,* Kitabistan (1st ed.), Allahabad, 1942, pp. 221, 217, 225.

59. Suhrawardy approached Barrister Longford James who appealed to the High Court, but it turned down the appeal. Even the Privy Council upheld the sentence of death. Barrister James then moved a mercy petition before the Governor of Bengal and the poor man's life could be spared. See *Hussain Suhrawardy,* The Morning News, Suhrawardy supplement, 5 December 1969; Rahman, Azizur, *Ajo mone pare* (We remember till today), Ittefaq: Suhrawardy ed., op. cit., p. 169.

60. Ahsan[a], op. cit., p. 19.

61. *Suhrawardy, personal notes (MS) left with his daughter, Begum Akhtar Sulaiman* (a copy is available with the Editor), p. 9.

62. See Part II of this book, Memoirs, p. 103.

63. Ahsan[a], op. cit., p. 19.

64. Ibid.

65. Ibid.

66. The leaders were: Maulana Abul Kalam Azad, Chowdhury Khaliquzzaman, Maulana Mohammad Akram Khan, Dr M.A. Ansari, Rafiq Ahmad Kidwai, Maulana Zafar Ali Khan, T.A. Sherwani and Sir Ali Imam.

67. *Suhrawardy's personal notes,* op. cit., p. 10.

68. Mujib[a], op. cit., p. 146.

69. Ahsan[a], op. cit., p. 19.

70. Ibid.

71. Ibid.

72. See Part II of this book, Memoirs, p. 114; Ahsan[a], op. cit., p. 19.

73. Ahsan[a], op. cit., p. 19.

74. Ibid., p. 20.

75. Ibid.

76. Fazal, op. cit., p. 138.

77. Sen, Rangalal, *Political elites in Bangladesh,* University Press Ltd., Dhaka, 1986, p. 40. See Part II of this book, Memoirs, p. 103; Ahsan[a], op. cit., p. 20. Both Sen and Ahsan name the party as 'Bengal Muslim United Party.'

78. The Muslim leaders of Bengal were more interested in rights for tenants, and, after the passing of the Bengal Tenancy Act of 1928, that gave more rights to landlords, most of whom were Hindus, they formed the *Nikhil Bango Proja Samiti* in 1929 with Sir Abdur Rahim as its President. Maulana Mohammad Akram Khan was elected Secretary. In 1935, there was another election and A.K. Fazlul Huq became its President. The next year, the name of the organization was changed to KPP to make it more popular among the peasants.

79. Ahsan[a], op. cit., p. 20.

80. Ibid.; Sen, op. cit., pp. 39–40.

81. See Part II of this book, Memoirs, p. 103.

82. Sen, op. cit., p. 40.

83. *Suhrawardy's personal notes*, op. cit., p. 13.

84. Sen, op. cit., pp. 40–42.

85. Ahmad[b], K., *Socio-political history of Bengal and the birth of Bangladesh,* Pioneer Printing Press (4th ed.), Dhaka, 1975, p. 34.

86. Sen, op. cit., p. 42.

87. Ibid., pp. 42–43.

88. Ahmad[b], op. cit., p. 44.

89. Quoted *in* Sen, op. cit., p. 48.

90. Ahmad[b], op. cit., p. 36.

91. *Huseyn Shaheed Suhrawardy,* Pakistan Publications, Karachi, April 1970, p. 10.

92. Fazlul Huq resigned from the Muslim League over the controversy of his joining the War Council constituted by the Viceroy of India to meet the Japanese threat. Fazlul Huq, Sir Sikandar Hayat Khan, Begum Shah Nawaz and a few other Muslim leaders had joined the National Defence Council on being invited by the Viceroy but without consulting the Muslim League. Jinnah called on them to resign and they did. Fazlul Huq resigned because, he said, his presence on the War Council would not serve any purpose under the present circumstances. He maintained that he was right in joining the National Defence Council as, he thought, during the war civil government was bound to be helpless if the head of such a government could not make his voice heard in the War Council. In that context he had to choose between loyalty to the Muslim League and loyalty to the people of Bengal of whom he was the leader.

    Why Fazlul Huq was ousted, or, as he claimed, resigned from the Muslim League only a year after he had moved the historic Lahore Resolution, is thought-provoking. Jinnah had certainly felt insulted at the Lahore Session of the Muslim League where, at the beginning of the session, disregarding his address which he was already making as chairman, the people of Lahore received the late-coming Prime Minister of Bengal with the full-throated slogan of 'Shere-e-Bangla, zindabad' and insisted on hearing him first. It took eight minutes for Fazlul Huq to convince them to hear the chairman first. Jinnah then remarked: 'When the tiger comes, the lamp should give way.' Probably he had not forgotten this insult to his pride and ousted Fazlul Huq from the Muslim League at the first opportunity. This was certainly a personality clash. Fazlul Huq, time and again, declared that he could put thousands of Jinnahs in his pocket.

    Suhrawardy respected Jinnah very much but always harboured the complaint against him that he never appointed him a member of the Muslim League Central Working Committee. Liaquat Ali Khan and Hassan Ispahani consistently opposed Suhrawardy's inclusion in the Working Committee of the Muslim League. Even when Suhrawardy was the only Muslim League Prime Minister in the whole of the subcontinent, he was not nominated as its member. Khwaja Nazimuddin and Ispahani, whether in power or in wilderness, were nominated to represent Bengal. For his conflict with Jinnah, see Sen, op. cit., pp. 53–7.

93. Ahmad[b], op. cit., 58.

94. The Food Conference was composed of representatives of all the provinces and (major Indian States), some of which were deficit and some surplus in foodgrains. The object of the conference was to assess surplus and scarcity and allocate surplus foodgrains to deficit areas. There were no reliable statistics. The surplus provinces toned down their surpluses as much as they could and the deficit provinces exaggerated their deficits.

95. *Suhrawardy's Personal notes,* op. cit., p. 15.

96. Mujibur[b] Rahman, Sheikh, *My leader: a messenger of peace,* The Morning News, Suhrawardy supplement, Karachi, 5 December 1969, p. 11.

97. Ibid.

98. Ahmad[b], op. cit., p. 59.

99. Suhrawardy assumed this non-cooperation was also due to Hassan Ispahani's appointment as the sole agent for procuring rice from this province and approached Ispahani to allow him to appoint a few Hindu handling agents. This angered and antagonized Hassan Ispahani, the most trusted friend of Jinnah in Bengal. He never forgave Suhrawardy for this. The powerful Ispahanis lent their support to Khwaja Nazimuddin and worked for his downfall in the contest for the parliamentary leadership after the 1946 election.

100. The Famine Enquiry Commission reports 1.5 million deaths, but well-informed public estimated the number of deaths exceeded 5 million. See Matinuddin Ahmed, *Bengal famine*

of 1943: British responsibility and social consequences, the Dhaka University Studies, Part A, Vol. 28, June 1978, p. 75. For the pathetic famine scenes see *Pakistan Art Folios* (Zainul Abedin). The Art Foundation, Pakistan Publications, Karachi, 1968. Moved by the agony of the starving humanity, Zainul Abedin, Bangladesh's foremost artist, vividly sketched the horror of this famine.

101. Quoted *in* Sen, op. cit., pp. 62–4.

102. *Huseyn Shaheed Suhrawardy,* op. cit., p. 15.

103. Hossain, Tofazzal (Manik Mia)[a], *Samudrer parimap jamon sambav noy* (As the measurement of the sea is impossible), Ittefaq: Suhrawardy ed., op. cit., p. 136.

104. Ahmad[a], Abul Mansur, *Shaheed Suhrawardy: the statesman,* Pakistan (now Bangladesh) Observer, Suhrawardy Supplement, 5 December 1969.

105. Islam, S., *H.S. Suhrawardy, a tribute, Pakistan* (now Bangladesh) Observer Suhrawardy Supplement, 5 December 1969, Dhaka.

106. The original letter, dated 2 July 1945, is available with Shamsul Hasan. He was the then office secretary of the AIML. Also see Syed Sharifuddin Pirzada, *The Lahore Resolution,* Pakistan Day Anniversary, *Dawn* Supplement, 23 March 1970.

107. Personal communication with the Suhrawardy family. Also see Ahmad[b], op. cit., p. 68; Sen, op. cit., pp. 65–6.

108. Ahmad[b], op. cit., p. 46.

109. Mansergh and Lumby (eds.), *Constitutional relations between Britain and India: Transfer of power, 1942–7,* Vol. VI, London, 1970, p. 196. Quoted *in* Sen, op. cit., p. 66.

110. Khan, Liaquat Ali, *The Resolution of the All-India Muslim League (1945–6), National Archives of Pakistan, Islamabad, Pakistan* (photostated copy), pp. 35–47. Also see, Ittefaq: Suhrawardy ed., op. cit., pp. 57–8.

111. Ibid.

112. The AIML, in its session held in Bombay on 29 July 1946, accepted the Mission Plan and, at the same time, adopted the Direct Action Resolution, saying: 'It calls upon the Muslim nation to stand to a man behind their sole organization—the Muslim League, and be ready for every sacrifice.'

113. Lieutenant General Sir Francis Tuker, GOC of the Eastern Command during the last eighteen months of British rule in India, writes: 'Hindu Mahasava was at the root but Hindu Police dominated the Intelligence Branch and the Criminal Investigation Branch of the police who kept the government in darkness.' See his book, *While memory serves,* Cassell and Company Ltd., London, 1950 (Quoted *in* Ahmad, op. cit., p. 72).

114. Hossain[a], op. cit., pp. 136–7. Tuker corroborates this refusal, saying that 'Brigadier Sixsmith gave Mr Suhrawardy the usual reply that the troops best fulfilled their task by keeping open the main routes and increased their effectiveness most economically by throwing out mobile patrols from these main arteries.' See his book, *While memory serves,* op. cit., p. 158.

115. Hossain[a], op. cit., pp. 136–7, 193.

116. Prominent leaders were Abul Hashim, Sarat Chandra Bose, Surendra Mohan Bose and Kiron Shankar Roy. See ibid., p. 137.

117. Tuker writes: 'Buses and taxis were charging about loaded with Sikhs and Hindus armed with swords, iron bars and fire arms.' About the number of dead, Tuker writes: 'I do not know—no one knows—what the casualties were.... All one can say is that the toll of dead ran into thousands.' See his book, *While memory serves,* op. cit., pp. 161, 163, 165.

118. Hossain[a], op. cit., pp. 136–7.

119. Ibid.

120. Ibid.

121. Ibid.

122. Ispahani, Hassan, *Quaid-i-Azam as I knew him,* Forward Publications Trust, Karachi, Pakistan, 1966, p. 193.

123. Rahman, op. cit., pp. 170–1.
124. Huda, M.H., *Suhrawardy-ke jamon dekhecchi* (As I saw Suhrawardy), Ittefaq: Suhrawardy ed., op. cit., p. 158.
125. Ahmad[a], op. cit., pp. 148–9.
126. Ibid., p. 149.
127. Ibid.
128. Ahsan[a], op. cit., pp. 20–1; Ahmad[a], op. cit., p. 149; Ahmad[b], op. cit., p. 72.
129. In the interim ministry Sri Jogendra Nath Mondal was nominated from Bengal which was a big farce in the then political situation and shows how apathetic and anti-Bengali were the Muslim League leaders from other provinces, especially Jinnah. Suhrawardy called this an injustice to Bengal, but Jinnah did it.
130. Ahsan[a], op. cit., p. 21.
131. Spear, Percival, *India: a modern history*, The Michigan State University, 1961, p. 416.
132. The fantastic speed at which Mountbatten effected the division of a subcontinent and its assets proved ominous and fears were justified when large Muslim majority areas were illegally handed over to India and partitioned Bengal. He connived at doing this in conjunction with the top Congress leaders and was handsomely paid for this betrayal by being appointed as the first Governor General of free India.
133. Ahmad[b], op. cit., p. 81.
134. Ibid., pp. 63, 78.
135. Ahsan[b], Raghib, *A note on the inner history of the United Bengal Scheme* (Draft Bengal Pact), Jinnah Awami Muslim League, Karachi, 1951 (The Editor holds a typed copy. Pages have been marked from there).
136. Ahmad[b], op. cit., pp. 88–9.
137. Hossain[b], Tofazzal (Manik Mia), *Pakistani rajnitir bish basar* (Twenty years of Pakistan politics), Bangladesh Books International Ltd., Edited by Golam Hafiz, 2nd ed., February 1984, p. 28.
138. Hodson in his book, *The Great Divide,* reveals that Jinnah even tried to give concessions to the Hindus of Bengal. At one stage he, in reply to a proposal about keeping Bengal united at the price of its staying out of Pakistan, said that he 'should be delighted. What is the use of Bengal without Calcutta? They had much better remain united and independent. I am sure they would be on friendly terms with Pakistan.' Hodson further said that the 'original plan for the transfer of power included an option for Bengal to decide on independence as a unit but Nehru opposed it.' Quoted *in* Ahmad[b], op. cit., p. 88.; Hossain[b], op. cit., p. 28.
139. Ahsan[b], op. cit., p. 5.
140. Ibid., p. 9.
141. Ahmad[b], op. cit., p. 63.
142. Ibid.
143. The three sections were: *Section A,* comprising Madras, Bombay, United Provinces, Bihar, Central Provinces and Orissa; *Section B,* comprising Punjab, NWFP and Sindh; and *Section C,* comprising Bengal and Assam.
144. 'His Majesty's government will have to consider to whom the powers of the central government in British India should be handed over, on the due date, whether as a whole to some form of central government for British India or in some areas to the existing provincial governments.' Quoted *in* Ahmad[b], op. cit., p. 78.
145. The proposed state was to be divided into three zones—*Central* (the Muslim majority districts of Chittagong and Dhaka, the Presidency and Rajshahi divisions and the district of Sylhet); *Eastern* (The whole of Assam without Sylhet district); and *Western* (Burdwan division and Purnea.).
146. Ahmad[b], op. cit., p. 81.
147. Ibid.

148. Ibid.
149. Hossain[b], op. cit., p. 29.
150. Ibid., pp. 29–30.
151. Ibid.
152. Ahmad[b], op. cit., p. 81.
153. Ahsan[b], op. cit., p. 10.
154. Ibid., pp. 11–12.
155. The outline read:
   1. The Muslim League government in Bengal shall continue to hold office, but, in place of Hindu ministers, new nominees of the Bengal Congress shall be appointed immediately;
   2. Bengal shall not join India or Pakistan and shall remain free. The question of Bengal joining Pakistan or India, or remaining independent shall be decided by the Constituent Assembly elected on the basis of universal adult franchise;
   3. Seats for the Muslims, the Hindus, the scheduled castes and other minorities shall be fixed according to their population basis;
   4. The Prime Minister shall be a Muslim; and
   5. Parity shall be maintained in the Council of Ministers.
156. Pyarelal, *Mahatma Gandhi—The last phase*. Quoted *in* Ahmad[b], op. cit., pp. 81–2.
157. Ibid., p. 82.
158. Ibid.
159. Ibid.
160. Ahsan[b], op. cit., 15.
161. Ahsan[b], op. cit., p. 18.
162. Mountbatten later admitted his nefarious role in the partition of Bengal. In his address to the Royal Empire Society in London on 6 October 1948, he said: 'He (Jinnah) produced the strongest arguments why these provinces (Bengal and the Punjab) should not be partitioned. He said they had national characteristics and that partition would be disastrous. I agreed, but I said how much more must I now feel that the same consideration applied to the partitioning of the whole of India. He did not like that and started explaining why India had to be partitioned, and so we went round the mulberry bush until finally he realized that either he could have a united India with an unpartitioned Punjab and Bengal or a divided India, with partitioned Punjab and Bengal, and he finally accepted the latter solution.' Quoted *in* Ahmad[b], op. cit., p. 83.
163. The 1905 partition of Bengal, creating the Muslim majority province of Eastern Bengal and Assam, was accentuated by two reasons: first, the British lately recognized the injustices which had hitherto been inflicted on Bengali Muslims. Second, the Bengal Presidency, which comprised, besides Bengal proper, Bihar and Orissa, was too unwieldy. See *Nawab Salimullah*, Pakistan Publications, February 1970, Karachi, pp. 1–2.
164. Although a minority (46%), since the Hindus were politically and economically far ahead of the Muslims, the formation of a Muslim League government must have caused disappointment to them.
165. The nationalization of landholdings was in the election manifesto of the KPP.
166. *Presidential addresses of the AIML 1936–44*, National Archives of Pakistan, Islamabad, pp. 27 ff; *A.K. Fazlul Huq*, Pakistan Publications, Karachi, 1970, p. 3.
167. Ahsan[b], op. cit., pp. 21–2; Hossain[a], op. cit., p. 136.
168. Ahsan[b], op. cit., p. 22.
169. Ibid.
170. When the AIML and the Congress were discussing the partition issues the Muslim League leadership was given by only Jinnah, Liaquat Ali Khan, and Sardar Abdur Rab Nishtar. There was no Bengali on the negotiation table. This encouraged Lord Mountbatten in doing great injustice to Bengal and Assam Muslims, particularly in awarding Calcutta to minority

West Bengal. If Calcutta was not given over to West Bengal, neither the Congress nor the Hindu Mahasabha would have felt encouraged to press their demand for the partition of Bengal. The AIML High Command, to kill two birds in one stone, encouraged the East Bengal Group of the BPML to leave its claim on Calcutta to isolate Suhrawardy and, at the same time, to frustrate any possible demand from East Bengal (or United Bengal) to make Calcutta the capital of Pakistan. The united stand of the Punjab Muslims had forced the British Viceroy to award Lahore to Muslim West Punjab when the Punjab province was similarly partitioned on the religious line.

171. Hossain[a], op. cit., p. 136.
172. Mujib[a], op. cit., p. 143; Ahmad[b], op. cit., p. 85; Hossain[a], op. cit., p. 136.
173. Ahmad[b], op. cit., p. 85.
174. In an emergency meeting held on 27 June, with only six members present, the East Pakistan Muslim League Working Committee resolved to make Dhaka the temporary headquarters of the province and abandoned any claim for compensation. Mujib[a], op. cit., p. 143; Hossain[a], op. cit., p. 136.
175. Ahsan[a], op. cit., p. 21.
176. Ibid.
177. Ibid.
178. Ittefaq: Suhrawardy ed., p. 86.
179. See Part II of this book, Memoirs, pp. 106, 109.
180. Hossain[a], op. cit., p. 136.
181. Mujib[a], op. cit., p. 143.
182. Ibid.
183. Ibid.
184. Hossain[a], op. cit., p. 136; Mujib[a], op. cit., p. 143.
185. A boundary force of 50,000 troops was constituted under General Rees and posted between West Pakistan and the western boarder of India. But it proved to be helpless because its sympathies were too sharply divided and the number of dead crossed the million mark. See Spear, op. cit., pp. 422–4.
186. Tuker, giving a pen-picture of the holocaust, says how village after village was exterminated by extremist Hindus. See his book, *While memory serves,* op. cit., pp. 161 ff. Also see Spear, op. cit., p. 424; Memoirs, pp. 105, 108.
187. Spear, op. cit., p. 424.
188. *The daily Azad,* 4 June, Dhaka, 1948
189. Ibid.
190. *The daily Azad,* 6 June, Dhaka, 1948.
191. Ahsan[a], op. cit., p. 19.
192. Ibid.
193. Memoirs, p. 112; Hossain[a], op. cit., p. 136.
194. Hossain[b], op. cit., pp. 39–40.
195. Ibid., pp. 35–42.
196. Ibid., p. 36.
197. Ibid., p. 36.
198. Ibid., p. 37.
199. Ibid.
200. Ibid.
201. Ibid.
202. Ahmad[b], op. cit., p. 93; Hossain[b], op. cit., p. 44.
203. Hossain[b], op. cit., p. 44.
204. Ahmad[b], op. cit., p. 93.
205. The Constituent Assembly of Pakistan was set up with 69 members, but when 8 million refugees entered West Pakistan, 10 more seats were allotted to her bringing the total number

to 79. East Bengal still had 44 seats; but, when Nazimuddin sacrificed more than half a dozen seats to West Pakistan, this rendered East Bengal a minority in the Constituent Assembly. He made this sacrifice at the request of Prime Minister Liaquat Ali Khan, who was among the recipients and was elected to the National Assembly from East Bengal. See Memoirs, p. 79.

206. Hossain[b], op. cit., pp. 38–42.

207. Ibid., p. 41.; Sen, op. cit., p. 82; Ahsan[a], op. cit., p. 22.

208. Hossain[b], op. cit., p. 41.

209. Sen, op. cit., p. 82; Ahmad[b], op. cit., p. 105; Ahsan[a], op. cit., p. 22.

210. Ahmad[b], op. cit., p. 105.

211. Besides Suhrawardy and Maulana Bhashani, the following persons were present: Ataur Rahman Khan, Abdus Salam Khan, Ali Ahmad Khan, Syed Abdur Rahim Mokter, Tofazzal Hossain (Manik Mia), Begum Anowara, Ajmal Khan, Molla Jalaluddin, Korban Ali, M.A. Wahed, Khandoker Mohammad Ilias, Almas Ali, Hamid Choudhury, Gazi Ghulam Mostafa. Sheikh Mujibur Rahman was serving a three-year jail term and was appointed as Joint Secretary of the newly-formed party. Shamsur Rahman was elected as General Secretary.

212. Sen, op. cit., p. 89.

213. I was then a college student and attended his public meeting in my home-town Sirajganj where, to the applause of his admiring audience, he uttered this.

214. Ahmad[b], op. cit., p. 106.

215. Ibid.

216. Tangail by-election was held in April 1949. Shamsul Huq, a young political worker, defeated Khurram Khan Panni, the candidate of the all-powerful Muslim League in the home district of the Chief Minister.

217. Hossain[b], op. cit., p. 16; Memoirs, p. 83.

218. The Population census of Pakistan, 1961., Vol. I, pp. 30–5.

219. Umar, B., Purbobanglar bhasa andolon o tatkalin rajniti (Language movement of East Bengal and politics of the time), Mowla Brothers, Dhaka, November 1970 (First Part), p. 50. The ruling Muslim League members from East Bengal refused to support the Congress move to make Bengali the official language of Pakistan.

220. Personal communication.

221. Umar, op. cit., pp. 50–1; Sen, op. cit., p. 98.

222. Sen, op. cit., p. 99; Ahmad[b], op. cit., pp. 99–100.

223. Umar, op. cit., pp. 77–8; Ahmad[b], op. cit., p. 100; Sen, op. cit., p. 101.

224. Kamruddin Ahmad was convener of the Committee of Action. See his book, op. cit., p. 99.

225. Ibid., pp. 100–1.

226. Speeches by Quaid-i-Azam Mohammad Ali Jinnah, Governor General of Pakistan, June 1947–August 1948, Karachi, 1948, p. 62.

227. Ibid., p. 67.

228. Maron, Stanley, 'The problem of East Pakistan,' Pacific Affairs, Vol. XXVII, June 1955, p. 132. Maron was a teacher of Philosophy in the University of Dhaka and had a first hand knowledge of the language movement.

229. The Times, London, 27 February 1952; Sen, op. cit., p. 108.

230. Ahmad[a], op. cit., p. 148.

231. Sen, op. cit., p. 118.

232. Mukherjee, Anil, Swadhin Bangladesh sangramer potobhumi (Background of Bangladesh independence struggle), 1379 BS, pp. 55–6.

233. Awami League, KSP, and Nizam-i-Islam Party.

234. Sen, op. cit., p. 118.

235. One year of popular government in East Pakistan, Government of East Pakistan, Dhaka, 6 September 1957, pp. 15–16.

236. *The statistical yearbook, 1954–5*, Government of East Pakistan, Dhaka.

237. Park, R.L., *East Bengal: Pakistan's troubled province, Far Eastern Survey*, Vol. XXIII, No. 5, May 1954, pp. 72–3; Callard, Keith, *Pakistan: a political study,* 1954, p. 94.

238. Park, op. cit., p. 70; *The Times,* London, 17 and 21 March 1954.

239. Hossain[b], op. cit., 50; Ahmad[b], op. cit., p. 114.

240. Sen, op. cit., p. 130.

241. Ibid.

242. 'It is important that the people of two Bengals should realize the fundamental fact that in order to live happily they must render mutual assistance to each other. Politicians had partitioned territories, but the common mass should ensure that everybody lived peacefully. Language proved to be the most important unifying factor in history and the people of two Bengals, bound together on common language, should forget political divisions and feel themselves to be one.' See Ray, J.K., *Democracy and nationalism on trial: a study of East Pakistan,* 1968, p. 98.

243. *The Morning News,* Dhaka, 5 May 1954.

244. Hossain[b], op. cit., p. 58; Sen, op. cit., p. 130.

245. *Dawn,* Karachi, 29 June 1954.

246. Huq 'refused that the communists were responsible and refused to agree to any general roundup.' Park, R.L. and R.S. Wheeler, *East Bengal under Governor's rule,* Far Eastern Survey, Vol. XXIII, No. 9, September 1954, p. 131.

247. *Dawn,* Karachi, 25 and 26 May 1954.

248. *The New York Times,* 23 May 1954. Callahan said he had 'gathered' the news from his talk with Chief Minister Fazlul Huq.

249. *The Times,* London, 30 May 1954.

250. *The Daily Worker* of London wrote on 1 June 1954 that 'Fazlul Huq, the United Front ministry and the people of East Bengal were the first to be slaughtered on the altar of the US-Pak military pact.'

251. *The Times,* London, 5 and 6 June 1954.

252. Ghulam Mohammad needed support from Bengal and he contacted Ataur Rahman Khan, the leader of the parliamentary group of the East Pakistan Awami League, through West Pakistani M.H. Usmani, then General Secretary of the Pakistan Awami League. Usmani warned him that if Ghulam Mohammad was not supported in Bengal, he would hand over the reins of government to the army. Ahmad[b], op. cit., p. 118; Hossain[b], op. cit., p. 62.

253. Referring to this incident, *Dawn* (Karachi) wrote editorially on 11 August 1957: 'There have indeed been times, such as that of October night in 1954 when, with a General to the left of him and a General to the right of him, a half-mad Governor General imposed upon a captured Prime Minister the dissolution of a Constituent Assembly and the virtual setting up of a semi-dictatorial Executive.'

254. The emissary was Ataur Rahman Khan, who went to Switzerland to discuss the matter with Suhrawardy.

255. Ahmad[b], op. cit., p. 119.

256. General Ayub Khan joined the cabinet retaining, at the same time, his position of the chief of the Pakistan Army.

257. That the suspicion seemed to have some basis was proved when Suhrawardy, as law minister, refrained from placing the Rawalpindi Conspiracy Tribunal Ordinance for validation. The Supreme Court had declared all acts and ordinances invalid, thus contributing to early release of the convicted generals.

258. Ibid., p. 119.

259. Only a year ago Bogra had dubbed Haq as a 'traitor'. Now, when he wanted to utilize him against Suhrawardy, he called him the 'Prince of patriots.' The KPP was renamed as KSP after the East Pakistan Assembly abolished *zamindari* in 1952.

260. Ahmad[b], op. cit., p. 119.

261. See Part II of this book, Memoirs, p. 87.
262. Tamizuddin Khan, president of the Constituent Assembly, had filed a petition contesting the dissolution of the Constituent Assembly, which was also the national parliament. After several causes and law suits, the following emerged:
    • Normally, the Governor General had no right to dissolve the Constituent Assembly, but, in view of certain special circumstances detailed in the statement made by the government, when seeking the advice of the Supreme Court, he was justified in doing so;
    • A new Constituent Assembly should be set up as soon as possible; and
    • All the laws passed by the Constituent Assembly were invalid, because the consent of the Governor General had not been taken.
    The judgement of the Supreme Court on the third point created considerable chaos and any number of ordinances had to be passed to legalize the laws and presidings.
263. See Part II of this book, Memoirs, p. 89.
264. The interim BPC reports evoked sharp reactions both from the anti-Muslim League and the Muslim League circles. See Choudhury, G.W., *Constitutional Development in Pakistan,* 1959, p. 109.
265. See Part II of this book, Memoirs, p. 88.
266. Constituent Assembly speech delivered as leader of the opposition, Karachi, 31 January 1956. Reproduced in *Morning News,* Suhrawardy Supplement, 5 December 1969, under the heading: *The constitution that I wanted.* Also see *Proceedings of the Constituent Assembly of Pakistan,* 31 January 1956, National Archives Library, Agargaon, Dhaka.
267. Ibid.
268. Hossain[b], op. cit., p. 71.
269. *The constitution that I wanted,* op. cit., pp. 1–12.
270. Ibid.
271. Ibid.
272. Ibid.
273. Hossain[b], op. cit., p. 72.
274. Ibid.
275. With the dismissal of the first democratically-elected Jukto Front government in East Bengal in May 1954, the Pakistan power elite adopted something called 'Controlled democracy, a brain child of Iskander Mirza, a regime that would be financed by America during the coming year, ie 1955, to the tune of US$105 million.' Deane, Philip, *The Reporter,* Vol. XII, No. 2, 27 January 1955, p. 33. Quoted *in* Sen, op. cit., p. 136.
276. *The Constituent Assembly of Pakistan Proceedings of 10 October 1956,* Dhaka. From his speech in support of joint electorate, reproduced *in* Ittefaq: Suhrawardy ed., op. cit., pp. 74–7.
277. It would appear that the basic philosophy of the two-nation theory, which connoted the right of self-determination by each group and, as a necessary corollary, the promise of a homeland for all the Muslims of the subcontinent of India, was abandoned when:
    • the decision whether the Muslim majority provinces would accede to Pakistan or to India was taken, not by the Muslims alone, but by a joint vote of the Hindu and the Muslim members of the legislatures.;
    • the fate of Sylhet and the NWFP was decided by the votes of the Hindu and Muslim inhabitants of these areas and not by the votes of Muslims alone;
    • It was agreed that there should not and could not be a general transfer of population between Pakistan and India. Pakistan would not form the homeland of all the Muslims of India and India would continue to contain such Muslims as were there at the time of partition. Pakistan, similarly, would continue to contain such Hindus as were in Pakistan at the time of partition.
278. Ahmad[b], op. cit., 126.

279. Within three days of his assumption of power, the Awami League in East Pakistan, headed by Ataur Rahman Khan, released all political prisoners totalling 500. See Hossain[b], op. cit., p. 78.

280. Ahmad[b], Abul Mansur, *Je mahan neta harailam* (The great leader we lost), Ittefaq: Suhrawardy ed., op. cit., p. 139. Ahmad was commerce minister in the Suhrawardy cabinet.

281. Ibid.

282. Ibid.

283. Ibid.

284. Ahmad[b], op. cit., p. 134.

285. Khan, Ataur Rahman, *Shaheed charitrer boishishta (Specialities in Shaheed's Character)*, Ittefaq: Suhrawardy ed., op. cit., p. 141. Ataur Rahman Khan was the Awami League chief minister of East Bengal during 1956–8. Praising Suhrawardy's greatness, he says, how, on becoming Prime Minister, he visited his province and granted several million rupees to combat the famine.

286. Ahmad[b], op. cit., p. 134.

287. Ibid.

288. *The Pakistan Quarterly*, spring 1957 issue, Pakistan Publications, Karachi, pp. 5–12, 43–4, 66–74.

289. Ahmad[b], op. cit., p. 127.

290. *The Pakistan Quarterly*, op. cit., p. 44.

291. In 1948, Russia had made a similar invitation to Prime Minister Liaquat Ali Khan, which he ignored and made Russia unfriendly towards Pakistan.

292. From his Paltan Maidan speech delivered on 14 June 1957. Reproduced *in* Ittefaq: Suhrawardy ed., op. cit., p. 26.

293. Ahmad[b], op. cit., p. 127.

294. Ittefaq: Suhrawardy ed., op. cit., pp. 40, 56.

295. Retranslated from Bengali, ibid.

296. *Foreign policy debate* (22–5 February 1957), reproducted *in* Ittefaq. Suhrawardy ed., op. cit., p. 47.

297. Four Muslim members of the Baghdad pact met in Tehran on 9 November 1956 and called upon Britain and France to withdraw their armies under a special arrangement and they withdrew greatly at the moral pressure of the 'zeroes'. *Foreign policy debate* (22–5 February 1957), Ittefaq: Suhrawardy ed., op. cit., pp. 48–9.

298. Ibid., pp. 27, 50.

299. Ibid., p. 50.

300. Ibid., p. 38.

301. Ibid., p. 48.

302. Siddiqui, Aslam, *Pakistan seeks security*, Karachi.

303. *Foreign policy debate* (22–5 February 1957), reproduced *in* Ittefaq: Suhrawardy ed., op. cit., p. 49.

304. Suhrawardy's predecessor, Chowdhury Mohammad Ali, had first offered the 'no-war pact' proposal to India. Ibid., pp. 51–2.

305. Hossain[b], op. cit., pp. 79–83.

306. *Foreign policy debate* (22–5 February 1957), reproduced *in* Ittefaq: Suhrawardy ed., op. cit., pp. 40–55. Also see *Proceedings of the Constituent Assembly of Pakistan*, National Archives Library, Agargaon, Dhaka.

307. Ittefaq: Suhrawardy ed., op. cit., pp. 40, 50.

308. Ahmad[b], op. cit., p. 115.

309. *Foreign policy debate* (22–5 February 1957), reproduced *in* Ittefaq: Suhrawardy ed., op. cit., pp. 37–45, 46–52.

310. The Bandung Conference, held in April 1955, fully reaffirmed the collective and individual rights of all states to enter into pacts for self-defence in accordance with Resolution 51 of the United Nations Charter.

311. *Foreign policy debate* (22–5 February 1957), reproduced *in* Ittefaq: Suhrawardy ed., op. cit., p. 40.

312. I gathered this news from Suhrawardy's only granddaughter, Shahida Munni.

313. *The Daily Telegraph,* London, 2 February 1957 (Editorial coment).

314. 'On a real view of its own interests, Delhi would surely be wise to welcome and explore Mr Suhrawardy's offer to let Pakistan troops in Kashmir be replaced by a United Nations force. That withdrawal would remove what Mr Menon, Mr Bakshi and other spokesmen for India call the only issue, and provide new hopes of ending a quarrel which only Russia—not even China—finds profitable.' *The Economist,* London, 2 February 1957 (Editorial comment).

315. *The New Times Magazine,* Chicago, 4 February 1957.

316. In 'Retrospect' to the book, Earl Attlee, Britain's Prime Minister during the partition days, corroborating Suhrawardy's view, says: 'I recall many, many long discussions with Mr Nehru on the vexed question of Kashmir, sometimes between the two of us, sometimes with other prime ministers, but they proved fruitless. Although we proposed every possible variant in order to have a fair plebiscite, to which he had already agreed in principle, we could not get acceptance from Mr Nehru. I have always considered this the blind spot of a great statesman. Whether it was due to his being a Kashmiri Brahmin by descent or to some other cause, Mr Nehru, so wise in other matters, was quite adamant on the question of Kashmir' (K. Katwar Singh, *The legacy of Nehru,* Vikash Publishing House, PVT Ltd., 1948, UP, India, p. 2).

317. He declared this at a public meeting held at the historic Paltan Maidan on 14 June 1957. Reproduced *in* Ittefaq: Suhrawardy ed., op. cit., p. 27.

318. Ahmad[b], op. cit., p. 118.

319. Ibid., pp. 118–19.

320. *Dawn,* Karachi, 5 March 1957.

321. Moniruzzaman, Talukdar, 'Group interests in Pakistan politics 1947–58', *Pacific Affairs,* Vol. XXXIX, Nos. 1 and 2 (spring-summer 1966), pp. 83–98; *The Pakistan Observer* (now Bangladesh), Dhaka, 18 April 1957.

322. Ahmad[b], op. cit., p. 132; Sen, op. cit., p. 153.

323. Ahmad[b], op. cit., p. 128.

324. *Dawn,* Karachi, 15 October 1957.

325. *Suhrawardy's personal notes,* op. cit., p. 48.

326. Ibid., p. 48.

327. Ibid., p. 49.

328. Personal communication with Rashid Suhrawardy.

329. Kamruddin Ahmad quotes from Major General Fazal Maqueem Khan's book, *The story of the Pakistan army,* to say that martial law in the country had received Commander-in-Chief Ayub Khan's final approval on the last day of September 1958. The fact is corroborated in *Friends, not Masters,* by Ayub Khan himself and, in *My Chief,* by Col. Mohammad Ahmad. See Ahmad[b], op. cit., p. 144.

330. *The Pakistan* (now Bangladesh) *Observer,* Dhaka, 8 October 1957.

331. Air Marshal Asghar Khan, an unwilling partner of the 1958 Revolution, tells the story of Ayub ousting his long-standing friend and principal partner in the Revolution from power. In the third week of October when Ayub Khan was on a tour of East Pakistan, President Iskander Mirza ordered the Air-force Chief of Staff, Air Commodore Maqbul Rabb, often Mirza's bridge-mate, to arrest Brigadiers Yahya Khan and Malik Sher Bahadur, with assistance from Brigadier Qayyum Sher, Commander of the Army garrison at Malir, a military base near Karachi. Rabb timely disclosed this to Asghar Khan as well as to the

two Brigadiers. Brigadier Yahya Khan controlled the military intelligence and he too intercepted Iskander Mirza's telephonic conversation with a certain Syed Amjad Ali, whose daughter was to be married with the President's son, that he would 'sort out Ayub Khan in a few days.' Ayub was duly informed of the latest developments and he, in a counter coup, ousted Iskander Mirza before the latter could 'sort him out.' See his *Generals in politics 1958–82,* University Press Ltd., Dhaka, 1982, pp. 8–9.

332. Ahmad[a], op. cit., pp. 143–4.

333. Personal communication with Rashid Suhrawardy.

334. Personal communication with Rashid Suhrawardy.

335. Suhrawardy, in See Part II of this book, (p. 167), as well as in his rejoinder (appendix I) to President Ayub, refers to this as the only real reason. However, it is also held that during his visit to the United States for massive military and economic aid, President Ayub Khan was told to first establish democracy in his country. A few weeks prior to this visit, Suhrawardy had visited the United States for his medical check-up. The President suspected this situation as Suhrawardy's work. Angered, and without waiting for evidence, he ordered his arrest on 26 January after his return from the Indian Independence Day celebration in Dhaka. However, since Governor Azam Khan refused to arrest him apprehending mass upsurge, Suhrawardy was arrested on 30 January after his return from a reception hosted by the American Ambassador in Karachi. This visit was one of the 'reasons' supplied to him as a ground for his arrest. See Ahmad[a], op. cit., p. 153.

336. Personal communication with Rashid Suhrawardy.

337. Ahsan[a], op. cit., p. 24.

338. Ittefaq: Suhrawardy ed., op. cit., p. 90.

339. Ibid.

340. Personal communication with Rashid Suhrawardy.

341. The letter has been reproduced *in* Ittefaq: Suhrawardy ed., op. cit., p. 118.

342. Fazal, op. cit., p. 134.

343. Personal communication with Rashid Suhrawardy.

344. Even the tribunal set up to try EBDO cases eulogized Suhrawardy's role in the creation of Pakistan.

345. Ahmed, op. cit., p. 139.

346. Brohi, A.K., *A tribute to Suhrawardy, The Morning News,* Karachi, Suhrawardy Supplement, 5 December 1969, p. v.

347. Hashim, Abul, *Amar dristitey marhum Suhrawardy* (The Late Suhrawardy in my own eyes), Ittefaq: Suhrawardy, ed., op. cit., p. 138.

348. Hossain[a], op. cit., p. 135.

349. Ibid., p. 136; Mujib[a], op. cit., p. 144.

350. Mujib[a], op. cit., p. 144.

351. Khan, Ataur, op. cit., p. 141.

352. Brohi, op. cit., p. v.

353. Ahsan[a], op. cit., p. 22.

354. Ahmad[a], op. cit., p. ii.

355. Brohi, op. cit., p. v.

356. Ibid.

357. Fazal, op. cit., p. 134.

358. Ahmad[a], op. cit., pp. 144–5.

359. Abul Fazal thinks that the national flag was, probably, lowered to half-mast to efface the ignominy of the moral defeat the Ayub administration suffered due to the illegal and unjustified incarceration without trial of such a great stateman like Suhrawardy and his humiliation during the past five years. See Fazal, op. cit., p. 134.

360. Suhrawardy's letter written from Zurich on 17 November 1963 has been reproduced *in* Ittefaq: Suhrawardy ed., op. cit., p. 117.

361. The election was, in fact, a vote for separation. The Awami League of Sheikh Mujibur Rahman fought the election on a clear-cut 6-point programme of achieving full autonomy for East Pakistan and won, in a 313-member assembly, 167 of the 169 seats allocated to East Pakistan but not a single seat in West Pakistan, while no West Pakistan-based party won a single seat in East Pakistan.

362. It was a great paradox that the East Pakistanis, who constituted 56% of the total population of Pakistan, had a nominal representation (Army 5%, Air force 16% and Navy 10%) in the powerful Pakistan army and held no commanding position in any one of the three services which allowed the West Pakistanis to militarily dominate the politically mature East Pakistanis.

PART II: MEMOIRS

1. The Presidency Division, comprising Murshidabad, Nadia, Calcutta and 24 Parganas—overwhelmingly Muslim—would have become part of East Bengal and Pakistan had not in the 1941 census the Hindu enumerators artificially inflated the number of Hindus. This obviously was done without Prime Minister Fazlul Huq's knowledge. He came to know of this when there was no time to rectify the misdeed.

2. The Front had captured 223 seats. See Supra, p. 44.

3. The One Unit was Daultana's brain-child as spelled out in his famous documents entitled 'Document X' and 'Documents A, B, and C'. He vigorously pursued it to establish 'an effective intelligent Punjabi leadership, both at the centre and at Lahore, and to isolate East Bengal through the introduction of separate electorates. Subsequently, General Ayub Khan went one step further, as is evident from Colonel Muhammad Ahmad's book, *My Chief,* to integrate the whole of Pakistan to establish a highly centralized military oligarchy. See Supra, pp. 77–8 and Ahmad[b], op. cit., pp. 141–2.

4. Khwaja Nazimuddin had contested the election from Patuakhali constituency. This was his own Zamindari and the Muslim League had found it the safest place for his election in view of Fazlul Huq's threatening that he would contest and defeat Nazimuddin from any corner of Bengal he contested. But even this safest place could not save him and he was defeated by Fazlul Huq by a margin of 24,000 votes. Suhrawardy offered one of his two seats and saved his political career. However, Nazimuddin paid back his benefactor by ousting him from East Bengal when the latter had come on a peace mission after the partition of India and Bengal.

5. The correct position was this: many Muslim members were elected as independents and they joined either the Muslim League or the KSP. A few members still remained independent. Subsequent position stood at 60 Muslim League and 54 KSP. See Supra, p. 16.

6. Suhrawardy gave asylum to 72,945 Muslim refugees (See Ittefaq: Suhrawardy ed., op. cit., p. 59) who fled Bihar and arranged their food and lodging in 40 camps. The unofficial number was 400,000.

7. The Liaquat-Nehru Pact was signed on 8 April 1950 in the spirit of Suhrawardy's 12-point Minority Charter, incorporating its salient points of communal harmony.

8. Suhrawardy was supposed to attend a communal harmony meeting in Manikganj, but Chief Minister Khwaja Nazimuddin first arrested him, charging him with sedition, attempting to unite both Bengals and later expelled him as an undesirable Indian *citizen at the instigation of Prime Minister Liaquat Ali Khan.*

9. With his entry into East Pakistan banned, Suhrawardy migrated to Karachi on 5 March and took up residence in his son-in-law's house.

10. Norman Brown writes: 'Liaquat Ali assailed in the most vigorous terms those who found other parties, calling them traitors, liars, and hypocrites, and singled out for specific attack

Huseyn Shaheed Suhrawardy and the Awami League. 'See his book, *The United States, India and Pakistan*, 1963, pp. 249–50.

11. Suhrawardy referred to an Arab saying: When your own existence is threatened you can even approach the devil for help.

12. Suhrawardy had ably convinced the United States government to approve the use of American military aid equipment against all aggression. The stand was revoked immediately after Suhrawardy's exit from power. See Supra, p. 60.

13. Suhrawardy addressed the Salimullah Muslim Hall students of Dhaka University and, on their request, submitted his views on the foreign policy of Pakistan which he based on four basic principles: Neutrality based on honesty and truth, maintenance of world peace and reduction of world tension, support to all United Nations resolutions and protection to national unity and freedom.

14. The Kagmari conference was held on 7–8 February 1957. See also Supra, p. 59.

15. The promised date was 28 November 1957. Subsequently, he resigned for his failure to amend the constitution accommodating separate electorate when the Republican Party changed its decision in favour of joint electorate.

16. Formerly Section 92-A of the 1935 constitution.

17. See Supra, note 340 (Part I).

18. Ayub sent the following generals to obtain President Iskander Mirza's signature on the document of his abdication: Major General Burki, Major General Azam Khan, Major General K.M. Sheikh and Brigadier Sher Bahadur.

19. The Canal Water Treaty, signed on 19 September 1960, settled the water dispute between India and Pakistan at a cost of US$1000 million financed through the World Bank.

20. This is now called the Bangladesh Academy for Rural Development (BARD).

21. There were a few, probably 2, from East Bengal.

22. This want of political consciousness resulted in Muslim League defeat in 1946 in all the provinces that later formed West Pakistan. In the general election held on the issue of Pakistan these Muslim majority provinces had voted against the Muslim League and Pakistan.

23. A very successful advocate subsequently appointed by the President as Chief Justice of the West Pakistan High Court amidst the protests of all the Bar Libraries of Pakistan which thought that the judiciary should be kept free from the political influence and should not be considered a prize for loyalty to the President.

24. The first meeting was held at Rawalpindi.

25. See Supra, pp. 68–9.

26. Nine leaders' statement was signed on 24 June 1962.

27. The President passed the Act on 15 July 1962.

28. *Lathies* are long poles made of bamboos, normally used by police to attack crowds and also carried by villagers in West Pakistan.

29. Major Ishaque and Major Aslam.

30. Nawabzada Nasrullah Khan was President of the West Pakistan Awami League.

31. Bhashani met Ayub on 22 August 1963 and was received at the doorstep. Ayub is reported to have extracted an assurance that Maulana Bhashani would counteract Suhrawardy and the NDF in East Pakistan.

32. The Karachi residence of Suhrawardy's son-in-law, Shah Ahmad Sulaiman. Suhrawardy used to stay in this house.

33. The Franchise Commission's report, which recommended adult franchise, was rejected by President Ayub.

Index

A

Aa'oraful Ma'rif, 1
Abdullah, Shaikh, 108
Abedin, Zainul, 20
Achakzai, Abdus Samad Khan, 99
Adamjee Jute Mills, 45
Advisory Council of Islamic Ideology (ACII),
   142, 143, 169, 171
Afghani, Jamaluddin, 5
Aga Khan, His Highness The, 14, 15, 103
Ahmad, Abul Mansur, 72, 89, 96
Ahmad, Maulana Mian Tufail, 201, 211
Ahmad, Sir Sultan, 14
Ahmadis/Qadianis, 121, 124, 143
Ahmed, Aziz, 38, 199
Ahsan, Maulana Raghib, 28, 40
Ainae-Ibrat, 5
Akbar the Great, 17
Ali Brothers, 9, 14
Ali, Chowdhury Mohammad, 38, 49, 51, 88,
   89, 90, 91, 92, 93, 94, 95, 96, 121, 156,
   190
Ali, Mahmud, 145, 177, 199, 204, 205
Ali, Maulana Athar, 85
Ali, Maulana Mohammad, 8, 14, 100
Ali, Maulana Showkat, 8, 15, 100
Ali, Syed Ameer, 2, 3
Ali, Syed Keramat, 2
All-Bengal Muslim Conference, 14
All-India Khilafat Conference, 14, 103
All-India Muslim Conference, 14
All-India Muslim League (AIML), 8, 15, 28,
   32, 33, 36, 37, 41, 100, 101, 102, 103,
   104, 194
All-India Muslim Volunteers' Conference, 14
All-Pakistan Muslim League Convention, 43
Alwar, Maharajah of, 11
Amin, Nurul, 29, 41, 43, 44, 45, 83, 176, 177,
   206, 207, 208, 194
Amrita Bazaar Patrika, 105
Ansari, M.A., 14
Ansars, 157
Arifin, Shamsul, 1

Assam Provincial Muslim League, 22
Attlee, Clement, 27
Awami League, 41, 44, 45, 47, 51, 53, 54, 59,
   65, 66, 83, 85, 86, 89, 94, 95, 114, 116,
   118, 122, 124, 126, 131, 147, 153, 167,
   173, 177, 190, 201, 204, 206, 207, 208,
   209, 211, 212; Council, 44; ministry, 54
Awami Leaguers, 21
Awami Muslim League, 40, 41, 112, 113
Ayub Khuhro ministry, 40
Azad Pakistan party, 84, 96
Azad, 146
Azad, Nawab of Dhaka Syed Mohammad, 6

B

Baghdad pact, 57, 58, 114, 115, 116
Bahar, Habibullah, 29
Balkan War, 5
Banerjee, Sir Surendranath, 104
Banu, Begum Khozesta Akhter, 5
Bari, Mian Abdul, 190
Basic Democracy system, 68, 138, 146, 147,
   148, 171, 179, 181, 191, 202
Basic Democrats, 67, 68, 135, 136, 140, 143,
   148, 152, 153, 166, 169, 170, 173, 179,
   180, 181, 182, 183, 184, 186, 187, 191,
   203, 206
Basic Principles Committee (BPC) Report, 48,
   81
Battle of Plassey, 30
Bell, John, 152
Bengal Pact, 9, 10
Bengal Provincial Muslim League (BPML),
   15, 16, 20, 21, 22, 28, 32, 37
Bengal Regiment, 157
Bengal Tenancy Amendment Bill of 1938,
   17
Bengali nationalism, 9, 31
Bengali, 22, 37, 42, 43, 44, 50, 89
Bengali-Bihari riots, 45
Bhashani, Maulana Abdul Hamid Khan, 14,
   22, 40, 43, 44, 45, 59, 85, 86, 88, 114, 116,
   117, 118, 197, 198, 199, 207, 208, 209,
   212

Bhutto, Zulfikar Ali, 71
Bihari, Sheikh Sharfuddin, 2
Bihi-Nur-Ki Dargah, 1
Bogra ministry, 48
Bogra, Mohammad Ali, 46, 47, 50, 66, 68, 69,
    83, 85, 86, 87, 88, 89, 90, 175, 176, 184
Bose, Sarat Chandra, 29, 30
Bose, Subash Chandra, 10, 24, 30
Boundary Commission, 31, 32
Bridges, Robert, 6
Brohi, A.K., 72, 73, 74
Bureau of National Reconstruction, 140, 143,
    147
Burki, General Wajid Ali Khan, 175, 177
Burrows, Frederick, 24, 25, 31, 32

C

Cabinet Mission, 23, 29
Callahan, John P., 46
CENTO, 115, 198, 208
Central National Mohammadan Association,
    3
Chakravarty, Babu Rajkumar, 36
Chattha, 192
Chistia Sheikhs, 1
Chittagong Armoury Raid convicts, 21
Chotonagpur adivasis, 28
Chou En-Lai, 55
Choudhury, Abdul Matin, 28
Choudhury, Hamidul Huq, 28, 29, 40, 177,
    207, 208
Chowdhury, Fazlul Qadir, 175, 193
Chowdhury, Hassan Ali, 184
Chowdhury, Yusuf Ali (alias Mohan Mia),
    177
Chundrigar, Ismail Ibrahim, 64, 65, 95, 121,
    122
Congress, 9, 12, 13, 14, 16, 17, 18, 20, 22, 23,
    24, 26, 27, 28, 30, 42, 67, 79, 104, 105,
    137
Congress-League joint committee, 30
Constitution Commission, 135, 152, 166, 169,
    182
Constitution of 1956, 63, 67, 77, 141, 167,
    169, 171, 188, 189, 201
Constitution of 1962, 141, 142, 146, 150, 170,
    176, 201
Convention of Councillors, 22
Cripps Plan, 28
Curzon partition line, 28

D

Daily Azad, The, 16
Dainik Ittefaq, 71
Das, C.R., 9, 10, 30, 72, 102
Datta, Dhirendranath, 42
Daud, Sardar, 57
Daultana, Mian Mumtaz Khan, 91, 93, 97,
    113, 118, 177, 192, 194, 201, 209, 211;
    ministry, 48
Dawn, 63, 145, 189
Debt Settlement Board, 17
Delhi Food Conference, 19
Delhi formula, 13
Democratic Youth League, 44
Denial Policy, 19
Dewan-i-Obaidi, 3
Dhaka Times, 146
Direct Action Day, 23, 24, 105; strategy, 26

E

East Pakistan Awami Muslim League, 40
East Pakistan Communist Party, 44
East Pakistan Industrial Development
    Corporation (EPIDC), 159
East Pakistan Muslim League (EPML), 41, 44,
    45, 83, 194
East Pakistan Rifles, 139
Eastern Examiner, 146
Eisenhower, Dwight D., 60
Election March 1954, 44
Elective Bodies Disqualification Order
    (EBDO), 66, 130, 173, 183; conviction,
    200;
politicians, 70, 183, 188, 210, 212; proceed-
    ings, 212
Ellahi, Chowdhury Fazal, 201
English, 43

F

Faiz, Faiz Ahmad, 96
Family Laws Ordinance, 152
Faqir of Ipi, 99
Faruque, G.M., 139, 140, 161
Fascism, 39, 44, 80, 82
Fatima, Begum Naiz, 6, 7
Fazlullah, Qazi, 209
Films Development Corporation, 54
Finance Commission, 156, 163
First World War, 8, 58, 100

Five-point agreement, 88, 198
Ford Foundation, 136, 137, 154
Forward Bloc, 18, 29, 30
Franchise Commission, 75, 182, 184, 185, 186
Friends' Association for the betterment of Bengali Muslims, 3
Front Ministry, 45, 46
Frontier Crimes Regulations, 164
Fundamental Rights Bill, 70

G

Gandhi Peace Mission, 33, 34
Gandhi, Mahatma, 9, 8, 14, 27, 29, 30, 33, 34, 35, 71, 100, 101, 102, 106, 107, 108, 109, 110, 198
Ghosh, P.C., 32, 59, 106
Ghosh, Surendra Mohan, 29
Government of India Act 1935, 14, 16, 17, 80, 103, 120, 170
Government of India Act of 1919, 100
Great Calcutta Killing, 27
Greater Bengal Scheme, 28
Gurmani, Nawab Mushtaq Hossain, 38, 88, 89, 92, 119

H

Haji Danesh (of Dinajpur), 204
Hakim, Abdul, 94
Hamid, Sultan Abdul, 5
Harvard University, 154
Hashim, Abul, 22, 29, 72
Hassan, Abul, 15
Hedayetullah, Sir Ghulam Hussain, 102
Hindi, 43
Hindu Mahasabha, 18, 29, 104, 108
Hitler, Adolf, 7
Home Rule, 100
Hossain, Colonel Abid, 201
Hossain, Tofazzal, 72, 116, 117, 144. *See also* Manik Mia
Huq, A.K. Fazlul, 6, 15, 16, 17, 18, 19, 21, 23, 31, 43, 44, 45, 46, 48, 49, 70, 85, 86, 87, 88, 89, 90, 94, 103, 104, 126, 177, 208
Huq, Sir Azizul, 19, 177
Hussain, Akhtar, 119, 173, 184
Hussain, Zakir, 138

I

Iftikharuddin, Mian, 84, 96, 97
Ikramullah, Begum Shaista, 6
Ikramullah, Mohammad, 6
Imroze, 96
Independence Act of 1947, 78, 80, 87, 201
Independent Muslim Party (IMP), 15, 103
Indian Franchise Commission, 186
Indian National Army, 24
Indian National Conference, 14
Indian National Congress, 10, 80, 100, 101, 118. *See also* Congress
Indus Basin scheme, 155, 156
Indus River Basin, 174
Inland Water Transport Authority, 54
Intelligence Branch, 24
International Cooperation Agency (ICA), 152
Iqbal, Allama, 13
Isa, Qazi, 118
Islamic Research Institute, 142
Ispahani, Hassan, 15, 26
Ispahanis, 15
Ittefaq, 117, 143, 145, 146

J

Jabres, Francois, 71
Jalal, Hazrat Shah, 2
Jamaat-i-Islami, 84, 121, 123, 131, 172, 173, 201, 206, 208, 209, 211, 212, 190
Jamiat-i-Ulema-i-Hind, 108
Jamil, Shahida Munni, 7
Jang, 145
Jang, Nizam ul-Mulk Asaf, 2
Jehal, 146
Jennings, Sir Ivor, 92
Jinnah Awami Muslim League, 40, 84, 113
Jinnah League, 40
Jinnah Muslim League, 40, 113
Jinnah, Fatima, 85, 187
Jinnah, Mohammad Ali, 11, 12, 13, 14, 15, 17, 20, 21, 22, 23, 26, 27, 28, 29, 30, 32, 33, 36, 37, 38, 39, 42, 43, 71, 73, 74, 80, 82, 100, 101, 103, 104, 105, 106, 109, 112, 113
Jinnah-Gandhi Bombay talks, 28
Jirga system, 164
Joint Electorate Bill, 53
Jukto Front, 45, 47, 53, 72

K

Kalat, Khan of, 127, 164, 165
Kashmir War, 34, 123
Kashmir, 27, 55, 56, 58, 59, 60, 61, 62, 79, 108, 116, 133
Keeler, Christine, 212
Khairuddin, Khwaja, 15
Khaliquzzaman, Chowdhury, 40, 46, 173, 191, 193
Khan Sahib, Dr, 51, 65, 87, 88, 89, 92, 93, 94, 95, 96, 102, 118, 119
Khan, Abdul Monem, 140
Khan, Agha Mohammad Yahya, 75
Khan, Ataur Rahman, 47, 73, 89, 95, 126, 147, 177
Khan, Brigadier F.R., 147
Khan, Chowdhury Zafrullah, 108
Khan, General Azam, 138, 139
Khan, General Mohammad Ayub, 47, 51, 59, 66, 67, 68, 69, 70, 74, 75, 77, 85, 87, 88, 89, 90, 93, 121, 124, 126, 128, 129, 133, 134, 135, 147, 157, 159, 162, 178, 179, 181, 182, 185, 188, 198, 199, 205, 206, 208, 209
Khan, General Mohammed Musa, 129
Khan, Iftikhar Ali (Nawab of Mamdot), 40
Khan, Khan Abdul Ghaffar, 51, 62, 87, 92, 96, 97, 99, 118, 164
Khan, Khan Abdul Qayyum, 79, 84, 91, 122, 173, 174, 177, 191, 192, 197, 201, 210
Khan, Khan Abdus Sabur, 176
Khan, Khan Habibullah, 192
Khan, Liaquat Ali, 20, 22, 32, 37, 39, 40, 42, 46, 47, 48, 71, 73, 79, 80, 81, 82, 84, 99, 106, 110, 111, 112; ministry, 46
Khan, Maulana Muhammad Akram, 16, 191, 194
Khan, Moulvi Tamizuddin, 87, 172, 112
Khan, Nawab Iftikhar Ali, 113
Khan, Nawabzada Nasrullah, 196, 201, 211
Khan, Sardar Bahadur, 93, 118, 178, 211, 213
Khan, Sirdar Nauroz, 164
Khan, Syed Ahmad, 2, 3
Khan, Zafrullah, 38, 59
Khattack, Yusuf, 201
Khilafat movement, 100, 101
Khilji, Sultan Alauddin Mohammad Shah, 1
Khrushchev, Nikita, 61
Khuhro, Ayub, 91, 209
Kirmani, 192

Kripalani, Acharya, 29, 110
Krishak Proja Party (KPP), 15, 16, 18, 21, 104
Krishak Samity, 198
Krishak Sramik Party (KSP), 48, 49, 85, 94, 103, 126, 127, 177, 206, 207, 208
Krugg, General, 54, 156

L

Labour Welfare Act, 16
Lahore Resolution, 17, 22, 31, 39, 51, 75, 104
Lari, Z.H., 200, 211, 212
Latif, Nawab Abdul, 3
Law Commission, 152
Linlithgow Commission, 14
Lodi, Sultan Bahlol, 1
Lucknow Pact, 12, 100

M

Mahmud, Hasan, 84
Mahmudabad, Raja Sahib of, 193
Makhazul Ulum, 2
Malay Constitution Commission, 57
Mamdot, Khan of, 97; ministry, 40
Mamdot, Nawab of, 113
Manik Mia, 71, 116, 144, 145, 146, 164. *See also* Hossain, Tofazzal
Manoki Sharif, Peer of, 40, 119
Mao Tse-tung, 116
Martial law, 66, 74, 88, 125, 127, 131, 132, 133, 134, 136, 137, 138, 140, 141, 145, 148, 149, 150, 152, 158, 164, 166, 168, 171, 172, 173, 174, 178, 180, 181, 182, 191, 194, 203, 211
Martyr's day, 44
Maternity Benefit Act, 16
Maudoodi, Maulana Abul Ala, 123, 171, 201
McConaughy, Walter P., 145
Mengal, Sardar Ataullah Khan, 211
Menon, V.P., 28
Minto, Lady, 5
Mirza, Iskander, 38, 46, 47, 49, 51, 57, 62, 63, 66, 74, 77, 85, 86, 87, 88, 89, 90, 91, 93, 94, 95, 96, 119, 121, 122, 123, 125, 126, 127, 128, 129, 180
Mohammad Ali formula, 29
Mohammad, Ghulam, 38, 46, 47, 48, 49, 59, 74, 82, 83, 85, 86, 87, 89, 90, 210, 211

Mohammadan Anglo-Arabic College, Aligarh, 3, 22
Mohiuddin (of Barisal), 204
Mohsenuddin, Pir, 177
Money Lenders Act, 17
Morning News, 146
Moscow Arts Theatre, 6, 7
Mountbatten, Lord Louis, 27, 28, 29, 30, 80
Mukherjee, Shyama Prasad, 18, 29
Multani, Sheikh Bahauddin Zakaria, 1
Murree pact, 48
Muslim Bengali Sepahis, 25
Muslim Cultural Centre, 6
Muslim League (Convention), 140, 146, 181, 193, 194, 195, 198, 206, 207, 210, 212
Muslim League (Council), 185, 194, 195, 200, 201, 206, 207, 209, 211, 212
Muslim League ministry, 67
Muslim League Parliamentary Party, 18
Muslim League, 14, 15, 17, 18, 20, 21, 22, 23, 24, 26, 28, 29, 30, 31, 32, 33, 37, 38, 51, 49, 64, 65, 72, 79, 80, 81, 82, 83, 84, 85, 86, 88, 89, 90, 92, 93, 94, 95, 96, 97, 99, 100, 101, 102, 103, 104, 105, 106, 111, 112, 113, 114, 116, 118, 119, 120, 122, 123, 131, 132, 135, 137, 167, 172, 173, 190, 191, 192, 194, 201, 206, 208, 211
Muslim Punjabi Sepahis, 25
Mutual Defence Aid agreement, 114

N

National Awami Party (NAP), 59, 62, 63, 96, 99, 118, 119, 124, 132, 145, 173, 177, 190, 195, 197, 198, 199, 200, 201, 204, 206, 207, 208, 209, 211
National Democratic Front (NDF), 69, 72, 177, 188, 194, 197, 198, 204, 205, 206, 209, 210, 211, 212
National Democratic Party, 207
National Home Guards, 41
National Labour Federation, 13
Navapanjika, 3
Nazimuddin, Khwaja, 15, 16, 18, 29, 32, 35, 39, 42, 43, 46, 48, 49, 70, 74, 82, 83, 85, 104, 105, 110, 111, 194, 195, 200, 206, 211
Nehru Report, 13, 103
Nehru, Jawaharlal, 23, 26, 27, 28, 30, 55, 58, 59, 61, 62, 105, 109
Nehru, Motilal, 13, 14
New Muslim Majlish, 15

New York Times, 46
Niazi, Maulana Abdul Sattar Khan, 209, 211
Nishtar, Sirdar Abdur Rab, 84
Nizam-i-Islam Party, 85, 177, 190, 206, 208
Noon, Malik Feroz Khan, 62, 65, 122, 125, 126, 127, 128

O

Ochterlony Monument Maidan, 24
October Revolution, 129
One Unit, 62, 63, 89, 118, 124, 133; Bill, 92, 93, 164, 165
One-Point Programme, 201, 204
Osmani, M.A., 33

P

Pakhtunistan, 97, 99
Pakistan Agricultural Academy, 136
Pakistan Awami Muslim League, 40
Pakistan Industrial Credit and Investment Corporation (PICIC), 154
Pakistan Industrial Development Corporation (PIDC), 139, 160, 161
Pakistan Industrial Finance Corporation (PIFCO), 154
Pakistan Muslim League (PML), 40, 41, 45, 80, 81
Pakistan Observer, 40, 146
Pakistan Resolution 1940, 23
Pakistan Times, The, 96
Pan Islamic Society, 5
Partition of Bengal, 28, 29, 30, 31
Patel, Sirdar, 28, 30, 34, 108, 109, 110
Pathans, 77, 90, 92, 97, 98, 99, 164, 200
Planning Commission, 136, 154, 155
Pocket Muslim League, 112, 194
Political Parties Act of 1962, 142, 173, 177, 183, 187, 193, 202
Proja-League: Coalition, 16; government, 31
Public and Representative Offices (Disqualification Act) of 1949 (PRODA), 40, 177
Public Offices Disqualification Order (PODO), 130, 210
Public Safety Act, 53, 86, 99, 131, 153, 173
Public Safety Laws, 112
Punjab Muslim League, 37

Q

Qadir, Manzur, 169, 171, 202, 212
Qasuri, Mian Mahmud Ali, 195, 196, 201, 208, 211
Qizilbash, Nawab Muzaffar Ali, 128
Quit India movement, 18
Quraishi, A.M., 189
Quraishi, I.H., 79

R

Radcliffe Award, 78, 79
Radcliffe, Cyril, 27
Rafiq, Khwaja Mohammad, 196, 211
Rahim, Sir Abdur, 6
Rahman, Fazlur, 28, 29, 85, 88
Rahman, Maulana Hafizur, 108
Rahman, Shah Azizur, 177
Rahman, Sheikh Mujibur, 13, 19, 40, 46, 70, 72, 75, 116, 117, 164, 177, 196, 207, 208
Raisman Award, 156
Rajagopalachari, 28
Rajpal, the author of *Rangila Rasool*, 10
Rangila Rasool, 10
Rashid Ali Day, 24
Rashid, Sardar Abdur, 91, 92, 96, 118
Rashtriya SwayamsevakSangha (RSS), 34, 35, 109
Reciprocal influence of Mohammadan and European Civilizations (essay), 2
Red Shirts, 80, 97
Reforms Act 1909, 12
Republican Party, 51, 62, 63, 64, 65, 93, 95, 96, 118, 119, 121, 122, 123, 126, 128, 208, 209
Riot Commission, 24
Round Table Conference (1933), 103, 203
Roy, Kiron Shankar, 29, 30
Russian Revolution, 6, 7
Russo-Chinese arms aid pact, 58

S

Sangbad, 146
Sarkar, Abu Hossain, 48, 87, 94, 95, 96, 126, 177
SEATO, 114, 115, 116, 198, 208
Second World War, 18, 24
Sengupta, J.M., 102
Shafi League, 14
Shah, King Zahir, 57

Shahnawaz, Begum Jahanara, 97
Shai (King's) jirga, 165
Shyama-Huq ministry, 18, 19
Siddique, Abdur Rahman, 15
Sikhs, 25, 97, 101, 108, 110
Simla Peace Conference, 12, 13
Simon Commission, 186
Sindhi, Shaikh Abdul Majid, 99, 118, 211
Singh, Maharaja Hari, 60
Sino-Pakistan relations, 55
Sixteen-point programme, 198, 204
Sodhpore *ashram* (hermitage), 33
Solaiman, S.M., 177
Soomro, Allahbux, 24, 102
South-East Asia Treaty Organization (SEATO), 58
Sovereign United Bengal scheme, 29, 30, 31
Sree Nivas, 19
Stanislavsky, Konstantin, 6
Staplestone, H. E., 2
Suez crisis, 56
Suhrawardia Order of Saints, 1
Suhrawardia, Akhter Jahan, 7. *See also* Sulaiman, Begum
Suhrawardy, Abdullah al-Mamun, 5, 6, 13
Suhrawardy, Aminuddin, 4
Suhrawardy, Hassan, 5, 6
Suhrawardy, Mahmud, 5, 6
Suhrawardy, Maulana Mobarak Ali, 4
Suhrawardy, Maulana Obaidullah al-Obaidi, 2, 3, 4, 5
Suhrawardy, Maulana Rukunuddin, 1
Suhrawardy, Professor Hassan Shahid, 6, 7
Suhrawardy, Rashid, 7, 68, 69, 70
Suhrawardy, Sheikh Shahabuddin Omar bin Mohammad Us-, 1, 2
Suhrawardy, Sheikh Zainuddin, 2
Suhrawardy, Zahid, 4, 36
Sulaiman, Ahmad, 75
Sulaiman, Begum, 68, 69, 71
Sulaiman, Shah Ahmad, 7
Sulaiman, Sir Mohammad, 7
Swaraj Party, 10, 30
Syed, G.M., 62, 99, 118

T

Tahzibul Akhlaq, 3
Tarkabagish, Maulana Abdur Rashid, 42, 177
Tehrik-i-Islam Party, 190
Tiwana, Malik Khizr Hayat Khan, 97, 102
Transfer of Power Bill, 37

Trevelyan, Charles, 2
Twenty-one-point programme, 44, 45
Two-nation theory, 52

U

Unionist Party, 94, 101; government, 97; ministry, 102
United Front, 44, 85, 86, 88, 90, 94. *See also* Jukto Front
United Nations, 56, 57, 61, 108, 109, 154, 155
United States Agency for International Development (USAID), 152

University of Dhaka, 41, 56
University of Karachi, 63
Urdu, 22, 37, 42, 43, 48, 50, 89
Usmani, M.H., 40
Usmani, Mahmudul Huq, 199, 200, 211

W

Waheeduzzaman, 176
Warsaw pact, 58, 115
Water and Power Development Authority (WAPDA), 139, 156, 162
Wavell, Lord, 23, 26, 27, 29
Whipping Bill, 9